THE BRONTËS

A TO Z

THE BRONTËS

A TO Z

The Essential Reference to Their Lives and Work

LISA PADDOCK and CARL ROLLYSON

Facts On File, Inc.

The Brontës A to Z

Copyright © 2003 by Lisa Paddock and Carl Rollyson

Facts On File, Inc.
132 West 31st Street
New York NY 10001

Library of Congress Cataloging-in-Publication Data

Paddock, Lisa Olson.
The Brontës A to Z / Lisa Paddock and Carl Rollyson.
p.   cm.
Includes bibliographical references and index.
ISBN 0-8160-4302-7 (alk.paper)
1. Brontë, Charlotte, 1816–1855—Encyclopedias. 2. Women and literature—England—History—19th century—Encyclopedias. 3. Authors, English—19th century—Biography—Encyclopedias. 4. Yorkshire (England)—In literature—Encyclopedias. 5. Women authors, English—Biography—Encyclopedias. 6. Yorkshire (England—Biography—Encyclopedias.
7. Brontë, Emily, 1818–1848—Encyclopedias. 8. Brontë, Anne, 1820–1849—Encyclopedias. 9. Brontë family—Encyclopedias.
I. Rollyson, Carl E. (Carl Edmund). II. Title.

PR4168 .P28 2002

823′.809—dc21   2002075446

Cover design by Nora Wertz
Map by Jeremy Eagle © Facts On File, Inc.

Printed in the United States of America

VB Hermitage 10 9 8 7 6 5 4 3 2 1

This book is printed on acid-free paper.

CONTENTS

INTRODUCTION

There were five literary Brontës: Patrick Brontë, the patriarch, and four of his offspring, Charlotte, Branwell, Emily, and Anne. With the exception of Patrick, who outlived his wife and all six of the children they had together, the Brontës lived brief lives. Charlotte, the longest lived of the Brontë siblings, died at 38. When her father died six years later, his passing marked the end of the Brontë line.

Still, the Brontës have, collectively, left the world an amazingly rich heritage. In addition to the poetry, pamphlets, and sermons created by Patrick, his young children—infected with what they called "scribblemania"—turned out numbers of tiny books chronicling the affairs of Angria and Gondal, the fully imagined—and imaginary—worlds they occupied. As the Brontë siblings grew older, their literary and artistic gifts sought other outlets. Branwell never fulfilled his early promise, but even he produced a variety of remarkable poems and drawings, while his three surviving sisters were responsible for such classic English novels as *Jane Eyre* (Charlotte), *Wuthering Heights* (Emily), and *Agnes Grey* (Anne).

During their lifetimes, the Brontës were notorious both for their personal eccentricities and for the unorthodox power of their artistic creations. Since their deaths, they have consistently been the objects of intense scholarly study and—in some quarters—nearly cultlike devotion. The myth of Charlotte Brontë commenced almost immediately after her death with the publication of Mrs.

Elizabeth Gaskell's worshipful biography, *The Life of Charlotte Brontë* (1857). Since then the flow of books, articles, stories, poems, plays, and motion pictures devoted to the Brontës has never ceased, reaching new heights in the 1990s with Hollywood's fifth film version of *Wuthering Heights* (1997), a traveling exhibition of Brontë memorabilia (including a pair of Charlotte's tiny gloves), and the publication in 1994 of Juliet Barker's thousand-page biography of the Brontë family. Barker's book, however, is hardly the last word. Since its publication, Lyndall Gordon has published an acclaimed biography of Charlotte Brontë (*Charlotte Brontë: A Passionate Life* [1997]), while Barker herself has edited *The Brontës: A Life in Letters* (1998).

A recent search of the Internet brought up more than 6,000 hits for the Brontës, among them several e-mail discussion groups devoted to their lives and works. Participants discuss biographical questions, literary criticism, relevant social and historical issues, recent books concerning the Brontës, movies, television programs, and audio recordings of works by the Brontës, as well as "Brontë-related travel suggestions."

Those scholars and other Brontë aficionados who operate in more traditional venues have also kept up a flurry of activity. The catalogue of the New York Public Library includes 490 entries under the subject heading "Brontë," with 85 items—ranging from *Haworth and the Brontës: A Visitor's Guide* (1967) to *Myths of Power: A Marxist Study of the Brontës* (1975)—devoted to the family

Brunty home, Ballynaskeagh, Ireland. Patrick Brontë's mother and father, Alice McClory and Hugh Brunty, moved their family to this larger and more comfortable home after Patrick was born. (Brontëana, 1898)

collectively. The holdings of the Library of Congress include a comparable number of Brontë-related items, including nine fictional works, such as Glyn Hughes's novel *Brontë* (1996), written by authors inspired by the Brontës. A search under the subject heading "Brontë" in the catalogue of a typical academic library (the City University of New York) turned up 1,300 entries.

We have drawn on useful reference books such as F. B. Pinion's *A Brontë Companion: Literary Assessment, Background, and Reference* (1975) and Barbara and Gareth Lloyd Evans's *Everyman's Companion to the Brontës* (1982), also published as *The Scribner Companion to the Brontës* (1982). In culling information from such great resources, we have tried to provide an up-to-date book that will help the common reader sort through this welter of material. *The Brontës A to Z*, therefore, enables general readers as well as Brontëmanes to access points of interest without having to make their way

through a dense thicket of ancillary material. Alphabetically organized, this volume's entries describe a wide variety of subjects related to the lives and works of this fascinating family. Touching on topics that range from a description of Emily's dog Keeper, who famously followed his mistress's coffin during her funeral procession, to the Luddite rebellion against industrialization that threatened Patrick Brontë's life and livelihood, *The Brontës A to Z* allows readers to investigate discrete points of interest quickly or to browse through a sequence of entries, following their interests. It is the first book devoted to the Brontës to offer such versatility.

All entries in *The Brontës A to Z* are complete in themselves, containing a discussion of how a character, term, place, historical figure, allusion, or reference functions in one or more of the Brontës' works. There is no need to consult charts or tables while reading an individual entry.

We cross-reference entries by using small capital letters; thus, for example, in a synopsis of Mrs. Gaskell's biography of Charlotte, "Sir Walter SCOTT" refers to an entry on Scott that will be found in the "S" section.

In addition to incorporating information of the kind found in earlier Brontë reference books, we have made a diligent effort to annotate the Brontës' biographies. Entries on their friends and family are extensive. The volume also reproduces drawings, illustrations, and paint-ings that help recapture the look and feel of the Brontës' world.

A chronology preceding the A-to-Z entries lists significant dates in the lives and careers of the family. The bibliography, which includes an inventory of reliable web sites, provides data on the most important scholarship about the Brontës and what Lucasta Miller recently called the "Brontë myth," in which Patrick, Charlotte, Branwell, Emily, and Anne have become characters as enduring as their fictional creations.

CHRONOLOGY

This chronology uses the following abbreviations:

AB   Anne Brontë
BB   (Patrick) Branwell Brontë
CB   Charlotte Brontë
EB   Emily Brontë
MB   Maria Branwell Brontë
PB   Patrick Brontë

1777
April 17: **PB is born in Emdale, County Down, Ireland.**

1783
April 15: **MB is born in Penzance, Cornwall, England.**

1789
French Revolution begins.

1798
William Wordsworth and Samuel Taylor Coleridge write *Lyrical Ballads,* a collection of poetry that marks the beginning of English literary romanticism.

1800
Napoléon Bonaparte becomes first counsel of France.

---

* Events that directly concern the Brontë family appear in **bold**.

1802–3
Sir Walter Scott's *Minstrelsy of the Scottish Border* (Volumes I–III) are published.

1804
Napoléon is proclaimed emperor of France.

1805
In the battle of Trafalgar, British admiral Horatio Nelson defeats the French fleet.

1808
Sir Walter Scott writes the poem "Marmion."

1809
During the Luddite riots, workers destroy machines in northern England.

1810
Durham miners strike.

1811
Jane Austen publishes her novel *Sense and Sensibility.*

Regency is established for the remainder of the reign of George III (1809–20) due to the king's insanity.

1812
December 29: **PB marries MB at Guiseley, near Bradford, Yorkshire, England.**

Lord Byron receives acclaim for Cantos I and II of *Childe Harold*.

1813

PB and MB make a home at Clough Lane, Hightown, Hartshead. PB writes *The Rural Minstrel: A Miscellany of Descriptive Poems*.

Jane Austen's *Pride and Prejudice:* and Robert Southey's *Life of Nelson* are published.

1814

April 23: **Maria Brontë is christened (birthdate unknown).**

PB writes *Lines Addressed to a Lady on Her Birthday* for MB.

Literary works of the year include *Mansfield Park* by Jane Austen, *Waverley* by Sir Walter Scott, and "The Excursion" by William Wordsworth.

1815

February 8: **Elizabeth is born (christened August 26).**

June 12: **Aunt Branwell joins the household.**

PB becomes clergyman at St. James's Church, Thornton, Yorkshire; writes *The Cottage in the Wood or the Art of Becoming Rich and Happy*.

The duke of Wellington, in charge of British forces, defeats Napoléon at Waterloo.

Sir Walter Scott writes *Guy Mannering*.

1816

April 21: **CB is born at Thornton (christened June 29).**

Aunt Branwell departs for Cornwall.

Jane Austen's *Emma*, Samuel Taylor Coleridge's "Kubla Khan," and Lord Byron's Canto III of *Childe Harold* and "Manfred" are published.

Blackwood's Magazine is founded in Edinburgh, Scotland.

1817

June 26: **BB is born at Thornton (christened July 23).**

Jane Austen dies.

Riots erupt in Derbyshire, England, over low wages.

1818

February 12: **MB becomes ill.**

June 30: **EB is born at Thornton (christened August 20).**

PB writes *The Maid of Killarney or Albion and Marina: A Modern Tale*; the second edition of *The Cottage in the Wood* is published.

Jane Austen's *Northanger Abbey* and *Persuasion* are published posthumously. Mary Shelley publishes *Frankenstein;* Lord Byron, Canto IV of *Childe Harold;* William Hazlitt, *Lectures on the English Poets*.

1819

Lord Byron writes Cantos I and II of *Don Juan*.

Peterloo Massacre in which 11 people are killed occurs at a public meeting in Manchester organized to demand parliamentary reform; Parliament passes several laws to reestablish order.

Burlington Arcade opens in Piccadilly, London.

1820

January 17: **AB is born at Thornton (christened March 25).**

April: **Family moves to Haworth: PB is appointed perpetual curate of St. Michael and All Angels Church.**

MB's illness worsens.

George III dies; accession of George IV.

John Keats writes "Ode to Nightingale"; Sir Walter Scott, *Ivanhoe*; Percy Bysshe Shelley, "Prometheus Unbound."

1821

Aunt Branwell arrives from Cornwall to care for her sister.

September 15: **MB dies, probably of uterine cancer; Aunt Branwell takes charge of household.**

John Keats dies.

Lord Byron writes Cantos III–V of *Don Juan;* Sir Walter Scott, *Kenilworth*; Percy Bysshe Shelley, "Adonais," an elegy for John Keats.

Manchester Guardian is founded.

Greek war of independence begins.

1822

PB proposes to Isabella Drury of Keighley and is rejected.

Percy Bysshe Shelley dies.

Lord Byron writes Cantos VI–XIV of *Don Juan;* Sir Walter Scott, *Quentin Durward.*

First iron railroad bridge is built on the Stockon-Darlington line in Britain.

Sunday *Times* is founded in London.

1823

PB proposes to Miss Burder July 28 and is rejected August 8.

Maria and Elizabeth contract measles and whooping cough.

1824

July: **Maria (10) and Elizabeth (9) enroll at the Clergy Daughters School, Cowan Bridge, Lancashire; CB (8) follows in August and EB (6) in November.**

PB engages Tabitha (Tabby) Aykroyd as family servant.

PB publishes *The Phenomenon: An Account in verse of the Extraordinary Disruption of a Bog which took place in the Moors of Haworth.*

Lord Byron dies.

Sir Walter Scott writes *Redgauntlet.*

Westminster Review is founded.

1825

May 6: **Having been sent home from school with tuberculosis, Maria dies.**

June 15: **Elizabeth, having been sent home with same disease, dies.**

CB and EB return to Haworth.

First passenger steam railway debuts in England, marking the beginning of the railroad building boom.

Trade unions are legalized in Britain.

Horse-drawn buses appear in London.

1826

PB brings home 12 wooden soldiers for BB; the children invent an imaginary world, Glass Town, and begin producing drawings, paintings, poems, magazines, and novelettes in home-made books.

Elizabeth Barrett Browning writes *Essay on Mind and other Poems.*

First railroad tunnel is built on the Liverpool-Manchester line.

1828

Aunt Branwell gives the children Sir Walter Scott's *Tales of a Grandfather.*

Duke of Wellington forms Conservative government.

The Spectator, a weekly magazine, is founded in London.

1829

CB and BB begin writing the *Glass Town* **and** *Angria* **sagas.**

Catholic Emancipation Act is passed; first Catholic is elected to Parliament.

English economist Thomas Attwood (1783–1856) establishes the Birmingham Political Union to advocate parliamentary reform.

1830

Alfred Tennyson's *Poems Chiefly Lyrical* is published.

William IV becomes king of England.

Revolutions occur in Europe.

Duke of Wellington resigns his ministry.

Ladies' skirts become shorter; sleeves and hats are larger and decorated with flowers and ribbons.

Steam streetcars are introduced in London.

1831

CB (14) enrolls at Miss Wooler's School at Roe Head (in Yorkshire) in January and wins silver medal for deportment; meets Ellen Nussey and Mary Taylor.

EB and AB, at home, create the fantasy world of Gondal.

1832

CB returns home from Roe Head in May to tutor her sisters.

Sir Walter Scott dies.

Alfred Lord Tennyson writes "The Lady of Shalott."

Reform Act gives the vote to the upper middle classes, increasing the number of eligible voters by at least 500,000.

1833

BB paints "gun group" portrait of the Brontë family (see p. 25) and famous pillar portrait of his sisters (see p. 17) in the next two years and plans to become an artist.

Thomas Carlyle writes *Sartor Resartus*.

Slavery is abolished in the British Empire.

Factory Act limits employment of children and sets up an inspection system.

1834

CB and BB create Angria, a new imaginary kingdom; EB and AB work on Gondal, their rival kingdom.

CB shows two of her paintings at Leeds Exhibition.

Samuel Taylor Coleridge dies.

Charles Dickens publishes *Sketches by Boz*.

Poor Law amendment stipulates that no able-bodied man can receive government assistance unless he enters a workhouse.

1835

William Weightman becomes curate at Haworth in April.

CB returns to Roe Head as a teacher; EB enrolls there (July–October), but her health deteriorates and she returns home; AB succeeds EB at Roe Head.

BB studies portrait painting with William Robinson at Leeds but fails to apply to the Royal Academy of Arts in London; turns to alcohol to soothe disappointment in himself and purchases Byron's *Childe Harold's Pilgrimage* May 30.

William Fox Talbot (1800–1877) produces the first photograph.

1836

April 25: **BB becomes a Freemason in Haworth.**

July 12: **EB writes her earliest dated poem.**

July 22: **AB writes the preface to the second edition of *The Tenant of Wildfell Hall*.**

BB writes to editor of *Blackwood's Magazine*, enclosing two poems.

Charles Dickens's novel *The Pickwick Papers* is published.

Chartism, a national working-class movement, demands political reform in Great Britain.

1837

January 19: **BB sends copies of his writing to William Wordsworth but receives no reply.**

AB visits with Moravian minister James de la Trobe while at Roe Head.

CB corresponds with poet laureate Robert Southey.

BB requests interview with the editor of *Blackwood's Magazine*.

Thomas Carlyle writes *The French Revolution*.

Victoria becomes British monarch.

1838

CB resigns position at Roe Head and returns home.

EB writes half of her surviving poems in the next four years and begins work as a schoolteacher at Law Hill School, Halifax.

BB starts taking opium and works as a portrait painter in Bradford.

AB leaves Roe Head School in December.

Charles Dickens writes *Oliver Twist*.

The Chartists issue the People's Charter, which demands universal male suffrage and parliamentary reform.

1839

CB rejects her first suitor, friend Ellen Nussey's brother; is unhappy as governess to the Sidgwicks of Stonegappe, near Skipton, Yorkshire; in August, rejects her second suitor, Reverend David Brice, an Irish curate.

AB takes position as governess for the Ingham family at Blake Hall in Mirfield.

BB renounces his artistic ambitions and goes into debt.

EB resigns from her teaching position at Law Hill.

Harriet Martineau writes *Deerbrook*.

Chartist National Convention sparks riots and strikes.

1840

AB becomes governess at the Robinson family home, Thorp Green Hall, Little Ouseburn, in August.

CB is governess from March to December at Upperwood House, Rawdon, near Leeds, for the Whites; longs to study abroad, rejecting Miss Wooler's offer of a school; sends Hartley Coleridge, son of poet Samuel Taylor Coleridge and nephew of poet laureate Robert Southey, copies of her poems, asking for an opinion.

BB is tutor to the Postlethwaite family at Broughton-in-Furness, Lake District, from January until June, when he is dismissed and works as assistant clerk-in-charge, Leeds-Manchester Railway at Sowerby Bridge near Halifax.

Harriet Martineau writes *The Hour and the Man;* Charles Dickens, *The Old Curiosity Shop;* Thomas Carlyle, *Chartism.*

Queen Victoria marries Prince Albert of Saxe-Coburg-Gotha.

Penny postage is established in England.

1841

June 5: First of 12 poems of BB are published in the *Halifax Guardian.*

BB is promoted to clerk-in-charge at Luddenden Foot Station near Sowerby Bridge.

CB, EB, and AB discuss plans to establish their own school; Miss Wooler proposes that CB take charge of her school.

CB asks Aunt Branwell to support a six-month stay in Brussels.

Thomas Carlyle writes *On Heroes, Hero-Worship, and the Heroic in History.*

1842

In February, CB and EB enroll at the Pensionnat Heger in Brussels. CB's teacher, Constantin Heger, recognizes her writing talent.

BB is dismissed in March from assistant clerk's position in a railway company; increases consumption of alcohol and drugs; sends more poetry to editor of *Blackwood's Magazine;* joins AB in December at Thorp Green as tutor.

October 29: Aunt Elizabeth Branwell dies; CB and EB return home from Brussels.

Robert Browning's *Dramatic Lyrics* and Thomas Babington Macaulay's *Lays of Ancient Rome* are published.

Britain bans child and female labor underground.

Chartist riots occur in British manufacturing towns.

Queen Victoria embarks on her first railway journey from Windsor to Paddington Station, London.

1843

CB returns to Brussels in January to teach English; falls in love with her teacher, Constantin Heger, director of the Pensionnat Heger; catches a glimpse of Queen Victoria visiting the city; lovesick and homesick, she goes to confession at Ste. Gudule Church and decides to go home but is dissuaded by M. Heger; leaves for home December 31.

BB, tutoring at Thorp Green, falls in love with Mrs. Robinson.

PB develops cataracts, and his eyesight deteriorates rapidly.

EB remains at home as housekeeper.

Robert Southey dies.

William Wordsworth is appointed English poet laureate.

Charles Dickens writes *Martin Chuzzlewit;* Thomas Carlyle, *Past and Present;* Harriet Martineau, *Life in the Sick Room.* The workers' cooperative society Pioneers of Rochdale is established in Britain.

1844

CB returns home in January; is angry at BB for his dissolute life and depressed about her love for M. Heger.

Sisters fail in attempt to start a school in Haworth.

EB absorbed in "Gondal" poems.

Benjamin Disraeli publishes *Coningsby;* William Makepeace Thackeray, *Barry Lyndon;* Elizabeth Barrett Browning, *Poems.*

Second railroad boom begins.

1845

AB leaves Thorp Green in June and returns home to complete *Agnes Grey.*

BB, emotionally attached to Mrs. Robinson, is dismissed from Thorp Green; is sent to Wales to recuperate but returns in poor condition; claims to be writing a novel about human feelings "veiled with deceit"; his poetry, written under a pseudonym, is published in the *Halifax Guardian*.

CB reads EB's poems; poems are submitted to publisher under the pseudonyms Currer, Ellis, and Acton Bell.

Arthur Bell Nicholls comes to Haworth as curate to PB.

Benjamin Disraeli publishes *Sybil, or The Two Nations,* Robert Browning, *Dramatic Romances and Lyrics.* Irish famine begins.

1846

Poems by Currer, Ellis, and Acton Bell is published in May.

CB completes *The Professor,* which remains unpublished after six rejections, and begins *Jane Eyre* while nursing PB after eye operation.

BB remains in "stupified condition"; is distraught when he learns Mr. Robinson's will prohibits Mrs. Robinson from having any contact with him.

Charles Dickens founds *Daily News,* the first inexpensive English newspaper.

George Sand writes *The Haunted Pool.*

1847

Agnes Grey (AB), *Jane Eyre* (CB), and *Wuthering Heights* (EB) are published; only *Jane Eyre* is a rousing success (three editions printed in six months); *Wuthering Heights* receives mixed reviews. Intense speculation begins on the true identities of the authors.

William Makepeace Thackeray writes *Vanity Fair*

Factory Act limits children and women to 10-hour workday.

1848

CB travels to London to corroborate separate identities of the Bells to her London publisher, Smith, Elder; sends copies of *Poems* to Hartley Coleridge, Thomas De Quincey, and J. B. Lockhart; continues to peddle *The Professor* to

publishers; visits London and attends the opera, the Great Exhibition, and other events.

AB's *The Tenant of Wildfell Hall* is published in June and "The Three Guides" in *Fraser's Magazine* in August.

September 24: **BB (31) dies of tuberculosis.**

December 19: **EB (30) dies of same disease.**

Poems by Currer, Ellis, and Acton Bell republished by Smith, Elder.

Elizabeth Gaskell writes *Mary Barton;* Karl Mary and Friedrich Engels, *Communist Manifesto.*

Revolutions occur in Europe; Third Republic is established in France.

First public health act is passed in Britain.

1849

May 28: **AB (29) dies.**

Shirley (CB) is published; CB travels to London and meets her literary hero, William Makepeace Thackeray, and Harriet Martineau; visits Parliament and meets several literary critics.

Matthew Arnold writes "The Strayed Reveller"; Charles Dickens, *David Copperfield;* Thomas Babington Macaulay, *History of England from the Accession of James the Second.*

Bedford College for Women is founded in London.

1850

CB befriends writer Harriet Martineau; meets Mrs. Gaskell, her future biographer; edits her sisters' work, adding a biographical note that initiates the Brontë legend; in London, visits the zoo, sees the Duke of Wellington, and George Richmond paints her portrait; visits Edinburgh in July.

Rooms in Haworth Parsonage are repainted.

William Wordsworth dies.

Elizabeth Barrett Browning's *Sonnets from the Portuguese,* William Makepeace Thackeray's *Pendennis,* Alfred Lord Tennyson's *In Memoriam,* and William Wordsworth's *The Prelude* are published.

1851

CB begins *Villette;* rejects third suitor, James Taylor, a manager at Smith, Elder, her publisher; interrupts work on her novel in distress

over unreciprocated love for her publisher George Smith; visits London, attends Thackeray's lectures and the Great Exhibition, and sees her publisher.

EB's dog, Keeper, dies.

Harriet Beecher Stowe writes *Uncle Tom's Cabin*.

1852

CB resumes work on *Villette* and rejects Reverend Nicholls's proposal after her father opposes the marriage; becomes ill with mercury poisoning.

Charles Dickens publishes *Bleak House;* William Makepeace Thackeray, *The History of Henry Esmond*.

French Third Republic falls; Napoléon III becomes emperor.

Duke of Wellington dies.

1853

Villette (CB) is published; CB goes to London and visits Newgate and Pentonville Prisons, the Exchange, and the Foundling Hospital; asks her father for permission to see Mr. Nicholls and then accepts his marriage proposal.

Matthew Arnold writes "The Scholar Gypsy"; Elizabeth Gaskell, *Cranford;* John Ruskin, *The Stones of Venice*.

Factory Act limits men to 10-hour workday.

1854

June 29: CB (38) marries Reverend A. B. Nicholls; honeymoons in Ireland.

Alfred Lord Tennyson writes "The Charge of the Light Brigade"; Charles Dickens, *Hard Times*.

Crimean War begins.

1855

February 17: Tabby dies.

CB becomes pregnant and ill, possibly with typhoid.

March 31: CB (38) dies after a six-week fever; leaves everything to her husband.

PB asks Mrs. Gaskell to write CB's biography.

1857

The Professor (CB) is published posthumously.

Mrs. Gaskell publishes her biography of CB and further embellishes the Brontë legend.

1861

June 7: PB dies.

CB's husband, Arthur Bell Nicholls, returns to Ireland.

Prince Albert dies.

1906

December 2: Arthur Bell Nicholls dies at Banagher, Ireland.

A-to-Z Entries

Abbott, Miss   Minor character in *JANE EYRE*. Miss Abbott, a servant, helps BESSIE subdue Jane after she has been attacked by John REED.

"Advantages of Poverty, in Religious Concerns"
Probably in 1815, Maria Branwell BRONTË wrote this unpublished article, which her husband, Patrick, carefully preserved in his papers, according to the biographer Juliet BARKER. In it, Maria argued that salvation was more easily obtainable by the poor because they suffered fewer temptations than the rich. This simple message also conveyed considerable compassion for those "daily & hourly sinking under the distresses & privations which attend extreme poverty." She urged that Christian charity be extended to the suffering poor, especially since poverty often led to bitterness: "It is surely the duty of all christians, to exert themselves, in every possible way, to promote the instruction, & conversion of the Poor; &, above all, to pray with all the ardor of christian faith, & love, that every poor man, may be a religious man." However conventional her sentiments, Maria counseled an active interest in the world and an involvement with the poor that her daughters would emulate.

Agnes   Minor character in *VILLETTE*. She is the old servant of Madame WALRAVENS.

Agnes Grey   Anne BRONTË's novel is based on her experience as a governess, although how closely *Agnes Grey* is modeled on actual persons and events has never been determined. Certainly the author drew from her experiences with the INGHAM and ROBINSON households in her depictions of the Murrays and the Bloomfields. The position of governess was not an easy one: On the one hand, she was responsible for disciplining and educating a family's children; on the other, she could have her regimen disrupted at any point by an interfering mother or father who often treated the governess as a servant to be ordered about. Perceptive children who observed their governess's subservience often succumbed to the temptation of disobeying and even baiting her.

For her novel Anne chose a female first-person narrator. The story is relatively subdued—less GOTHIC and ROMANTIC than Charlotte's or Emily's tales. *Agnes Grey* almost reads like a primer on what it means to behave properly: to have a just sense of religion and of society and to assume one's duty to family and employer. In this respect, her work is reminiscent of Samuel RICHARDSON's novels aimed at instructing young women how to comport themselves, although Anne avoids Richardson's strong vein of melodrama and sentimentality.

As Juliet BARKER observes, *Agnes Grey* has a quiet strength and authority, revealing much more about the life of a governess than can be discovered in *JANE EYRE*. Agnes herself is not a remarkable beauty or an outspoken critic—that is, not among her employers. In her narrative, on the other hand, Agnes is both amusing and critical, resembling Jane AUSTEN's narrators in her assessment of social behavior, although Anne's writing lacks Austen's fierce wit and satirical style.

If Anne's work seems sober next to her sisters' novels, it is also far more realistic. It has a cumulative persuasiveness akin to Anthony TROLLOPE's. Like him, she rarely relies on powerful dramatic scenes or flashy, intense characters. Instead, there is an equilibrium in the writing, a balancing of character and event, a steady vision and command of her material, resulting in an authentic narrative grounded in everyday experience.

SYNOPSIS

Chapter 1: The Parsonage
The novel's opening sentence sets the tone for the manner and substance of the work: "All true

histories contain instruction." Agnes confesses that she wants to be useful and entertaining, writing with a candor for the public that she would not employ even among her closest friends. She writes behind the shield of changed names, the "lapse of years," and her own obscurity. It is, then, a true tale that the narrator need not exaggerate.

Through Agnes, Anne describes her family background. The father, Richard GREY, is a clergyman in the north of England. The mother, Alice GREY, is the daughter of wealthy aristocratic parents who disown her when she marries her beloved but decidedly poor Richard. The couple have six children, only two of whom survive past infancy: Agnes and her older sister, Mary. Agnes is treated as the baby of the family. She feels frustrated because neither her mother nor her sister is willing to give her any responsibility. They only succeed, in Agnes's view, in making her seem more helpless than she is.

Disaster strikes the family when the father makes an imprudent investment, all of which is lost when the ship he has helped to outfit is destroyed in a storm, thus demolishing the family's dreams of a fortune as well. Agnes's mother and sister resort to needlework to bring in income, but it is supposed that Agnes can do nothing to help a family in reduced circumstances. Agnes proposes herself as governess, only to be greeted by her family's skepticism. Nevertheless, Mrs. Grey agrees to find a "situation" for Agnes and eventually secures one with Mrs. BLOOMFIELD at Wellwood House. As Agnes leaves home she sees a sinking sun and ventures forth into "gloomy shadow."

Chapters 2–5: First Lessons in the Art of Instruction, A Few More Lessons, The Grandmamma, The Uncle
Although Agnes has sought a position as a governess, she worries that she is not prepared. She is not quite 19 and knows that even some girls of 15 have had more experience of the world than she has had. Nevertheless, she hopes that Mrs. Bloomfield, her employer, will prove a "kind, motherly woman."

Telling herself to remain calm, Agnes manages to subdue her unease at Mrs. Bloomfield's "chilly" reception. Matters are worsened when Agnes finds it nearly impossible to converse while struggling with the tough beefsteak Mrs. Bloomfield has given

her to eat. The unsympathetic employer ignores Agnes's discomfort while informing her that the children are "not very far advanced in their attainments," but that they are clever. Her boy Tom is "noble-spirited," and daughter Mary Ann is a "very good girl," although she will require watching. Agnes draws her own conclusions about the other children: Fanny ("a very pretty little girl") and Harriet ("a little broad, fat, merry, playful thing"). Tom is the oldest at seven, followed by Mary Ann (six), Fanny (four), and Harriet (two).

As Agnes watches the children interact, she sees that Tom is bossy and cruel and Mary Ann lacks discipline. Almost immediately Tom tries to boss Agnes, who tries to take a firm line with him, disapproving of his trapping birds and torturing them. Tom retorts that both his father, Mr. BLOOMFIELD, and his uncle Robson approve of his behavior. Agnes fortifies herself with her mother's advice not to criticize the children in front of their mother, since "people did not like to be told of their children's faults."

In spite of a disconcerting introduction to the household, Agnes awakes the next day with a hopeful spirit. Soon, however, she discovers that Tom, who is a tyrant, is rarely able to concentrate on his studies, and Mary Ann can hardly read. Even worse, Mr. Bloomfield speaks rudely to Agnes while treating his children with the utmost respect. The children seem like "unbroken colts" to Agnes, who finds more and more to deplore in their characters and in their parents' indulgent treatment of them. Agnes can barely control her charges and often has to run after them. She enjoys a respite when Tom settles down to study, but Mary Ann seems almost constitutionally incapable of studying for any length of time. When Mary Ann shrieks in frustration, Mrs. Bloomfield criticizes Agnes for not being able to teach her daughter. Fanny often enters the schoolroom and disrupts whatever semblance of order Agnes has managed to create. The children seem to be getting "worse and worse," Mrs. Bloomfield tells Agnes. Only the desire to help her family by bringing in an income keeps Agnes in the Bloomfield household.

After a Christmas holiday at home Agnes returns to more trying episodes with the Bloomfield children. In one especially vexing incident, the children rifle through her workbag and then rush out into snow. Agnes wonders whether to run after them, or whether that would simply stimulate more disobedience. Before she can decide, Agnes is berated by Mr. Bloomfield for not keeping the children in order. Even worse, Agnes overhears the children's grandmother question whether Agnes is a "proper person." Agnes, whose own grandmother has always treated her kindly, is shocked to encounter a "glare of Gorgon ferocity." She realizes that flattery might soften the grandmother, but such a strategy is against her principles. Mr. Bloomfield continues to hector Agnes about the lack of discipline in her schoolroom. Only Betty, the household nurse, seems to understand and sympathize with Agnes's impossible position.

The affected uncle Robson visits. He has encouraged Tom's cruelty to animals and is proud of his efforts to make his nephew a man not subject to "petticoat government." Even so, Agnes makes progress, however slow, with her pupils. Ironically, this is the very point at which Mrs. Bloomfield dismisses Agnes, complaining that the children have not learned enough during Agnes's tenure in the household.

Chapter 6: The Parsonage Again
Agnes is ashamed of her failure in the Bloomfield household, but she returns home to a happy reception, with no one faulting her for her dismissal. Financial reverses have worn down Richard Grey, who worries about his family's future should he die. Agnes announces her resolve to take another position as a governess, and her mother is heartened by her daughter's refusal to be discouraged. An advertisement of Agnes's qualifications leads to her employment in the home of Mr. MURRAY of Horton Lodge. The Murrays appear to be a better family than the Bloomfields, and Agnes is determined this time to thrive in her position.

Chapter 7: Horton Lodge
One of Mr. Murray's servants meets Agnes at the railway station. She is taken to the house and shown her quarters by Matilda, one of the Murray girls, who asks that a cup of tea be sent up for Agnes. Alone in her room, Agnes feels the full weight of her "retired, stationary life." The next day she descends to the schoolroom "with no

remarkable eagerness to join my pupils." She finds Mr. Murray the very picture of "blustering, roystering, country squire" and Mrs. MURRAY a "handsome, dashing lady of forty." Mrs. Murray is curt with Agnes and seems interested only in having her girls acquire some polish and refinement. She counsels Agnes to be patient with her son Charles and the other children. Agnes notes that Mrs. Murray does not spend a moment considering what might make Agnes comfortable or happy.

Rosalie MURRAY, at 16, is the eldest child, pretty and well formed but without a matching disposition. "She seldom lost sight, for above half an hour at a time, of the fact of my being a hireling and a poor curate's daughter," Agnes observes. Like other members of the household, Rosalie has no principles and makes no effort to "make inclination bow to duty." Indeed, she is "swallowed up in the all-absorbing ambition to attract and dazzle the other sex."

Matilda, two years younger than Rosalie, is like "an animal . . . full of life, vigour, and activity." She is unladylike and rambunctious, exhibiting almost no ability to reason or to control her behavior.

Eleven-year-old John is a good-natured boy but "rough as a young bear": "boisterous, unruly, unprincipled, untaught, unteachable." He eventually is sent away to school—to Agnes's immense relief.

Charles is his mother's "darling." At 10, he is a "pettish, cowardly, capricious, selfish little fellow." He does not read properly and has almost no capacity to concentrate on his studies.

Agnes finds it necessary to "smother her pride" in dealing with such a undisciplined lot and putting up with the servants who treat her disrespectfully. Her only consolation is that Horton Lodge itself is a more pleasant and more spacious domicile than Wellwood House.

Chapters 8–10: The "Coming Out,"
The Ball, The Church
Rosalie is set to make her debut in fashionable society. She teases Agnes about the long letters she receives from home and insensitively suggests that Agnes should tell her family not to write so much. Rosalie only wants to talk about the ball and afterward insists that Agnes hear every word of her account about the gentlemen she flirted with. She shocks Agnes by announcing she wants to make as

many conquests as possible and is not concerned that she might be hurting her suitors' feelings.

She is contemptuous of Sir Thomas ASHBY, Sir Hugh Meltham, and Sir Broadly Wilson because they are "old codgers." Mr. GREEN has money but his family is not distinguished, and he seems "stupid—a country booby." Mr. HATFIELD, the rector, seems a rather proud suitor, and his new curate, Mr. WESTON, Rosalie dubs "an insensate, ugly, stupid blockhead."

After a visit to church, Rosalie asks Agnes to confirm her opinion that Mr. Weston is ugly. Agnes refuses, saying she cannot tell his character from his face but liked his "style of reading." Hearing Weston preach another time, Agnes is taken with the "evangelical truth of his doctrine," which is a relief from Mr. Hatfield's harangues about the "atrocious criminality of dissent." Agnes points out that Hatfield is hard on people and does little to help them. In the meantime, Rosalie and Matilda squabble over Sir Henry Meltham and whether his attentions are directed at one sister or the other.

Chapter 11–13: The Cottagers, The Visit, The Primroses
Agnes accompanies the Murray sisters on visits to the cottagers on their father's estate. Although they are supposed to perform acts of charity, the sisters rarely take any real interest in the poor or the sick, and Agnes prefers to make such visits by herself. Agnes especially enjoys the company of Nancy BROWN, a widowed cottager with an eye infection. Nancy is lively and speaks her mind with Agnes's encouragement. They discuss the rector, Mr. Hatfield, and Mr. Weston. Nancy derives little spiritual guidance from Hatfield, who seems haughty and little interested in Nancy's concerns, whereas Mr. Weston is sympathetic, polite, and engaging. Agnes, who often feels lonely, thinks a good deal about Mr. Weston and his sensitive, compassionate conduct. She is isolated and can open her heart to no one except Nancy. She worries that the bad company of the Murrays will bring her to their low level. Weston, "appearing like the morning-star in my horizon, to save me from the fear of utter darkness," provides a counter example.

On her next visit to Nancy, Agnes encounters Mr. Weston, who acknowledges her with a "slight bow." Agnes comments, "I should have been invisible to Hatfield, or any other gentleman of those parts." Weston has come to say he has pre-

vented the gamekeeper from shooting Nancy's cat, which has strayed. When Agnes returns to the Murrays, Matilda scolds her for being away when she was wanted.

Agnes feels her plight strongly on an outing with the Murray sisters: "To submit and oblige was the governess's part," she reminds herself. "It was disagreeable, too, to walk behind, and thus appear to acknowledge my own inferiority." Agnes dreams of home and of familiar sights, and in this mood she encounters the kind Mr. Weston, who offers to gather wildflowers for her. In his company, she imagines how delightful it would be to have her home and to . . . She does not complete her thought: "I began this book with the intention of concealing nothing," she remarks, "but we have *some* thoughts that all the angels in heaven are welcome to behold, but not our brother men—not even the best and kindest among them." Worse yet, Agnes has to contend with the taunting of Murray sisters, who make fun of her growing attachment to Mr. Weston.

Chapter 14: The Rector
Rosalie continues with her plan to flirt with as many men as she can before she marries. She remains unconcerned by how she might injure a man's feelings, including Mr. Hatfield, who seems smitten with her. She scorns the idea of falling in love and looks only to set herself up in a comfortable establishment.

When Rosalie sees Mr. Hatfield approaching the house, she sends Agnes off to see Mark Wood, a poor laborer suffering from CONSUMPTION. On her way, Agnes meets Mr. Weston, also on his way to see the unfortunate man. On her return she is approached by Rosalie, in triumph over her conquest of Mr. Hatfield. She reports that she has rejected his suit and that the outraged man has criticized her for "arrant flirting." He makes her promise not to tell anyone about his proposal to her, yet, as Agnes points out, Rosalie has already broken her promise not to say anything by confiding in Agnes. "Oh! It's only to you," Rosalie replies. Agnes is "disgusted" at Rosalie's "heartless vanity."

Chapters 15–17: The Walk, The Substitution, Confessions
Agnes is out walking alone when she encounters Mr. Weston. He observes that Agnes is alone and

inquires about her friends. She makes clear that given her station in life, it is difficult to have friends. He replies that fault may be both in society and in herself and then asks if she reads much when she is by herself. It is her favorite occupation, she responds. She wonders why he takes such an interest in her: "what is it to him what I think or feel?" she asks herself. "And my heart throbbed in answer to the question," she adds.

When Agnes concludes her walk by joining Rosalie, who has been visiting friends, Weston attends them. After he leaves, Rosalie declares that she will "fix that man" so that "he will go home and dream of me. I have shot him through the heart!" Agnes is skeptical but also concerned that Rosalie would trifle with Mr. Weston's feelings.

Agnes then begins to confront more directly her own attachment to Weston, lecturing herself that "it is not the man, it is his goodness that I love." Yet she confesses: "I may as well acknowledge that, about this time, I paid more attention to dress than ever I had done before." In the meantime, Rosalie accepts the proposal of Lord Ashby and looks forward to a June wedding and her role as the mistress of Ashby Park.

The malicious Murray sisters taunt Agnes, saying they have told Mr. Weston that he never sees Agnes because she only likes her books and takes no pleasure in anything else. They tell the same story to Nancy Brown. Agnes is irritated but does not show it: "I was accustomed, now, to keeping silence when things distasteful to my ear were uttered." Agnes is made even more disconsolate when she hears news from home that her father is gravely ill.

Chapter 18: Mirth and Mourning

On June 1 Rosalie becomes Lady Ashby. All Agnes can think of is Mr. Weston. She longs to meet him again on one of her walks. Instead she is treated to a lecture from Mrs. Murray, who is displeased that her younger daughter, Matilda, has not made enough progress in her studies or in her deportment as a lady. "Try to exert yourself a *little* more," Mrs. Murray urges Agnes. "Then I am convinced, you would soon acquire that delicate tact which alone is wanting to give you a proper influence over the mind of your pupil."

Agnes meets Weston on one of her walks. He candidly tells Agnes that Rosalie has been thrown away on a husband who will not be able to appreciate her, yet he wants to believe Sir Thomas Ashby is a better man than he supposes. Weston sounds satisfied to learn from Agnes that she opposed the idea of the marriage. "At least, you will have the satisfaction of knowing that it is no fault of yours," he tells Agnes. Their conversation is interrupted by Matilda, who has just watched a dog hunt and kill a hare. Agnes is revolted at Matilda's reveling in the cruelty of the hunt, but on a later part of the walk she seizes an opportunity to reply to Mr. Weston's belief that she is a "perfect bookworm." She calls the term a "scandalous libel. These young ladies are too fond of making random assertions at the expense of their friends." Agnes retires for the week immensely satisfied that she has been able to correct Weston's misapprehension. She feels the "flame of hope" kindled in her, but then she must rush home to see her ailing father. Her mother and sister tell her he has died.

Chapters 19–20: The Letter, The Farewell

Mrs. Grey receives a letter from her father saying that she can resume her title as a lady and he will remember her daughters in his will if she will only write to say that she regretted the marriage and the spurning of his advice. The indignant Mrs. Grey shares her reply with her daughters, who see that their mother is determined not only to honor the late Mr. Grey and their marriage but also to support herself by establishing a school.

When Agnes returns to conclude her employment with the Murrays, she has a conversation with Mr. Weston, who supposes she will be happy to leave because she has made no friends. Agnes pointedly says that she does not always expect to have friends near her but that she could not "live contentedly without a friend in the *world*." Agnes finds her attachment to Weston has deepened: "To be near him, to hear him talk as he did talk; and to feel that he thought me worthy to be so spoken to—capable of understanding and duly appreciating such discourse—was enough." Yet she chastises herself for "false hopes and vain delusions." When Weston bids her good-bye, Agnes breaks down: "I could not keep the water out of my eyes." She walks away with Matilda, "turning aside my face."

Chapters 21–23: The School, The Visit, The Park

Agnes leaves the employ of the Murrays with Mr. Weston's words in mind: "It is possible we may meet again . . . will it be of any consequence to you if we do or not?" She regards his question as a "secret solace and support." She scolds herself not to hope, yet she finds it difficult to obey "my own injunctions." A listless Agnes receives a letter from Rosalie, now Lady Ashby. She importunes Agnes to visit her, writing "Alas! how far the promise of anticipation exceeds the pleasure of possession." Vowing to spend only a few days away from home and school, Agnes embarks on a visit to Rosalie, hoping that she might also meet Mr. Weston.

Agnes learns that Rosalie is indeed unhappy with her unresponsive husband. Agnes also learns that Mr. Hatfield disliked Mr. Weston because "he had too much influence with the common people" and was not as tractable and submissive as the rector required. Agnes despairs of seeing Mr. Weston as she thinks of her "quiet, drab-colour life."

As Lord Ashby rides by on his horse, Agnes is shocked to hear Rosalie say that she detests her husband. Agnes tries to comfort her by enjoining her to do what is right and to hate no one, but Agnes doubts that her former pupil will able to follow such advice.

Chapters 24–25: The Sands, Conclusion
Shortly after her return to home and school, Agnes takes an early-morning walk. The sea air invigorates her, and she is able to forget her cares. A dog appears, snuffling behind her. It is her old pet terrier, Snap, which she had had to give away when she became a governess. She then looks up to see that its master is Mr. Weston. He tells her he has found a position just two miles from her. Agnes is overwhelmed: "The flash of his dark eyes seemed to set my face on fire." They walk along the sands arm in arm. He asks if he might visit her and her mother at their school. Agnes assents, and as they part, she asks him when he will make his visit. "To-morrow—God willing," he replies. She is once again happy and prays that her hopes will not be disappointed.

Mr. Weston makes several visits to the Grey household, winning the approval of Agnes's mother and becoming an "expected guest." When he proposes to Agnes, she learns that he has already consulted her mother, and to his question "You love me then?" she replies, "Yes."

Agnes concludes her story, explaining she became the wife of Edward Weston, who makes surprising reforms in his parish and is "esteemed and loved by its inhabitants." The couple have three children, Edward, Agnes, and little Mary. The family lives a modest but comfortable existence. "And now I think I have said sufficient," remarks Agnes at the end.

PUBLICATION HISTORY

Publisher T. C. NEWBY accepted *Agnes Grey* for publication in 1847, but not on favorable terms. Both Anne and her sister Emily, whose *Wuthering Heights* had also been accepted, were required to advance the publisher 50 pounds, which would not be refunded until sales of their novels equaled their advance. Issued in three volumes, *Agnes Grey* received few reviews, but those it did receive found the novel pleasant, if not as powerful as *Wuthering Heights.* One reviewer negatively compared Anne's work to Jane Austen's.

Compared to sister Charlotte's *Jane Eyre,* which was a huge success in 1847, *Agnes Grey* sold poorly, as did *Wuthering Heights.* Anne's novel fared better in 1850 when it was issued in a cheap single-volume format with a preface by Charlotte. A decade later, in 1858, *Agnes Grey* was reprinted in an edition of 15,000 copies.

Ainley, Miss Mary Ann   Minor character in *SHIRLEY.* Shirley KEELDAR gives Miss Ainley 300 pounds to dispense good works (charity) to the poor.

Alexander, Christine, and Jane Sellars   In their book *The Art of the Brontës* (1995), Alexander and Sellars provide not only a meticulous study of the family's paintings and drawings (reproduced both in black and white and in color), documenting many new discoveries and discussing work attributed to the Brontës, but also well-informed assessments of their subjects' understanding of the visual arts. The book includes separate sections on Charlotte, Branwell, Emily, and Anne; a catalogue of Brontë drawings and paintings; an essay on how the visual arts influenced the Brontës; a bibliography; a chronology; and several indexes. It is an essential guide for anyone interested in the visual aspects of the Brontës' work.

Ambleside   Village in the Lake District of England. Charlotte Brontë had occasion to visit this picturesque spot on Lake Windermere twice in 1850. In August of that year she stayed first with Sir James and Lady Janet KAY SHUTTLEWORTH, would-be patrons of Charlotte's, at their lakeside retreat, Brierly Close, where she first met Mrs. Elizabeth GASKELL. Charlotte then visited for a week with Harriet MARTINEAU at Martineau's Lakeland stone villa, The Knoll.

Andrews, Miss The demanding teacher at COWAN BRIDGE who was the model for Miss SCATCHERD in Charlotte Brontë's *JANE EYRE*.

Angelique Minor character in *VILLETTE*. She is one of three students who try to disrupt Lucy SNOWE's lesson, but Lucy deals with the students firmly.

Anglican Church *See* CHURCH OF ENGLAND.

Angria This imaginary kingdom, created in 1834, evolved from the GLASS TOWN saga and represented a convergence of Charlotte and Branwell Brontë's fictional characters. In Charlotte's story "High Life in Verdopolis," the duke of Zamorna, winner of a great victory over the Ashantes, is given the kingdom of Angria by the grateful marquis of Douro. While Branwell worked out the plot, Charlotte focused on Angria's characters. The tensions between the two siblings over creative control of their juvenile dramas is played out in Angria; for example, Charlotte's Zamorna, the love object of several women, is challenged by Branwell's earl of Northangerland (Alexander Percy) in a civil war. Into Zamorna and her characters Charlotte poured her passions: Her letters reveal that she identified intensely with them and called Zamorna her "mental king," grieving when Branwell's plot inventions harmed her hero.

Politics as well as romance caught the attention of brother and sister, who subjected Angria to the same rises and falls of governments that England experienced in 1834 and 1835. A new parliament in Angria called forth speeches from Zamorna, which Northangerland rebutted. Northangerland also canvassed the countryside, successfully regaining his premiership—still opposed by Zamorna, who demanded his resignation. Branwell countered with a plot twist that had Zamorna and Angria ejected from their political union with Verdopolis.

In *Caroline Vernon,* a short novel completed early in 1841, Charlotte returned to her romantic theme by having Zamorna seduce Northangerland's former mistress. This story marked a critique of Charlotte's former adolescent passion for romantic heroes, however, for Zamorna has degenerated into a seeker of vicious and corrupt pleasures, and his conquest is excessively emotional. Charlotte had instead turned to a much more realistic style of fiction, signaled in her story "The Farewell to Angria," completed early in 1841.

While Branwell and Charlotte devoted themselves to the kingdom of Angria, sisters Emily and Anne broke away in 1834 to found the independent world of GONDAL. *See also* "HISTORY OF YOUNG MEN, THE."

Antigua In *VILLETTE*, the ship that Paul EMMANUEL was supposed to sail on to the West Indies until he decided to delay his trip.

antinomian A term that came into use in the 17th century to describe Christians who felt themselves exempt from moral laws by the action of divine grace. In *SHIRLEY*, the term is used to describe anyone of radical political or religious views.

Arabian Nights A collection of tales, also called *Thousand and One Nights,* set in several Middle Eastern lands. These folk tales, anecdotes, and fables arose from a rich oral tradition and became part of written literature over many generations. The stories of Aladdin and his magic lamp, Sindbad the sailor, and flying carpets have intrigued readers across the world. The Brontë children were attracted not only to the exotic locales but also to the frame story: the efforts of Scheherazade to tell a new enchanting story every night to keep her husband, the king, from killing her, as he did with all his other wives. The enchanting power of literature is certainly one of the lessons the Brontës learned from their reading of the *Arabian Nights,* as well as the notion that art can, in a sense, prolong life and even impose a kind of victory over death. It was a powerful model indeed for the budding artists. After all, Scheherazade does not merely postpone her execution; she is rewarded with life because of her storytelling ability.

Archer, Dame   Minor character in *WUTHERING HEIGHTS*. Dame Archer assists at the birth of Hareton EARNSHAW, brings the infant downstairs, and shows him to his father.

"Arthuriana"   In 1833 Charlotte BRONTË worked on several incomplete stories and poems that revealed her gradual shift from an interest in the supernatural to settings and characters closer to home and connected to British history. The GOTHIC atmosphere and ghost-story setting of Brushwood Hall (slightly foreshadowing the gloom in *Jane Eyre*) eventually gave way to the poem "The Red-Cross Knight" and images of the Crusades: "To the desert sands of Palestine / To the Kingdoms of the East / For love of the cross & the holy shrine / For hope of heavenly rest / In the old dark times of faintest light / Aye wandered forth each Red-cross Knight." Some of the pieces were set in GLASS TOWN. She collected and organized these fragments into "Arthuriana, or Odds & Ends." The "Arthuriana" were never published in Charlotte's lifetime.

art of Anne Brontë   Thirty-seven of Anne Brontë's pictures survive, five in watercolor and the rest in pencil. Like her sisters, Anne made copies from prints and engravings. She produced portraits, studies of landscapes (oaks, elms, rocks) or buildings (a church, a cottage), and occasionally drawings created from her own observations. Compared to Emily's work, Anne's compositions are far more detailed, demonstrating her interest in registering all aspects of a scene studiously. Her work seems careful; Emily's, somewhat hasty. As is pointed out in *The Art of the Brontës*, by Christine ALEXANDER and Jane Sellars, Anne had a sensitivity to landscape, especially trees, that is also revealed in her poetry and fiction, especially in *THE TENANT OF WILDFELL HALL*. Compared to Emily, however, Anne's feeling for nature is gentle and compositional. She sees in it a symphony of the senses, a way of ordering one's perceptions of life—not an elemental force opposed to society as portrayed in Emily's *Wuthering Heights*.

Anne's work shows that she had an artist's eye, if not a trained artist's hand. How seriously she took her own pictures is not clear, although she appears to have viewed her work with some ambivalence if we read between the lines of her written work. The heroine of *The Tenant of Wildfell Hall* is a painter who cannot fully enjoy her own talent for representing nature: "I am always troubling my head about how I could produce the same effect on canvas; and that can never be done, it is mere vanity and vexation of spirit. . . . Well, after all I should not complain: perhaps few people gain their livelihood with so much pleasure in their toil as I do."

art of Branwell Brontë   Like his sisters, Branwell Brontë combined an interest in the visual and the literary arts. That he had promise as an artist is indisputable, judging from his evocative group portrait of his sisters and the fragmentary but sensitive depiction of Emily. At an early age, Branwell was drawing based on the books he read but also from his observations of life. In this respect, his range and capacity exceeded that of his sisters, who began in the conventional manner of copying from books exclusively.

Branwell was the only member of the family to paint in oils and to pursue a professional career as a painter, and his early pen-and-ink drawings have a power unrivaled by his sisters. In the group portrait of his sisters (see p. 17), he captures the personality of each by positioning their figures at different angles. Anne, at the extreme left, seems almost fierce in her concentrated gaze, which wards off any quick reading of her character. Emily, just above Anne, seems to look outward, perhaps more aware of the world that views her, while Charlotte, on the right, seems less distant than her sisters, although all three share an inaccessible self-composure that resists interpretation. The poor physical condition of the picture suggests neglect. It is known that Charlotte did not like it and did not take care of it, yet the very scuffing and scratching of the surface adds a kind of mysterious, archival atmosphere to the work. It has become a portrait that exhumes these lives while it simultaneously represents Branwell's erasure from the Brontë tableau: It is also known that he painted himself out of the picture.

Branwell's "gun group" family portrait (see p. 25) exists only in poor reproductions (no original has survived). Some critics claim that the picture can be read as an assertion of his male dominance: He meets the viewers gaze, whereas his sisters interact with each other. This work, as so many of his other drawings, shows he had a fluidity and subtlety that his sisters could not match. If his work does not show unmistakable signs of genius, it has been deemed good enough by several authorities to suggest he could have established himself as a professional artist—if he only had had the discipline to curb his temptations. For a thorough discussion and reproductions of his work, see *The Art of the Brontës* by Christine ALEXANDER and Jane Sellars.

art of Charlotte Brontë Charlotte Brontë's skill as an artist was recognized when her publisher asked her to illustrate the second edition of *JANE EYRE*. In 1834 two of her drawings were also shown in the summer exhibition of the Royal Northern Society for the Encouragement of the Fine Arts in Leeds. If Charlotte recognized her own talent, she nevertheless regarded it as conventional and without originality. Yet the variety of her work—drawings, watercolors, needlepoint—and the range of her subject matter—portraits, landscapes, architectural studies—are a valuable record of her precise powers of observation and her intense imaginative activity. In *Jane Eyre*, she recognizes the importance of artistic effort when she has Mr. Rochester examine and comment on Jane's drawings. In *VILLETTE* as well, Lucy Snowe is an ardent, self-critical artist.

Although Charlotte began in the conventional way, learning at school to copy engravings and other works of art, it is clear from her pencil portrait of Mr. Brocklehurst that she came to rely more and more on her own power of observation and invention. Like William Crimsworth in *THE PROFESSOR*, she came to value an art "pencilled after nature." Christine ALEXANDER and Jane Sellars's *The Art of the Brontes* includes an extensive discussion of Charlotte's techniques and subject matter as well as a comprehensive illustrated catalogue of her work.

art of Emily Brontë As in her writing, Emily Brontë's illustrations show a special sensitivity to the natural world and to animals. Most of her work is in pencil and watercolor. Like her sisters, she copied popular engravings, but she was more likely to take her subject matter from the world she observed around her. Her sketches of a winged serpent and of a man abusing a child, for example, suggest how alert she was to the cruelty and force of nature that so mark her novel *WUTHERING HEIGHTS*. Her pictorial work has a spontaneous, unfinished quality, but whether this is the result of a relative lack of training or of a different attitude toward her art is not clear. How far Emily meant to take her art is also not certain. Unlike Charlotte, she did not carefully preserve her work in a portfolio.

In the pen-and-ink drawing of herself and her animals, Emily sets herself to the side in the bottom right corner, apparently at work at her portable desk. This image of solitude accords well with the remote, inaccessible character Emily appears to have assumed, even with her family. The scene is presented in outline with no effort to embroider detail. It is tempting to see in this scene the starkness of Emily's vision.

Emily's sketches and paintings reveal her great, imaginative energy and independence and her preference for natural surroundings over social settings. In *The Art of the Brontës*, the most comprehensive treatment of Emily's exercises in the visual arts, authors Christine ALEXANDER and Jane Sellars point out that Emily titled many of her works "from nature," as if to suggest "her wish to underline the genuineness of both her portrayal and the nature of her subject." Such comments call to mind the portrait of a hypocritical and effete society that emerges in *Wuthering Heights*. Emily accorded great respect to animal instincts. Given such a view of society, it is no wonder that Emily remained the enigmatic sister, the one least likely to share with anyone her own thoughts.

Ashby, Sir Thomas Rosalie MURRAY's suitor in *AGNES GREY*. Although Rosalie is bored by Sir Thomas, she covets his large estate (Ashby Park) and his fortune. After they marry, she finds him a dull man who takes no interest in her.

aurora borealis Sometimes referred to as the northern lights, the aurora borealis is a diffuse colored light in the upper atmosphere, the product of charged particles from the Sun interacting with nitrogen and oxygen atoms. Sight of the aurora borealis stimulates Lucy SNOWE in *VILLETTE* to resolve to start new life in London after the death of Miss MARCHMOUNT.

Austen, Jane (1775–1815) English novelist born at Steventon, Hampshire, where her father was a REC-TOR. She later lived in Bath, Southampton, Chawton, and Winchester, where she died. Four of her novels were published anonymously during her lifetime: *Sense and Sensibility* (1811), *Pride and Prejudice* (1813), *Mansfield Park* (1814), and *Emma* (1815). *Persuasion* (1818) and *Northanger Abbey* (1818) were published under her name after her death. Austen's work represents the pinnacle of the novel of manners. Her deft style and satiric touch remain the standard by which subsequent novelists writing about society are measured. Anne Brontë was frequently compared to Austen and found wanting in so far as she lacked Austen's keen wit and comic gift. On the other hand, Anne shared Austen's astute judgment of human character and ability to blend narrative and character. Charlotte thought Jane Austen overrated and told Mrs. Elizabeth GASKELL that Austen was clever but not a literary genius.

Aykroyd, Tabitha (Tabby) Servant at HAWORTH PARSONAGE who came to work for the Brontë family in 1824 and died in the household in 1855. Charlotte's letters make several references to Tabby, who became an integral member of the family. She is mentioned often in *THE LIFE OF CHARLOTTE BRONTË*.

Aylott & Jones Publisher of *POEMS*. Charlotte Brontë first wrote to this small publishing firm, located at 8 Paternoster Row in London, on January 28, 1846, inquiring whether the firm would be interested in publishing a one-volume collection of short poems either at the publisher's risk or if the authors shared in it. The firm accepted, but only if the Brontë sisters paid in advance for the costs of publication. When the volume appeared in May 1846, the authors were also obliged to pay to advertise it. Unfortunately, only two copies of the book were sold then, but after the success of *JANE EYRE*, Charlotte's new publisher, Smith, Elder & Co., took over the remainder of the print run of *Poems* from Aylott & Jones.

Baptist An adherent of the Baptist Church, which originated in the 17th century. Baptists are Christians who anchor their beliefs in the rite of baptism accompanied by the believer's personal profession of faith in Jesus Christ. Baptists rely on the authority of the Bible and on the faith of the individual instead of subscribing to the authority of an established church such as the Church of England. Baptists, like METHODISTS, were considered DISSENTERS in England of the Brontës' time. There are scattered references to Baptists throughout the works of the Brontës.

Barker, Juliet Author of *The Brontës* (1994) and *The Brontës: A Life in Letters* (1998). The former is the most comprehensive one-volume treatment of the Brontë family; in addition to her narrative of the family's life, Barker includes maps of the Brontës' home and surroundings, many important illustrations, detailed notes, a list of characters and places in the juvenilia, and an extensive index. In the latter, she includes the most important Brontë letters arranged chronologically, a Brontë chronology, important illustrations, a list of correspondents, an index of correspondents, and an index of proper names.

Barraclough, Moses Minor character in *SHIRLEY*. He is described as a "preaching tailor," and he invokes the suspicion of the three Church of England curates because he is a METHODIST.

Barrett, Mrs. Minor character in *VILLETTE*. After Miss MARCHMOUNT dies, Lucy SNOWE consults with Mrs. Barrett, a housekeeper in London, about her future.

Bassompierre, M. de *See* HOME, MR.

Bassompierre, Miss de *See* HOME, PAULINA.

Bates, Mr. Minor character in *JANE EYRE*. He is a surgeon who visits Jane's friend Helen BURNS on her deathbed.

Batley, Dr. The doctor at COWAN BRIDGE, he served as the model for Mr. BATES in *JANE EYRE*.

Beck, Madame Major character in *VILLETTE*. Madame Beck is headmistress of the boarding school in the town of Villette. She takes pity on Lucy SNOWE, who turns up at the school hoping to find employment. Madame Beck favors English students and teachers, and Lucy is grateful for her generosity. At the same time, Madame Beck spies on her pupils and teachers, even going so far as to search through their belongings. Lucy dislikes this surveillance but learns to tolerate it because of Madame Beck's good qualities.

Madame Beck becomes jealous of Lucy because she attracts the attention of Professor Paul EMMANUEL, with whom Madame Beck is in love. In fact, Madame Beck does everything in her power to keep M. Paul and Lucy apart. But their love triumphs over Madame's maneuvers, and Lucy—aided by M. Paul—eventually leaves Madame Beck's pensionnat to start her own school.

The character of Madame Beck was suggested by Clair Zoe HEGER, the headmistress of the PENSIONNAT HEGER, where Charlotte and Emily Brontë went to study and where Charlotte later became a teacher. Although Madame Heger welcomed Charlotte and Emily into the school and praised their work, Charlotte came to believe that Madame Heger did not like her and conspired against her when she realized that Charlotte had fallen in love with her husband, Constantin George Romain HEGER, a renowned teacher in the school.

Belgium *See* BRUSSELS.

Bell, Currer, Ellis, and Acton Pseudonyms employed by Charlotte, Emily, and Anne Brontë, respectively. In 1845, when Charlotte proposed to her sisters that they seek a publisher for a selection of their poetry, Emily and Anne agreed on the condition that the three use pseudonyms. They chose androgynous names, but as Charlotte later wrote, the choice was "dictated by a sort of conscientious scruple at assuming Christian names positively masculine, while we did not like to declare ourselves women." Charlotte's choice of "Currer" may have been taken from Frances Richardson Currer, a philanthropist whose largesse had graced such familiar establishments as COWAN BRIDGE and the KEIGHLEY MECHANICS INSTITUTE. It was also a name Branwell had bestowed on Haworth Currer Warner, a character in his juvenile production the "Life of Warner Howard Warner." "Ellis" was another name familiar to locals, as the Ellis family owned a mill not far from Haworth, and Ellis Cunliffe Lister-Kay was a Liberal member of Parliament who represented the town of BRADFORD after passage of the REFORM BILL OF 1832. Anne may have taken the name "Acton" from the then-popular poet Eliza Acton (1777–1859). The Brontës appended their pen names to their collective *POEMS. JANE EYRE, SHIRLEY,* and *VILLETTE* were published under Currer Bell; *WUTHERING HEIGHTS,* under Ellis Bell; and *AGNES GREY* and *THE TENANT OF WILDFELL HALL.* under Acton Bell.

The sisters might not have intended their pen names to hide entirely their identities or their gender, but such was the effect. Critics not only assumed Currer, Ellis, and Acton Bell to be male, some even believed the three names belonged to one individual. The Brontë sisters hid their true identities from both their reading public and their publisher, Smith, Elder, until 1848, when the advertisement of Anne's second novel, *The Tenant of Wildfell Hall,* indicated that it was another work by Currer Bell rather than Acton Bell. Determined to set the record straight, Charlotte and Anne went to London (Emily, as usual, refused to leave home) and introduced themselves to George Smith. That same year, when Smith, Elder published a third edition of *Jane Eyre,* Charlotte wrote an introductory note indicating that Currer Bell's "claim to the title of novelist rests on this one work alone." Still the critics continued to conflate the three Bells. Charlotte made yet another attempt at

clarification in 1850, when as Currer Bell she wrote a "Biographical Notice of Ellis and Acton Bell" as a preface for a dual reprint of *Wuthering Heights* and *Agnes Grey* in which she identified Emily and Anne by name.

Benson Minor character in *THE TENANT OF WILDFELL HALL.* Benson is the butler at GRASSDALE MANOR, the family seat of Arthur, Lord HUNTINGDON. Despite his position, Benson is sympathetic to the lot of Helen HUNTINGDON, and when she finally flees her abusive husband together with her young son and her maidservant, Benson helps her steal away by secreting her bags and boxes and loading them onto the coach that spirits them away.

Bessie Character in *JANE EYRE.* A servant in Mrs. REED's household, Bessie treats Jane roughly at first. But Jane's good nature and sincerity win Bessie's heart, and the servant not only looks after Jane but later visits her at LOWOOD.

Blackhorse Marsh Location in *WUTHERING HEIGHTS.* When HEATHCLIFF kidnaps Catherine LINTON and Nelly DEAN toward the end of the novel, inhabitants of GIMMERTON, the village nearest WUTHERING HEIGHTS, speculate that the women are lost in this forlorn area near the moor.

Black Tom Parsonage cat that died at HAWORTH in June 1841.

Blackwood's Magazine Founded by the publisher William Blackwood in 1817, this periodical was a TORY organ. It featured contributors such as Sir Walter SCOTT (a Brontë favorite) and attacked radicals such as Lord BYRON. Branwell Brontë encouraged his sisters to create their own journal (see *BRANWELL'S BLACKWOOD'S MAGAZINE*) in the *Blackwood* format of polemical journalism, fiction, and book reviews.

Blake Hall The home of the INGHAM FAMILY, who employed Anne Brontë as governess in 1839. This grand estate in a small wooded park in Mirfield stood three stories high and had an 18th-century facade.

Blanche Minor character in *VILLETTE.* Along with ANGELIQUE and VIRGINIE, Blanche attempts to disrupt Lucy SNOWE's classroom. Lucy acts decisively by tearing up Blanche's "stupid" composition book, thereby bringing order to the classroom. Lucy's methods are similar to William CRIMSWORTH's in *THE PROFESSOR*.

Blanche, Mademoiselle A resident teacher at PENSIONNAT HEGER, she became the model for Mademoiselle Zéphyrine in *THE PROFESSOR* and Mademoiselle Zélie de St. Pierre in *VILLETTE*.

"Blatant, Mr." Minor character in *THE TENANT OF WILDFELL HALL*. "Mr. Blatant" is the name Arthur, Lord HUNTINGDON jestingly gives Mr. Leighton, the pastor of Mr. and Mrs. MAXWELL's church.

Bloomfield, Fanny Minor character in *AGNES GREY*. Only four years old, Fanny is one of four children Agnes GREY meets on her first day in the employ of the Bloomfield family.

Bloomfield, Harriet Minor character in *AGNES GREY*. Only two years old, Harriet is jolly and high spirited and, Agnes GREY believes, too young to teach.

Bloomfield, Mary Ann Minor character in *AGNES GREY*. Six-year-old Mary Ann seems to have no powers of concentration and no ability to learn her lessons. Mary Ann quarrels with her brother when she is not scheming with him to disturb Agnes GREY's peace of mind.

Bloomfield, Mr. Character in *AGNES GREY*. Agnes GREY's employer, he is intolerant and highly critical, expecting her to teach his unruly and spoiled children to be obedient. A fretful, inattentive father, he shows little understanding of Agnes's plight or of his wild children.

Bloomfield, Mrs. Character in *AGNES GREY*. As Agnes GREY's new employer, she welcomes Agnes rather coldly to her household and gives her a tough beefsteak to eat. Mrs. Bloomfield expects Agnes to perform her duties without complaint. She attributes any problems with the children to Agnes's inability to teach and to control them. Eventually Mrs. Bloomfield dismisses Agnes, complaining that she has seen virtually no improvement in the children.

Bloomfield, Tom Minor character in *AGNES GREY*. Seven-year-old Tom is a little tyrant who has been taught by a relative to torture birds and to think it is manly not to care about the feelings of other creatures. He acts superior to his siblings and expects Agnes GREY to be interested in all his activities.

Boarham, Mr. Minor character in *THE TENANT OF WILDFELL HALL*. Boarham is a wealthy elderly man who is an old friend of Helen HUNTINGDON's aunt and uncle. When Helen is first on the marriage market, Boarham courts her, going so far as to ask her uncle (who is also Helen's guardian) for her hand. Helen, who is years younger and has other, more attractive suitors, refers to the old fellow as "Bore'um" and refuses his offer of marriage.

Boissec, M. Minor character in *VILLETTE*. One of two examiners invited by Paul EMMANUEL to test Lucy SNOWE's command of French, M. Boissec seems to take sadistic delight in her struggle to complete her composition. During the examination, Lucy realizes that Boissec is one of the two men who harassed her when she tried to make her way to Madame BECK's school.

Bonaparte, Napoléon (1769–1821) Historical figure mentioned in *SHIRLEY*. The career of the Corsican-born general, consul, and emperor of France was made possible by the French Revolution. He rose in the ranks, famed for his brilliant victories in war. He instituted the Napoleonic code of laws and embarked on a series of wars across Europe. In England, he was both championed as a man of destiny who brought republican government to Europe and attacked as a ruthless dictator determined to destroyed England's power. England's two political parties—(TORY and WHIG)—tended to divide on the question of Napoléon. The Tories regarded him as a menace, and the Whigs, as a savior. In *SHIRLEY*, Matthewson HELSTONE and Robert MOORE quarrel, the former taking the Tory view of Napoléon, and the latter, the Whig position.

Bossuet, Jacques Bénigne (1627–1704) A French clergyman and author, he is best known for his philosophical treatises on the nature of history. In the *Life of Charlotte Bronte*, Mrs. Elizabeth GASKELL mentions that Charlotte read Bossuet on Oliver CROMWELL.

Boultby, Dr. Thomas   Minor character in *SHIRLEY*. The narrator refers to him favorably as one of the clergymen, like Cyril HALL, who are deemed "infallible to their admirers."

Boultby, Mrs.   Minor character in *SHIRLEY*. She idolizes her husband, Dr. Thomas BOULTBY, observing that he looks like an angel when he falls asleep after dinner.

bourgeois   Term used in *THE PROFESSOR* to describe the social class of many of the students. This French word was originally applied to the artisans and craftsmen of medieval towns whose socioeconomic position put them between the nobility (landed class) and the peasants. By the 19th century, the terms *bourgeois* and *bourgeoisie* became synonymous with "middle-class" and "the middle class," respectively, representing a broad range of people who had moved out of the lower peasant class into urban occupations and various kinds of businesses and manufacturing. In *VILLETTE*, Lucy SNOWE uses the term *bourgeois* to describe Madame BECK's style of dress.

Bradford   Town in Yorkshire, situated six miles east of Haworth. Bradford was the nearest metropolitan center to the Brontë home. When Branwell Brontë embarked in 1838 on his short-lived career as a portraitist, he set up shop in the rapidly growing manufacturing town, where he also was introduced to opium. Later, in the 1850s and 1860s, Bradford became a stop on the lecture circuit for such literary lights as Charles Dickens, John Ruskin, and William Makepeace THACKERAY.

Bradley, Reverend James Chesteron   The curate of Oakworth, near HAWORTH, he became the model for David SWEETING in *SHIRLEY*. Charlotte was greatly amused by the pompous curates who came to visit her father. She satirized them mercilessly in her novel.

Branderham, Rev. Jabes   Fictitious personage in *WUTHERING HEIGHTS*. When Mr. LOCKWOOD is forced to stay overnight at WUTHERING HEIGHTS, he sleeps in the paneled bed that had belonged to Catherine EARNSHAW. There he finds a small

library, including the volume *SEVENTY TIMES SEVEN, AND THE FIRST OF THE SEVENTY-FIRST. A PIOUS DISCOURSE DELIVERED BY THE REVEREND JABES BRANDERHAM, IN THE CHAPEL OF GIMMERDEN SOUGH*. Falling asleep, Lockwood dreams that he is forced to sit through one of the reverend's sermons and is persecuted for his inattention.

Branii Hills   *See* GLASS TOWN.

Branwell, Elizabeth (Aunt Branwell) (1776–1842)   The older sister of Maria Branwell BRONTË, Elizabeth came to live with Patrick BRONTË and his children after Maria's death. She was a strict, pious woman. She did not like having to move from Cornwall to Yorkshire but did her Christian duty, teaching the Brontë sisters how to sew and supervising them in household tasks. She seemed to

A silhouette of Elizabeth Branwell (Aunt Branwell), who cared for the Brontë children after their mother's death in 1821 (Life and Works of Charlotte Brontë and Her Sisters [1872–73], illustrations by E. M. Wimperis)

like the quiet Anne the best, and Anne seemed to appreciate her aunt's attention. The other children obeyed her, but there seems to have been little affection on either side, although she encouraged them to read and gave Charlotte financial assistance when she and Emily attended the Pensionnat Heger in Brussels. Apparently a well-informed woman, Aunt Branwell often discussed politics with Patrick.

Branwell's   Blackwood's   Magazine   Branwell BRONTË's precocious imitation from 1829 to 1831 of a popular journal, *BLACKWOOD'S MAGAZINE*. In articles such as "Journal of a Frenchman," "The Swiss Artist," "Review of the Causes of the Late War," and "The Bay of Glass Town"—not to mention his poetry and paintings—Branwell shows off his extraordinary understanding of European history and culture. He even invents a French poet, YOUNG SOULT. *See also* GLASS TOWN; JUVENILIA; *YOUNG MEN'S MAGAZINE, THE*.

Braun, Anna   Minor character in *VILLETTE*. She is Polly HOME's German teacher.

Bravey, Sir William   *See* GLASS TOWN.

Bretton, John Graham (Dr. John)   Character in *VILLETTE*. The son of Mrs. Louisa BRETTON, he is known as Dr. John by the townspeople he serves as doctor of VILLETTE but is called Graham by those close to him. He is a kind, energetic man who first falls in love with Paulina (Polly) HOME when she comes to stay with his mother. When Polly leaves with her father, and Mrs. Bretton's goddaughter, Lucy SNOWE, moves on to make her living in the world, he is educated as a doctor. In Villette, he meets Lucy one night, but they do not recognize each other after the separation of many years. Lucy knows him only as a kindly stranger who points the way to the school where she hopes to find employment. Later he becomes her good friend. Dr. John brings her back to health after she suffers a complete mental and physical breakdown. He seems unaware that Lucy has fallen in love with him. After a brief but intense infatuation with Ginevra FANSHAWE, a pupil at the pensionnat where Lucy teaches, he falls in love again with Polly, who has become Miss de Bassompierre since

her father inherited a French title. After some initial resistance from M. de Bassompierre, John succeeds in marrying Polly.

Bretton, Mrs. Louisa   Character in *VILLETTE*. She is Lucy SNOWE's godmother and benefactor. Lucy, poor and friendless, comes to stay with this kindly woman and her son, John Graham BRETTON. After Lucy leaves the Bretton household to make her own way in the world, she does not see Mrs. Bretton again until the latter arrives in Villette to make a home for her son. Lucy is again taken up by Mrs. Bretton. She and her son restore Lucy's health when she suffers what amounts to a nervous breakdown.

Briarmains   The home of Mr. and Mrs. YORKE in *SHIRLEY*.

Briggs, Mr.   Minor character in *JANE EYRE*. On behalf of his client, Richard MASON, the attorney Mr. Briggs objects in church to the marriage between Mr. Edward ROCHESTER and Jane EYRE. As the ceremony gets under way, he announces that Mr. Rochester gets already married to Bertha MASON, Richard Mason's sister. Later, at THORN-FIELD, he also informs Jane that her uncle, John EYRE, is a friend of Richard Mason's, and that when her uncle received her letter announcing her marriage to Mr. Rochester, her uncle said as much to Richard Mason, who then took legal action against the marriage.

Broc, Marie   Minor character in *VILLETTE*. She is a cretin whom Lucy SNOWE must care for during the school's September holidays.

Brocklehurst, Mr.   Character in *JANE EYRE*. An EVANGELICAL clergyman, he comes to GATESHEAD HALL at the invitation of Mrs. REED to see if Jane EYRE is an acceptable candidate for his charity school, LOWOOD. Mrs. Reed tells him that Jane is an ungrateful girl who is not to be trusted. He agrees to take the child and make known at the school Jane's unreliable character. At Lowood, Mr. Brocklehurst makes Jane stand in front of her schoolmates and teachers while he calls her a liar and demands that she be treated with suspicion and strict discipline. A religious tyrant, Mr.

Brocklehurst demands that all the girls at the school be fed only the minimum amount of food, and he ignores reports that even the poor quantities are so badly prepared as to be inedible. When several children die as a result of his incompetent and cruel supervision, reforms are instituted, and Jane's later years at Lowood are markedly better.

Brocklehurst, Mrs.   Minor character in *JANE EYRE*. She is the wife of Mr. Brocklehurst.

Brocklehurst, Naomi   Mentioned in *JANE EYRE*. She is the founder of LOWOOD, and her son, Mr. BROCKLEHURST, is the school's treasurer and manager.

Brocklehurst children   Minor characters in *JANE EYRE*, they are the children of Mr. and Mrs. BROCKLEHURST: Augusta, Broughton, and Theodore.

Charlotte Brontë's drawing of the tyrannical Mr. Brocklehurst, headmaster of Lowood in Jane Eyre
(*Life and Works of Charlotte Brontë and Her Sisters* [1872–73], illustrations by E. M. Wimperis)

Brontë, Anne (1820–1849)   The youngest of the Brontë children, Anne was always delicate of constitution, and in tow of her sisters she followed her father's lead in keeping to herself and seldom visiting the village of Haworth. From an early age she collaborated with sister Emily, to whom she seemed to gravitate in childhood, on the GONDAL saga, inspired by the Arctic expeditions of Sir James Clark Ross and Sir William Edward Parry. Anne has been described as the best looking of the Brontë sisters with her fine skin and well-shaped eyebrows. Like her sisters, she learned to sew and do other household tasks under the watchful eye of her Aunt Branwell. Although quiet and the favorite of an aunt who taught submission rather than assertion of the will, Anne would prove resourceful and self-reliant.

At 16, Anne was sent to the ROE HEAD school to study with Miss WOOLER. She managed to stay there nearly two years, but then—like Emily before her—was sent home in a state of collapse. Brontë biographer Lyndall GORDON suggests that by this time the bond between Anne and Emily was fixed, and the excluded Charlotte (also at Roe Head) showed little sympathy for Anne, whom Charlotte deemed competition for Emily's affection. At any rate, Charlotte never explained why Anne was allowed to deteriorate so badly at the school.

Anne returned home to roam the moors with Emily; however, she seemed determined to demonstrate her independence from the family circle, as well as to contribute to its support, by taking a position as a governess, at the age 19, with the INGHAM family. As she would dramatize in *AGNES GREY*, she was treated as no better than a servant and came to regard her employment as a humiliating confinement. A second post as governess to the ROBINSON family proved hardly more satisfactory, though the experience also contributed material to *Agnes Grey*, which conveys the impression of a shrewdly observant mind.

As was the case for her sisters, Anne became increasingly disturbed over the behavior of her brother, Branwell. His drinking coarsened him, and Anne's second novel, *THE TENANT OF WILDFELL HALL*, explored the life of a woman married to an alcoholic. Since women in England had few rights at the time, they were helpless in such a situation, and the frustrations of the sisters with their

The famous pillar portrait of the three Brontë sisters (from left to right: Anne, Emily, and Charlotte) was painted by Branwell Brontë, who had originally painted himself into the picture and later took himself out. There is still an outline of his form in the pillar. Branwell's destructive behavior troubled Anne, and she later wrote about alcoholism in The Tenant of Wildfell Hall. (Hulton/Archive by Getty Images)

brother are clearly transformed into the tragedy of a woman who attempts to flee and re-create her own life. The protagonist, Helen HUNTINGDON, shows a resourcefulness that also reflected Anne's spirit, which enabled her to endure more than four years as a governess, a period of employment much longer than her other sisters could manage. After Charlotte's *Jane Eyre, The Tenant of Wildfell Hall* marked the greatest success among readers and critics that the sisters would enjoy during their short careers.

In June 1848, Anne's delicate health began to break down, and she took on the pale, exhausted look that Charlotte ascribes to Caroline HELSTONE in *Shirley*. Charlotte attributed Anne's terrible cough to asthma. It became painful for Anne to breathe, although Charlotte noted that her sister never complained and bore her suffering stoically.

But it was TUBERCULOSIS, not asthma, that was killing Anne. She could not sleep, and she spent her days in a depressed, languid state. To Charlotte it seemed as if Emily's death in December 1848 somehow brought on Anne's final decline, particularly because Anne and Emily were always so close.

In the spring of 1849, Charlotte managed to take the weakening Anne to the sea for a last look at the Yorkshire coast. On May 27, Anne was able to watch a brilliant sunset from her chair near a window. She died the next day, exhorting Charlotte to "take courage." It was, in Lyndall Gordon's words, a "patient, Christian death."

Brontë, Branwell   *See* BRONTË, PATRICK BRANWELL.

Brontë, Charlotte (1816–1855)   The third of six children, Charlotte was the last surviving child of Patrick and Maria Branwell Brontë. Like her older sister Maria, Charlotte was a precocious and pious child, and like her younger sisters, Emily and Anne, she had considerable literary gifts, expressed early in her ANGRIA saga. Early on, she seems to have competed with her youngest sister, Anne, for the affection of Emily, the most strong willed and intensely imaginative member of the family.

Charlotte's mother died in 1821, when Charlotte was five and the family had just taken up residence in HAWORTH parsonage, her father having obtained what was called a "perpetual curacy." Aunt Branwell, her mother's sister, came to live in the house, supervising Charlotte and the other children and making sure the girls were versed in the domestic arts.

Charlotte was educated first at the Clergy Daughters School at COWAN BRIDGE, a dreadfully run institution with an unsanitary kitchen. Both of Charlotte's older sisters, Maria and Elizabeth, died shortly after coming home from the school, their tuberculosis exacerbated by conditions of neglect and incompetence there.

Later Charlotte was sent to Miss WOOLER's school at Roe Head, a much more competently run institution, where she thrived. Miss Wooler employed her as an assistant teacher from 1835 to 1838; however, Charlotte found teaching a burden and did not feel she had any special gift for it. As

Following the success of Jane Eyre, *Charlotte Brontë traveled to London, where she met several literary figures, including her hero, William Makepeace Thackeray, and Elizabeth Gaskell, her future biographer.* (Library of Congress)

HEGER, a dynamic teacher whom she re-created in the characters of Edward CRIMSWORTH in *THE PROFESSOR* and Paul EMMANUEL in *VILLETTE*. Charlotte attended the pensionnat between 1842 and 1844 but returned home when the tension between her and Monsieur Heger's wife became intolerable.

Plans for the Brontë school never materialized—in part because Anne sought employment as a governess and in part because the family did not have the financial means and often suffered illnesses that made a consistent plan of action impossible. Throughout these early years the Brontë sisters and their brother, Branwell, wrote poetry and fiction and formed inchoate desires to attain literary distinction and even fame. Charlotte, Anne, and Emily finally published, in 1846, a volume of poetry, *POEMS*, under the pseudonyms of Currer, Ellis, and Acton Bell, but their effort went virtually unnoticed.

Undaunted, they continued to write, and in 1847 Charlotte scored a phenomenal success with *JANE EYRE*, her second novel. (She could not find a publisher for her first novel, *THE PROFESSOR*.) The ROMANTIC, melodramatic story became an instant classic, although Charlotte was heavily criticized for what certain critics deemed her coarseness. Standards of the day—both literary and social—called for more genteel subjects than those that the Brontës usually chose.

Charlotte's sisters did not achieve similar recognition with their first novels—Emily's *Wuthering Heights* and Anne's *Agnes Grey*—although Anne's second novel, *The Tenant of Wildfell Hall*, almost rivaled Charlotte's sudden success. Emily and Anne died in quick succession, in 1848 and 1849, shocking Charlotte into a prolonged period of depression and psychosomatic illness made worse by mercury poisoning, resulting from prescription medication. Although she continued to write—producing two more superb novels, *SHIRLEY* and *VILLETTE*—and received the flattering attention of such literary masters as William Makepeace THACKERAY and Harriet MARTINEAU, she was reclusive and devoted to her father, who suffered many illnesses.

In 1853 Charlotte accepted the marriage proposal of Reverend Arthur Bell Nicholls, who had worked for her father at Haworth. At first, Patrick Brontë very much opposed the marriage, but he

an alternative she tried work as a governess in 1839 and again in 1841, but both times she found her positions humiliating and tiresome. As her sister Anne learned, Charlotte discovered that governesses were treated with little respect and were considered no better than servants whom their charges did not have to obey.

Like her other sisters, Charlotte found time spent away from home an ordeal, so she, Emily, and Anne conceived of a plan to establish their own school. Although their father did not have the means to help them monetarily, they enlisted the support of their Aunt Branwell. But first Charlotte and Emily set off for BRUSSELS to attend the PENSIONNAT HEGER school, where they could strengthen their knowledge of languages, in particular French and German. There Charlotte fell love with Constantin George Romain gradually relented, after assurances that his privacy would be respected when Nicholls joined the household and that everything possible would be done to ensure his comfort. By all accounts the marriage was a success, with Charlotte enjoying a degree of happiness new to her.

Charlotte's sudden death in 1855—perhaps brought on by complications during her pregnancy—was a shattering blow and an injustice that her biographer Elizabeth GASKELL was determined to rectify. Thus, not only Charlotte but all the Brontës were memorialized in *THE LIFE OF CHARLOTTE BRONTË* (1857), one of the great biographies of the 19th century. Mrs. Gaskell's mission was not merely to document Charlotte's life but to make her an exemplary figure of a suffering woman and an aspiring writer.

The response to Mrs. Gaskell's biography was extraordinary. She put the Brontës on the literary map of England with Charlotte as the starring figure, devoted to her father and the memories of her siblings, a belatedly fulfilled wife, and an independent and brilliant artist. Many critics who had previously decried Charlotte's work repented in print, testifying that in the conditions of her life they had found the key to the style of her novels.

Brontë, Elizabeth (1815–1825)   The second child of Patrick and Maria Branwell Brontë, Elizabeth was viewed by her father as less intelligent than the others and best fit for housework. Little is known about her, although biographers suggest she was rather docile, displaying perhaps some of Anne's stoicism as well. She was nine years old when her father asked her how to educate a woman, to which Elizabeth replied that she should be taught to govern her house well.

In July 1824 Elizabeth was sent to the Clergy Daughters School at COWAN BRIDGE, run incompetently by William Carus WILSON. The children were fed poorly prepared food in unsanitary conditions and fell ill with diseases such as typhus and TUBERCULOSIS. Although Patrick Brontë visited the school, he somehow did not observe that an epidemic had caused many pupils to waste away. Elizabeth was sent home in May 1825, already far gone with consumption. She died in June, at age 10, just a month after her sister Maria passed away from the same disease.

Brontë, Emily Jane (1818–1848)   Although she produced what is unquestionably one of the masterpieces of English romanticism, the novel *WUTHERING HEIGHTS*, little is known about the actual biography of the second-eldest surviving Brontë sister. One reason for the paucity of information is her early death at age 30, when she succumbed to TUBERCULOSIS, the disease that killed most members of her immediate family. Another is her self-containment and reclusiveness. When in 1845 her sister Charlotte discovered a manuscript of her verse, Emily accused her sister of invading her privacy. Although Charlotte ultimately prevailed upon Emily to publish her poetry, the former had learned a hard lesson—one that led, in all probability, to

Branwell Brontë painted this portrait of his intensely private sister Emily in the early 1830s. (National Portrait Gallery, London)

her destruction of nearly all of Emily's correspondence and diaries upon her death.

In life Emily Brontë's society consisted almost exclusively of her family; she seems to have been particularly close to her sister Anne, with whom in youth she shared the imaginary world of GONDAL, created as a counterpart to Charlotte and Branwell's fabulous ANGRIA. But it is arguable that the members of the household to whom Emily felt closest were the Brontë animals. Some of the most memorable and telling anecdotes that survive about Emily concern her relationship to nonhuman beings, as when she self-cauterized a wound incurred during an encounter with a strange dog or when she broke up a fight between her dog KEEPER and another large canine using only her own strength and a box of ground pepper, which she liberally applied to both dogs' snouts. The latter incident was recorded by a local merchant, who commented on Emily's apparent obliviousness to the local men who looked on but did not dare interfere with the dog fight. This merchant is only one of many observers to mention the mannish quality that set Emily apart from her sisters and other women of her station. Constantin George Romain HEGER, her teacher in Brussels in 1842, would later remark unequivocally, "She should have been a man—a great navigator. Her powerful reason would have deduced new spheres of discovery from the knowledge of the old; and her strong, imperious will would never have been daunted by opposition or difficulty. . . ."

Emily's nine-month sojourn in BRUSSELS, where she went with Charlotte to study, was the only time that she left England and—aside from three months spent at a local boarding school and a six-month stint as a teacher, both of which ended when she returned home ill—the only extended

Emily Brontë's sketch of herself drawing. She is seated at her writing desk with her dog, Keeper, to her left and with Anne's dog, Flossy, and a cat on the bed. (*The Art of the Brontës*, 1995)

period she spent away from her HAWORTH parsonage household. Far from the only environment where she felt comfortable, and more particularly far from her beloved moorlands, Emily distinguished herself in Belgium by her nonconformity and unsociability. She apparently made no attempt to make herself likable and refused to go along with her sister's adoption of more fashionable Continental fashions. Her refusal to bend, to sacrifice any part of her powerful sense of personal integrity, prompted her schoolmates to taunt her. Emily's response was anger and the altogether characteristic statement, "I wish to be as God made me."

This wish to be in some sense "natural"—as evident in her physicality and her affinity for animals and the out-of-doors—is part of what makes Emily at once unique among her peers and also a true ROMANTIC. Her unwillingness or inability to break free of Gondal and her otherworldly, almost mystical nature reflect the same desire to escape the self and individual identity expressed, for example, in William WORDSWORTH's "Snowdon" vision in *The Prelude*. But in her writing she often couples a longing for release from corporeal existence with a decidedly earthbound, sensual vision of eternity. A verse like "Yet none would ask a Heaven / More like this Earth than thine" leads us directly into *Wuthering Heights* and Cathy Earnshaw's dream of dying and going to heaven, only to beg the angels to let her come back to her earthly paradise amidst the heath, where she and Heathcliff are one.

Like her doomed lovers, Emily herself seemed to yearn for a world beyond this one—whether it be Gondal, the moor, or some other place outside space and time. Charlotte wondered at her sister's bravery in the face of early and certain death, but Emily clearly did not look on her demise as an end to anything. Charlotte's "Biographical Notice of Ellis and Acton Bell," written as a preface to the one-volume second edition of *Wuthering Heights* and sister Anne's *Agnes Grey*, conveys a sense of Emily's attitude toward death as less acceptance than anticipation: "She made haste to leave us. Yet, while physically she perished, mentally, she grew stronger than we had yet known her. . . . I have seen nothing like it; but, indeed, I have never seen her parallel in anything. Stronger than a man, simpler than a child, her nature stood alone."

Brontë, Maria (1814–1825) The eldest child of Patrick and Maria Branwell Brontë. Charlotte Brontë said she provided a portrait of Maria in Helen BURNS of *Jane Eyre;* just as Maria was persecuted by Miss ANDREWS at COWAN BRIDGE, so was Helen by the teacher Miss SCATCHERD at LOWOOD. According to Elizabeth GASKELL, Charlotte told her that Maria had a formidable intellect and took an active interest in current affairs—she read the newspaper to her younger siblings—but got into trouble for her untidiness.

The children at Cowan Bridge were poorly fed in unsanitary conditions, and Maria became ill. She had remembered her mother's religious injunctions and endured her illness with the same fortitude as she had her punishment at school. She succumbed to TUBERCULOSIS in May 1825, when she was only 11. Biographers have described her passing almost as the sacrifice of a saint. Charlotte remembered Maria as taking the place of her mother, for Maria had a maturity far beyond her years. Although none of her siblings would attain the kind of religious sublimity Maria exemplified, she was their model in the sense that she inspired a calm air of resoluteness and independence.

Brontë, Maria Branwell (1783–1821) Maria Branwell married Patrick Brontë on December 29, 1812. She was just shy of 30, a small and elegant woman from a merchant family of Methodists. Beginning in 1814, she had a baby a year. In 1820, her husband, Patrick, was offered the parish of HAWORTH, a rather remote village with polluted water and high rates of early death, even for the early 19th century. By January 1821 Maria had been diagnosed with cancer and was confined to her room. She exhorted her children to be quiet and not disturb their father, or herself. She died in September, lamenting, "Oh God, my poor children!"

Brontë, Patrick (1777–1861) Born on April 17, Patrick was the eldest of 10 children of Irish parents living in County Down, Northern Ireland. Sources indicate several variants of his family name, including Brunty, Bronty, Branty, Bronte, Prunty, or perhaps even O'Prunty. It was Patrick himself who settled on Brontë, apparently while a student at Cambridge, in England.

Early on, Patrick developed a passion for poetry, especially John MILTON's *Paradise Lost,*

Patrick Brontë was born in this cottage in Elmdale, County Down, Ireland, in 1777. (*Brontëana*, 1898)

which Shirley KEELDAR criticizes in Charlotte's novel *Shirley.* At 12, he was a blacksmith's assistant, but the precocious Patrick's early career was as a teacher. Around 1800 he was sponsored by Reverend Thomas Tighe, a wealthy landowner, who became impressed with Patrick while he was tutoring Tighe's son. With Tighe's assistance, Patrick attended Cambridge, an extraordinary privilege for a young man from the Irish peasant class.

Confirmed in his career as a clergyman, Patrick took holy orders in 1806. He married Maria Branwell in 1812, and in 1820 they settled in HAWORTH. It has been reported that by the time he became curate at Haworth, Patrick had lost all trace of his Irish accent. His life and his children's was transformed by the death of his wife in 1821. Without her tempering presence, the household became more insular. Patrick impressed on his children a sense of religious duty and a distrust of society that became manifested in their desire to stay close to home and to defer to his wishes. At the same time,

Patrick shared his keen intellect and intense curiosity with them. The very idea of an independent, critical mind had an overwhelming impact, especially on his strong-willed daughter Emily, though hardly less so on the more sociable Charlotte and the quiet but determined Anne. Maria, the eldest, seems to have delighted her father because she absorbed his piety so early in her short life. Not surprisingly, his only son, Branwell, would take pride of place in his father's plans for the future.

After his wife died, her sister, Elizabeth Branwell, came to superintend the house and children. A woman of firm Christian principles, she seems to have suited Patrick, even though she did not care much for Haworth or Yorkshire manners. Although he was to enjoy a long life, Patrick was often struck by illness, and his almost perpetual infirmities deeply affected his children, especially Charlotte, who considered it her duty to attend to her father after the deaths of her siblings. She often feared for her father's life and at one point thought he might be going blind. After a successful cataract operation, however, his sight was restored, and though he remained only fitfully healthy, the example of his daily courage in facing adversity won Charlotte's absolute love.

If Charlotte seemed inordinately attached to her father, it was in part because he had shown remarkable interest in her plans to establish a school. He had accompanied her and Emily to Belgium where the sisters enrolled in the PENSION-NAT HEGER in order to refine their language skills and acquire the credentials required to establish their own school.

Not that Patrick actively approved of literary careers for women. This aspect of his daughters'

lives was vouchsafed to him only in rare moments of candor. Charlotte, for example, read a few of the interesting reviews of *Jane Eyre* to him when she first disclosed that she was its author. Patrick's response was telling: He mildly accepted the fact and expressed only faint surprise. He later told the biographer Mrs. Elizabeth GASKELL that he had suspected that Charlotte and her sisters were writing. At least one biographer, Rebecca FRASER, believes Patrick was teasing Charlotte by not reacting strongly to her news.

At any rate, visitors to Haworth could see that Patrick was extremely proud of Charlotte and delighted to hear reports of her success. As she grew older, he also shared confidences with her

The library at St. John's College, Cambridge. Patrick Brontë was able to enroll at St. John's with the assistance of Reverend Thomas Tighe, a wealthy landowner who took notice of Patrick's intellect and curiosity while he tutored Tighe's son.
(*A History of the University of Cambridge,* 1815)

Reverend Patrick Brontë, who outlived his wife and six children, died in 1861 at the age of 84. (Hulton/Archive by Getty Images)

and gave her her mother's letters to read. That he was a demanding father who asserted extraordinary privileges is clear from Charlotte's awareness that he would object to the marriage proposal she received from Arthur Bell NICHOLLS. Nicholls, who had been Patrick's assistant and knew the family well, told Charlotte that he had been afraid to ask for her hand, and when Charlotte consulted her father, he expressed vehement objections to Nicholls. Yet the patient Charlotte apparently knew her father well: Over several months, Patrick, assured he would still have a treasured place in the home Nicholls would be joining, eventually relented.

Patrick survived even the death of Charlotte, his last child. Although he was hurt by some of Mrs. Gaskell's comments about his role in Charlotte's life, he praised the biography when it came out in 1857 and seemed to think that on balance it had done Charlotte and her family justice. He affirmed that the biographer had ensured his daughter's fame. He also continued to exert an almost terrifying hold over Nicholls, who stayed on at Haworth.

Patrick died after a very harsh winter on June 7. His death certificate specified the cause as "chronic bronchitis; dyspepsia, convulsions, duration nine hours."

Brontë, Patrick Branwell (1817–1848) The only son and the fourth child of Patrick and Maria Branwell Brontë. Not much is known about Branwell's earliest years, although it is clear that the birth of a male child gave his father and sisters much pleasure. Patrick referred to his son as having been a "naughty child," but too much may have been made of that in light of Branwell's subsequent delinquencies. From his own testimony and from poetry he wrote, it is clear that Branwell was profoundly affected by the deaths of his sisters Maria and Elizabeth and had vivid memories of their struggle for life, a struggle evoked, for example, in the line "The voiceless gasp—the sickening chill."

As was typical of the time, it was Branwell, the male child of the family, who studied Greek, not his sisters. But like them he took to writing poetry and fiction early on and would later write letters to

The only male child in the Brontë family, Branwell worked as a writer, portraitist, tutor, and railway clerk, though he never found great success in any particular occupation. Portrait medallion by J. B. Leyland (Life and Works of Charlotte Brontë and Her Sisters [1872–73], illustrations by E. M. Wimperis)

After he painted the "gun group" portrait of the Brontë family in 1833, Branwell decided to become an artist; in 1835, he wrote a letter requesting admission to the Royal Academy of Arts in London but never attended. (*Haworth Past and Present,* 1879)

famous writers such as William WORDSWORTH in the hope of obtaining a sponsor for his work. He urged his sisters to collaborate on a periodical that imitated *BLACKWOOD'S MAGAZINE.* He wrote poems, tales, and reviews and drew pictures for BRANWELL'S BLACKWOOD'S MAGAZINE. He adopted pseudonyms, such as Captain John Bud, a historian, and Young Soult, a poet. He sometime acted as an editor introducing his sisters' writings. After six months of work on the journal he issued a farewell message. The biographer Juliet BARKER finds this behavior typical of Branwell: initial enthusiasm followed by boredom and plans for yet another new venture.

Although Branwell continued to write, his new ambition was to be an artist, and accordingly, in 1835 he wrote a letter addressed to the Royal Academy in London requesting admission as a "probationary student." Accounts vary as to what happened next: Some biographers suggest that Branwell went to London, was overwhelmed by the talent he saw there, and in a panic, went on a

drinking spree and wasted his father's money. Others believe this inference unfounded or lacking in evidence, since there are no extant letters that clear up exactly why Branwell's plans went awry, or even if he actually traveled to London. It is possible that the letter to the academy was never sent. At any rate, the episode, like so many others in his life, is a tale of hopes unfulfilled.

Branwell then turned to a number of occupations: portraitist (1838), tutor (1839), railway worker (1840), and back to tutor (1842). He was dismissed from his positions for either incompetence or drinking that led to other irregularities. He had an affair with Lydia ROBINSON, the mother of a boy he was tutoring. There seems to be no doubt that Branwell loved Mrs. Robinson and that she professed the same feelings for him; his poetry certainly reflects his obsession with her. But when her husband died, she did not marry Branwell, apparently because the will specifically stated that if she ever saw Branwell again she would not inherit her husband's estate.

Branwell was never able to reconcile himself to the loss of Mrs. Robinson. Although he fitfully tried to resume a career as a writer, much of his remaining five years was a sorry record of self-degradation and self-pity. Over and over again he turned to drink and opium to salve his sorrow. He wrote letters to friends and family asking for money; once his father's favorite, he was now considered a lost cause. Branwell himself became obsessed with the subject of death, and in 1848 Patrick, who had attended the deathbeds of many of his parishioners, now had to watch his son die. Shortly before his end, Branwell said to a friend, "In all my past life I have done nothing either great or good." With the family gathered around him, he suddenly started up, then collapsed, and died of TUBERCULOSIS at age 31.

It is hard to gauge just how angry Branwell must have made his sisters. As the favored one, he had had all the privileges yet had ruined his life. Only after his death was Charlotte able to forgive him, writing, "All his errors—to speak plainly—all his vices seemed nothing to me in that moment; every wrong he had done, every pain he had caused, vanished; his sufferings only were remembered."

Brontë juvenilia   *See* JUVENILIA.

Brontë Society   Established in Haworth in 1893, this organization of Brontë lovers has been responsible for preserving Brontë manuscripts and other items owned by or associated with the family. The society created a museum at Haworth Parsonage, which became a pilgrimage site for Brontë readers, writers about the Brontës, and a general public fascinated with the family and their life. Indeed, when Virginia Woolf visited the museum in 1904, she remarked that it emphasized the writers' lives more than their works.

Broughton House   Branwell Brontë tutored the children at this 18th-century estate at Broughton in Furness.

Brown, Martha   A servant at HAWORTH PARSONAGE, she witnessed Branwell Brontë's attacks of delirium, observed Emily's decline and death, and was present when Charlotte made her will and

died. Brown received a legacy from Patrick Brontë and accompanied Charlotte's widower, Arthur Bell Nicholls, to Ireland after Patrick's death.

Brown, Mr.   Minor character in *THE PROFESSOR*. He is an associate of HUNSDEN. Mr. Brown helps William CRIMSWORTH find employment at a private school in BRUSSELS.

Brown, Nancy   Character in *AGNES GREY*. Both Agnes GREY and Mr. WESTON take an interest in the widowed cottager (who suffers from an eye infection) after Mr. HATFIELD rudely ignores her and her troubles. Through Nancy, Agnes is able to gauge Mr. Hatfield's insensitivity and Mr. Weston's compassion.

Brussels   The capital of Belgium. In Charlotte Brontë's *THE PROFESSOR*, William CRIMSWORTH goes to Brussels to find employment and is hired to teach in a school with Belgian, French, English, and German students. Chapter 7 of the novel presents a portrait of Brussels, where Charlotte and sister Emily attended a school, PENSIONNAT HEGER, to perfect their French and German and to learn more about private education so that they might set up their own school. Crimsworth describes his journey through central Belgium, the Flemish farmhouses, and the fertile fields. He finds Brussels a charming "little city," commenting on picturesque sights that remind him of Dutch paintings.

Buckworth, Reverend John   A friend of Patrick Brontë. It was Buckworth who first brought Patrick to Yorkshire, where the latter worked as his assistant from 1809 to 1810. Later, Patrick would in gratitude dedicate the first of his *Cottage Poems* to Buckworth.

Bud, Captain John   *See* GLASS TOWN; "HISTORY OF YOUNG MEN, THE."

Burder, Mary   Patrick Brontë proposed to her twice, in 1806 or 1807 and again in 1823. The two seem to have become engaged in 1807, but then the relationship broke off. The reasons for their parting remain uncertain, but Mary Burder was obviously still bitter about their breakup in 1823, when she firmly rejected Patrick's second proposal.

Burns, Helen Character in *JANE EYRE*. Helen becomes Jane EYRE's best friend at LOWOOD. Whereas Jane is fiery and cannot accept injustice and humiliation, Helen is patient and stoical. She advises Jane to accept her punishment and to treat everyone with Christian charity. When Jane learns that Helen is dying of CONSUMPTION, she joins Helen on her deathbed. The two girls fall asleep together, and the following morning Jane is carried away from Helen's bed, where Helen has died during the night.

Byron, George Gordon (Lord Byron) (1788–1824) A daring and controversial English writer with a reputation for ruining women. Byron wrote fierce satires and love poetry and is renowned as one of the greatest poets of the ROMANTIC period. His work often features intense, moody, and sometimes threatening figures who have come to be called "Byronic heroes." He is perhaps best known for such longer works as *Manfred* (1817) and *Don Juan* (1819–24). In *THE PROFESSOR*, William CRIMSWORTH mentions that Frances Evans HENRI becomes "excited" when reading Byron. *See also* GLASS TOWN.

Lord Byron. Francis Evans Henri reads Byron in The Professor. *Mr. Rochester and Heathcliff have often been called Byronic heroes.* (Library of Congress)

Carlyle, Thomas (1795–1881) The Brontës read the work of this important essayist, who was born in Scotland but became a fixture of English literary life. Writing in a florid style about German history, Oliver CROMWELL, and the French Revolution, among other subjects, Carlyle is best known for his "great man" theory of history, which propounds that history is largely the biography of great men. Elizabeth GASKELL mentions Charlotte's reading of Carlyle in the *Life of Charlotte Brontë*.

Caroline (1) Minor character in *THE PROFESSOR*. One of three students who disrupt William CRIMSWORTH's class. Like EULALIE and HORTENSE, Caroline is not a serious student. She is sensuous and tries to flirt with Crimsworth. He believes she has the kind of nature that will become coarser as she grows older.

Caroline (2) Character mentioned in *THE TENANT OF WILDFELL HALL*. Caroline was the fiancée of Lord LOWBOROUGH before he lost his fortune to drink, drugs, and gambling debts. Losing his income resulted in his losing Caroline, too.

Caroline Vernon *See* ANGRIA.

Carter Minor character in *JANE EYRE*. A surgeon, he is fetched by Mr. ROCHESTER to attend to Richard MASON's wound.

Cartwright, William The owner of Rawford's Mill, near HAWORTH, he served as the model for Robert MOORE in *SHIRLEY*. Like Cartwright, Moore is shot at by LUDDITES. Patrick Brontë undoubtedly supported the mill owner, although he was not without sympathy for the Luddite cause, a popular one in his parish.

Castlereagh, Robert Stewart (1769–1829) British statesman. As part of the Tory administration, he opposed Napoléon BONAPARTE and set up alliances against him. In *SHIRLEY* he is criticized by Mr. Hiram YORKE, a Whig.

Catholicism Doctrines and organization of the Roman Catholic Church. There is a strong anti–Roman Catholic strain in *THE PROFESSOR* and *VILLETTE*. The roots of Charlotte Brontë's antipathy seem to stem from her experience at the PENSIONNAT HEGER in BRUSSELS. Although Clair Zoe HEGER, the Catholic headmistress, did not force Charlotte or Emily to observe Catholic services or practices, Charlotte saw the regimen of the religion, and especially the role of the priesthood, as coercive. She favored the Protestant idea of the individual who is bound by his or her own conscience and not subservient to a centralized church in Rome. Charlotte viewed Roman Catholicism as enforcing a conformism on the individual. At the pensionnat, Charlotte was devoted to her teacher, Constantin George Romain HEGER, and although there is no evidence that Monsieur Heger tried to convert Charlotte, in *Villette*, Lucy SNOWE's teacher, Paul EMMANUEL, tries (with the aid of a priest, Pere SILAS) to convert her to Catholicism. Furthermore, there is a sense in *The Professor* and *Villette* of Roman Catholicism, or Romanism, being a "conspiratorial religion"—as Lucy calls it—in which the powerful conspire against individuals for the good of the faith. Thus, Romanism is associated with tyranny and thought control. Indeed, to Lucy the very idea of Catholicism seems to undermine the individual will. Lucy is horrified after she resorts to the Catholic confessional to relieve her suffering over her unrequited love for John Graham BRETTON—just as Charlotte had done when she was tormented by her love for the married Monsieur Heger. The biographer Juliet BARKER suggests that this momentary capitulation to the spell of Catholicism strengthened Charlotte's suspicion of it.

Chambers, Robert One of the publishers of the literary periodical *Chambers's Edinburgh Journal,* he responded helpfully to Charlotte Brontë's request for advice about publishing. She later remembered his "brief and business-like but, civil and sensible reply." His letter has not survived.

Chantry, Henry *See* GLASS TOWN.

Chapel Royal Charlotte Brontë attended services at this Anglican church in BRUSSELS.

Chapter Coffee House Following their father's lead, Charlotte and Emily Brontë stayed at this inn near St. Paul's Cathedral during their visits to London.

Charles Character mentioned in *VILLETTE.* He is Lucy SNOWE's uncle. She hears of him from a waiter at a London inn that Charles favored.

Charlie Dog in *WUTHERING HEIGHTS.* Charlie is one of two pointers—the fiercer of the pair—that set out with the 13-year-old Catherine LINTON from THRUSHCROSS GRANGE. Cathy's caretaker, Nelly DEAN, imagines the girl is off on a picnic, but the simple outing, for Cathy, turns into an exploration of the world beyond the parklands around her home. When Nelly goes out to look for Cathy, the first indication that Cathy has ended up at nearby WUTHERING HEIGHTS is the sight of Charlie lying under a window at the Heights, with a swollen head and a bleeding ear. Charlie and the other pointer, PHOENIX, have apparently been bitten by the fierce dogs that stand guard at the Heights.

Chatterton, Thomas (1752–1770) A precocious English poet, Chatterton was steeped in medieval literature and first made his reputation with his purported discovery of the work of Thomas Rowley, a 15th-century monk. Chatterton's ruse was eventually discovered, but only after he had successfully duped important literary figures in London. He continued to write essays, stories, and poetry, this time under his own name, but could not sell much and in despair committed suicide. The romantic intensity of his work—including the Rowley writings—influenced later writers, including the Brontës. In *THE LIFE OF CHARLOTTE BRONTË,*

Elizabeth GASKELL mentions that Charlotte visited Chatterton's rooms on a trip to London.

Cholmodeley, Mrs. Minor character in *VILLETTE.* One of Ginevra FANSHAWE's chaperons, the fashionable Mrs. Cholmodeley introduces Ginevra to the social life of VILLETTE. Ginevra takes advantage of this lady by ordering all sorts of fancy dresses and other presents.

Church of England England's official national church was established between 1632 and 1634, when Henry VIII severed his country's connection to the Roman Catholic Church. Also called the Anglican Church, the Church of England contains elements of both Catholic and Protestant Christianity. The monarch of England is the official head of the church. To belong to the Church of England in the period of the Brontës meant subscribing to not only religious but also political principles—to affirm one's support of the status quo. Mr. HATFIELD, the rector in *AGNES GREY,* considers opponents of the Church of England (called DISSENTERS) dangerous and evil influences, as he tells his congregation.

Clergy Daughters School *See* COWAN BRIDGE.

Colburn, Henry London publisher who rejected Charlotte Brontë's *The Professor,* Emily's *Wuthering Heights,* and Anne's *Agnes Grey* when Charlotte sent the manuscripts to him in 1846.

"Cold in the earth—and the deep snow piled above thee" Poem by Emily BRONTË. Entitled "Remembrance" in the 1846 *POEMS* collection, it is an amended version of a poem written March 3, 1845. The original poem, titled "R. Alcona to J. Brenzaida," was a continuation of the GONDAL saga in which the heroine of the epic, Rosina of Alcona, mourns the loss of her husband, Julius of Brenzaida, some 15 years after his assassination. Before publication, Emily was careful to change a reference to "Angora's shore," in Gondal, to the less specific "northern shore." Other alterations seem to have been made simply for poetic effect; for example, "Severed at last by Time's all-wearing wave" was changed to "Severed at last by Time's all-severing wave." Cited by critics for the directness of its language and the strength of its emotion, "Cold in the earth" is generally considered one of Emily's most powerful poems. And as is the case with many of the works that make up the extant Gondal saga, lines such as the following seem to anticipate the immortal bond between Cathy EARNSHAW and HEATHCLIFF in *WUTHERING HEIGHTS*.

Cold in the earth, and fifteen wild Decembers
From those brown hills have melted into spring—
Faithful indeed in the spirit that remembers
After such years of change and suffering!

Coleridge, Hartley (1796–1849)   Son of the poet and critic Samuel Taylor Coleridge and an editor and critic himself. Both Branwell and Charlotte Brontë sent him samples of their work; Branwell met him in 1840.

consumption   The word commonly used in the 19th century for TUBERCULOSIS.

Coriolanus   Shakespeare based his play *Coriolanus* on this Roman figure described in Plutarch's *Parallel Lives*. A Roman war hero of the fifth century B.C., he turned against his native town and sided with its enemies, the Volscians, whom he had earlier defeated in battle. After pleas from his wife and mother, he spared Rome. In *SHIRLEY*, Robert MOORE is compared to Coriolanus because he has the Roman's proud personality and his contempt for common people.

Cornhill   A section of east central London associated with such literary figures as William Makepeace THACKERAY and Anthony TROLLOPE, who published in *CORNHILL MAGAZINE*. In *VILLETTE*, Lucy SNOWE includes Cornhill on her tour of London.

Cornhill Magazine   Founded in 1860 by Charlotte Brontë's publisher, George SMITH, this periodical featured serialized novels by Elizabeth GASKELL, Anthony TROLLOPE, and other important writers. William Makepeace THACKERAY, who was its first editor, published *EMMA*, Charlotte's last work, along with his reminiscences of her, in the magazine. The magazine was published until 1975.

Cottage in the Wood, The   Patrick BRONTË's prose piece about the devout Mary, daughter of a poor cottager, dates to 1815. In the story, Mary has to fend off the advances of a wealthy drunkard. She rejects his offers to support her family and spurns his offer of marriage because he is an immoral atheist. Her example eventually converts the dissolute rich man, and he wins Mary in the end. Blessed with long lives and happy children, the couple die almost at the same time.

The story emphasizes the importance of piety and education through Sunday schools. Its clear, unadorned style attracted readers, and it was reprinted in 1817 and 1818.

Cottage Poems   *See* POEMS OF PATRICK BRONTË.

Cowan Bridge   School that was the real-life model for LOWOOD in *JANE EYRE*. Maria, Elizabeth, Charlotte, and Emily Brontë were sent to this dreadful institution where many students succumbed to typhoid fever, the result of unhealthy drinking water and a poor diet. Mrs. Elizabeth GASKELL renders a vivid account of the school's miserable conditions in her biography, *LIFE OF CHARLOTTE BRONTE*.

Cowper, William (1731–1800)   English poet. Cowper is most famous for his comic ballad *John Gilpin* (1782) and *The Task* (1785), a celebration of rural life. He helped to redirect 18th-century poetry toward personal expression and domestic life, thus heralding the ROMANTIC age. Charlotte Brontë found much solace in his work during her period as a governess. In *SHIRLEY* he is one of Shirley KEELDAR's favorite writers.

Crimsworth, Edward   Major character in *THE PROFESSOR*. He owns an apparently prosperous business and hires his younger brother, William CRIMSWORTH, to work in his office. Edward distrusts William and accuses his younger brother of spreading lies about him. William is innocent of the charges and has been a model employee. In a confrontation with Edward, William stands up to his older brother, then leaves his job. Later William learns from HUNSDEN, his benefactor and a critic of Edward's, that Edward has gone bankrupt and his handsome estate, Crimsworth Hall, has been sold.

Crimsworth, William   Main character and narrator of *THE PROFESSOR*. With no relatives he can rely on, William has to make his own way in the world first as an office employee of his hostile brother, Edward CRIMSWORTH, then later as a teacher in a school in BRUSSELS. The latter position he acquires with the aid of HUNSDEN, a wealthy land- and factory owner who takes an interest in the independent Crimsworth. At the school, Crimsworth falls in love with Frances Evans HENRI, a pupil-teacher, the daughter of a French father and English mother. Frances calls Crimsworth her master; Crimsworth admires her vibrant intellect and wit. Eventually the couple establish their own school. After a decade of success, they achieve Frances's dream of retiring to England, the country in which she has always dreamed of living.

Cromwell, Oliver (1599–1658)   Leader of the English civil war (1642–48), which led to the decapitation of Charles I and the establishment of a Puritan state headed by Cromwell as lord protector (1653–58). Although Cromwell's reign was succeeded by the restoration of Charles II, his legacy included a reform of Parliament to make it more representative of the British people, an increase in religious toleration, and the strengthening of England's role in European and world affairs. Important writers such as Thomas CARLYLE wrote admiring biographies of Cromwell, and Elizabeth GASKELL in the *Life of Charlotte Brontë* mentions that Charlotte Brontë read Jacques Bénigne BOSSUET's study of Cromwell.

Crosby, Dr. John   The ROBINSON FAMILY physician, he became Branwell Brontë's confidant and perhaps a go-between during Branwell's affair with Lydia ROBINSON.

Crystal Palace   Designed by Sir Joseph Paxton to house the Great Exhibition of 1851, this iron-framed structure of glass was erected in Hyde Park in London to celebrate "The Works of Industry of All Nations," organized by Prince Albert. Charlotte Brontë visited it several times, calling it a "mixture of a Genii Palace and a mighty Bazaar."

Daniel   The biblical story of Daniel in the lion's den is one of Polly HOME's favorites in *VILLETTE*. King Darius throws Daniel into the lion's den to see if the God Daniel serves will save him. The next day Daniel announces that the Lord has sealed the lions' mouths. Convinced that Daniel is protected by God, the king throws Daniel's accusers into the lion's den, and they are devoured. The king proclaims that Daniel's God is the living God and his "dominions shall be even unto the end."

"Day at Parry's Palace, A"   *See YOUNG MEN'S MAGAZINE, THE.*

Dean, Ellen (Nelly)   Character in *WUTHERING HEIGHTS*. Nelly Dean, who serves as a family retainer at both WUTHERING HEIGHTS and THRUSHCROSS GRANGE, is a principal witness to the drama that swirls around HEATHCLIFF and Catherine EARNSHAW. Later, she relates her version of the events to an outsider, Heathcliff's tenant Mr. LOCKWOOD, and becomes the primary narrator of the novel. By the time she serves as Lockwood's housekeeper and informant, Nelly Dean has grown into a pious old woman, but her narrative indicates that she has always been sanctimonious. In particular, she seems to have always disapproved of the central characters in the story, repeatedly criticizing them for their willfulness and solipsism. Her status as a busybody also helps to move the plot along at several points, for she cannot help interjecting herself into the lives of those she serves.

"Death is here I feel his power"   Poem by Charlotte Brontë composed in August 1830 and published in 1942. Appearing as part of a longer piece titled "A Frenchmen's Journey Continued by Tree" in the November 1830 issue of *THE YOUNG MEN'S MAGAZINE* (Charlotte's title for her brother's juvenile production *Branwell's Blackwood's Magazine*),

this brief five-stanza poem has some biographical interest because it is addressed to a dead sister.

De Lisle, Frederick   *See GLASS TOWN.*

Dent, Colonel   Minor character in *JANE EYRE*. He is one of the neighbors Mr. ROCHESTER invites to THORNFIELD for a party. Jane EYRE mentions his "soldierly" bearing.

Dent, Mrs. Colonel   Minor character in *JANE EYRE*. She arrives with her husband for a party at THORNFIELD. She makes a pleasant impression on Jane EYRE, who describes her as "ladylike" and well dressed.

Desiree   Minor character in *VILLETTE*. She is Madame BECK's eldest daughter, a bad-tempered child who smashes items in the kitchen and blames the servants. Madame Beck tries to excuse her daughter's behavior, observing that Desiree needs to be watched more closely.

Dindonneau, Duc de   Character mentioned in *VILLETTE*. Lucy SNOWE notes that he accompanies his mother and father, the king and queen, to the same concert where Lucy sees Paul EMMANUEL and his niece, Justine Marie, whom Lucy mistakenly assumes M. Paul will marry.

dissenter   A term applied to those who disagreed with the doctrines of the CHURCH OF ENGLAND. Also called nonconformists, dissenters objected specifically to the teachings of the Anglican Church and the idea of an established national church or religion. In *AGNES GREY*, Mr. HATFIELD lectures his Anglican congregation about the evils of dissent.

Dolores   Minor character in *VILLETTE*. This "unruly Catalonian" student is so persistently disruptive that

Lucy SNOWE locks her in a closet. Because Dolores is an unpopular student, Lucy's action earns the class's approval.

Donne, Joseph Minor character in *SHIRLEY*. Donne, the curate of Whinbury, is one of three clergymen (along with Peter Augustus MALONE and David SWEETING) satirized in the novel for their contentious, narrow-minded ways.

"Doubter's Hymn, The" Poem by Branwell BRONTË. This is one of the poems Branwell selected for his 1837 notebook, which included verses he compiled and often heavily revised as part of an apparent attempt to publish his work and make a living as a man of letters. The poem dates from November 1835 and was composed as part of "The Life of Field Marshall, The Right Honorable Alexander Percy, Earl of Northangerland," which narrates events relating to Branwell's juvenile alter ego, Alexander Percy. In the context of the 1837 notebook, however, "The Doubter's Hymn" bears no traces of ANGRIA and Branwell's childhood obsessions. Instead, the poem speaks of a crisis of faith that was probably only too real for Branwell, as it was for Charlotte. But whereas Charlotte resolved hers through strength of character, turning her back on both her religious doubts and her involvement with a world of fantasy, Branwell never conquered his inner demons. Perhaps for this reason the conclusion of this poem, written by a man who both feared and courted death, continues to seem so haunting:

> How will that Future seem?
> What is Eternity?
> Is Death the sleep?—is Heaven the Dream?
> Life the reality?

Douro, marquis of *See* ANGRIA; GLASS TOWN; *YOUNG MEN'S MAGAZINE, THE*.

Dronsart, Adele Minor character in *THE PROFESSOR*. She is a rather suspicious student whom other students try to avoid.

Drury, Isabella A woman of independent means from KEIGHLEY, she rejected Patrick BRONTË's marriage proposal in 1822.

Earnshaw, Catherine (Cathy) Character in *WUTHERING HEIGHTS*. Cathy grows up at WUTHERING HEIGHTS, the younger sister of Hindley EARNSHAW and the playmate of HEATHCLIFF, a street urchin her father brings home from Liverpool when she is six years old. From the outset Cathy and Heathcliff are soulmates, wild children who spend much of their time together out on the moor. When Cathy is on the threshold of womanhood, however, events conspire to separate her from Heathcliff. First, her father dies, then when Hindley succeeds him as master of the house, Hindley banishes Heathcliff from the family living quarters. Furthermore, when Cathy is injured at nearby THRUSHCROSS GRANGE and forced to convalesce there for a number of weeks, she is introduced to a more refined way of life, epitomized by the epicene Edgar LINTON. When Edgar proposes to her, Cathy accepts, but not before voicing her misgivings to Nelly DEAN and fervently asserting that she and Heathcliff will always be one. After Cathy marries Edgar, her husband and Heathcliff compete for her affections. Torn between the two, Cathy willfully breaks her own heart. Mortally ill, Cathy—joined by Heathcliff—vows that their love shall outlast the grave. She dies directly after delivering a premature infant, Catherine LINTON. Her spirit haunts Heathcliff the rest of his life.

The character of Cathy may have had its origins in the fictional Augusta Romana di Segovia, the tempestuous and destructive first wife of Branwell Brontë's hero Alexander Percy of ANGRIA, or in other Percy wives, such as Mary Henrietta Percy or Lady Zenobia of GLASS TOWN, who also appears in Charlotte and Branwell's novella "The Foundling." Certainly Cathy is a creature of the passionate, timeless worlds that preoccupied all the Brontë children in their youth and which Emily in particular never left. For Cathy—and perhaps for her creator— paradise is the natural world writ large, a never

ending moor on which she and Heathcliff can roam forever.

Earnshaw, Frances Character in *WUTHERING HEIGHTS*. When Hindley EARNSHAW returns to WUTHERING HEIGHTS for his father's funeral, he brings his young bride with him. Frances is cheerful and attractive—and already afflicted with the TUBERCULOSIS that will soon take her life. At first delighted with her younger sister-in-law, Cathy EARNSHAW, Frances quickly tires of the girl and of HEATHCLIFF, retreating into her illness and her pregnancy. Not long after giving birth to Hareton EARNSHAW, the last of the line, Frances succumbs to consumption.

Earnshaw, Hareton Character in *WUTHERING HEIGHTS*. The only offspring of Hindley and Frances EARNSHAW, Hareton is the last of the Earnshaw line. He bears the same name that appears over the threshold of his ancestral home, but he is nearly a grown man before he learns to read the inscription for himself. When his mother dies shortly after his birth, Hareton's father turns to drink, eventually mortgaging his household to HEATHCLIFF. With ownership of WUTHERING HEIGHTS, Heathcliff gains control over little Hareton, whom he loathes and loves at the same time. As part of his vengeance on Hindley, Heathcliff turns Hareton into a brutish servant, re-creating the treatment he had experienced at Wuthering Heights in his youth. Still, the boy feels some affection for his oppressor, who is also the only father figure he has ever known. For his part, Heathcliff cannot help but see his own youthful self in Hareton. But whereas Heathcliff is damned by his love of Catherine EARNSHAW, Hareton is redeemed by his love for her daughter and namesake, Catherine LINTON, who teaches him to read the legend over the portal to Wuthering Heights.

Earnshaw, Hindley Character in *WUTHERING HEIGHTS*. Hindley is Catherine EARNSHAW's brother and HEATHCLIFF's oppressor. He leaves home when the foundling Heathcliff supplants him in his father's affections, only returning to WUTHERING HEIGHTS after his father's death three years later. His old jealousy of Heathcliff causes the new master of the house to banish the youth from the family's living quarters, obliging him to work out of doors as a servant. This vengeful treatment backfires, however: After Hindley's wife, Frances EARNSHAW, dies, he spirals into alcoholism, while Heathcliff, who has temporarily left Wuthering Heights, returns an educated, moneyed individual. As such, Heathcliff is able to take advantage of Hindley, gradually assuming control of the Earnshaws' ancestral home. Such developments naturally add to Hindley's hatred of Heathcliff, and he resolves to kill the man he continues to regard as an interloper. Instead, Hindley only succeeds in drinking himself to death six months after his sister dies: He is only 27 years old and is survived by one son, Hareton EARNSHAW.

Earnshaw, Mr. Character in *WUTHERING HEIGHTS*. Old Mr. Earnshaw is father to Hindley EARNSHAW and Catherine EARNSHAW, to whom he brings, as a kind of present, a street urchin he has found during a trip to Liverpool. He names the orphan HEATHCLIFF, after a son who died in childhood. Old Mr. Earnshaw dotes on the boy, who gradually assumes the place of Hindley in his father's affections. After Hindley is sent away to school, his father dies, with Catherine and Heathcliff at his feet. Old Mr. Earnshaw's death signals the end of the status quo, as Hindley returns to take control of WUTHERING HEIGHTS and Cathy turns elsewhere for affection previously found in Heathcliff.

Edinburgh The capital of Scotland and a commercial and cultural center that Charlotte Brontë visited briefly in 1850.

Emma Charlotte BRONTË's last piece of writing is a manuscript of approximately 5,000 words that was first published in *CORNHILL MAGAZINE* with an introduction by William Makepeace THACKERAY. *Emma* seems to be the beginning of a novel in the vein of *JANE EYRE*. It is set in a girl's school and centers on Matilda Fitzgibbon, a wretched, cast-off girl. But is she? The plot takes a dramatic turn when Miss Wilcox, the headmistress, who does not like Matilda, writes to her father at May Park. The letter is returned, address unknown.

The critic Rebecca FRASER deems this fragment "repetitious," but she concedes there is not enough of it to say what Charlotte might have made of the story.

Emmanuel, Josef Minor character in *VILLETTE*. The brother of Paul EMMANUEL, He accompanies Paul on important family occasions and to public events.

Emmanuel, Paul (M. Paul) Major character in *VILLETTE*. He is a professor at Madame BECK's school. Opinionated, intense, and fitful, he both attracts and repels Lucy SNOWE. She gradually earns his admiration for her intelligence and pertinacity; indeed, she becomes his favorite pupil and colleague (Lucy gives and takes lessons at the school). When Lucy realizes that her love for Dr. John Graham BRETTON will never be reciprocated, she transfers her affections to M. Paul, who takes an avid interest in her life. As she learns of his benevolent disposition, and as she makes him, a Catholic, respect her Protestant principles, they draw closer together. In the end, he secures a building for the school Lucy has always wanted to establish, and after a three-year absence on business, he returns to marry her. M. Paul is based on Constantin George Romain HEGER, the teacher at the PENSIONNAT HEGER in Brussels who encouraged Charlotte Brontë's writing and became her severe but supportive critic, as well as the object of her affections.

Eshton, Amy Minor character in *JANE EYRE*. She accompanies her sister, Louisa ESHTON, and their parents to THORNFIELD. Jane EYRE describes her as small and childlike.

Eshton, Louisa Minor character in *JANE EYRE*. She accompanies her sister, Amy ESHTON, and their parents to THORNFIELD. Jane EYRE describes her as taller than Amy and more sophisticated.

Eshton, Mr. Minor character in *JANE EYRE*. Mr. ROCHESTER invites him and his family to THORNFIELD for a party. Eshton is a magistrate and appears to Jane EYRE the very image of the distinguished, white-haired, noble judge.

Eshton, Mrs. Minor character in *JANE EYRE*. Mr. ESHTON's wife, whom Jane EYRE describes as handsome and well preserved. She and her daughters accompany Mr. Eshton on a visit to THORNFIELD.

Eton College In *THE PROFESSOR*, William CRIMSWORTH attends Eton, the largest and most famous of the English public schools, founded in 1440 by King Henry VI. (Public school in England is the equivalent of a private school in the United States.) One of the country's most prestigious schools, Eton has produced many leaders and other outstanding men. That Crimsworth has attended Eton means not only that he has received a first-class education but also that he has the manners and attitudes of a gentleman. It is therefore surprising to his aristocratic uncles (Lord TYNEDALE and the Hon. John SEACOMBE) that Crimsworth should desire to pursue a career in trade, since commercial activities were deemed vulgar by the upper class.

Eulalie Minor character in *THE PROFESSOR*. Along with HORTENSE and CAROLINE, Eulalie forms a triangle of female students who try to bedevil teacher William CRIMSWORTH. A tall and well-shaped girl, she shows little personality and is so without expression that Crimsworth compares her to a wax figure.

evangelical Proponent of a zealous, missionary type of Christianity embraced by Patrick Brontë. In *JANE EYRE*, Jane EYRE is sent to LOWOOD, a charity school run by Mr. BROCKLEHURST, an evangelical clergyman. Evangelicals believe in the primacy of the Scriptures, so Jane and the other students are instructed each day in passages from the Bible. Evangelicals also put a good deal of emphasis on the sincerity of the believer—what Martin Luther called "justification by faith." The evangelical believes in a personal conversion experience, or what has been called in modern times "born-again" Christianity. When Mr. Brocklehurst questions Jane at GATESHEAD HALL about her reading of the Bible, her reasoned answers disappoint him because she shows none of the fervor and personal commitment to the Scripture that an evangelical craves seeing in a Christian. He forms a poor opinion of Jane's religious convictions.

Evans, Miss Anne The superintendent of COWAN BRIDGE, she was the model for Miss TEMPLE in *JANE EYRE*.

Eyre, Jane Narrator and title character of Charlotte Brontë's novel *JANE EYRE*. The plain-featured orphan Jane, abused at GATESHEAD HALL, punished but ultimately triumphant at LOWOOD, and suffering because of her love for Mr. ROCHESTER at THORNFIELD, overcomes all her humiliations and emerges as her beloved's wife. Jane's ability to overcome every obstacle under slavelike conditions has made her an emblem of independent and passionate women.

Eyre, John Character in *JANE EYRE*. Jane EYRE's uncle, a wine merchant, seeks her at Mrs. REED's but is told she has died.

F —— Place in *THE TENANT OF WILDFELL HALL.* F—— is the lovely seaside watering hole to which Helen HUNTINGDON and her aunt, Mrs. Peggy MAXWELL, and Esther HARGRAVE repair after the death of Helen's uncle. It resembles in many respects the coastal village of SCARBOROUGH, which Anne Brontë loved so much and where she died and was buried.

F ——, Lady   Character mentioned in *THE TEN-ANT OF WILDFELL HALL.* Lady F—— is the married woman with whom Arthur, Lord HUNTINGDON was romantically involved before marrying Helen HUNTINGDON.

Fairfax, Mrs.   Character in *JANE EYRE.* The friendly housekeeper of THORNFIELD, Mrs. Fairfax makes Jane EYRE welcome and becomes her confidant and helper. Mrs. Fairfax is distantly related to the Rochesters and gives Jane her first bit of information about Mr. ROCHESTER, her employer and future husband.

Fairy Cave   Location in *WUTHERING HEIGHTS.* Catherine EARNSHAW mentions the cave under the PENISTONE CRAGS when she becomes delusional during her final illness. Later, a maid at THRUSHCROSS GRANGE mentions it to the young Catherine LINTON, who explores the cave's mysteries with her cousin Hareton EARNSHAW.

Fanny (1)   Dog in *WUTHERING HEIGHTS.* Fanny is Isabella LINTON's springer, which HEATHCLIFF hangs from a bridle hook when he and Isabella elope from THRUSHCROSS GRANGE.

Fanny (2)   Minor character in *SHIRLEY.* She is a servant in Matthewson HELSTONE's home.

Fanshawe, Ginevra   Major character in *VILLETTE.* Lucy SNOWE meets this lively but exceedingly vain young woman on her way to the Continent. Lucy hopes to secure employment, and Ginevra tells her about the school where she studies. When Lucy secures a position there, she becomes Ginevra's confidante. Lucy, however, disapproves of the willful, devious Ginevra, who delights in flirting with men. One of her conquests is Dr. John Graham BRETTON, with whom Lucy has fallen in love. Eventually Dr. John realizes how frivolous Ginevra is and loses interest in her, transferring his affections to Polly HOME. Ginevra eventually elopes with Alfred de HAMAL, a titled Frenchman. Her note to Lucy indicates that she remains the same flighty and narcissistic person without any concern for others' feelings.

"Farewell to Angria, The"   *See* ANGRIA.

Farren, William   Minor character in *SHIRLEY.* An unemployed mill worker, he argues with Robert MOORE about the responsibilities of a mill owner to his workers. Farren believes Moore has a responsibility to safeguard his employees, but Moore counters that the economic problems of his workers cannot be solved by one employer. Nevertheless, Farren's argument and manner impress Moore, who goes out of his way to make sure that Farren does find work. Farren is a favorite of Shirley KEELDAR's and in her presence he displays good sense and humor, a side of him Moore has never seen.

Fénelon, François de Salignac de la Mothe (1651–1715)   French writer and liberal theologian. In spite of the Roman Catholic Church's opposition to Fénelon's ideas, they changed the cultural atmosphere of his country. He came from a noble family and was ordained a priest in 1675. He was known for instructing women converts to the church, which is why in *VILLETTE,* Lucy SNOWE compares Pere SILAS, a Catholic priest seeking to subvert her Protestantism, to Fénelon. He held many distinguished positions in the church. He also wrote a novel, *Telemachus* (1699), advocating his belief in the fraternity of nations, as well as a *Treatise on the Education of Girls* (1687), in which he defended the education of women. His pacific and gentle view of humankind makes him an appealing model for Lucy, who is falling in love with her teacher and colleague Paul EMMANUEL, a Catholic.

Ferndean   In *JANE EYRE*, the modest manor house to which Mr. ROCHESTER retires after the devastating fire at THORNFIELD.

Fernley Manor, Cumberland   Title of a painting by Helen HUNTINGDON in *THE TENANT OF WILDFELL HALL*. Helen must sell paintings of WILDFELL HALL to support herself and her young son, but she is obliged to give Wildfell another name in order to keep her whereabouts secret from her husband.

Fieldhead   Shirley KEELDAR's home in *SHIRLEY*.

Fifene   Minor character in *VILLETTE*. When Fifene, Madame BECK's second daughter, breaks her arm, she is attended by Dr. John Graham BRETTON, whom Lucy SNOWE recognizes as the man who guided her to the school when she first arrived in Villette.

Finic   *See* GLASS TOWN.

Fitzgibbon, Matilda   *See EMMA.*

Flossy   Anne Brontë's dog. The ROBINSON FAMILY gave Flossy to Anne in June 1843, when she worked as their children's governess at THORP GREEN. Flossy outlived her mistress by several years, finally succumbing to old age in 1854.

Flower, Captain John   *See* GLASS TOWN.

"Foundling, The"   *See* GLASS TOWN.

Frank   Character mentioned in *VILLETTE*. He is the young man whom Miss MARCHMOUNT loved. He died after what she describes as "twelve months of bliss."

Fraser, Rebecca   Brontë biographer. Fraser's *The Brontës: Charlotte Brontë and Her Family,* although not as extensive as Juliet BARKER's study of the clan, is a lively and scrupulously researched account. Her detailed notes, useful bibliography, and index make this a key resource.

Fraser's Magazine   This periodical began as a TORY publication in 1830, but by the mid 1850s it had become a Liberal (WHIG) organ. Its early reviews of Charlotte Brontë's novels were highly critical of what was deemed her "coarseness," that is, her frankness in addressing subjects such as mad women in the attic (Bertha Rochester). In 1848, *Fraser's* also published two of Anne Brontë's poems. Its last edition appeared in 1882.

Gale, John Minor character in *SHIRLEY*. A "small clothier" and friend of Peter Augustus MALONE.

Gale, Mrs. Minor character in *SHIRLEY*. She is Peter Augustus MALONE's landlady.

Garrs, Nancy Nurse to the Brontë children from 1816 to 1824, when she left HAWORTH PARSONAGE to get married. The biographer Juliet BARKER calls her a "good and loyal servant."

Garrs, Sarah A servant in the Brontë household from 1818 to 1824, she left HAWORTH PARSONAGE after her sister Nancy GARRS married. Sarah taught the Brontë sisters how to sew.

Gaskell, Elizabeth (Mrs. Gaskell) (1810–1865) English novelist and biographer of Charlotte Brontë. Born in the Chelsea section of London, Elizabeth Gaskell was brought up in Cheshire by her mother's sister, after her mother died in 1811. Educated at home until she was 12, she was then sent to boarding school, the setting for some of her novels, which often feature motherless girls. In 1832 she married William G. Gaskell, who was a Unitarian minister, as was her father, William S. Holland.

Rather than hindering her talent, Mrs. Gaskell's marriage seemed to foster it. She was happy, even though she lost a son in infancy and wrote in part to assuage her grief. A prolific author of short stories and novels, she is best known for *Mary Barton* (1848) and *North and South* (1855), both of which include female characters that are the dominating forces in men's lives.

Mrs. Gaskell did not identify herself as a feminist, but she did admire strong women and resented male interference, a theme that also pervades her classic *THE LIFE OF CHARLOTTE BRONTË*. Like her novels, the biography is sympathetic to a woman's quest for creative freedom.

Elizabeth Gaskell. While in London in 1850, Charlotte Brontë met Mrs. Gaskell, who wrote The Life of Charlotte Brontë *(published in 1857) upon Patrick Brontë's request. George Richmond's* Portrait of Mrs. Gaskell *(1851) depicts Charlotte's first and most important biographer.* (National Portrait Gallery, London)

Gasper HAWORTH PARSONAGE dog from 1831 to 1837 or 1838. Emily drew a picture of the dog in 1834.

Gateshead Hall The estate of Mrs. REED, the aunt who provides a miserable home for the young Jane in *JANE EYRE*.

Georgette Minor character in *VILLETTE*. She is Madame BECK's youngest daughter, who is treated by Dr. John Graham BRETTON for a fever. Georgette's illness allows Lucy SNOWE to see more of the doctor.

Gérin, Winifred One of the most important Brontë authorities, Gérin published in 1967 a landmark biography, *Charlotte Bronte: The Evolution of Genius,* considered by many scholars to be the best since Elizabeth GASKELL's. This work had been brilliantly preceded by Gérin's meticulous biographies of Branwell and Anne. Gérin lived near HAWORTH to immerse herself in the environment of her subjects. Her books combine intense emotional empathy with scrupulous documentation; indeed, her work lifted Brontë studies out of the sentimentalism and farfetched speculation that had marred earlier critical work.

Gifford, John *See* GLASS TOWN.

Gill, Mrs. Minor character in *SHIRLEY*. She is Shirley KEELDAR's housekeeper.

Gimmerton Location in *WUTHERING HEIGHTS*. Gimmerton is the village closest to WUTHERING HEIGHTS and THRUSHCROSS GRANGE.

Glass Town An imaginary world created by Charlotte and Branwell Brontë. This creative project apparently derived from a gift of 12 wooden soldiers that Patrick Brontë brought home from Leeds for his nine-year-old son. During the children's games, these soldiers became a contingent for forces led by Charlotte's hero, the duke of WELLINGTON. These soldier-explorers set off for Africa, founding a colony, eventually named Glass Town. The names of characters would change, depending on the children's fancy and on their reading. Branwell called one of his characters Buonaparte, the Corsican spelling of Napoléon BONAPARTE's surname. All of the Brontë children were fascinated with the idea of conquest and heroic adventures and with exotic locales, in part stimulated by their reading of the *ARABIAN NIGHTS*. Branwell even invented an imaginary language, a code of laws (including a constitution), and a geography for the colony, and demonstrated an obsession with the land's history and day-to-day

happenings. The autobiographical nature of his characters is evident in Captain John Bud, an excessively finicky and verbose historian of Glass Town, who, like Branwell, tended to carry his enthusiasms to a pedantic extreme. Similarly, Young Soult, a poet, shared his creator's emotional, melodramatic, and rather untidy side; indeed, Young Soult is prophetic of Branwell's later lack of discipline and self-control. Much like Branwell, his literary alter egos consider themselves men of destiny.

The colony became a country complete with maps, place-names, and sites such as Branii Hills (on the northern border of Glass Town); Philosopher's Island (a college campus); Quaximina Square (where antiquarians and historians met); the Tower of All Nations (the tallest building in the capital city); and Waterloo Palace (the duke of Wellington's residence). The array of Glass Town inhabitants is impressive: Sir William Bravey, a founder of the colony; Sergeant Bud, Captain Bud's son and a shifty attorney; Henry Chantry, a sculptor-protégé of the marquis of Douro; Frederick De Lisle, a celebrated artist; the beautiful Lady Zenobia Ellrington; Myrtillus, Lady Ellrington's silly younger brother; Finic, the deformed servant of Lord Charles Wellesley who is discovered to be the illegitimate son of the marquis of Douro; Captain John Flower, historian of Verdopolis; John Gifford, the conceited antiquary; Quashie, king of the Ashantes; John Sneaky, eldest son of the king of Sneakysland, who becomes the marquis of Douro's ally; and Vernet, a painter of animals.

The Glass Town world continued to engage the Brontë siblings well into their 20s, with Lord BYRON gradually becoming their inspiration for creating rebellious, anarchistic heroes. They also wrote magazines full of Glass Town doings, jokes, poetry, and puns; for example, one magazine issue featured Wellington discussing the art of war, politics, and cultural subjects, while another featured reviews of art. During one of Charlotte's absences from home (1830–32), Branwell invented Alexander Rogue, a Byronic hero who displaced the original Glass Town ruling party, headed by the duke of Wellington. Charlotte's response was to create a romantic play, "The Bridal," featuring the marquis of Douro, an art connoisseur, and his courtship of

Lady Zenobia. But Charlotte did not forsake the saga; she later collaborated with Branwell on "The Foundling," a boisterous novella celebrating crass low-life scenes, apparently inspired by Byron's obstreperous epic *Don Juan*. Glass Town eventually metamorphosed into other kingdoms, the most important of which was ANGRIA. Emily and Anne broke away in 1834 to found the independent world of GONDAL.

The Brontës clearly took this early work seriously: Branwell sent off poetry derived from the Glass Town saga to BLACKWOOD'S MAGAZINE, and Charlotte sent hers to Robert SOUTHEY, the poet laureate. By their early teens, the Brontës had already developed an extraordinarily sophisticated notion of the power of fiction. Thus Charlotte has one of her Glass Town characters, Wellesley, wonder if he might be the "mere idea of some other creature's brain. The Glass Town seemed so likewise." *See also* "HISTORY OF YOUNG MEN, THE."

Gnasher Dog in WUTHERING HEIGHTS. Gnasher is one of the guard dogs at WUTHERING HEIGHTS that JOSEPH (1) calls to attack Mr. LOCKWOOD, because he thinks the visitor is making off with the house lantern.

Goldsmith, Oliver (1730–1774) English historian. In JANE EYRE, Jane EYRE reads his *History of Rome* and compares the bullying John REED to such Roman emperors as Nero and Caligula.

Gondal All four of the surviving Brontë children—Charlotte, Branwell, Emily, and Anne—afflicted with what they called "scribblemania," began writing at an early age. Many of their literary efforts went into fleshing out two fantasy worlds they invented beginning in the mid-1820s. While Branwell and Charlotte devoted themselves to the kingdom of ANGRIA, Emily and Anne broke away in 1834 to found the independent world of Gondal. Envisioned as a large island in the north Pacific, it had snowcapped mountains, ruined castles, and wandering deer unknown in Yorkshire but borrowed from the novels of Sir Walter SCOTT. Gondal's capital was Regina, and fittingly for a world created by two female minds, it was ruled by a series of strong and ambitious queens.

Although Emily and Anne continued to engage in interplay centering on Gondal well into adulthood (for example, during a railway journey they took together in their middle 20s, they passed the time pretending to be Royalist prisoners escaping from Gondal), by 1845 Anne had become disinterested in the game. Emily, however, proved incapable of leaving either her home or the world of Gondal. Any prolonged period away from HAWORTH PARSONAGE produced serious illness, whereas at home she was free to indulge her Gondal fantasies, which she at times seemed incapable of distinguishing from the world around her. Many of the most accomplished works Emily contributed to the Brontë sisters' first publication, *POEMS* under the pseudonyms Currer, Ellis, and Acton Bell, came directly from her Gondal works, as did many elements of her masterpiece, WUTHERING HEIGHTS.

Gordon, Lyndall In *Charlotte Brontë: A Passionate Life* (1994), Lyndall Gordon has written an elegant and moving biography that is up to date and useful, with extensive illustrations, a chronology, source notes, and bibliography. Her work goes beyond Winifred GÉRIN's in exploring the creative process of her subject.

gothic Term applied to works of European and American literature that emphasize one or more of the following elements: the supernatural, the medieval past, a family curse, a sinister but often charismatic hero, an air of mystery and suspense, and a style that is intense and melodramatic. Novels such as Emily Brontë's WUTHERING HEIGHTS and sister Charlotte's JANE EYRE have often been called gothic because of such characters as Heathcliff and Mr. Rochester, and because the authors' styles heighten and exaggerate family conflicts and the mysterious role of the past in their fiction. The term *gothic* derives from the development of what became known as the gothic novel in the late 18th and early 19th centuries. Gothic fiction, like ROMANTIC works of literature, challenged the 18th century's reliance on reason and explored, instead, the irrational side of human nature.

Goton Minor character in *VILLETTE*. She is Madame BECK's faithful servant who attends Lucy SNOWE during her serious illness.

Graham, Arthur *See* HUNTINGDON, ARTHUR.

Graham, Helen Alias assumed by Helen HUNTINGDON in *THE TENANT OF WILDFELL HALL* when, as a fugitive from her abusive marriage, she takes up residence in the ruins of WILDFELL HALL. Although she keeps her given name, she uses her deceased mother's maiden name as a surname.

Grame, Mr. Character in *SHIRLEY*. He is Sir Philip NUNNELY's steward.

Grange, the *See* THRUSHCROSS GRANGE.

Grassdale Manor In *THE TENANT OF WILDFELL HALL*, Grassdale is the ancestral home of Arthur, Lord HUNTINGDON. He and Helen HUNTINGDON settle at the country estate after they marry in December 1821.

Graves, Mr. Minor character in *SHIRLEY*. He is Mr. MACTURK's stony young assistant.

Greaves, Mrs. Minor character in *THE TENANT OF WILDFELL HALL*. She is one of Arthur, Lord HUNTINGDON's servants at GRASSDALE NANOR.

Green, Mr. (1) Character in *AGNES GREY*. He is the "country booby" who courts Rosalie MURRAY.

Green, Mr. (2) Minor character in *WUTHERING HEIGHTS*. On his deathbed Edgar LINTON attempts to contact the GIMMERTON lawyer Mr. Green in order to change his will to benefit his daughter, Catherine LINTON. Paid off by HEATHCLIFF, however, Green does not appear at THRUSHCROSS GRANGE until after Edgar has died.

Green Dwarf, The This short novel by Charlotte BRONTË features Captain Andrew Tree, a writer and rival of Captain John Bud, Branwell's alter ego. *See YOUNG MEN'S MAGAZINE, THE*.

Greenwood, John A stationer in HAWORTH, he kept a diary describing the Brontës. He reported on Charlotte's health and helped Elizabeth GASKELL with *The Life of Charlotte Brontë*.

Grey, Agnes Narrator and title character of *AGNES GREY*, a novel by Anne Brontë. She is the younger of two daughters, pampered by both her mother, Alice GREY, and older sister, Mary GREY. She wishes to be mature and help support the family by working as a governess when her father, Richard GREY, suffers financial reverses. A determined young woman, Agnes struggles to maintain her dignity and principles in households that do not respect her role as governess and undermine her attempts to discipline her pupils. Although Agnes has contempt for her employers, Mr. and Mrs. BLOOMFIELD and Mr. and Mrs. MURRAY, she fulfills her responsibilities admirably and is rewarded in the end by the respect of a local clergyman, Mr. WESTON, whom she falls in love with and marries.

Grey, Alice Agnes GREY's mother in Anne Brontë's novel *AGNES GREY*. Alice marries her husband, Richard GREY, a clergyman, for love, thereby cutting herself off from her aristocratic father and family, who disapprove of the marriage. Alice is happily married, and the couple have six children, only two of whom survive into young adulthood. When her husband suffers financial reverses and then dies, Alice is forced to find employment. Alice copes with every misfortune and tries to shield her younger daughter Agnes from adult responsibilities. But after Agnes insists that she wishes to help her family, Alice is able to secure her daughter work as a governess. Eventually Alice starts her own school, which Agnes helps her manage.

Grey, Mary Agnes GREY's older sister in Anne Brontë's novel *AGNES GREY*. Mary, like her mother, Alice GREY, treats Agnes as the baby of the family. When Agnes expresses her wish to contribute to the family's finances after her father, Richard GREY, suffers a total loss of his fortune in the sinking of a ship he has invested in, Mary, like her mother, doubts that Agnes has any practical skills. But Mary learns to respect her sister's desire to become a governess, and they remain close, seeing each other when Agnes returns home for holidays.

Grey, Richard The father of Agnes GREY in *AGNES GREY*. Agnes's mother, Alice GREY, has married him in spite of her aristocratic father's warning that she will be cut off from her family and fortune should she make such a lowly match. It is a happy marriage, marred only by Richard Grey's financial misfortune. He invests in a ship that is lost at sea, and his family, including his two daughters, go to work to support themselves. Worried by his setback, Richard Grey eventually becomes ill and dies, forcing his wife and children into working even harder. But the loss of this good man grieves the family, and his wife refuses to accept her father's offer that she be readmitted to her family after she acknowledges that marrying Grey was a mistake.

Grimalkin Cat in *WUTHERING HEIGHTS*. A brindled gray cat in the kitchen at WUTHERING HEIGHTS is given this generic feline name by Mr. LOCKWOOD.

Grimsby, Mr. Character in *THE TENANT OF WILDFELL HALL*. Grimsby is one of Arthur, Lord HUNTINGDON's drunken and corrupt friends. He conspires with others to keep Huntingdon and Lord LOWBOROUGH inebriated as often as possible in order to continue their good times. Unlike some of the others in this group, Grimsby dies under circumstances much as he has lived; he is murdered during a drunken brawl.

Grove, the Place in *THE TENANT OF WILDFELL HALL*. The Grove is home to Mrs. HARGRAVE and her family in Grassdale.

Gryce, Miss Minor character in *JANE EYRE*. She is the Welsh cook at LOWOOD.

Guadeloupe Island in the West Indies to which Paul EMMANUEL travels in *VILLETTE* on a mission to secure the property of Madame WALRAVENS, the grandmother of Justine Marie SAVEUR (1). M. Paul had been in love with Justine Marie, but she died as a nun after her family refused to consent to her marrying him.

Gulliver's Travels Novel by English author Jonathan SWIFT published in 1726. A classic story of adventure, travel, and fantasy, it is one of Jane EYRE's favorite books, perhaps because Gulliver learns to question societal customs and is skeptical of people in power and of authority figures.

Gustave Character mentioned in *VILLETTE*. Dr. John Graham BRETTON is attending Gustave when he sees a small casket thrown from a window. The casket incident is the cause of some intrigue, which he refuses to explain to Rosine MATOU, the portress, or to Lucy SNOWE.

Halford, J., Esq. Character mentioned in *THE TENANT OF WILDFELL HALL*. Halford is a friend of the narrator, Gilbert MARKHAM, and the recipient of a series of letters in which Markham relates the tale of Helen HUNTINGDON. At the end of the novel Halford marries Markham's sister, Rose MARKHAM.

Halifax Emily Brontë taught for six months at the Law Hill School in this industrial town 10 miles from HAWORTH.

Halifax Guardian Branwell Brontë published two poems in this newspaper. Later this same paper published letters protesting Charlotte's portrait of William Carus WILSON, founder of the Clergy Daughters School, as Mr. BROCKLEHURST in *JANE EYRE*.

Hall, Cyril Minor character in *SHIRLEY*. This middle-aged, bald man provides a welcome relief to Caroline HELSTONE, who finds the three curates David SWEETING, Peter Augustus MALONE, and Joseph DONNE, a trial during a social call.

Hall, Margaret Minor character in *SHIRLEY*. Her devoted brother, Cyril HALL, befriends Caroline HELSTONE.

Hamal, Alfred de Minor character in *VILLETTE*. He is one of Ginevra FANSHAWE's suitors. Both a doctor and a dandy, he eventually sneaks into the school where Ginevra studies and elopes with her.

Hargrave, Esther Character in *THE TENANT OF WILDFELL HALL*. Esther is the younger sister of Helen HUNTINGDON's friend Milicent HARGRAVE. Helen sees much of herself in the young Esther, who resists her family's attempts to marry her off to a much older man. Eventually Esther marries Helen's brother, Frederick LAWRENCE.

Hargrave, Milicent Character in *THE TENANT OF WILDFELL HALL*. Milicent is a great friend of Helen HUNTINGDON, with whom she has much in common, especially after Milicent marries one of Arthur, Lord HUNTINGDON's drunken and rowdy cronies, Ralph HATTERSLEY. Her husband, however, eventually sees the error of his ways and settles down to be a good husband to his long-suffering and adoring Milicent.

Hargrave, Mrs. Minor character in *THE TENANT OF WILDFELL HALL*. She is the mother of Helen HUNTINGDON's friends Milicent HARGRAVE and Esther HARGRAVE and of Walter HARGRAVE, who tries to insinuate himself into Helen's affections. Mrs. Hargrave attempts to force Esther into an unsuitable marriage with a much older man simply because he is well heeled.

Hargrave, Walter Character in *THE TENANT OF WILDFELL HALL*. One of several men who fall in love with the striking and forthright Helen Lawrence (later Helen HUNTINGDON), Walter is the brother of Helen's friend Milicent and as such is frequently in Helen's company. For Helen's part, he is around too much of the time, and she finds his attentions both cloying and overbearing. He is, however, genuinely concerned about the abuse she endures at the hands of her husband, Arthur, Lord HUNTINGDON. Walter is part of Huntingdon's circle and therefore knows firsthand the drinking, gambling, and infidelity in which Huntingdon and his cronies indulge. It is Walter who warns Helen repeatedly about Huntingdon's affair with Annabella WILMOT, now the married Lady Lowborough. Helen's dislike of Walter clearly stems in part from his role as the bearer of such unwelcome news, but she also cannot escape the notion that he tells her negative things about her husband so that he can prey upon her weakness.

Harriet Minor character in *VILLETTE*. She is Polly HOME's nurse in the Bretton household.

Hartley, Mike Minor character in *SHIRLEY*. The local curates view him, a disgruntled weaver, with suspicion, declaring that his violent protests against working conditions make him an ANTINOMIAN, JACOBIN, and LEVELLER.

Hatfield, Mr. Major character in *AGNES GREY*. He is a RECTOR who proposes to Rosalie MURRAY, who spurns him. Mr. Hatfield is a pompous, insensitive clergyman who shows little interest in his flock and is downright rude to its humbler members. He takes little notice of Agnes GREY, in contrast to the humane clergyman Mr. WESTON, whom Agnes grows to love.

Hattersley, Helen Character in *THE TENANT OF WILDFELL HALL*. Helen is the daughter of Ralph HATTERSLEY and his wife, Milicent HARGRAVE, who names her child after her close friend Helen HUNTINGDON. Young Helen will grow up to marry Helen Huntingdon's son, Arthur HUNTINGDON.

Hattersley, Milicent *See* HARGRAVE, MILICENT.

Hattersley, Ralph Character in *THE TENANT OF WILDFELL HALL*. Ralph Hattersley is the son of a rich banker and is married to Helen HUNTINGDON's close friend Milicent HARGRAVE. He is also a friend of Helen's husband. Initially he is no better than Arthur, Lord HUNTINGDON and his circle, but Hattersley comes to realize—with Helen's urging—that his behavior is ruining not only his own health but also that of his marriage. He reforms, settling down to become a country squire and a renowned horse breeder.

Haworth English village and home of the Brontë family. Patrick Brontë held a ministry at Haworth from 1820 to 1861. In the second decade of the 19th century the village had just under 5,000 inhabitants. The nearest large town (a few miles away) was KEIGHLEY. Situated on a major route between Lancashire and Yorkshire, the village was in a region with a plentiful water supply and thus experienced the effects of the industrial revolution. The Brontës were well aware of the developments in the mills—a subject of Charlotte's *VILLETTE*—and Patrick traveled a wide circuit that took him into both Yorkshire and Lancashire. To some extent, therefore, the legend of Haworth's and the Brontës' isolation is just that—a legend. Of course, the landscape included plenty of wild and bleak scenery associated with *WUTHERING HEIGHTS*, and the constantly shifting colors of the sky above Haworth surely contributed to the moodiness of Brontë novels. Mrs. Elizabeth GASKELL provides a vivid contemporary portrait of Haworth in her biography, *The Life of Charlotte Brontë*.

Haworth Moor Open land near the Brontë home in HAWORTH, Yorkshire. HAWORTH PARSONAGE abutted this open tract of land on the border of Yorkshire and Lancashire, and the moor could be seen clearly from the back windows of the Brontë residence. The series of bleak but starkly beautiful rolling hills was beloved by all the younger Brontës but is especially associated with Emily. As Charlotte wrote in 1850 to James TAYLOR, "My sister Emily had a particular love for [the moors], and there is not a knoll of heather, not a branch of fern, not a young bilberry leaf, not a fluttering lark or linnet, but reminds me of her." Emily transformed Haworth Moor into a virtual character in *WUTHERING HEIGHTS*, adopting the hilltop farmhouse, known as TOP WITHENS, as a model for WUTHERING HEIGHTS and incorporating natural features such as the rocky outcrop Ponden Kirk, called PENISTONE CRAGS in the novel, into the story line. For Cathy EARNSHAW the moor is a kind of heaven on earth, just as it was for her creator. As Cathy tells Nelly Dean, "'I dreamt, once, that I was [in heaven] . . . and I broke my heart with weeping to come back to earth; and the angels were so angry that they flung me out, into the middle of the heath on the top of Wuthering Heights, where I woke sobbing for joy.'"

Haworth Parsonage (the Parsonage) Brontë family home. Situated at the apex of the village of HAWORTH, on the edge of the Yorkshire and Lancashire moors, the Parsonage was home to the family beginning in April 1820, when Patrick Brontë was appointed to a perpetual curacy as minister to Haworth, including the privilege of residing rent free at the Parsonage for the remainder of his life. He and his family would live there until his death in June 1861. When Arthur Bell Nicholls, Charlotte's widower, lost in the bid to succeed Patrick as curate, he left the Parsonage in September 1861, turning over the clergy residence to another occupant.

Built in 1779 of limestone, like most of the other dwellings in Haworth, the Parsonage was two stories high, rectangular in shape, and Georgian in design. During his residence, Patrick had a large wash kitchen added to the back of the house, and the backyard included both an outdoor privy and a well. The front garden of the Parsonage was somewhat neglected, but the interior of the residence was reportedly austere and scrupulously clean. The downstairs was divided by a central hallway into two main living rooms, a family parlor, and Patrick's study. Situated behind these rooms were a pantry and a kitchen. The second floor housed four bedrooms, two larger ones in front and two smaller at the rear of the house. Above the hallway was an open area that served as the children's study.

When Patrick and Maria Branwell Brontë arrived in 1820, their household included six children and two young servants. In September 1821, Maria died, and after Patrick failed in his attempts to remarry, Maria's sister, Elizabeth Branwell, who had nursed Maria during her final illness, stayed on to mind the children. Aunt Branwell remained at the Parsonage until her own death in 1842. The sisters Nancy and Sarah GARRS were the first of a

The Brontë family moved to Haworth in April 1820, three months after Anne was born. The Parsonage remained the family home until Patrick's death in 1861. (*The Costume of Yorkshire,* 1814)

small number of household helpers who also lived at the Parsonage. When the Garrs left in 1824, they were replaced by Tabitha AYKROYD, who stayed at the Parsonage for three decades, and Martha BROWN, the daughter of a parish sexton who would serve the Brontës until 1861, when she left for Ireland with Arthur Nicholls to continue in his employ. A number of dogs and cats made up the balance of the household during the Brontë years.

In 1928 the Parsonage became the Brontë Parsonage Museum, administered by the BRONTË SOCIETY. Every effort was made to restore the dwelling to its state during years of the Brontë family residence. Brontë furniture fills the rooms, which are used to display items such as the tiny books produced by the Brontë children and Branwell's finely drawn portraits of local people.

Heald, Reverend William Margetson Vicar of Birstall, in Yorkshire. In *SHIRLEY*, Charlotte Brontë used him as the model of the autocratic Cyril HALL, the vicar.

Heathcliff Major character in *WUTHERING HEIGHTS*. Early in the novel Old Mr. EARNSHAW brings home from Liverpool a dirty, homeless boy with a dark, scowling demeanor and an unrecognizable language. He names the child Heathcliff after his son who died in childhood. This is, as Nelly DEAN tells readers of the novel, the only name he will ever have. It seems altogether appropriate that Heathcliff should serve as both first and last name for this character, who is less an individual than half of an entity that also consists of Catherine EARNSHAW. As Cathy confesses to Nelly, Heathcliff is "'more myself than I am,'" later adding, "'Nelly, I *am* Heathcliff.'"

But as Cathy and Heathcliff become in an almost literal sense soul mates, Heathcliff and her brother, Hindley EARNSHAW, become mortal enemies. Jealousy of Heathcliff causes Hindley to relegate his foster brother to the status of a servant. When Cathy agrees to marry the wealthy Edgar LINTON, Heathcliff becomes the embodiment of vengeance. Returning to WUTHERING HEIGHTS after three years elsewhere, during which he has gained wealth and a measure of polish, Heathcliff gradually takes over the ancestral Earnshaw home

from the now dissolute Hindley and his son Hareton EARNSHAW, the last of the line. By marrying Isabella LINTON, Heathcliff gains a purchase on the nearby Linton home, THRUSHCROSS GRANGE. The death of Cathy—seemingly brought about by the contest between Heathcliff and Edgar for her affections—only fuels Heathcliff's determination to ruin both houses. Ultimately, both survive in the marriage of Hareton Earnshaw and Cathy's daughter, Catherine LINTON, who manage to experience in the mundane world the kind of peace and unity that Heathcliff and Cathy find only in death.

The flamboyant, Byronic hero of Wuthering Heights grew directly out of larger-than-life characters such as Northangerland and Zamorna, who dominated the imaginary worlds of GONDAL and ANGRIA created by the Brontës in their youth. Of all the Brontë children, Emily retained the strongest ties with these worlds, and it is no accident that it was she who made the best use of these sources in creating an unforgettable character.

Heathcliff, Catherine *See* LINTON, CATHERINE.

Heathcliff, Isabella *See* LINTON, ISABELLA.

Heathcliff, Linton Character in *WUTHERING HEIGHTS*. The son of HEATHCLIFF and Isabella LINTON, Linton is a sickly child. When his mother—having left Heathcliff shortly after their marriage—dies prematurely, Linton is retrieved by his uncle, Edgar LINTON, but almost immediately reclaimed by his father. At WUTHERING HEIGHTS, Linton grows older but not healthier. His illness is exacerbated by a peevish temperament, which alienates those around him, most especially his father. Heathcliff's only interest in his son is as a pawn in his elaborate plan to gain control of both Wuthering Heights and THRUSHCROSS GRANGE, a plan that apparently succeeds when he forces Linton to marry Catherine LINTON just days before the youth dies of TUBERCULOSIS.

Heger, Clair Zoe (Madame Heger) Headmistress of the PENSIONNAT HEGER, where Charlotte and Emily Brontë studied in Brussels. Although Charlotte initially considered Madame Heger a supportive presence in the school, ultimately she concluded that Madame did not like her. Part of the problem stemmed from Charlotte's refusal to socialize with students and fellow teachers— an aloof stance that Madame Heger criticized. The headmistress could not have failed to notice, as well, how Charlotte doted on her husband, Constantin George Romain HEGER. Charlotte grew to distrust Madame Heger, and her caustic portraits of the headmistresses Madame BECK in *VILLETTE* and Mademoiselle Zoraide REUTER in *THE PROFESSOR* owe much to her suspicions about Madame Heger.

Heger, Constantin George Romain (Professor Heger, Monsieur Heger) A distinguished teacher at the PENSIONNAT HEGER in Brussels where Charlotte and Emily Brontë studied and husband of Clair Zoe HEGER, headmistress of the school. Charlotte admired Monsieur Heger as a profound teacher, although she also described him as "choleric and irritable." He clearly is the model for M. Paul EMMANUEL in *VILLETTE* and William CRIMSWORTH in *THE PROFESSOR*. He was a brilliant professor of composition, and his rigorous discussion of classical texts contributed to Charlotte's growing mastery of literary form and style. He expected his students to write their own compositions, drawing on the models he had presented to them. This method is also pursued by the fictional Crimsworth and Emmanuel. A ruthless critic, Heger taught Charlotte and Emily the virtues of an economical style, although his influence is more strongly visible in the evidence that remains in the essays Charlotte wrote for him. She exulted in her status as one of Professor Heger's best pupils.

At some point, her devotion to learning became adoration of her teacher. After leaving the school she wrote him passionate letters, and her idealization of him is reminiscent of the love her heroines have for Crimsworth and Emmanuel. The extent to which Professor Heger encouraged Charlotte's attachment has never been determined. His letters to her have not survived. Her letters suggests he was never less than professional and proper in his treatment of her.

Heights, the *See* WUTHERING HEIGHTS.

Helstone, Caroline Major character in *SHIRLEY*. The 18-year-old Caroline lives with her uncle, Matthewson HELSTONE. She knows little about her parents, who separated after her birth, and her uncle refuses to tell her very much. Indeed, he largely ignores his niece, and she finds comfort in the household of Robert MOORE, a distant cousin, with whom she falls in love. She also forms a close friendship with Hortense MOORE, Robert's sister.

Caroline's world is shattered when her uncle requests that she no longer visit the Moore household. He despises Robert's politics and does not want his niece to come under her cousin's influence. But Caroline is deeply in love with Robert and pines away, especially when it seems that Robert is very much taken with the wealthy landowner Shirley KEELDAR.

Caroline becomes so distraught that she is taken ill, and for a time it is feared that she will die. She slowly recovers when Mrs. PRYOR, who is nursing the sick young woman, reveals that she is in fact Caroline's mother. After Robert Moore is shot by a disgruntled mill employee, Caroline visits him and realizes that he is not in love with Shirley but with her. She marries Robert and learns that Shirley has been in love all along with Robert's brother, Louis MOORE, Shirley's former tutor.

Helstone, James Character mentioned in *SHIRLEY*. He is Caroline HELSTONE's father, who abandons her mother, Mrs. PRYOR, shortly after Caroline is born.

Helstone, Matthewson Character in *SHIRLEY*. The rector who provides a home for Caroline HELSTONE, Mr. Helstone, an indifferent husband and uncle, is a TORY. He forbids Caroline to visit her cousin Robert MOORE, a Whig, and refuses to tell Caroline anything about her parents. Despite his political views, he sides with Moore in Moore's conflict with his employees, who resist Moore's efforts to modernize the mill and bring in new machinery.

Henri, Frances Evans Major character in *THE PROFESSOR*. Frances, the daughter of a Belgian father and an English mother, comes to Mademoiselle Zoraide REUTER's school as a pupil-teacher:

She teaches the other girls lace mending while she takes lessons in English from William CRIMSWORTH. Although Frances has never been to England, she dreams of living there someday. She speaks perfect English and wants to be able to write better in the language. William becomes fascinated with Frances. She is more serious than the other students, and she treats him with profound respect, calling him her master. When Mademoiselle Reuter realizes that William is falling in love with Frances, she discontinues Frances's employment at the school. But Frances sends a note to William, and he is able to find her, despite Mademoiselle Reuter's refusal to give him Frances's address. William marries Frances, and after 10 years of teaching in Belgium, the couple leave for retirement in England.

Henri, Julienne   Character mentioned in *THE PROFESSOR*. She is Frances Evans HENRI's deceased mother.

Henry   Minor character in *SHIRLEY*. He is Joe SCOTT's son.

Highlander   Term used to describe people from the Scottish Highlands. Still a remote region in the mid-19th century, the Highlands were considered wild and backward. Disaffected Highlanders supported the Roman Catholic Stuart pretenders to the British throne and were involved in efforts by the Stuarts to regain the throne in 1715 and 1740. In *VILLETTE*, Mr. HOME notes John Graham BRETTON's Highlander descent, implying that he is a rebel against the established order—in this case, a pretender to his daughter Polly HOME's hand in marriage.

"High Life in Verdopolis"   *See* ANGRIA.

"History of the Year, The"   In one of the surviving bits of Brontë JUVENILIA, Charlotte Brontë recounts the plays that she and her siblings wrote and critiqued among themselves. Her awareness of contemporary events and her literary ambitions are evident. Just as important, however, is her self-conscious awareness that her literary life had a history worth recording. She also provides a vivid account of the 12 wooden soldiers Patrick Brontë bought for Branwell that stimulated the children to begin childhood sagas such as GLASS TOWN, ANGRIA, and GONDAL. Charlotte later described the arrival of the toy soldiers: "Emily and I jumped out of Bed, and I snat[c]hed up one and exclaimed this is the Duke of Wellington it shall be mine!! When I said this Emily likewise took one and said it should be hers[;] when Anne came down she took one also. Mine was the prettiest of the whole and perfect in every part[.] Emilys was a Grave Looking fellow we called Gravey[.] Anne's was a queer little thing very much like herself he was called waiting Boy[.] Branwell chose Bonaparte[.]"

"History of Young Men, The"   Branwell BRONTË wrote this story in 1830–31 and signed it John Bud, Esq. (also known as Captain John Bud), "the greatest prose writer"—an action often interpreted by biographers as signifying his rebellion against his bossy sister Charlotte and his own literary ambitions. The story is violent (wars, killings, cannibals, devils, and monsters abound) and is set in the 18th century. It is part of the GLASS TOWN saga.

Hogg, Mrs.   Minor character in *SHIRLEY*. She is Joseph DONNE's landlady.

Home, Mr. (M. de Bassompierre)   Character in *VILLETTE*. The father of Paulina (Polly) HOME, he visits his daughter at Mrs. Louisa BRETTON's house. She has kindly offered to look after the child while Mr. Home travels abroad to recover his health. He eventually returns to take Polly away with him. Later Mrs. Bretton and her son, John Graham BRETTON, meet the Homes in France, where Mr. Home has inherited the title of the Bassompierre family. John resumes his childhood friendship with Polly and falls in love with her. Mr. Home, now M. de Bassompierre, is a doting father reluctant to see his daughter married, but he eventually consents to the match, and the couple are happily united.

Home, Mrs.   Character mentioned in *VILLETTE*. She is the mother of Polly HOME. Mrs. Louisa BRETTON calls the recently deceased Mrs. Home a silly mother and a careless person.

Home, Paulina (Polly Home, Miss de Bassompierre)   Character in *VILLETTE*. She stays with Mrs. Louisa BRETTON after her mother's death because her father is in ill health. Mrs. Bretton's son, John Graham BRETTON, finds Polly a fascinating playmate, but the two are separated after Mr. Home returns for Polly and John goes on to medical studies. Later the two are reunited in France, where John works as a doctor and Polly is visiting as Miss de Bassompierre (her father has inherited a French title). Dr. John, as Bretton is called, falls in love with Polly and succeeds in overcoming the doting father's initial qualms. Polly is a lively young woman. As a child she seems willful to Lucy SNOWE, who also stays with Mrs. Bretton, Lucy's godmother. But Lucy, later reunited with Polly in Villette (where Lucy teaches at a school), observes a maturing young woman deserving of Dr. John's affection.

Horsfall, Mrs.   Minor character in *SHIRLEY*. She is the stout, reliable nurse who attends Robert MOORE after he has been shot.

Hortense   Minor character in *THE PROFESSOR*. Along with EULALIE and CAROLINE, she is one of three girls who do their best to disrupt William CRIMSWORTH's class. Hortense is stout, lacks grace, and likes to stir up mischief.

Hunsden, Mr.   Character in *THE PROFESSOR*. A mill owner and manufacturer, he is impressed with William CRIMSWORTH and in turn deplores William's older brother, Edward CRIMSWORTH, for exploiting the labor of his younger brother. When William leaves Edward's employ, Hunsden provides him with a recommendation to employers in France. Later Hunsden visits William to see how he is getting along. Although Hunsden often seems harshly critical of William, he is in fact William's benefactor, and he grows gruffly fond of William's wife, Frances Evans HENRI. Hunsden loves to argue and finds that not only William but also Frances are quite willing to stand up to him. Hunsden becomes the Crimsworths' closest friend.

Huntingdon, Arthur (Arthur Graham)   Character in *THE TENANT OF WILDFELL HALL*. Young Arthur is the only child of Arthur, Lord HUNTINGDON and Helen HUNTINGDON. His mother, deeply attached to him and fearful that he will be corrupted by his father's bad influence, spirits him away. In hiding, he and his mother go by the last name Graham. He serves as a kind of unconscious go-between, helping to bring his mother and Gilbert MARKHAM together. Young Arthur grows up to marry Helen HATTERSLEY, his mother's namesake and the daughter of her oldest friend, Milicent HARGRAVE.

Huntingdon, Arthur, Lord   Character in *THE TENANT OF WILDFELL HALL*. Arthur Huntingdon is a member of the landed gentry, with a country seat at GRASSDALE MANOR. When Helen Lawrence (see HUNTINGDON, HELEN) meets him during her first London season, she is smitten with his good looks and lively manner. As a result, she pays little heed to her aunt's warning that Lord Huntingdon is, in addition to being profligate, destitute of principles. After they marry Helen learns the truth of this warning, for although Huntingdon clearly loves her in a possessive way, he is unwilling to devote much time or attention to her. Instead, he leaves her at Grassdale for months on end while he indulges in excessive drinking and gambling with a dissolute lot of cronies in London.

Later, when Huntingdon insists on bringing his friends to Grassdale, Helen learns that her husband is also guilty of adultery. Stung by this knowledge and fearful that her husband might corrupt their young son, she leaves Huntingdon. When his excesses result in mortal illness and his friends have deserted him, however, Helen returns to Grassdale to nurse him and attempt to save his soul. His dissolute life and agonizing death owe much to those of Branwell Brontë, whose escapades and end Anne Brontë witnessed directly.

Huntingdon, Helen (Helen Lawrence, Helen Graham)   Major character in *THE TENANT OF WILDFELL HALL*. Helen Huntingdon, born Helen Lawrence, also appears in the novel as Helen Graham, an alias she uses when she becomes the tenant of Wildfell Hall. Although she presents herself as a widow, neighborhood gossip has it that she is involved in an illicit romance with her landlord, Frederick LAWRENCE, who in fact is her brother. The narrator of the novel, Gilbert MARKHAM, falls in love with her and is the first to discover her secret: Helen has run away from an abusive husband, taking her young son, Arthur HUNTINGDON, with her to the derelict old manor.

Raised in comfort by her aunt and uncle, Helen possesses both money and fine looks when she is presented to London society as an eligible young woman. She is also proud, and her pride blinds her to the faults of one of her attractive suitors, Arthur, Lord HUNTINGDON. Arthur's true dissolute and selfish character makes itself known almost immediately after Helen marries him, but Helen stays with him, believing she can reform him. When she finally leaves, she does so because she fears for her child.

Helen is unquestionably a strong woman. In leaving Huntingdon, she not only betrays convention but also exhibits a profound faith in her own abilities. Although she brought a considerable amount of money to her marriage, it now belongs to Huntingdon, and Helen is obliged to make a living for herself and young Arthur with her own artistic talent. When she inevitably falls in love with her smitten neighbor, Gilbert Markham, she is able to resist his offer to save her, suggesting instead that they remain spiritual intimates. When Huntingdon becomes mortally ill, she finds the will to return to him and nurse him on his deathbed. After Huntingdon dies and Helen is once again a rich woman, Markham's self-consciousness prevents him from contacting her, and when the two eventually meet again, it is Helen who makes the first move.

Notwithstanding her abiding faith in God, Helen Huntingdon is a thoroughly unconventional 19th-century heroine. Her self-reliance and iron will, almost as much as the portrayal of Huntingdon's debauchery, scandalized readers and reviewers when *The Tenant of Wildfell Hall* first appeared.

Ingham family In writing *AGNES GREY*, Anne Brontë drew on her experience as a governess with the Ingham family at Blake Hall. She secured her position in March 1839, and like Agnes GREY, her fictional counterpart, she seems to have looked forward to leaving home so that she could contribute to her family's finances. The Inghams were an aristocratic family with an impressive residence. Like Agnes, Anne had to care for very young children, and she evidently performed her duties at Blake Hall with the same quiet, determined manner of Agnes. According to Charlotte, Anne did not have the authority to punish the children, a restriction that hampered her effectiveness, as it does Agnes's. Indeed, pampered and undisciplined children became the bane of both Anne's and Agnes's experience as governesses. Mr. and Mrs. BLOOMFIELD's children in the novel are roughly the same age as Anne's pupils at Blake Hall, and stories that were later told about Anne's stay there suggest a close correspondence between her fiction and her life.

Ingram, Blanche Character in *JANE EYRE*. The daughter of Lord and Lady INGRAM and one of the group of neighbors Mr. ROCHESTER brings to THORNFIELD for a party. The beautiful Blanche is greatly admired and seems destined to become Mr. Rochester's bride. She is haughty and treats Jane EYRE with contempt. Rochester later tells Jane that he rejected Blanche because she was mercenary and was only interested in him so long as she thought he had a large estate and vast sums of money. Blanche's interest in him ends when he puts about a rumor that he is not as wealthy as was generally supposed.

Ingram, Lady Minor character in *JANE EYRE*. She arrives at THORNFIELD with her husband, Lord INGRAM, and two daughters, Blanche and Mary. Lady Ingram has a fine figure but is excessively proud, and Jane EYRE does not like her "fierce hard eye."

Ingram, Lord Minor character in *JANE EYRE*. He is one of the neighbors Mr. ROCHESTER invites to THORNFIELD for a party. He is accompanied by Lady INGRAM and their daughters Blanche and Mary. Jane EYRE regards him as tall and handsome but also "listless."

Ingram, Mary Character in *JANE EYRE*. She is Lord and Lady INGRAM's daughter and among the group of neighbors Mr. ROCHESTER brings to THORNFIELD for a party. Jane EYRE finds Mary slimmer and less physically appealing, but also milder and softer, than her sister Blanche INGRAM.

Jacob Character mentioned in *THE TENANT OF WILDFELL HALL*. Jacob is a workman apparently standing nearby when Eliza MILLWARD gives Gilbert MARKHAM the unwelcome (and untrue) news that Helen HUNTINGDON is to be married for a second time.

Jacobin A member of the most radical revolutionary group in the French Revolution. The name stems from the group's development in the Dominican, or "Jacobin," monastery in Paris in 1789. The Jacobins spearheaded the repressive Reign of Terror (1793–94), and their name became synonymous with left-wing extremism. In *SHIRLEY*, the term is used interchangeably with ANTINOMIAN and LEVELLER to describe anyone opposed to the status quo, the Church of England, and the political establishment.

Jane Eyre Charlotte BRONTË's novel is often called GOTHIC and ROMANTIC because of the haunted atmosphere of THORNFIELD and the dark, brooding, even menacing presence of its owner, Mr. Edward Fairfax ROCHESTER. However, the novel is also a vibrant revelation of its heroine's passions and independence. It is true that Jane EYRE submits to her master, yet her submission is possible only because Rochester acknowledges her independence. Over and over again he exults in the fact that Jane is different from other women and that she will not submit to his will—or rather, she will acknowledge his authority only on her own terms. Such is the paradox of this traditional yet unconventional feminist novel. What other fictional heroine before Jane declares early in her narrative that there are millions of women like her—women who do not want to lead conventional lives, women who want to pursue an education and to do work worthy of an independent adult?

Of course, the novel is also a fairy tale, a wish fulfillment of the kind common in romance novels. It is the story of beauty and the beast—although Jane is no beauty and Rochester is no beast. Those words are best applied to his mad wife, a former beauty who has turned into a beast, laughing like a demon and literally setting her world on fire, making Thornfield a living hell for its inhabitants.

It has been said that as a Byronic hero, Rochester has much in common with Emily Brontë's HEATHCLIFF in *WUTHERING HEIGHTS*, although Rochester becomes domesticated and a better, more civilized man due to Jane's influence. Jane is more outspoken about her society than any male character in the novel. If she values the sentimental ties of marriage and of having a man in her life, her view of conventions, of religion, and of her world are hardly sentimental. She speaks her mind, and that is why certain contemporary critics called Charlotte's novel "coarse." The novel simply did not fit the mold of pious Victorian fiction, and it broke the mold of the conventional romantic and gothic novel, because its outspoken heroine criticized polite society and social conventions.

SYNOPSIS

Preface
Charlotte thanks the public, the press, and her publishers for taking such interest in an unknown and unrecommended author. To her potential critics, she defends her reputation, arguing that "conventionality is not morality"; her novel may be unconventional, she argues, but it is not immoral. She takes as her model William Makepeace THACKERAY, the famous Victorian novelist whose satire, especially in *Vanity Fair*, she warmly recommends to her readers.

Charlotte Brontë's Jane Eyre *was published in 1847. The story of the independent, outspoken title character met with huge success. The 1970 film version, directed by Delbert Mann, featured George C. Scott as Mr. Rochester and Susannah York as Jane.* (moviegoods.com)

Chapters 1–3

The novel begins with Jane Eyre's plight at GATESHEAD HALL. An orphan, Jane has been taken in by her widowed aunt Mrs. REED, whose husband had promised his dying sister to take care of her child. But Jane finds herself at the mercy of a chiding servant, BESSIE, and Mrs. Reed's bullying son, John REED. Jane is also made to regard her plain features as a negative trait, especially when compared to Mrs. Reed's daughters, Eliza and Georgiana REED.

Jane's reading in the breakfast room is interrupted by John Reed, a 14-year-old ruffian. Jane reports that Mr. Miles, John's schoolmaster, has advised John's mother to curb the boy's appetite, but Mrs. Reed indulges her boy in everything. John starts to abuse Jane and hits her, claiming he is punishing her for speaking impudently to his mother.

John also condemns her for reading the family's books, saying her dependent status deprives her of any rights or any share in the family's pleasures. "You ought to beg," he declares. He makes her stand by the door to the room. As she turns her back, he throws a book at her, and she falls, striking her head against the door and cutting herself. "Wicked and cruel boy!" Jane exclaims, calling him a slave driver. She compares him to the Roman emperors Nero and Caligula, about whom she has been reading in Oliver GOLDSMITH's *History of Rome*.

Hearing the ruckus, Mrs. Reed enters and assumes Jane is at fault. Mrs. Reed orders Jane locked up in a chilly part of the house called the red room.

Jane, quite hysterical herself, resists being carried away, and the servants deplore her shocking conduct. They even threaten to tie Jane up, but she promises to calm down and is left with Bessie's admonition that she should be grateful to Mrs. Reed; otherwise Jane would find herself in the poorhouse. Jane is told not to think of herself as an equal to the Reed children. Miss ABBOTT, another servant, advises Jane to repent.

The red room is where Mr. REED died, and Jane is fearful that she will encounter his ghostly presence. Feeling terribly isolated and abandoned, Jane frets over her ill treatment and inability to please the family, not only John Reed and his mother, but also the headstrong and selfish Eliza and the spoiled Georgina. With an aching head, Jane rails against the injustice of her incarceration. She knows that her position would be better if only she were prettier.

Jane imagines that if Mr. Reed were alive, he would treat her more kindly. Thinking of him, however, increases her dread of seeing his ghost. When a light seems to enter the room, she panics and beats against the door, arousing the attention of the servants. They judge her screams a deliberate act of perversity, and Mrs. Reed refuses Jane's plea that she be punished some other way.

Still shut up in the room, the terrified Jane loses consciousness. When she awakes, she finds herself cared for by Bessie and Mr. LLOYD, an apothecary. Bessie has softened considerably toward Jane, and the kindly Mr. Lloyd draws out of Jane the story of John Reed's tormenting behavior. Bessie brings Jane her favorite book, Jonathan SWIFT's *GULLIVER'S TRAVELS*, which attracts her in part because of Gulliver's account of his long voyages away from England.

Mr. Lloyd inquires about Jane's family and learns that she knows nothing about them. He asks if she would like to go to school. After thinking about it, Jane enthusiastically declares she would. She later learns from a conversation between Bessie and Miss Abbott that her mother married a poor clergyman and that her family was so upset that they cut off Jane's mother from all support. Both of Jane's parents later died of typhoid fever.

Chapter 4

After Jane recovers, Mrs. Reed treats her coldly, Eliza and Georgina ignore her, and John Reed avoids her after she hits him in the nose. This last act stimulates Jane's rebellious nature, and she decides the Reed children are not fit to associate with her. She even reproaches Mrs. Reed for her abusive behavior and receives, in turn, Mrs. Reed's blows on her ears. Jane remains excluded from all household activities and from parties and other social engagements. To her, however, this is no punishment. The 10-year-old Jane plays with her doll and is warmed by Bessie's increasingly affectionate attention.

Jane's life is suddenly changed by a visitor, Mr. BROCKLEHURST, who has come to inspect Jane as a candidate for his charity school, LOWOOD. He warns Jane that naughty girls go to hell, and he is outraged at her reply that she will have to take care not to die. Under his further examinations, Jane reveals an independent spirit and a thoughtful intelligence that clash with his demand for strict obedience and conventional behavior.

Mr. Brocklehurst and Mrs. Reed agree that Jane should be sent to the school as soon as possible. He says he will inform Miss TEMPLE, the school's superintendent, of Jane's imminent arrival.

Incensed, Jane confronts Mrs. Reed. She denies Mrs. Reed's charge that she has been deceitful: It is Georgiana who is a liar. Jane confesses she does not love Mrs. Reed and that the only person she dislikes more is John Reed. Jane says she is glad that she is not related to Mrs. Reed and also declares that she will tell everyone just how badly Mrs. Reed has treated her. When Mrs. Reed wonders at Jane's accusations, Jane recalls how Mrs. Reed locked her up in the red room and showed no pity for her sufferings.

The long speech of denunciation liberates Jane, who says, "my soul began to expand, to exult, with the strangest sense of freedom, of triumph, I ever felt." Mrs. Reed counters that Jane is mistaken; she decries Jane's passionate nature and tells her to lie down. Jane refuses. Mrs. Reed mutters that she will indeed send Jane to school soon. Jane feels like the "winner of the field."

After this long battle—the hardest Jane feels she has ever fought—she goes to Bessie, the only person in the household who treats her kindly and in whom Jane can confide. Bessie recognizes Jane's new assertiveness, calling her a "little sharp thing!" The two of them share a happy time together, with Bessie singing and telling Jane stories.

Chapters 5–6
On a cold day in January, Jane leaves for school. Saying goodbye to Bessie, Jane starts out for a moonlight ride in a coach. She falls asleep during the 50-mile journey and arrives at Lowood, where she is greeted by Miss MILLER, who gives her a meal. Another woman, who Jane later learns is Miss Temple, asks her if she can read, write, and sew. Jane explains that she has no parents.

The next day Jane begins to learn the school routines, the lessons and prayers, but is still exhausted from her journey. The rooms are cold, and the discipline is strict. The girls are expected to memorize passages from the Bible. The breakfast meal of burned porridge is inedible. Jane becomes aware that the other students dislike Mr. Brocklehurst.

Exploring the grounds, Jane finds a sign that reads "Lowood Institution." She then meets Helen BURNS, a young girl reading Samuel Johnson's *RASSELAS*, which looks "dull" to Jane's taste, since it seems to have nothing in it about fairies or the kind of bright variety she craves in her reading.

Helen explains the nature of the institution, what it means to be a charity child, and that a new part of the institution was built by Naomi BROCKLEHURST, the mother of Mr. Brocklehurst. He is the treasurer and manager of the school. Helen also identifies the teachers and the subjects they teach.

Jane ends the day disturbed by the punishment of an older girl, who is made to stand in the middle of the room. Jane declares that she could not bear the humiliation, and she marvels that the girl is able to remain so calm.

The next day Jane begins her courses. Miss SMITH gives her two yards of muslin, a needle, and a thimble and sets her to work on sewing. Miss

SCATCHERD gives a history lesson and chastises Helen for failing to keep her head up. Helen knows her lesson well, but Miss Scatcherd becomes upset because Helen's nails are dirty. Jane is astonished when Helen does not explain that she could not bathe that morning because the water was frozen. Miss Scatcherd punishes Helen by striking her a dozen times on the neck with a bundle of twigs. Helen remains quiet, and the teacher calls her a "hardened girl!" Only a single tear reveals to Jane Helen's distress.

During the play period Jane talks to Helen about Miss Scatcherd's cruelty. Helen replies that the teacher is severe because she hates Helen's faults. Helen expresses no resentment, pointing out that the Bible says to return good for evil. Jane declares that she would not stand for such punishment and could not bear the humiliation. Helen insists it is her duty to bear it.

Helen acknowledges that she does have faults that need to be corrected. Unlike Jane, she cannot focus on her lessons. Jane finds it hard to accept Helen's doctrine of Christian forgiveness and her injunction to love one's enemies. Jane thinks of Mrs. Reed, whom she finds impossible to love. Helen suggests that Mrs. Reed simply does not like Jane's cast of character. In the long run, Helen advises, Jane will be happier if she gives up her grievances.

Chapters 7–8
Jane describes her first three months at Lowood. The students are poorly clothed and fed but encouraged by Miss Temple to move along like stalwart soldiers. Academic lessons are supplemented with lectures on the Scriptures and sermons by Miss Miller.

Mr. Brocklehurst's first visit to the school is mortifying for Jane. After reprimanding Miss Temple for being too indulgent with the girls—he wants them to be hardy, patient, self-denying—and instructing that the girls' hair must be clipped short to present a modest appearance, he singles out Jane, makes her stand on a stool before the whole school, then denounces her as a liar. He warns the girls to shun Jane's company and directs that no one speak to her for the rest of the day.

By the end of the day Jane is weeping steadily, and Helen Burns tries to comfort her with food and kind words. But Jane despairs that anyone will now consort with her. Helen points out that Mr. Brocklehurst is not a god and not even much admired by the pupils. His words will have only a temporary impact, and Jane will not be without friends.

Helen's words calm Jane, and then Miss Temple consoles her as well, saying that all Jane needs to do is behave and she will prove herself a good girl. Jane tells Miss Temple the story of her life at Gateshead Hall and of Mr. Lloyd's kind treatment of her. Miss Temple knows Mr. Lloyd and tells Jane she will write to him and seek to clear Jane's reputation. Miss Temple invites Jane and Helen to tea in her apartment.

A week later Miss Temple assembles the whole school and announces that she has investigated and cleared Jane of the charges against her. A grateful Jane renews her studies and thrives, concluding, "I would not now have exchanged Lowood with all its privations for Gateshead and its daily luxuries."

Chapter 9

By spring, Jane's spirit has reawakened, and Lowood itself seems more pleasant during this brilliant season until an outbreak of illness devastates the school, leaving more than half of the 80 girls infected, and killing several. Mr. Brocklehurst and his family never appear during this ghastly period.

Jane makes a new friend, Mary Ann WILSON, who is "shrewd" and "observant." Jane likes Ann's

In this scene from the 1944 film Jane Eyre, *Mr. Brocklehurst (played by Henry Daniell) cuts Helen Burns's (Elizabeth Taylor) hair while a young Jane (Peggy Ann Garner) looks on.* (Movie Star News)

stories and wit. Jane misses Helen, who is ailing and confined to bed. Then Jane learns that Mr. Bates, the surgeon, has been to see Helen. Late that evening Jane sneaks out of the dormitory to visit Helen, who asks Jane if she has come to say good-bye. At first Jane is puzzled and presumes Helen must be leaving the school. But Helen is in no doubt that she is dying and tells Jane that she is going to "my last home." She is serene in her faith in God, and the two girls fall asleep together. The next day Jane awakes and realizes she is being taken away from Helen, who has died during the night.

Chapter 10
Jane reports that the typhoid fever that swept the school caught the public's attention, and an investigation exposed the poor diet, unhealthy drinking water, and wretched clothing and accommodations that contributed to so much death among the students. Although Mr. Brocklehurst was not removed from his post (his eminent position protects him), he is now assisted by an inspector who greatly improves Lowood's living conditions.

Jane quickly recounts the eight years she has spent at the school. An excellent student, she becomes a teacher there in her last two years. Miss Temple leaves the school and marries the Rev. Mr. Nasmyth, provoking in Jane a desire to leave as well and experience something of the larger world. She desires her liberty, "or at least a new servitude!" she declares.

Jane is inspired to advertise for a new position in a newspaper. Now 18, Jane seeks a position as a governess and emphasizes her abilities in French (taught to her by Madame PIERROT), drawing, and music. A week later she receives a letter concerning a teaching post for one pupil; the pay will be 30 pounds a year. Jane is directed to have her references sent to Mrs. FAIRFAX at Thornfield.

Jane is excited at the prospect of living nearer to London (Thornfield is 70 miles from the city) with a higher salary (twice what she receives at Lowood). When she learns that her references have been accepted, Jane busies herself in preparation to leave Lowood. Then, to her surprise, a visitor asks for her. It is Bessie, who has come to see how Jane is getting on and to give her news of

Gateshead. Jane learns that Bessie is married and has children, that Georgiana is as handsome as ever, and that John Reed has been expelled from college and has done little with his life. Jane also learns that one of her uncles (her father's brother) has visited Gateshead, inquiring about her. Receiving a cold reception from Mrs. Reed, he leaves without making contact with Jane, who has never met him and still knows almost nothing about her family. Saying good-bye to Bessie, Jane enters her coach for the journey to Thornfield.

Chapters 11–13
On her journey Jane speculates about the character of her employer, Mrs. Fairfax. She dreads the idea that she will encounter "a second Mrs. Reed." At Thornfield she is directed to a snug, small room where she meets Mrs. Fairfax, the neatest imaginable little elderly lady. Jane is surprised by how warmly she is received, expecting more formal treatment as a governess. She inquires about her pupil, whom she calls Miss Fairfax. Mrs. Fairfax corrects her, "You mean Miss Varens!" Jane learns that Mrs. Fairfax has no family. Jane asks no questions, not wanting to be thought rude. Mrs. Fairfax arranges a late-night supper for Jane and considerately proposes they retire for the night. Jane is overwhelmed by her kindness and the cozy room Mrs. Fairfax has arranged for her.

The next day Jane arises to take a good look at Thornfield. It is a substantial edifice, three stories high—a manor house, not a nobleman's estate. She admires the mighty old thorn trees, "as broad and knotty as oaks," and its secluded location in the hills. Mrs. Fairfax agrees with Jane that it is a "pretty place," but it is "getting out of order" because Mr. Rochester does not "reside here permanently . . . Great houses and fine grounds require the presence of the proprietor."

Suddenly Jane realizes that Mrs. Fairfax is not the lady of the house. Mrs. Fairfax explains that she is only the housekeeper, although she is distantly related to the Rochesters. Jane's pupil, Mrs. Fairfax explains, is Mr. Rochester's ward. He has commissioned Mrs. Fairfax to find a governess for Adèle VARENS.

Adèle is delighted to meet Jane and to learn that her governess speaks such perfect French.

Jane and Adèle get acquainted, and Jane gives Adèle her first lesson. Adèle is docile enough and ready to take instruction, but she is not disciplined or used to rigorous lessons.

Curious about her employer, Jane asks Mrs. Fairfax if Mr. Rochester is a fastidious man. Not particularly, Mrs. Fairfax answers, but he does like to see his house in order and ready to receive visitors. Mrs. Fairfax is careful not to shut up rooms or cover the furniture, especially since he is apt to visit without any notice. Jane wants to know more about his character, but Mrs. Fairfax says little in answer to Jane's question about his peculiarities except that it is difficult to read Mr. Rochester's moods, whether he is speaking in jest or earnest, whether he is pleased or the contrary.

Jane turns her attention to the house, wanting to know more about its history. Mrs. Fairfax mentions that the Rochesters have had a violent history but are quiet now. Jane wonders aloud if there are ghosts in the house. Mrs. Fairfax cannot think of any instances, then Jane hears a strange, loud, preternatural laugh. Mrs. Fairfax suggests it is one of the servants, Grace POOLE, whose behavior is not always proper. To confirm her suspicion, Mrs. Fairfax knocks on a nearby door, and Grace materializes, curtseying silently when Mrs. Fairfax tells her she is making too much noise.

Jane accustoms herself to the daily routine at Thornfield Hall, confirming that Mrs. Fairfax is as pleasant as she seemed, and Adèle as obedient and unambitious as she first appeared. Jane enjoys walking the grounds. She also walks along the corridors of the house's third story, feeling restless and thinking about the millions of human beings, especially women, who are too confined, too rigidly relegated to conventional roles that provide no outlet for their energy or talents. They stagnate in a narrow-minded culture. Why should they be condemned, Jane wonders, for wanting to learn and do much more than is customary for women? Jane's thoughts are disturbed only by Grace Poole's unearthly laugh, yet Jane cannot connect the plain sight of Grace, who excites no misgivings in a person, with the unnerving sound.

Three months of this routine bring Jane to a day in January when Adèle has a cold. Acceding to Mrs. Fairfax's wishes, Jane gives her pupil a holiday and takes a letter from Mrs. Fairfax to the post office in the village. On her way, Jane discovers a horse and rider who have slipped and fallen on an icy patch of road.

The traveler's dog fetches Jane, who hears the traveler swearing at his misfortune. She offers help, but he requests only that she stand aside. When he attempts to right himself and mount his horse again, he discovers that he has badly sprained an ankle. Jane observes his "dark face, with stern features and a heavy brow." He looks angry. A man of middle height, he has a powerful looking chest. She imagines him to be about 35.

Jane insists she cannot leave the injured man. He asks her where she lives, and if she knows Mr. Rochester or anything about him. She answers that she does not and explains that she is the governess. Finally, he leans on her for support in mounting the horse, then rides away.

On her return to Thornfield, Jane feels reluctant to enter the house; it now appears stagnant to her—dark, silent, and lonely. She lingers outside, looking at the moon and the stars.

Coming into the house Jane is surprised to see the dog, PILOT, from the road. She learns from a servant, LEAH, that Mr. Rochester has returned home and that the rider who fell and whom she helped is, in fact, her employer.

The next day Jane and Adèle are invited to tea with Mr. Rochester. At their first meeting, Jane finds him abrupt to the point of rudeness. He questions her gruffly, asking her whether she likes gifts, and Jane rejoins that it depends on what the gift signifies. He appears nettled by her careful replies, but he also compliments her on the improvement he sees in Adèle. Next he questions Jane about her years at Lowood and her family. She is frank about her dislike of Mr. Brocklehurst. He then directs her to play the piano but stops her when he discovers she has no special talent. Finally, he examines her drawing, judging that while she is no artist, she does have great powers of observation.

Apparently satisfied that he has taken Jane's measure, he dismisses her and Adèle for the evening. Jane observes to Mrs. Fairfax that Mr. Rochester is rather peculiar. Mrs. Fairfax says that she is so used to his ways that she has never considered the point. She also notes that he has had family troubles and mentions an elder brother, Rowland, with whom Mr. Rochester quarreled. Mr. Rochester's unsettled life, she notes, is the result of having broken with his family. Mrs. Fairfax also suggests that he does not spend more time at Thornfield because he finds it gloomy.

Chapters 14–16

Jane sees little of Mr. Rochester in the following days, until one day, after he has shown visitors Jane's portfolio of drawings, he summons her and Adèle. He bids Adèle amuse herself with a doll, then proposes to enjoy himself in conversation with Jane. He notices that Jane is examining him carefully, and he asks her if she thinks him handsome. She says she does not. "By my word! there is something singular about you," he confesses. Jane apologizes, but he presses her to continue her assessment of him. He is again caught by surprise when she asks him if he is a philanthropist. "Another stick of the penknife," he exclaims, apparently enjoying Jane's directness and independence. After more efforts to elicit conversation from Jane, he tries to make her agree that he has a right to be abrupt given his age, worldly experience, and position. Jane counters that his authority should rest on what he has made of his experience and position. He points out that to accept her terms is to acknowledge his faults. He succeeds in making her agree that she will take his manner as informal and not insolent.

After Mr. Rochester comments on Jane's youth, Jane observes that no matter how he has failed, in time he can correct his behavior and remedy the faults of character he regrets. He acknowledges the possibility but is struck by how somber Jane is: "Do you never laugh, Miss Eyre?" He suggests that the constraints of Lowood still cling to her and that she has not allowed herself to speak freely or move quickly. He believes that in time she will liberate herself and soar cloud-high. As for himself, "my Spring is gone," he concludes. At the close of the evening he says he will tell her how he became Adèle's guardian. The girl's energetic entrance into the room brings a close to the evening.

Later Mr. Rochester explains to Jane that Adèle is the daughter of Céline VARENS, a French opera singer for whom he had a "*grande passion.*" So smitten was he with Céline that he made her his mis-

tress and set her up in an apartment in Paris. Then one night he discovered her in the company of another man, a rather feeble figure whom Mr. Rochester wounded in a duel. Céline had pleaded with Mr. Rochester not to give her up, but he had overheard her disparaging him to the other man, and he realized he could never love a woman who could take as her lover a man she did not respect. He was not jealous; he was contemptuous.

Mr. Rochester says he was foolish to ruin himself and spend his fortune on an unworthy lover. He also explains that when Céline abandoned her child, he felt he had to adopt her, even though he did not believe Céline's claim that Adèle was his child. Now that Jane has learned of her pupil's scandalous background, she will wish one day to find other employment, Mr. Rochester suggests. But Jane replies that Adèle is not answerable for either her mother's fault or his. On the contrary, Jane says her regard for her pupil is even stronger now that she knows Adèle is parentless, forsaken by her mother and disowned by Mr. Rochester.

Jane retires to her room and ponders what Mr. Rochester has told her. Although he seemed now reconciled to his past, she perceives in him some anxiety about his current situation. She is encouraged by the confidence he places in her and admits she likes to hear him talk. She praises his open mind and her keen delight in receiving the new ideas he offers. His easy manner relieves her "painful restraint." Jane also confesses to a delight in his physical presence. Although he can be moody and harsh, she believes in better tendencies and dedication to higher principles. She suspects something in his experience accounts for his darker emotions and wonders what alienates him from his own house.

Musing on the evening, Jane falls asleep—only to be awakened by a "demoniac laugh." When she hears the sound again, she thinks of Grace Poole. She hears a door creaking open. Now fully awake, she finds the hallway full of smoke and the door to Mr. Rochester's room ajar. He is in a deep sleep in the midst of a raging fire. She awakens him and has water brought to put out the flames.

Mr. Rochester questions Jane closely about whether she saw the person who started the fire. Jane supposes it was Grace Poole, and Mr. Rochester quickly supports her speculation. When Jane bids him good night, he is reluctant to let her go: "Why, you have saved my life—snatched me from a horrible and excruciating death! And you walk past me as if we were mutual strangers!" He says good night to his "cherished preserver." Jane returns to her room but cannot sleep.

The new intimacy disturbs Jane. The next day she longs to see him, but he does not appear. She is surprised instead to see Grace Poole, who has not been dismissed for her presumed crime. Jane begins pondering Mr. Rochester's relationship with Grace Poole. Grace is not young or handsome, and it hard to believe there has been a closeness between her and Mr. Rochester.

That evening Mrs. Fairfax informs Jane that Mr. Rochester has gone off on a journey and will be bringing back several guests for a party. Mrs. Fairfax tells Jane about Blanche INGRAM, a beautiful, much admired young woman who once sang a duet with Mr. Rochester. Jane is surprised to learn that Mr. Rochester can sing, and she is intensely curious about Blanche. She learns from Mrs. Fairfax that Blanche is not married, and Jane suggests to Mrs. Fairfax that Mr. Rochester might think of marrying her. Here Jane first intimates that she has fallen in love with Mr. Rochester but criticizes herself for thinking she could be of any importance to him. She instructs herself not to take his praise seriously. She even directs herself to draw a picture: *Portrait of a Governess, disconnected, poor, and plain.* She also decides to draw a picture of Blanche based on Mrs. Fairfax's description. This portrait will serve to remind Jane that she is an "indigent and insignificant plebeian." In this way she hopes to "discipline" her feelings.

Chapter 17

Over the next several days Jane torments herself with her passionate feelings for Mr. Rochester. She counsels herself to give up her love for him, since she cannot expect him to return it. After two weeks, Mrs. Fairfax receives a letter from her master that he will arrive in three days with a company of guests. The figure of Grace Poole continues to trouble Jane, especially when she hears a charwoman say to the servant Leah, "Doesn't she [Jane] know?" Jane realizes "there was a mystery at Thornfield; and that from participation in that mystery I was purposely excluded."

Everyone dresses up for the day of Mr. Rochester's arrival with his guests. Jane tries to calm an excited Adèle, who loves social gatherings and dressing up. Jane tells her stories, then walks with her in the house's gallery. Jane again questions Mrs. Fairfax about the likelihood of Mr. Rochester marrying Blanche Ingram. Mrs. Fairfax does not think it likely, although she concedes it would be a good match.

Mr. Rochester arrives with a party of eight. Jane observes Mrs. ESHTON and her two daughters. Amy ESHTON seems rather small and childlike, whereas Louisa ESHTON is taller and more elegant. Lady LYNN enters, a woman of 40 elegantly dressed and with an erect, haughty bearing. Mrs. Colonel DENT appears less arrogant, more gracious, and also well dressed. The most spectacular guests, however, are Lady INGRAM and her two daughters. The mother has kept her figure, but it is spoiled, for Jane, by her haughtiness and fierce, hard eye. The star of the gathering is Blanche, whom Jane likens to the goddess Diana. Jane observes that Blanche is quite conscious of her appeal and exploits it. Although most of the guests greet Adèle affectionately, it is clear that Blanche finds her tiresome.

Jane turns her attention to the men, describing Henry LYNN and Frederick LYNN as "dashing sparks" and Colonel DENT as having a very "soldierly" appearance. Mr. ESHTON, a magistrate, is the image of the white-haired wise man. Lord INGRAM is tall and handsome but also rather passive. Mr. Rochester dominates the scene, for Jane, and she describes him in detail: "massive brow, broad and jetty eyebrows, deep eyes, strong features, firm, grim mouth—all energy, decision, will." Although he is not a conventionally handsome man, he has a striking force that is in sharp contrast to Ingram's languid manner and the Lynns' gallantry. Clearly, Jane is devoted to this mercurial man who changes from melancholy expressions to vivid smiles. He is a much more substantial figure than the rest.

The guests banter and inquire about Adèle. The ladies trade unflattering comments about governesses. Jane grows uncomfortable and tries to slip away, but Mr. Rochester accosts her and asks her how she is. He observes that she seems pale, but she replies that nothing is the matter. He insists that she looks depressed, and although

Charlotte's novel was so well received that the London publisher Smith, Elder issued a second printing within three months of its publication. The 1944 film version, directed by Robert Stevenson, starred Orson Welles as Mr. Rochester and Joan Fontaine as Jane Eyre. (Movie Star News)

he excuses her for the evening, he expects her to be in the drawing room while his guests remain at Thornfield.

Chapters 18–20
Jane describes the bustling, "merry days" at Thornfield, including an elaborate game of charades, the first she has seen. She comments on Blanche Ingram's behavior, which she finds insincere and lacking distinction, in spite of the young woman's polish and high manner. Jane doubts Miss Ingram has any true affection for Mr. Rochester, and she concludes that both he and Miss Ingram are simply following the dictates of their upbringing, which decrees that people of the

same position should marry. As Jane admits, she is now so attached to her master that she quite willingly forgives him his faults; indeed, when Mr. Rochester is absent from the room, Jane feels the energy level fall.

A man who announces himself as an old friend of Mr. Rochester's joins the festivities. Jane notes that he speaks with an unusual accent, but he accommodates himself to the party quickly. Jane learns that his name is Mason (see MASON, RICHARD) and that he comes from the West Indies, which surprises her, since Mr. Rochester had not spoken of traveling so far from home.

The party is interrupted by the announcement that a gypsy fortune-teller has arrived and insists on consulting the ladies. One by one they have their fortunes read and return amazed that the gypsy is able to tell them so much about themselves. Finally, the gypsy insists on seeing Jane, who complies, even though the gypsy proceeds to cross-examine her in a very free manner, commenting on Jane's independence of mind and suggesting she is cold, silly, and sick. "Prove it," Jane retorts. The gypsy explains that Jane is cold because she is alone, sick because she had been denied the "best of feelings, the highest and sweetest given to man," and silly because she has it within her power to experience those feelings. Jane observes that as much could be said of anyone in her circumstances. The gypsy doubts there is another person placed precisely in Jane's circumstances; she also admits that she has had some inside information from Grace Poole and that Grace can be relied on.

The gypsy then asks Jane what she knows of Mr. Rochester and his marriage plans. Jane says that it seems he will marry Blanche Ingram, but she reminds the gypsy she has come to hear her fortune, not Mr. Rochester's. The gypsy replies that Jane's future is doubtful and that it is up to her to grasp her happiness. Under the spell of the gypsy Jane almost thinks she is dreaming until the gypsy reveals herself to be Mr. Rochester. He asks the surprised Jane if she will forgive him. She doubts that what he has done is right.

Jane says she must return to the new guest. When Mr. Rochester is told the guest's name, he is shocked and says, "Jane, I've got a blow—I've got a blow, Jane!" and he leans on her as he did after his riding accident. A glass of wine restores him, and he questions Jane closely about the new arrival. He asks her, "If all those people came in a body and spat at me, what would you do, Jane?" She replies that she would turn them out of the room and would stay with him and comfort him. Then Jane hears a restored Mr. Rochester heartily welcome Mason.

Jane is awakened that night by a savage cry. She hears shouts for help and Colonel Dent angrily asking for Mr. Rochester. Rochester calls for calm, explaining that a servant has cried out during a nightmare, and firmly tells everyone to return to bed. Afterward, he requests Jane's aid. She accompanies him to a room to minister to a wounded Mason, who fears he has been mortally injured. Rochester assures him that his wound is not seri-

ous and that a surgeon will be brought to attend to him. He warns Mason not to speak to Jane, tells her he will be gone for perhaps two hours, then leaves Mason in her care.

The two hours pass slowly, and Jane begins to fret. But Mr. Rochester returns with CARTER, a surgeon, who confirms that the wound is not serious in spite of the blood loss. He observes that the wound could not have been done by a knife, and Mason remarks, "She bit me." Mr. Rochester allows Jane to think that the "she" is Grace Poole. After having Jane bring a potion that calms Mason, Mr. Rochester asks the surgeon to take Mason with him. Mason bursts into tears and says, "Let her be taken care of." Mr. Rochester replies, "I do my best, and have done it, and will do it." As Mason leaves, Mr. Rochester adds, "Yet would to God there was an end of all this!"

After Mason's departure, Mr. Rochester assures Jane he is in no danger from Mason and that he will make sure Grace Poole does not harm anyone again. He alludes to some great error he has made that accounts for the present circumstances. Then he changes the subject and refers to the possibility of marrying Miss Ingram. He tells his guests that Mason got an early start and was gone before sunrise.

Chapters 21–22

Robert LEAVAN, the coachman from Gateshead Hall, arrives to tell Jane that Mrs. Reed is dying and that she has asked to see Jane. He also tells Jane that John REED has died after having squandered his fortune. Jane asks Mr. Rochester to spare her for the time it takes to see her aunt at Gateshead. Rochester reluctantly gives his consent but makes Jane promise that she will return to Thornfield as soon as possible. She is doubtful, however, about her future at Thornfield now that Mr. Rochester has intimated that he will marry Miss Ingram. Jane expresses her desire to leave if that happens, and Mr. Rochester—after rejecting her plan to advertise for a new position—promises that he will find her suitable new employment.

At Gateshead, Jane receives a cold reception from Georgiana and Eliza and at first cannot communicate well with a delirious Mrs. Reed. Eventually Jane hears her aunt criticize Jane's poor appearance and rebelliousness. Mrs. Reed reveals that she turned away one of Jane's relatives, an uncle named John EYRE, who declared his intention to leave Jane his fortune. When Jane asks why she was never told of this visit, her aunt replies, "Because I disliked you too fixedly and thoroughly ever to lend a hand in lifting you to prosperity." Indeed, Mrs. Reed informed Jane's uncle that Jane had died of typhus at Lowood.

Although Jane forgives her aunt, who is near death, Mrs. Reed continues to reiterate how much she always has hated Jane. After Mrs. Reed's death, her two daughters quarrel and take advantage of Jane's goodwill in helping them organize their affairs. Jane consents only because she knows her involvement with them is temporary, even though it delays her return to Thornfield. The sisters show some appreciation of Jane's good nature, and she parts with them on good terms.

Not wanting any fuss made over her, Jane returns to Thornfield unannounced. She enjoys her approach to the grounds and tries to avoid Mr. Rochester, who is seated on the stone steps with a book and pencil, but he sees her and teases her about her month away. He also alludes to his upcoming marriage, which she acknowledges as she thanks him for his kindness.

That evening she resolutely tries to face her future, which seems one of "coming grief." Nothing more is said of Mr. Rochester's marriage, however, and she is puzzled that he makes no visits to Ingram Park, which is not far away.

Chapters 23–24
Jane describes the loveliness of England in midsummer. Again she tries to evade Mr. Rochester's attention, for like her he is outside enjoying the weather. He sees her and begins to question her about her attachment to Thornfield. She acknowledges it and asks "Must I leave Thornfield?" He says she must, and she feels his words like a blow. He reaffirms that he will be married soon. He tells Jane he has found a place for her in Ireland, and she points out it is a long way off from him. To his comment that she will forget him, she replies *"never."* Each word from her master stirs Jane's intense emotions, and she exclaims, "I grieve to leave Thornfield: I love Thornfield."

Mr. Rochester suddenly declares that she must stay. After prolonging her agony by observing that she can determine her destiny, he tells her that she is the wife he had in mind. Jane, who cannot seem to understand his avowal of love, says "your bride stands between us." After more misunderstanding, Rochester finally breaks through her disbelief, and she accepts him. They embrace and kiss, and Jane notices that Mrs. Fairfax has observed part of this scene.

The next morning Jane wonders if she has been dreaming. She goes to breakfast and is greeted by a wary Mrs. Fairfax. An exuberant Mr. Rochester speaks of sending for jewels he means Jane to have, but she is adamantly opposed to what seems "unnatural and strange." He speaks of touring all the capitals of Europe with her. She asks him why he pretended to be courting Blanche Ingram. He replies that he only wanted to make Jane as madly in love with him as he was with her. Jane chides him for vexing her and for toying with Miss Ingram's feelings. Rochester retorts that Miss Ingram is a proud woman whose feelings he could not hurt, since she never really cared for him.

When Mr. Rochester tells Mrs. Fairfax that he is going to marry Jane, Mrs. Fairfax is astounded and tells Jane she can hardly believe it. Indeed, Mrs. Fairfax is concerned about the match and fears that Jane will be disappointed. She also fears that Jane's youth and inexperience will lead her into trouble. She advises Jane to keep some distance from Mr. Rochester: "Distrust yourself as well as him. Gentlemen in his station are not accustomed to marry their governesses." Jane confesses to the reader her irritation, but in fact she takes Mrs. Fairfax's advice, restraining Mr. Rochester's desire to dress her up.

Although Mr. Rochester is irritated by Jane's aloofness, he is also intrigued and entertained by it. He does, after all, value her independence, and Jane realizes that a slavish respect for his desires would only foster his despotism.

Chapter 25
The month of Jane's courtship is almost over. She is excited but also anxious. An event the previous night has aroused her uneasiness. She describes a beautiful July day that ends with the sight of a blood-red, half overcast moon. She walks through the orchard on an evening that has turned gloomy. She returns to Thornfield in a gale accompanied by rain, and she thinks again of the

event of the previous evening. Her troubled thoughts are relieved when Mr. Rochester appears on his horse and sweeps her up for a ride home. Yet her prospects seem "unreal" to her. He tries to dismiss her gloom, calling it "hypochondria." To reassure her, he asks her to tell him about the event of the previous evening.

Jane describes a day that started well with preparations for her wedding. That night— another gusty, rainy one—she slept fitfully and dreamed she was following the windings of an unknown road with a little child in her charge. She sensed that Mr. Rochester had been on this road earlier and that she could not catch up to him. Indeed, her movements were somehow fettered, and he seemed to withdraw farther and farther every moment.

Rochester interrupts her to reaffirm his love for her, but she continues with the story of another dream. This time it is about a Thornfield in ruins. Jane still has her little child, and she hears a gallop that she believes is Mr. Rochester's horse. He is going away and will not return for many years. She tries to go after him, but the child clings to her neck, almost strangling her. As she tries to climb a wall after him, the child falls. Jane loses her balance, falls, and awakes from her dream.

When Mr. Rochester asks if that is all, Jane tells him that as she awoke she became aware of a presence in the room near her wedding veil. She calls out the name of the family servant, Sophie, but there is no answer. Eventually Jane makes out that the person in the room is no one she has met in the household. She sees, instead, a savage face, fearful and ghastly, with rolling red eyes. The dark presence reminds her of a vampire.

Although Mr. Rochester dismisses the figure as the creature of an overstimulated brain, Jane denies that she was overwrought—and besides, when she awoke from her swoon of terror, her wedding veil had been torn in two. Rochester says that if anything malign came near her, it was fortunate that only the veil was damaged. He recommends that Jane share her bed with Adèle, where Sophie also sleeps.

Chapters 26–27

It is Jane's wedding day. At the church communion rail Mr. wood, the clergyman, instructs the

couple that they must confess now to any impediment to their marriage. When Mr. Wood pauses, a "distinct voice" says, "The marriage cannot go on: I declare the existence of an impediment." Mr. Rochester ignores the voice and tells Mr. Wood to proceed. Mr. Wood replies that he cannot without investigating the assertion that has just been made.

The speaker, Mr. briggs, a lawyer who represents Richard Mason, announces that Mr. Rochester is already married. He then reads out Richard Mason's written statement: Mr. Rochester married his sister, Bertha mason, in Spanish Town, Jamaica. When Mr. Rochester challenges Briggs to produce his witness, he does. Richard Mason steps forward. Confronted with the witness, Rochester decides to tell all. He calls off the wedding and admits that he was about to commit bigamy. He invites the wedding party to Thornfield, where he shows them his mad wife. At the same time, Briggs tells Jane that Richard Mason learned of her marriage to Mr. Rochester because she wrote a letter to her uncle, John Eyre, announcing her plans, and her uncle told his friend, Richard Mason. After the party leaves, a disconsolate Jane retires to her room feeling bitter, her "love lost," her life "lorn."

The next afternoon Jane ponders what to do. Her expectations now seem only a dream, and she resolves that she must leave Thornfield at once. After several hours she leaves her room and finds that Mr. Rochester has been sitting next to her door. He is surprised that she has not been crying and that she does not reproach him. Saying he never meant to hurt her, he asks for her forgiveness. "Reader, I forgave him at the moment and on the spot," Jane admits. When Jane nearly faints, he revives her with a glass of wine. When she does not respond to him with her former affection, he presumes she is resentful. But she replies, "All is changed about me, sir, I must change, too." He tells her of his plans to send Adèle to school, to shut up Thornfield, and to keep his wife well away from everyone. When Jane protests that he is too hard on Bertha Mason, he says that it is not because she is mad that he hates her, arguing that if Jane were crazy, he would still love her.

Rochester's plan is to go into seclusion with Jane, but she rejects his offer, even though she admits that she still loves him. He explains in detail how he came to be married. He describes himself as an inexperienced son whose avaricious father determined that his elder son, Rowland, would inherit all the property so that it would be kept intact. For Edward, he designed a marriage in the West Indies to a wealthy Creole family. Rochester describes how he visited the island and was charmed by Bertha Mason, unaware that her family had a history of madness and that she would prove a most unsuitable wife, with whom he would not be able to hold a civilized conversation. After the marriage, her behavior became increasingly erratic and eventually she became mad. After four years of coping with her fits, he decided to seclude her at Thornfield and resume his life as a single man. He made sure that Grace Poole, a qualified nurse, looked after Bertha, but he did not see how he could spend his whole life chained to youthful error. Leaving Bertha was the only way he could rouse himself from his despair. When he returned from his travels to find Jane installed as governess, he was immediately captivated. Soon he found he could not do without her stimulating company, and he fell in love.

Jane listens to Edward Rochester's tale with great sympathy, but she cannot alter her resolution to leave Thornfield. Rochester yields to her determination, asking her only to think over her decision that night in the hope that she will reconsider.

To avoid yet another painful meeting with Rochester, Jane leaves Thornfield shortly before dawn. She takes virtually nothing with her and spends her last 20 shillings on a coach ride.

Chapters 28–30
Two days later the coachman sets Jane down at a crossroads called Whitcross. There are no people in sight, and she strikes out across the heath. Jane has no idea what to do or where to go. She sleeps out of doors that night, still tortured by her thoughts. The next day she begins to feel keen hunger. She enters a village and a shop. She has no money and can think only of exchanging her gloves or a silk handkerchief for the rolls she has seen in the window. But the idea seems absurd to her, and she asks only if she can sit down. She asks the shopkeeper if there is any work to be had, but the woman provides no useful information, and a

depressed Jane leaves and tries a private home. The woman who answers the door cannot help her. Jane is now reduced to the thought of begging for her bread. Another attempt at seeking aid at a clergyman's home is fruitless (he is away). Then a farmer gives her some of his bread when she asks him for it, and at another home she obtains some cold, hardened porridge that was about to be thrown out.

Seeking shelter for the night, she approaches another house, where she can hear two women, who we later learn are Diana and Mary RIVERS, talking about some German literature they are reading. When Jane knocks on the door, the servant Hannah answers and refuses Jane's request to speak to the young ladies. Jane declares she is too weak to go on in the rain and will die if she is turned away, but the skeptical Hannah, thinking Jane might be part of a gang of housebreakers, turns her away.

A despairing Jane is rescued by St. John RIVERS, the young ladies' brother, who comes home just in time to overhear Hannah spurn Jane. He takes her in, and he and his two sisters feed her. But she is silent when they inquire about who she is and where her friends are. She pleads exhaustion, and they agree to provide her shelter, withdrawing to discuss her in another room.

Jane overhears the family sharing their impressions. Diana and Mary feel pity and want to help her. St. John agrees. Jane, as she is restored to health over a three-day period, becomes more confident, and from Hannah she learns about the family's situation. The sisters and brother do not permanently reside in the house but have come home after their father's recent death (their mother died years ago). St. John is a clergyman, and the family has only modest means. The family name is Rivers, a distinguished name, and at one time a prosperous one.

St. John asks Jane pointed questions as his sisters protest that he is taxing her too much. But he is persistent, and Jane finally agrees to tell as much of her story as she can without hurting other people or compromising her own privacy. St. John agrees to help her find employment, although he warns her that a man in his modest position will not be able to provide her a highly placed position. Jane, however, is agreeable and wants nothing better than to serve, no matter how humble the capacity.

Jane's fondness for the Rivers family grows. She enjoys talking with the sisters, and she is deeply respectful of St. John's principles and his zealous work as a clergyman. She is delighted when he is able to find her a post as a teacher. He doubts she will stay at it long because he believes she has a passionate, if not an ambitious nature.

As the time approaches for Diana and Mary to leave home (they must earn a living), St. John announces that their Uncle John has died. They are disappointed because he has left them nothing and given his fortune to another relative. St. John explains that his father had quarreled with Uncle John, his mother's brother, and they had never reconciled.

Jane is pleased to have not only her teaching post but also a modestly furnished little cottage. Mr. Rochester is still very much on her mind even as she tries to begin her life anew. She assures the skeptical St. John that she is quite content with her new surroundings. He confesses that he has had worldly ambitions and has only recently learned to govern them in favor of his dedication to missionary work. Their conversation is interrupted by Miss Rosamond OLIVER, a beautiful woman from a wealthy family. St. John seems disconcerted in her presence, and soon Jane realizes that he is in love with her.

Chapters 31–32
Although Jane finds her pupils dull at first, she gradually begins to see that all are not so, and she is heartened by the welcome she is given in the community. Rosamond Oliver also befriends her and takes an interest in her teaching. Mr. OLIVER, Rosamond's father, speaks highly of St. John, thus increasing Jane's wonder that St. John does not court Rosamond, for a match with her would solve his family's financial problems.

As Jane is reading Sir Walter's SCOTT's long poem *MARMION*, St. John examines a portrait she had been making. It is a likeness of Rosamond Oliver, and Jane takes the opportunity to sound out St. John about his feelings for Rosamond. He admits his love for her, but he regards his attraction as a mere weakness of the flesh, since he does not regard Rosamond's personality as suitable for

the kind of wife he desires. He needs a woman who can serve with him in his missionary work. Jane wonders why he must pursue such work, and he replies, "Relinquish! What! My vocation? My great work? My foundation laid on earth for a mansion in heaven?" He believes his wife must share his EVANGELICAL fervor, and nothing Jane can say sways him from his purpose.

Chapter 33
Jane receives a surprise visit from St. John Rivers. After some rather aimless talk, he begins to tell the story of an orphan girl. The details correspond to Jane's life: her years at Gateshead, Lowood, and Thornfield. Eventually Jane learns that Mr. Mason's lawyer, Mr. Briggs, had contacted St. John as one of the clergymen in the area. Jane is only concerned to learn of Mr. Rochester's fate, and St. John is keen to tell her that her uncle, John Eyre and the same uncle John the Riverses refer to, has died and left her a fortune of 20,000 pounds. As soon as Jane fully absorbs that she has indeed inherited this money, she promptly announces that she will share it with St. John and his sisters. While he protests and says she must take more time to consider the matter, she is insistent that she must share her new wealth with her newfound family. To Jane, 20,000 pounds is an extravagant sum, and she will only feel right when her cousins receive their part of it.

Chapters 34–35
The Christmas holidays approach. Jane is well satisfied with the progress of her pupils, and she agrees to stay on until her replacement is found. Although Jane now feels close to the Rivers family, she notices that St. John is not as affectionate with her as he is with his sisters and that he does not quite partake of the intimacy that Jane enjoys with Diana and Mary. Diana notices St. John's aloofness and bids him kiss Jane as he does Diana and Mary. He complies, but Jane recognizes what a trial he would have been as a husband to Rosamond Oliver. He thinks only of his missionary work. He presses Jane to give up learning German and to learn Hindustani instead; his reason becomes apparent when he proposes to her. He tells her she would make a proper wife for a missionary. As much as she respects St. John, she does not love him, nor does she think he loves her. She observes

no passion in his proposal, no romantic strain in his character. His proposal becomes an ordeal; the more insistent he becomes, the more Jane shrinks from him, offering only to go with him on his missionary work as his sister, not his wife. He rejects her counteroffer as impractical and unwise, since he must present no appearance of impropriety by traveling with a woman who is not his wife. Jane can only say,"I am ready to go to India, if I may go free." St. John reiterates, "A part of me you must become." Jane rejects him then, saying "I scorn your idea of love." Although they part on apparent good terms, Jane senses that she has offended him and that he will no longer give her his confidence.

The next day St. John is polite but cold to Jane. He again tries to argue her into marriage. She renews her idea of becoming his partner, but not his wife; he still finds her suggestion lacking in common sense. He then accuses her of thinking only of Mr. Rochester. Jane replies that she must find out what has become of him.

When St. John leaves, Diana questions Jane and confirms her suspicion that her brother has asked Jane to marry him. It is what Diana and Mary have hoped for, but Diana is shocked when she learns that her brother wanted Jane to accompany him to India. Jane explains that she does not love St. John, and she does not believe he loves her. Jane believes he only sees her as a "useful tool" and Diana agrees such an attitude is "insupportable— unnatural—out of the question!" Jane concedes that he is a handsome, even a great man, but she cannot accept his terms.

That evening, after St. John had made yet one more effort to persuade Jane to marry him, Jane hears a voice cry out "Jane! Jane! Jane!" She cries, "I am coming!" A superstitious feeling sweeps over her and she feels the need to leave her cousins.

Chapters 36–37
It is now June, and Jane departs for Thornfield. It is a 36-hour journey. As she nears her goal, she meets an old man who was once butler to Edward Rochester's father. He tells her what has happened at Thornfield since she left. There has been a terrible fire, the house is a ruin, Bertha Mason has perished in the conflagration, and Edward Rochester was blinded and lost a hand in his efforts to get everyone safely out of the house.

Mrs. Fairfax has been pensioned off, Adèle has been sent off to school, and Rochester remains secluded at FERNDEAN, a modest manor house on the grounds of his devastated estate.

Jane approaches Ferndean with great joy. That Rochester may have turned into a gloomy tyrant does not concern her; in fact, she observes him at a distance and confirms that he has the same strong and stalwart contours as ever. Only in his face does she see the signs of his suffering, which remind her of a sightless Samson.

Rochester is attended by his faithful servant JOHN (1) and John's wife, MARY. His dog, Pilot, is also at his side. After Mary and John get over their initial shock at Jane's arrival, they tell her that their master sees no one. But Jane brings in a tray to him, and when she begins to speak, he is agitated and wonders who is speaking. He is overjoyed when she confirms his suspicion that it is Jane Eyre. He asks her to tell him what has happened to her. Minimizing her own suffering, she tells him about the fortune she has inherited and the cousins who have helped her.

The next day Rochester tells Jane how much he suffered when he realized that Jane had left Thornfield and had not taken anything with her. He also cross-examines her about St. John. Jane teases him by calling St. John handsome, learned, and an achiever. Rochester accuses her of being unfaithful to him, but Jane then frankly explains that she turned down the proposal of a man who did not love her and whom she could never love. Rochester asks Jane to marry him, and she accepts. Then they share their mysterious experiences, her tale that she heard someone calling out her name and his tale that he heard someone say, "I am coming." Rochester affirms that he did call out her name at the very hour she heard the voice summon her.

Chapter 38
"Reader, I married him," Jane writes, describing the day of their wedding. She also explains that she visited Adèle at school and did not like what she saw. Installing Adèle in a new school, she devotes the next 10 years of her life to Rochester. After the first two years of their marriage, he regained his sight in one eye. She also reports that St. John pursued a successful missionary career in India but that he never married. He now seems

close to death, evidently exhausted from his labors. The last words of the novel are St. John's dying words: "My Master . . . has forewarned me. Daily He announces more distinctly, 'Surely I come quickly' and hourly I more earnestly respond, 'Amen; even so, come, Lord Jesus!'"

PUBLICATION HISTORY

Jane Eyre, Charlotte's second novel and first to be published, appeared under the name of Currer Bell on October 16, 1847, in an edition of approximately 2,500 copies. Within three months, the publisher Smith, Elder issued a second printing, followed by a third in April 1848. Accolades came from William Makepeace Thackeray and important critics such as George Henry LEWES. A tremendous critical and popular success, the novel nevertheless provoked attacks that it was improper—largely because Jane, as narrator, was so outspoken and because Charlotte embedded considerable criticism of society in her narrative. The author was nettled enough by such criticism to defend herself in a preface to the second edition (1848), which sold as well as the first. Another sign of its great popularity was its dramatization as *The Secrets of Thornfield Manor* on the London stage in February 1848. A French translation of *Jane Eyre* quickly followed. In May 1850, Smith, Elder published a cheap edition of the novel, which testified to its continued hold on the public's imagination.

Jenkins, Reverend Evan   Chaplain of the Royal Chapel, Brussels. Patrick Brontë consulted Jenkins about schools in Brussels for Charlotte and Emily, and Jenkins accompanied Patrick and Charlotte to the PENSIONNAT HEGER in February 1842.

Jenny   Minor character in *WUTHERING HEIGHTS.* Jenny is a servant to old Mr. LINTON at THRUSHCROSS GRANGE.

Jesuit   A member of the Jesuit order of the Roman Catholic Church. The order, which was established by St. Ignatius Loyola in 1534, was known for its emphasis on education and its aggressive desire to increase the power of the papacy as a religious, educational, and political force. Consequently, the Jesuits encountered con-

siderable opposition and prejudice, for they were deemed unscrupulous and dishonest in intellectual and religious debate. The twisting or manipulation of ideas came to be known as Jesuitical. Thus in *VILLETTE,* Lucy SNOWE believes she must defend Protestantism against "Jesuit slanders."

Job   In the Bible, Job is the righteous man whom God deprives of all his worldly possessions and who is made to suffer terribly in a test of his faith. In *VILLETTE,* the lonely Lucy SNOWE describes herself as "poor as Job."

John (1)   Minor character in *JANE EYRE.* He and his wife, MARY, are servants to Mr. ROCHESTER; they stay with him even after THORNFIELD is destroyed in a fire.

John (2)   Minor character in *THE TENANT OF WILD-FELL HALL.* John is one of Arthur, Lord HUNTINGDON's many servants at GRASSDALE MANOR.

John (3)   Minor character in *WUTHERING HEIGHTS.* He is one of old Mr. LINTON's retainers at THRUSHCROSS GRANGE.

John, Dr.   *See* BRETTON, JOHN GRAHAM.

Joseph (1)   Character in *WUTHERING HEIGHTS.* This old manservant at WUTHERING HEIGHTS has long been an Earnshaw family retainer. His broad Yorkshire accent and sour disposition make him an embodiment of the bleak, forbidding atmosphere of the place, as Mr. LOCKWOOD first finds it. Although Joseph's overt piousness makes him in a sense a foil to the godless HEATHCLIFF, the two men are equally impersonal in the roughness with which they treat others.

Joseph (2)   The biblical story of Joseph is one of Polly HOME's favorites in *VILLETTE.* He is sold into slavery in Egypt by his brothers and is mourned by his father Jacob, who tears his clothes and refuses to be comforted, declaring: "I will go down into my grave unto my son mourning."

Juno   Dog in *WUTHERING HEIGHTS.* This "liver-colored bitch pointer," mother to a new batch of puppies, attacks Mr. LOCKWOOD on his first visit to

WUTHERING HEIGHTS, then reluctantly wags her tail at him on his second visit.

juvenilia In June 1826, Patrick Brontë purchased for his nine-year-old son 12 wooden soldiers. All of his surviving children—Charlotte (10), Branwell (9), Emily (8), and Anne (6)—were well used to making up childhood games and stories. With this gift, however, the soldiers became a focal point for their creation of stories, plays, poems, newspapers, magazines, illustrations—indeed, virtually every medium available at the time to children inclined toward literary and artistic interests. Moreover, the children created a world of their own not only in the invention of GLASS TOWN, ANGRIA, and GONDAL but also in booklets written in small, almost indecipherable letters meant to keep their writing a secret from their father and to mimic the printed page.

As the oldest, Branwell and Charlotte took charge of what amounted to an exclusive society of storytellers. They modeled themselves after characters in the *ARABIAN NIGHTS*: Branwell became the Chief Genius Brannii; Charlotte, the Chief Genius Tallii; and Emily and Anne, Emmii and Annii Branwell. The cooperation and rivalries of these siblings manifested the children's extraordinary ambition and imagination.

Unlike the juvenilia of other authors, these early productions do not represent a stage of creative life that the Brontës left behind. Even as adults, they continued to expand on their sagas, and aspects of the juvenilia appeared to varying degrees in their mature work; for example, Cathy EARNSHAW and HEATHCLIFF in Emily's WUTHERING HEIGHTS bear close resemblance to a number of characters who peopled the Angrian and Gondal sagas. The juvenilia is an integral part of what Lucasta MILLER calls the "Brontë myth" because it shows from the earliest ages that their lives were dedicated to literature and to making a literature out of their lives. *See also* "ARTHURIANA; "HISTORY OF THE YEAR, THE"; "HISTORY OF YOUNG MEN, THE"; "TALES OF THE ISLANDERS"; "WE WOVE A WEB IN CHILDHOOD"; *"YOUNG MEN'S MAGAZINE, THE."*

Kay Shuttleworth, Sir James and Lady Janet   The Kay Shuttleworths lived at Gawthorpe Hall, near Burnley in Lancashire. Sir James, a retired physician, persistently attempted to draw his neighbor, the literary celebrity known as Currer BELL, into his orbit, but he had only limited success. Charlotte Brontë met Elizabeth Gaskell when staying as a guest at the Shuttleworth home. Charlotte made several visits to the Shuttleworths', who provided her with respite from her duties at Haworth. Later Mrs. Gaskell also became friends with the Kay Shuttleworths, who provided her with some assistance when she was writing Charlotte's biography, *The Life of Charlotte Brontë.*

Keeldar, Shirley   Title character in Charlotte Brontë's *SHIRLEY*. She is a landowner of independent means who helps Robert MOORE, a local mill owner, remain in business after the attack of his LUDDITE workers. She also befriends Robert's cousin, Caroline HELSTONE, who has fallen in love with Robert but thinks Robert and Shirley are in love. In fact, Shirley loves Louis MOORE, Robert's brother and her former tutor. Shirley and Caroline engage in spirited discussions of a woman's role and the nature of men. As independent as Shirley is, she declares her desire for a man who would be worthy of becoming her master. She does not want to enslave herself to a male but instead find a great man to whom she can devote her considerable energies and intelligence. At first, she suspects that Louis Moore, in his position as tutor, will not assert himself and propose to her. He rises to the occasion, however, and she defies her family—chiefly her uncle, Mr. SYMPSON—by announcing that she and Robert will marry.

Keeper   Emily Brontë's dog. Keeper was a large mastiff who was as profoundly attached to his mistress as she was to him. Emily made a drawing of him "from life" on April 24, 1838, when he was a year old. When Emily died in 1848, Keeper made up part of the funeral procession that followed her coffin to the graveyard in Haworth. During the service that followed, he sat in the Brontë family pew. He died of old age in December 1851.

Keighley   The nearest major town to HAWORTH, three miles away. The Brontë children took advantage of some of the cultural activities available in Keighley, including drawing lessons offered by the Keighley Mechanics Institute.

Keighley Mechanics Institute   Educational institution founded in 1825 in the village of KEIGHLEY, three miles west of HAWORTH. The institute was intended primarily to serve the working classes. It did, however, open its lectures and library to ladies and gentlemen. Patrick Brontë became a member in 1833 to provide his family with access to its library, and for the next decade he and his children made use of its collection.

Kenneth, Mr.   Minor character in *WUTHERING HEIGHTS*. Mr. Kenneth, a plain-spoken, rough individual, is the local doctor. He is summoned from his home in GIMMERTON for all the births, deaths, and major illnesses of the characters in the novel.

Kint, Victor   Minor character in *VILLETTE*. He is Madame BECK's brother and Paul EMMANUEL's friend.

Knoll, the   Harriet MARTINEAU's home in AMBLESIDE, which Charlotte visited in December 1850.

Koslow, Aurelia   Minor character in *THE PROFESSOR*. A flirt, she tries to interrupt the concentration of her teacher, William CRIMSWORTH.

L—— Place in *THE TENANT OF WILDFELL HALL*. L—— is a market town about seven miles from WILDFELL HALL where Helen HUNTINGDON switches from a coach to a common cart in the midst of her flight from her abusive husband.

Law Hill *See* HALIFAX.

Lawrence, Frederick Character in *THE TENANT OF WILDFELL HALL*. Frederick Lawrence is Helen HUNTINGDON's brother. When she moves to the Lawrence family home, the near-derelict WILDFELL HALL, he becomes her landlord. Although Lawrence is a reserved, gentlemanly sort, local gossip links him romantically with Helen, who is posing as the widowed Mrs. Graham. The gossip harms them both. The local farmer Gilbert MARKHAM, for example, who loves Helen and is convinced Lawrence is taking advantage of her, physically attacks Lawrence. Soon thereafter, Markham learns the truth about Helen, and he and Lawrence become friends. Lawrence even becomes a kind of conduit between Markham and Helen, and Markham in turn saves Lawrence from a potentially regrettable marriage to Jane WILSON. In the end Lawrence marries Helen's young friend Esther HARGRAVE.

Lawrence, Helen *See* HUNTINGDON, HELEN.

Leah Minor character in *JANE EYRE*. A servant at THORNFIELD, she is aware of the "mystery" involving Grace POOLE, who is suspected of creating the disturbances at night that trouble Jane EYRE.

Leavan, Robert Minor character in *JANE EYRE*. The coachman at GATESHEAD HALL, he comes to THORNFIELD to announce that Mrs. REED is dying and has asked to see her niece, Jane EYRE.

Leigh household In *VILLETTE*, the household where Lucy SNOWE's friend, Mrs. BARRETT, works. Lucy observes the nurse in the household; she seems to do well and is treated kindly by the family. Searching for some means of employment, Lucy thinks to go abroad and perhaps obtain a similar position.

Leighton, Mr. *See* "BLATANT, MR."

leveller The term was first used during the English Civil War and the period of Oliver CROMWELL's rule to describe members of a political movement that wanted to enforce a state of equality, with everyone but the poorest man having the right to vote. Levellers also believed in religious toleration and the abolition of the monarchy and the House of Lords. In *SHIRLEY*, the term is used along with ANTINOMIAN and JACOBIN to describe anyone of radical political and religious views who is opposed to the Church of England and to the establishment.

Lewes, George Henry (1817–1878) English historian, biographer, novelist, and critic. He is best known for his 24-year liaison with the writer George Eliot (Mary Ann Evans). An influential reviewer, he took notice of Charlotte Brontë's novels and corresponded with her. Charlotte rejected his advice that she write more like Jane AUSTEN. Elizabeth GASKELL discusses Charlotte's response to Lewes in *THE LIFE OF CHARLOTTE BRONTË*.

Life of Charlotte Brontë, The Elizabeth GASKELL's biography of her friend Charlotte BRONTË began as a memoir, when she decided to write down all she could recollect—beginning with their first meeting in the Lake District—and to copy out extracts from Charlotte's letters that revealed her character. Although she received much assistance from Charlotte's rather forbidding father, Patrick BRONTË, and her husband, Arthur Bell NICHOLLS, Mrs. Gaskell soon realized the dangers of relying too closely on the family, who might be offended by the kind of personal material that inevitably becomes part of the public record in a biography. She sought, instead, to interview friends of the family who supplied her with letters and reminiscences. Even here, though, the noted novelist found it difficult to extract documents from those wishing to protect Charlotte's reputation. The farther away Mrs. Gaskell moved from family informants, the more she had to count on testimony from those unsympathetic to Charlotte's father and husband.

There were other frustrations: Some of Charlotte's correspondents had destroyed her letters, figures such as Clair Zoe HEGER refused to see the biographer because they felt Charlotte had portrayed them unfavorably in her novels, others censored letters or offered only excerpts, new material came to light that meant significant portions of the biography had to be rewritten, and Mrs. Gaskell's publisher, George Smith, objected to her portrayal of Patrick Brontë, because he thought it harsh. But the biographer triumphed through perseverance and shrewdness, modifying her description of Patrick and paying a surprise visit to him in the company of the distinguished Sir KAY SHUTTLEWORTH, who helped entice from the old patriarch the valuable manuscripts of *THE PROFESSOR* and an unfinished work, *EMMA*.

In general, Mrs. Gaskell learned how to manipulate her sources, wrest evidence from reluctant witnesses, and preserve her own vision of Charlotte even when it conflicted with those close to her. Although critics and biographers have pointed out instances of bias and misinterpretation in *The Life of Charlotte Brontë*, it remains a founding text of Brontë biography and a key source for subsequent accounts of the family's life and art.

SYNOPSIS

Chapter 1
Mrs. Gaskell begins her biography by describing the road to HAWORTH village, the site of the

Brontë home. She describes nearby KEIGHLEY, an old-fashioned town falling fast to modern times. The few miles from Keighley to Haworth have lost their country look. Workers' homes and worsted factories now mark the landscape. As she nears the village, she describes the purple HAWORTH MOOR, the long narrow street into the village, and the feeling of solitude and bleakness the gray land evokes.

The biographer then approaches HAWORTH PARSONAGE, meticulously describing the old stone-gray, tidy house, the location of Mr. Brontë's study, and the air of purity that envelops the scene. Just above the house is the little church and its graveyard, a medieval place. In this historic setting, inside the church, is a tablet commemorating the Brontës who have come and gone: Patrick's wife, Maria Branwell BRONTË, and their children Maria, Elizabeth, Patrick Branwell, Emily Jane, and Anne BRONTË. The lines of the stone are cramped as one name quickly succeeds another with the inscribed dates of each one's birth and death, until no more room is left after Anne's name. The biographer notes that a separate tablet, next to the one that records the lives of five motherless children, is one commemorating Charlotte Brontë, the sixth Brontë child to die and the wife of Reverend Arthur Bell NICHOLLS.

Chapter 2
Mrs. Gaskell explains that in order to understand the life of her "dear friend, Charlotte Brontë," the reader must know Brontë's family background and the people of Haworth and its environs. The biographer takes special note of Yorkshire self-sufficiency and independence. The character of JOSEPH in *WUTHERING HEIGHTS*, Mrs. Gaskell observes, exemplifies both the virtues and vices of the Yorkshire character, which is at once so self-contained and strong, yet stubborn and often incapable of cooperating with others. Feuds often lead to fights.

Mrs. Gaskell describes Yorkshire as a hardy world where woolen mills were established in the days of Edward III and prospered under Oliver CROMWELL. The region remembered Cromwell's rule with stubborn loyalty even after the monarchy was restored under Charles II. Yorkshiremen are not sentimental; indeed, they are stoical and to an outsider seem even brutal and rude in their reactions to human suffering. Mrs. Gaskell relates an anecdote in which a young boy jumps into a stream full of broken glass, severs an artery, and almost bleeds to death. The crusty old doctor hardly cares whether the boy lives or dies, and a relative remarks that it will save a good deal of trouble if the boy does not recover.

The biographer attributes this rough-hewn character to the remote, mountainous character of the area. Bad roads make communication with the rest of the world difficult. The cold and the snow contribute to a feeling of isolation and alienation in the pockets of hill villages. Solitary inhabitants—not bound by intercourse between individuals in communities—develop manias and eccentricities. By way of illustration, Mrs. Gaskell tells the story of a dying squire who was fond of cockfighting and had the cocks brought into his bedroom so he could watch them tear each other apart. This kind of story, she adds, will not surprise readers of *Wuthering Heights* and THE TENANT OF WILDFELL HALL.

Haworth has also been the site of religious fanaticism, which Mrs. Gaskell relates in her sketch of the life of the Reverend William Grimshaw, who often preached in private homes 20 and even 30 times a week, warning people that they were going to hell. He strictly enforced the sabbath and was even known to whip reluctant parishioners into church.

The biographer next describes the clergyman who preceded Patrick Brontë in the parsonage at Haworth: She dwells on the experience of Mr. Redhead, whose unruly congregation walked out on his sermons and even contrived situations that threatened his physical safety. But Mr. Redhead persevered and was able to consign a well-ordered parsonage in February 1820 to Patrick Brontë, who arrived with a wife and six small children. "One wonders how the bleak aspect of her new home—the low, oblong, stone parsonage, high up, yet with a still higher background of sweeping moors—struck on the gentle, delicate wife, whose health even then was failing," Mrs. Gaskell concludes.

Chapter 3
Patrick Brontë and his family history and Irish ancestry are the focus of this chapter. Mrs. Gaskell remarks that Patrick maintains in old age a physical presence that suggests he was a very handsome young man. Born on March 17, 1777, Patrick was a precocious youth. By the age of 16 he was running his own school. After a position as tutor for a family, he entered Cambridge University in 1802, obtaining a B.A. four years later at the age of 29.

By the time he settled as a curate in Hartshead, a small village in Yorkshire, Patrick showed in his speech and habits no traces of his Irish origins. He remained in Hartshead for five years, wooing and marrying Maria Branwell, the third daughter of Thomas Branwell, a merchant in the seaside resort of Penzance, which in the 18th century was the scene of smuggling and violent criminal activities. Through her mother's sister, Charlotte no doubt heard vivid stories about Penzance that Mrs. Gaskell speculates helped shape the girl's imagination.

As Mrs. Gaskell would have it, the elegant, if not beautiful Maria Branwell fell in love with the outgoing Irishman, Patrick Brontë. He, in turn, loved her simple, yet stylish manner. Patrick and Maria were married on December 29, 1812, the same day Maria's younger sister, Charlotte, was married in Penzance. In the years the couple lived at Hartshead, Maria gave birth to two daughters: Maria and Elizabeth.

Charlotte Brontë was born on April 21, 1816, in THORNTON, where Patrick next served as curate in the parish of Bradford. Patrick Branwell, Emily Jane, and Anne were born after Charlotte in quick succession, seemingly contributing to Maria's steady decline in health. Except for a few extracts from Maria's letters, however, Mrs. Gaskell reports only that she was an agreeable, pious, well-read, and apparently a "well-balanced and consistent woman." Much of her short life after her marriage was the sad story of an invalid.

Charlotte was six when the family moved to Haworth on February 25, 1820. Even at this early age, accounts mentioned her grave, thoughtful personality. For such a sensitive child there was to be no normal childhood, Mrs. Gaskell suggests. The biographer describes the stone house with its four bedrooms upstairs, a large parlor, window seats, and a pleasant garden.

The people of Haworth did reasonably well working in the worsted mills and operating small shops. BAPTISTS, METHODISTS, and ANGLICANS all worshiped in the same community, and Patrick Brontë had good relations with them all, although his family was known for preserving a certain aloofness. But in Yorkshire, Mrs. Gaskell pointedly remarks, people are expected to mind their own business.

All the Brontë children particularly enjoyed playing on the moors. Because their mother was slowing dying of cancer, they often seemed rather somber and quiet for their years. They lived in a house where their mother never came out of her bedroom. Adding to their soberness was Patrick Brontë's belief in an austere household, which included dinners that consisted only of potatoes. He believed his children should be hardy and self-sufficient—once even going so far as to burn their boots because he thought them "too gay and luxurious" for children. Patrick Brontë, Mrs. Gaskell suggests, had suppressed his Irish background and favored a dour stoicism in hopes of appearing more "English." The only outlet he permitted himself was the firing of pistols when he was upset.

A vigorous man, Patrick walked the moors for hours. A keen observer of nature, he was also fearless in the expression of his opinions. Mill workers disliked his lack of sympathy for men protesting the introduction of new machines. At one point, he carried pistols, ready for an attack because of his outspoken view that the LUDDITES should be prosecuted promptly. At another time, he took the side of striking workers and was heavily criticized by the mill owners. The biographer does not profess to understand why Patrick often held seemingly contradictory opinions, but she emphasizes that he never acted for worldly gain and was always a man of principle. Both his fearlessness and his frankness contributed greatly, Mrs. Gaskell believed, to Charlotte Brontë's character.

Charlotte's mother died in September 1821. The children seemed even more subdued; later Charlotte would say that she retained only a few vivid memories of her mother. Patrick, now suf-

fering from some kind of intestinal complaint, took his dinners alone, away from his children. His habits inevitably made their household an isolated one—another factor in the formation of Charlotte's imagination, Mrs. Gaskell suggests. What the children did learn of the world often came from Maria, the oldest child, who read the newspapers to her siblings. The Brontë servants Mrs. Gaskell interviewed said they were impressed with the solidarity and intelligence of these children. They conducted their own dramatic performances. Patrick, realizing their incipient talent, encouraged it, developing the ingenious device of a mask behind which they were free to speak their minds. He was struck by their answers to his questions: Charlotte said the Bible was the best book in the world; Branwell said the differences between men's and women's minds was traceable to their different bodies; Emily advocated reasoning with the naughty Branwell or whipping him if he would not listen to reason; Anne wished for "age and experience." Maria impressed her father with her knowledge of worldly affairs. Lacking childhood playmates the children relied on one another and their father's stimulus.

Chapter 4
The family gained a new member after Patrick lost his wife. Maria's sister, Elizabeth BRANWELL, arrived to take charge of the household and the children. Mrs. Gaskell suggests that Aunt Branwell was conscientious but also put off by the region's rough manners and the cold, bleak Yorkshire landscape. Haworth Parsonage seemed isolated compared to the sociable, temperate climate she was used to. The children honored her efforts, even if they could not love her.

Maria and Elizabeth Brontë entered the COWAN BRIDGE school in July 1824. The school served as a model for LOWOOD in *JANE EYRE*, and the biographer reports that Charlotte later regretted that her fictional school should have been so absolutely identified in certain readers' minds with its real-life counterpart. Allowances have to be made in fiction, Mrs. Gaskell implies, that would not be tolerated in a work of history.

William Carus WILSON, the founder of the school, is both praised for his resourcefulness in establishing an institution for the education of clergymen's children and criticized for weak administrative abilities that led to incompetence in certain departments of the school. Funding was in short supply for the seven cottages that made up the school, which Mrs. Gaskell describes in meticulous detail. Food was of good quality but poorly prepared. Basic sanitary procedures were not followed, and meals were often inedible. Wilson would not believe reports that children went hungry; he replied that they were not to be pampered. Poor feeding resulted in many illnesses, especially in a cold climate where children in a malnourished state were exposed to daily walks.

By September, Charlotte and Emily were also pupils at the school. Maria Brontë (Helen BURNS in *Jane Eyre*) became ill and was treated badly by a teacher. Although she could hardly rise from her bed, Maria was punished for arising late. Charlotte was incensed at her sister's treatment, but she was also, Mrs. Gaskell speculates, aware that Cowan Bridge was the best education her father could provide for his children.

By spring 1825, several girls in the school were ill with fevers. Eventually a doctor determined that about 40 girls had been sickened by the school's food, and the cook was dismissed. Although the meals afterward were better prepared, in general Mr. Wilson still did not realize how injurious his staff's behavior had been to the welfare of the school's hundred or so pupils.

Mrs. Gaskell reports that Maria was intelligent but also untidy. Almost nothing is known of Elizabeth's behavior, although the school headmistress, Miss TEMPLE, reported that her head had been cut in some kind of accident. Five-year-old Emily was something of a school pet. Charlotte was considered the most talkative sister and very bright.

Maria grew more ill, and by the late spring of 1825 she was sent home, where she died a few days after her arrival. She evidently suffered from consumption (TUBERCULOSIS), a disease that also afflicted Elizabeth, who died in the early summer of the same year. Although Emily and Charlotte returned to Cowan Bridge after their summer vacation, they were removed from the school before the winter recess, since it had been decided that the damp conditions there "did not suit their health."

Chapters 5–6

Mrs. Gaskell describes Charlotte Brontë at the age of 15 in 1831. She had extraordinarily expressive eyes and delicate, if not beautiful features. She gave the impression of neatness and liveliness, yet she had a gravity that reminded her biographer-friend of a Venetian portrait. It was a demeanor worthy of an elder sister who now had to care for her siblings.

In January 1831, Charlotte was sent to Miss WOOLER's school, a cheerful house. With more open country than the land around Haworth, Roe Head, where the school was situated (on the road to Leeds), provided grassy views and pleasant country houses that inspired the setting and the characters of *SHIRLEY*.

Miss Wooler was kindly and accepted only seven to 10 pupils at any one time, so Charlotte felt comfortable and got to know the local children. According to accounts from school friends, Charlotte arrived with some apprehension. Her fellow pupils found that although a good reader, she was otherwise not well educated. Miss Wooler ministered to Charlotte's concerns by allowing her to make a private study of those subjects in which she was deficient. The students soon learned she had an impressive command of literature and was a master storyteller, supplementing her tales with fine drawings.

Charlotte got into arguments at school about the REFORM BILL OF 1832, expressing her staunch support for the duke of WELLINGTON. She told one friend that she had been interested in politics since the age of five and learned a good deal from reading her father's newspapers. She missed her two dead sisters terribly and talked about her dreams of them. She was a serious student and awkward at games. Miss Wooler challenged Charlotte with harder and harder reading assignments. In general, Charlotte and the school benefited from a teacher who knew how to motivate the desire for learning.

At Roe Head, Charlotte heard the story of Mr. Cartwright, a local mill owner, who had invited trouble by introducing new machinery that provoked an assault by his workers. She visited the sites where he had rebuffed his adversaries and heard about another mill owner who was shot and killed in a similar incident. These events became the basis of *Shirley,* as did the opinions of the DISSENTERS in the area surrounding the school. Their radical, outspoken opinions also influenced the dialogue of her novel. Altogether, Charlotte spent two years at the school, enjoying its cozy, tight-knit world.

Chapter 7
Charlotte left Roe Head having made two friendships for life, with young women whom Mrs. Gaskell identifies only as "Mary" and "E." Perhaps because of the early death of her sisters, the biographer speculates, Charlotte did not hold out much hope for her own life. At any rate, by July 1832 she was at home teaching her younger sisters. Her father also employed an instructor for drawing, which Charlotte and her sisters enjoyed as a form of relaxation. The girls stayed among themselves, walking on the moors and rarely venturing down to the village. They remained a literary household, owning volumes of poetry by William WORDSWORTH, Sir Walter SCOTT, and Robert SOUTHEY, and taking other books out of the library.

When one of Charlotte's friends from Roe Head came to visit, she observed a shy Anne and a reserved Emily. Charlotte wrote her friend that everyone had enjoyed her visit; indeed, Charlotte wrote frequent letters, trying to imagine the great metropolis of London, which her friend had visited and which Charlotte could only think of as an immense center of business and a proving ground for characters who could easily be corrupted by the city's distractions.

Charlotte's teenage letters, quoted by Mrs. Gaskell, show strong literary likes and dislikes: Avoid the comedies of Shakespeare, she advises, and Lord BYRON's *Don Juan;* read fearlessly about evil in Shakespeare's tragedies and history plays. Scott's novels seemed the only worthy fiction to her; in nonfiction she admired James Boswell's *Life of Johnson,* Southey's *Life of Nelson,* and John Gibson Lockhart's *Life of Burns.* She disliked moralistic attitudes and saw nothing wrong with dancing, a harmless amusement.

Charlotte rarely visited friends—a fact Mrs. Gaskell attributes to her "lack of hope," her dread lest she love too strongly those whom death might take away at any time. Her father believed that too much society was not good for the soul, yet Char-

lotte kept her interest in politics and the greater world, especially in regard to her hero, the duke of Wellington.

Branwell, now 18, was proving to be a problem. He had no profession as yet, and his father seemed oblivious to his son's faults. Although he may have been the most brilliant of the children, Branwell dissipated his time and did not take his lessons seriously. He was the artist of the family, it was thought, especially when it came to his drawing and painting.

Branwell's would be a blighted life, the biographer remarks, but in 1835 his future still seemed bright; he anticipated going to London to study at the Royal Academy, thus fulfilling his dreams of becoming a great painter. Emily was about to attend Roe Head, and Charlotte would take up Miss Wooler's offer to teach at the school.

Chapter 8
On July 29, 1835, 19-year-old Charlotte became a teacher at Miss Wooler's school. Emily accompanied her but quickly became homesick and returned to Haworth after only three months of schooling. Emily missed the moors and a life in which she had the liberty to be herself. Charlotte thought Emily would perish at the school; indeed, Emily, who did her share of housework at Haworth, never reconciled herself to leaving home and would spend only two notable extended periods away from it, Mrs. Gaskell reports.

While at Miss Wooler's Charlotte heard the story that would become the germ of *Jane Eyre.* It involved a man who had married a governess in his family. After a year of marriage it was discovered that in fact he already had a wife. He pleaded the excuse that his first wife had become deranged.

Although Charlotte knew the school well and Miss Wooler was attentive and kind, the new teacher found it difficult to be happy. She saw her teaching only as a duty. Gradually she became despondent and found solace in the poems of William COWPER, whose melancholy suited hers. Mrs. Gaskell prints several of Charlotte's letters that reflect her sense of isolation and lack of interest in any sort of recreation that might relieve her depression.

At Christmas 1836 Charlotte returned home for a holiday with her family. Emily had tried another period away from home, this time teaching at a school in Halifax, but her schedule was too demanding and she had returned home after six months of work. Like Charlotte, Emily had tried to work to help relieve her father of supporting her. He had only a small stipend to rely on, but the salaries the sisters earned were so meager that accruing savings seemed nearly impossible.

Charlotte attempted to change the trajectory of their lives by writing to Robert Southey in an effort to interest him in their budding literary efforts. She enclosed some of her poems. Branwell also wrote to William Wordsworth, enclosing some of his poems and entreating the poet to advance an opinion that might help the young writer make his own way in the world. Mrs. Gaskell could find no evidence that Wordsworth answered the letter.

While Charlotte awaited a reply from Southey, she found solace in Mary, a friend from Miss Wooler's school. Although the two young women quarreled about politics—Mary was from a radical, dissenting family, and Charlotte remained a staunch Tory, reflecting her father's conservative views—they enjoyed each other's company.

In March 1837 Southey's letter arrived. He cautioned Charlotte against dreams of a literary career, which would make her unfit for a woman's duties. He softened this conventional advice by acknowledging she had a gift for writing and that she should continue it so long as she did it for the sake of writing alone and not to achieve a degree of fame or recognition. Mrs. Gaskell later observed Charlotte's reaction to the letter; Southey's advice was "kind and admirable; a little stringent, but it did me good," Charlotte remarked. At the time of his letter, she wrote him a gracious and grateful reply, explaining the circumstances of her life. Southey wrote another, warmer letter inviting her to come see him. Charlotte, however, could not afford to do so, and then Southey died.

Southey's letter persuaded Charlotte that she would have to put her literary ambitions aside at least for the time being so that she could return to teaching, which continued to wear her down.

Emily and Anne stayed at home, forming an even closer bond with each other—the former a deliberate recluse, the other too diffident to venture out into the world. Anne became a special cause of concern when she began to develop symptoms of consumption, which had caused the deaths of her sisters Maria and Elizabeth. Branwell's future remained in limbo since he had not pursued his idea of studying at the Royal Academy. Charlotte's melancholy increased, and she was easily unnerved. Home for the summer of 1838, she restored herself. She had a suitor (unidentified in Mrs. Gaskell's narrative) whom she liked but could not think of as a husband. "Matrimony did not enter into the scheme of her life," comments the biographer, yet teaching, the only independent source of income for a woman, did not suit her either. Mrs. Gaskell doubts that Charlotte had the knack to convey knowledge to others or that she had any particular interest in children.

In April 1839 Anne summoned her courage and took a position as a governess. Her first reports were promising, and shortly afterward Charlotte found similar employment. Both sisters gradually realized that their positions were untenable and degrading in a way that was worse than teaching in a school. Mrs. Gaskell learned from Charlotte that much of what Anne described in *AGNES GREY* was "literally true." Although the setting was beautiful, the governess was treated as an inferior and often scolded for disciplining unruly, even violent children. Only visits home restored her spirits, and only there could she express her full personality. Although plain looking, Mrs. Gaskell emphasizes, Charlotte's liveliness excited male interest, and she turned down another marriage proposal. Mrs. Gaskell quotes from one of Charlotte's letters: "I am certainly doomed to be an old maid. Never mind. I made up my mind to that fate ever since I was twelve years old."

When Tabby (see AYKROYD, TABITHA), the faithful household servant, became too lame to continue her duties, the Brontë sisters took over such chores as baking and ironing. They had nursed Tabby even after their father had tried to send her off, but now she was simply too weak to work at all. Domesticity did not daunt Charlotte—better housework than being a governess, she wrote to a friend.

Chapter 9

Mrs. Gaskell speculates that Branwell's plans to attend the London Academy came to grief because of the expenses that his father could not possibly afford. Such a disappointment must have hit him hard, the biographer speculates, since he so looked forward to London as an outlet for his rambunctious personality. An exceedingly handsome young man, he nevertheless appeared to Mrs. Gaskell as weak willed because of the set of his loose lips. She also interpreted the coarseness of his mouth as a sign of his flawed character. He was frank and genial, if self-indulgent. He aspired to fame and continued to send his verse to Wordsworth and Samuel Taylor Coleridge, who evidently encouraged his talent.

Aunt Branwell, who continued to oversee the household, favored the quiet Anne over the more outspoken Charlotte and Emily, although she reserved her greatest admiration for Branwell, the only member of the family she recognized as talented. There is no doubt that Miss Branwell enforced a sense of neatness, order, and decorum in the household.

By 1840 the sisters were thinking of establishing their own school. Their chief problem was finding the capital to begin, so Charlotte sought yet another position as a governess. She also resumed her writing and sent part of a story to Wordsworth. The idea of creating her own world, as she confessed to the poet, was quite stimulating. She also had fun over Wordsworth's attempt to discover whether she was a man or a woman. As Mrs. Gaskell observes, Charlotte's response was more playful and showed the personality that is evident in *Shirley*. She had begun to satirize the curates who helped her father and who would figure in her later novel.

Chapters 10–11

Mrs. Gaskell observes that Charlotte, so used to leisure at home and so unacquainted with child-rearing practices, found it a trial to be a governess, even in the best-run households. Introducing Charlotte's letters from this period (early 1841), the biographer begs the reader to understand from her "mount of observation" that whatever pain Charlotte's experience as a governess caused her, it did not prevent her from fulfilling her duties.

Charlotte was considerably relieved when she found that her employers (Mrs. Gaskell does not identify the family) welcomed visits from her friends. Still, Charlotte worried about reports of Anne's illness, and a visit home in summer 1841 confirmed her fears that her sister was not strong. If only there were some way for the three sisters to live together and pursue their dream of a literary career, Charlotte confided in a letter to a friend. And there was also the project of their school, although they did not yet have the capital to start one. Her hopes began to rise when Aunt Branwell promised the sisters a loan.

Charlotte returned to her position as governess in late summer 1841. While her situation was comfortable, she chafed when plans for the sisters' school seemed to founder. No location or situation seemed quite suitable—not even Miss Wooler's offer of a school, since enrollment there had fallen—and it would be an arduous task to find pupils. Charlotte admitted in the fall of 1841 that she still had not made a decision yet about establishing a school, in part because of Anne's delicate state of health and her retiring nature.

Charlotte's employers, sympathetic to her plans, suggested that a six-month course of study in a school on the Continent would better prepare Charlotte for the rigors of running a school. She thought Brussels, where she had a friend with English contacts, would be the cheapest and most useful venue for her educational improvement. She anticipated that her father might think her plans a wild scheme, but in a letter to Aunt Branwell she contended that her ambitions were no greater than his in leaving Ireland and attending Cambridge. "I want us all to get on," she emphasized.

In the event, Charlotte's father agreed to her plan, and Charlotte left her employment as a governess to return home for Christmas 1841. Shortly after the holiday season, Charlotte received word from Mrs. Jenkins, wife of the chaplain at the British embassy in Brussels, there would be two places available at the PENSIONNAT HEGER for her and Emily. Charlotte made her arrangements through Mrs. Jenkins's brother, who lived not far from Haworth and was a friend of her father's.

Patrick accompanied his two daughters to Brussels, staying only a day before making his return to

Haworth. Mrs. Gaskell comments on the momentous change in Charlotte's and Emily's lives—the extraordinary contrast between the city and their native moors. Charlotte later wrote that the transition was hardest on Emily, who dearly missed her "desolate Yorkshire hills." The taciturn Emily rarely spoke, even to Mrs. Jenkins on their visits to her. If they were awed by the Roman Catholic churches, they were also repelled and took refuge in their sturdy, independent Protestantism, the biographer reports.

The school was a handsome building with four flights of stairs and an impressive walled garden. It stood on an ancient site, once the grounds of a ducal palace, then a hospital, and later an archery ground, where a mansion for the master archer was built. This eventually became the Pensionnat Heger, in which Charlotte and Emily enrolled in February 1842. Constantin George Romain HEGER, Madame Heger's husband, tutored both Charlotte and Emily in French and other subjects. Although Mrs. Gaskell is discreet, it is clear that Charlotte soon developed an extravagant attachment to Monsieur Heger.

Although Monsieur Heger rated both Charlotte and Emily highly, he thought Emily superior in the force of her will and ability to argue. He decided that the usual grammar drills in French would not do for such sophisticated pupils and decided instead to read the French classics with them, devoting lessons to the style, structure, strengths, and weaknesses of the texts. Emily thought it a poor plan, complaining that it would stifle their originality. Charlotte, too, was doubtful but expressed a willingness to try it.

Both young women stood out at the school because they were so earnest and said so little to their Belgian classmates. In her mid-20s, Charlotte found it odd to be a student again, and to take rather than give orders. In letters home she described a pleasant Madame Heger, who seemed happily married, and her three teachers, Mademoiselle Blanche, Mademoiselle Sophie, and Mademoiselle Marie. Charlotte did not see much distinction between the first two, whereas Mademoiselle Marie showed some originality, if also an irritating arbitrariness. The school also had seven masters teaching French, drawing, music, singing, writing, arithmetic, and German. Charlotte was

conscious of the Protestant minority she and Emily represented, but she liked the school. The sisters remained in good health.

Charlotte lingered in her descriptions of Monsieur Heger, a temperamental, demanding man, prone to fits of anger. Emily found his lessons ever heavier going. He made few concessions to their poor background in French and even, at one point, forbade Charlotte to use a dictionary. However, Mrs. Gaskell says, the teacher was boldly attempting to imbue his pupils with the spirit of the language rather than tie them down with grammatical rules and literal translations. Charlotte's increasing command of French, the biographer suggests, proves that Monsieur Heger's methods had some success, which she illustrates by reprinting one of Charlotte's translations and her teacher's comments on it. Emily's work, Mrs. Gaskell contends, was even better than Charlotte's.

Monsieur Heger next progressed to what the biographer calls "synthetical teaching," reading to his students several accounts of the same event while pointing out discrepancies between them and directing his students to ask why the accounts differed. He had them compare, for example, Thomas CARLYLE's and Jacques Bénigne BOSSUET's account of Oliver Cromwell. Eventually Charlotte and Emily were required to put together a synthesis of different sources. Charlotte seemed to excel at this kind of exercise, according to Mrs. Gaskell. Indeed, both Charlotte and Emily were soon invited to become teachers at the school as well as to continue lessons in French and German. Charlotte liked Brussels, and although she missed home, she was proud of her adaptation to a new environment. Emily remained aloof even as she proved her brilliance as a student.

Charlotte found little to admire in her fellow students, calling them "singularly cold, selfish, animal, and inferior." She considered Catholicism an infantile religion, but she allowed that there were many good people among Catholics—better even than some Protestants.

Mrs. Gaskell describes the school day, the size of the classes, how Charlotte and Emily stayed together off to the side. It was a full day of lessons, physical exercise in the garden, meals, and other gatherings that lasted past eight in the evening. The girls slept in a large dormitory room, but Charlotte's and Emily's beds were positioned so that they formed what amounted to a separate apartment.

Mrs. Gaskell interviewed pupils at the school, who confirmed that Charlotte was a firm teacher who knew how to keep order. As always, Emily kept to herself and let Charlotte do the talking. Their good time there was marred by the death of their English friend Martha TAYLOR, who, the biographer notes, is commemorated in a passage in *Shirley,* which Mrs. Gaskell quotes. Then the sisters received word that their Aunt Branwell was dying. They departed hurriedly from Brussels, not certain when they would return; just before leaving, however, they learned that their aunt had died. She had kept the household together for 20 years, Mrs. Gaskell notes, and it was not certain how life at Haworth would now proceed.

Emily decided to remain at Haworth to take the place of her aunt. Charlotte's plans were not clear, although a letter from Monsieur Heger figured in her deliberations. Expressing his sorrow over the family's loss, he also paid tribute to the sisters' scholarship and proposed that Charlotte return for a second year to continue her impressive progress. After much discussion among family members, it was agreed that Charlotte should return to Brussels.

In spite of Aunt Branwell's death, the reunited family, including Branwell, who had come home from his job at the railway for the holidays, rejoiced. They were fully aware of Branwell's failing (Aunt Branwell had favored him but had not remembered him in her will because of his recklessness), but they still hoped that he would become the family standard-bearer and do them proud.

Chapter 12

Mrs. Gaskell points out that *VILLETTE* includes an episode that closely resembles Charlotte's trip to London to embark for Brussels. She arrived late in the day and had a waterman row her out to her vessel. Fearing a return to London, where she would have to find a hotel at a late hour, she prevailed on the suspicious ship captain to accommodate her for the evening, although he had initially

stated that no passengers could be put aboard until the next morning.

At school, she settled into her routine of taking French and German lessons and teaching English. In March 1843 she wrote home that she had begun giving Monsieur Heger and his brother-in-law English lessons. She found their efforts to achieve English accents amusing, yet her letters also reveal loneliness. She respected only Monsieur and Madame Heger; most of her English friends had left the city. Most rooms in the school were occupied and she had little privacy. She thought of herself as a Robinson Crusoe figure and scorned the idea of marriage as a way to relieve her solitude. Although Mrs. Gaskell does not remark on it, clearly the focus of Charlotte's feelings were on the only deserving person in her ken, Monsieur Heger.

Charlotte worried about Emily's health and how her father was getting along, but she also made great progress in her French lessons, which the biographer demonstrates by including her French composition on the death of Napoléon BONAPARTE. Mrs. Gaskell adds that Charlotte seemed more keen to praise her hero Wellington than to delve into Napoléon's fate. With such progress made in French, Charlotte now redoubled her efforts in German, although her health began to fail.

By August 1843 Charlotte was writing home about her profound depression. She hoped that just a few more months at the school would suffice in her quest to master German. After the pupils left for their summer vacations, she fell ill with fever. Restless, she roamed the streets and parks of Brussels, until her illness forced her to bed. By early October Charlotte announced her intention to return home but was dissuaded from giving her notice by a vehement Monsieur Heger.

To make matters worse, an estrangement began to develop between Charlotte and Madame Heger, which the biographer attributes to Charlotte's loathing of Heger's Roman Catholicism. A devoted Catholic, Madame Heger was offended by Charlotte's contempt for her religion, and Charlotte found herself even more alone and worrying about her father, whose eyesight was failing. In a letter to Emily she imagined herself home at Haworth, cooking in the kitchen, and watched over by the family pets, Tiger and Keeper. By the end of the month she was back at Haworth, with a diploma in hand certifying her ability to teach French, and determined to look after her father. She wrote to a friend of her surprise that her Belgian pupils seemed to regret her leaving.

Charlotte reveled in reuniting with her family. Mrs. Gaskell dwells on the affection she also bestowed on animals, and how that affection is reflected in *Shirley*—as is Emily's powerful devotion to the family pets, especially their dog, Keeper. Charlotte drew on many of Emily's experiences for her novel and told Mrs. Gaskell that Emily's feelings ran far deeper for animals than for human beings.

Chapter 13

Charlotte and Emily walked the moors discussing their future. They agreed that Charlotte should ask her friends and former employers if they would send any of their children to Haworth as pupils. By the end of the summer, however, the sisters reluctantly realized that people were unwilling to send their children to a place as remote as Haworth.

Branwell's unruly behavior proved a trial for the sisters and may even have contributed to their failure to attract pupils. He had become romantically involved with Mrs. ROBINSON, whose son he was tutoring. Mrs. Gaskell does not name her but alludes to a "bold and hardened woman" who did not bother to conceal her affection for Branwell in front of her children. The liaison had become, in other words, a public scandal. The infatuated Branwell was no longer, as the biography tersely puts it, the "family pride."

By spring 1845 Charlotte's spirits were low indeed. Her plans for a school had foundered, her father's eyesight had grown worse, and Branwell showed no sign of giving up Mrs. Robinson. The sisters worried but rarely discussed openly their brother's outrageous behavior. Charlotte felt isolated and feared she would eventually suffer from the blindness overtaking her father.

In August 1845 Branwell returned home and confessed the sordid details of his affair with Mrs. Robinson. The whole family deeply felt what the biography refers to as Branwell's "disgrace," yet he

yearned for his mistress. "We have had sad work with Branwell. He thought of nothing but stunning or drowning his agony of mind," Charlotte confessed to a friend. Branwell's case, she feared, was hopeless.

By the end of the year, Mrs. Robinson's husband had died, and Branwell hoped now to be reunited with her. The terms of her husband's will, however, stipulated that she never see Branwell again. Deprived of hope, Branwell was driven again to opium and drink. He would die three years later, as Mrs. Gaskell's describes it, with his paramour's letters in his pockets.

Chapters 14–16

In January 1846 Charlotte's feelings took an entirely different tack when she discovered the poems Emily had been writing. They struck her as remarkably vigorous and quite unlike any poetry by a woman she had ever read. Although Emily was averse to the idea of publication, Charlotte reminded her of their earlier plans to one day become published authors. Then Anne showed her own poetry to Charlotte, and the sisters set about, with some difficulty, finding a publisher. Later Charlotte would write, as Mrs. Gaskell reminds her readers, that this first volume of poetry, issued under the pseudonyms of Currer, Ellis, and Acton BELL, attracted virtually no attention.

So secretive were the sisters about their writing that not even Robert CHAMBERS, the stationer from whom they bought their paper, knew for certain what purpose they put it to. A friend of Anne's suspected that the sisters were writing for magazines when Anne expressed satisfaction in seeing a poem of hers in print in *Chamber's Journal*. Charlotte handled publishing arrangements discreetly, even negotiating the price of paper and other details since the sisters would have to defray the costs of their first publication.

Branwell continued to degenerate, prompting Charlotte's observation to Miss Wooler, "You ask me if I do not think that men are strange beings? I do, indeed. I have often thought so; and I think too that the mode of bringing them up is strange: they are not sufficiently guarded from temptation." Charlotte thought it absurd that women should be protected as if they were the weaker sex. She admired most those women who made a life for themselves without the traditional support of a husband.

Branwell remained, in Charlotte's words, a "hopeless thing." In a letter to a friend she described his stupefied state. What little money he had, he spent on drink. Although he had decent offers of work, he did not stir. Charlotte and her sisters, meanwhile, busied themselves with reading proofs of their new book, with Charlotte handling correspondence and pretending to act as an "agent for the real author." She also took charge of sending out review copies and arranging for advertisements, although she strictly limited her budget for such promotion to two pounds. She would be able to spend more if the work was a success.

When the volume appeared in late May 1846, it received a decent notice in the *Athenaeum*. The reviewer assumed the three Bells were brothers. Ellis's work seemed the most powerful and most original to the reviewer. But the book's publication did little to change matters at Haworth. Household work, as Charlotte made clear to friends, was still in the hands of their "poor old servant Tabby," who was beginning to fail, having had a fit and a "swelling in her knee." Mrs. Gaskell supposes, based on Charlotte's letters in July 1846, that the book did arouse in the sisters thoughts of independent careers and lives not so bound by duty and home. Yet, as Charlotte noted, the "right path is that which necessitates the greatest sacrifice of self-interest—which implies the greatest good to others." Charlotte resolved to stay at home and help her father. She advised the same to a friend with an aged mother.

Charlotte was preoccupied with her father, whose cataracts had made him virtually blind. Otherwise unimpaired, Patrick continued to deliver crisp, timely sermons that lasted exactly 30 minutes. His blindness curbed the range of his activities among his parishioners, but he bore his burden patiently, although he did suffer from depression, according to Mrs. Gaskell.

By the end of August 1846, the sisters had arranged for their father to see Mr. WILSON, a surgeon in Manchester, who removed the cataracts. Charlotte marveled at how her father "displayed extraordinary patience and firmness" during the

15-minute operation. Heavily bandaged, Patrick had to wait several days before he would be able to test the results of the operation.

In spite of the anxieties of this period, all three sisters were at work on novels: Emily on *Wuthering Heights*, Anne on *Agnes Grey*, and Charlotte on *The Professor*, the last of which was published posthumously. Only after Charlotte's first novel received several rejections did she begin *Jane Eyre*. This second work, Charlotte told her biographer, proceeded by fits and starts, whenever she could find time for it amidst her other duties and responsibilities. Tabby, now 80, required the help of a servant girl as well Charlotte's own tactful efforts to avoid injuring the pride of the old family retainer.

As the sisters discussed their literary work, Charlotte told Mrs. Gaskell that occasionally ideas would spring out of these conversations. During one evening of talk, for example, Charlotte decided to make the heroine of Jane Eyre "plain, small, and unattractive, in defiance of the accepted canon."

The end of September, Patrick was at home recovering from his operation, the results of which were uncertain. Charlotte had resolved to stay home even if it meant ending her dream of starting a school. The cold winter was taking its toll on Anne's delicate health. She was prone to coughing fits and asthmatic attacks. She improved, but then Patrick was struck by influenza. In poor spirits, Charlotte developed a toothache, exacerbated by the cold winter. Branwell added to her misery by accumulating fresh debts. The sisters helped their father on visits to the parish school, while Charlotte wrote her novel and her sisters made preparations for publishing theirs. Charlotte's hopes brightened when she received a letter from the publishing house Smith, Elder. Although George SMITH rejected *The Professor*, he did so in measured terms that promised continuing interest in her work. Charlotte wrote to the firm again, describing her work on *Jane Eyre*, which she believed would have a "more vivid interest" than her earlier work.

The sisters remained secretive, so much so that although their father had some suspicion of their writing activity, when the sisters' novels were published he was stunned to see their work in print and amazed at the success of *Jane Eyre*. By September 1846, Mrs. Gaskell notes, Smith, Elder had accepted *Jane Eyre* for publication, impressed with its magnetic effect on readers at the firm. Initial reviews were "cautious," Mrs. Gaskell reports, but the library demand for it was so high that by early December 1846 the "rush began for copies."

In Charlotte's letter to her publishers she seems to have taken the reviews in stride, commenting that if the book was any good it would weather negative reviews like the one in the *Spectator.* Mrs. Gaskell reports asking Charlotte if she was surprised by her novel's popularity. Charlotte replied that she expected the book to have a powerful impact on readers but never predicted that a book by an unknown author would reach such a large audience.

At this point the sisters still had not taken their father into their confidence, not wanting to trouble him if their literary endeavors proved fruitless. Patrick later told Mrs. Gaskell that he had had suspicions. After the success of *Jane Eyre,* however, Emily and Anne urged Charlotte to reveal all to their father. The biographer presents the scene, with an uncomprehending Patrick asking, "How can you get a book sold? No one knows you or your name." Charlotte then read him some of the reviews. Later, at tea, Patrick addressed Emily and Anne: "Girls, do you know Charlotte has been writing a book, and it is much better than likely?"

Jane Eyre's success, Mrs. Gaskell points out, was aided by the mystery surrounding the author. Who was Currer Bell? Even the publisher could not say for sure whether the author was male or female. Speculation spread. The author of the novel received respectful, admiring letters from distinguished critics such as George Henry LEWES, who expressed his enthusiasm and delight while warning the author to beware of melodrama and to stick to the ground of "real experience." Charlotte penned a shrewd reply: "Is not the real experience of each individual very limited? . . . Then too imagination is a strong, restless faculty, which claims to be heard and exercised: are we to be quite deaf to her cry, and insensate to her struggles?"

With the success of her book Charlotte hoped to do something more for her sisters, especially for the ailing Anne. An alarmed Charlotte reported to a friend that Anne had difficult walking and keeping in good spirits. Neither Anne's nor Emily's novel achieved initial success. Mrs. Gaskell quotes Charlotte's later words about Emily's isolated, towering genius, her tendency to create a somber story out of her observations of local characters. She was not much moved by criticism of her book, since she never relied on the world's opinion.

The biographer defends all three sisters from the charge of coarseness, observing that their own suffering and experience of the world justified the narratives they produced. They followed the "stern dictates of their consciences." They could have been mistaken, but they were possessed of "wonderful gifts" and exercised them with a "feeling of responsibility for their use."

The biographer quotes at length Charlotte's continuing correspondence with Lewes. A deferential Charlotte was nevertheless firm when responding to his advice, suggesting, for example, it did not do much good to urge her to write like Jane AUSTEN, since each writer has his or her own masters and impulses he or she must follow. "And should we try to counteract this influence? Can we indeed counteract it?" she asked shrewdly. Austen seemed, in fact, entirely too mild for Charlotte's sensibility. She thought *Pride and Prejudice* a "carefully-fenced, high-cultivated garden, with neat borders and delicate flowers; but no glance of a bright, vivid physiognomy, no open country, no fresh air, no blue hill, no bonny beck." She preferred Scott's *Waverley* novels or Henry Fielding's *Tom Jones.* "These observations will probably irritate you, but I shall run the risk," she concluded. When he wrote several more letters arguing with her points, she stood her ground, stating her preference of George SAND and William Makepeace THACKERAY to Austen, who lacked poetry: "I submit to your anger, which I have now excited (for have I not questioned your daring?) the storm may pass over me." Impressed with Charlotte's intellectual abilities, Mrs. Gaskell includes a long letter she wrote to another party about Lewes's novels.

Illness prevailed at Haworth in the winter of 1847–48, due in part, Mrs. Gaskell's suggests, to the proximity of the graveyard to the parsonage, an unsanitary situation that Patrick pointed out to the Board of Health. But taxpayers did nothing to ameliorate the deplorable conditions, and Anne suffered from a cough and a fever.

The dethronement of Louis Philippe of France in February 1848 occasioned a letter by Charlotte in which she characterized revolutions as the sickness of civilization: "That England may be spared the spasms, cramps, and frenzy fits now contorting the Continent, and threatening Ireland, I earnestly pray. With the French and Irish I have no sympathy. With the Germans and Italians I think the case is different; as different as the love of freedom is from the lust for license."

Charlotte and her sisters still wished to preserve their privacy, and Charlotte rebuffed all queries from friends about her authorship of *Jane Eyre.* Anne, in spite of her illness, was working on her second novel, *The Tenant of Wildfell Hall.* When rumors continued to circulate that Currer, Ellis, and Acton Bell were really one author, the sisters determined that Charlotte and Anne travel to London to meet with their publisher and prove their separate identities. The sisters arrived at Smith, Elder unannounced, and Charlotte put Mr. Smith's last letter to her in his hand. At first he did not believe the sisters could be the Bells, but after further explanation, he quickly accommodated himself to their identities and made plans to entertain them in London. He took them to the opera (where they felt somewhat self-conscious in their country clothes), to the Royal Academy, the National Gallery, and to dinner at several different houses. Mr. Smith invited them to be guests at his home, but the sisters preferred to stay at the CHAPTER COFFEE HOUSE on Paternoster Row in the heart of the city, where their father had stayed on visits to the city and where Thomas CHATTERTON and other famous writers had lived. The biographer points to a passage in *Villette,* in which this part of the city is praised for its "business, its rush, its roar," and deep excitement. Of this visit to Mr. Smith, Mrs. Gaskell gleaned from several interviews that Charlotte made quite an impression as a person with "clear judgment and fine sense."

Mr. Smith sent the sisters home "laden" with books, and they returned exhausted from their excitement. As Charlotte said when entering the opera house, "I am not accustomed to this sort of thing." Back at home she confronted the sad story of Branwell and reflected, "has not every house its trial?" He was confined to his bed for long periods; Emily had an obstinate cold; Anne's condition remained delicate. The weather by late October turned quite harsh. Emily worsened, stopped going out of doors after Branwell's death, and by late November found it difficult to breathe, yet even while in pain she refused to see a doctor and remained stubbornly independent. She died of tuberculosis on December 21, 1848; Charlotte wrote a friend that her family was calm and relieved that Emily suffered no more. Anne's already fragile health deteriorated further.

Chapter 17

Mrs. Gaskell excoriates the impertinent reviews that speculated on the identity of the author of *Jane Eyre,* especially at a time when Charlotte experienced such sorrow over Emily's death and Anne's rapid decline. The biographer quotes extensively from Charlotte's letters during this period when she was nursing Anne. Charlotte's moods swung from hope to despair, depending on the daily changes in Anne's condition. Often in pain herself, Charlotte tried to look forward to better times. By March, a doctor's examination confirmed that Anne was suffering from an advanced stage of tuberculosis. Unlike Emily, however, Anne spoke freely with Charlotte about her illness and welcomed the proposal that they visit the seashore in an effort to restore her health. Charlotte's only concern was if Anne could withstand the journey. Mrs. Gaskell cites Anne's last poem, which expresses her desire to live but her resignation to God's will: "Whether thus early to depart, / Or yet a while to wait." The doctor was not hopeful.

Anne's condition did not improve with the spring weather, but the sisters attempted the trip to SCARBOROUGH anyway. Anne had lost a good deal of weight, and after a momentary revival at the outset, she died four days after leaving home. She had been able to walk on the beach one day and to watch a beautiful sunset from her window. She had wanted to go to church, but Charlotte thought her too weak to attempt it. On her final day, Anne awoke and realized she would die soon. A truthful doctor confirmed her diagnosis, and she hoped she would have enough time to return home. But there was no time, and she died urging Charlotte to "take courage."

Charlotte heeded her sister's words. In spite of this loss, she wrote to a friend: "But crushed I am not; nor robbed of elasticity, nor of hope, nor quite of endeavour." She would "get on."

Chapter 18

Mrs. Gaskell relates how Charlotte began to work on *Shirley,* basing many of its events on the Luddite riots and on characters like the three curates who visited her father. Emily served as a model for certain features of the novel's heroine, but an Emily "placed in health and prosperity." Charlotte wanted to imbue the novel with a sense of history and of realism, in part as a reply to critics of *Jane Eyre,* yet she denied to her publisher that the book would be recognized as an account of actual places and persons. She had little experience of the world, and even when she had modeled her characters on certain people, the story itself was her invention and not likely to be associated with the lives of others.

When *Shirley* appeared October 26, 1849, George Henry Lewes wrote to Charlotte saying he wished to review the book in the *Edinburgh Review.* After expressing her regret that reviewers thought of her as a woman (Charlotte had not yet divulged her identity), since that meant they would not judge the book on its own merits, Charlotte encouraged Lewes to give his candid opinion of the novel. She did not expect, nor would she appreciate, flattery. It was too late, however, for Charlotte to expect that she could conceal her true identity, Mrs. Gaskell observes. In fact, a Haworth man had already come close to guessing the book's author.

By the end of November Charlotte had traveled to London, in part to see if medical attention there could relieve the headaches and sense of exhaustion she suffered from at Haworth, where the elderly Tabby and her younger helper had been ill. In London Charlotte met her literary hero William Makepeace Thackeray and worried whether she had made a good impression. On a second meeting, she thought he had come to see how she had coped with a negative review of *Shirley* in the *Times.* She had been provoked to tears by the attack but had recovered her composure by the time of his visit.

Charlotte had sent Harriet MARTINEAU a copy of her new novel, commenting that she had admired Martineau's novel, *Deerbrook,* and Charlotte was now gratified to make her acquaintance. They met in early December, and when Charlotte introduced herself to Martineau and her friends, Charlotte effectively abandoned the pseudonym of Currer Bell.

When she returned home and had time to reflect on her trip, Charlotte wrote to an old friend that "Thackeray is a Titan of mind." Of all her new acquaintances, he was the only one who made her feel "fearfully stupid."

Chapters 19–21

Charlotte resumed her quiet life at Haworth, with the "postman's call the event of her day." Although she confronted another harsh, cold winter, her health improved, perhaps, Mrs. Gaskell speculates, because of the medical advice Charlotte had received in London. Still mourning the loss of her sisters, she took refuge in books, especially several sent to her by new friends such as Martineau and her publisher Smith. To the latter she wrote about her continuing admiration for Thackeray, even though his latest novel, *Pendennis,* revealed a tired author not in the mood to write. She took much pleasure in titles such as William Hazlitt's *Essays,* Ralph Waldo Emerson's *Representative Men,* and Scott's *Suggestions on Female Education.*

Charlotte's fame had become such that even the servants at Haworth had heard that she had published two books and she was gratified by the attention and respect her work elicited, especially from a common workman whose written thoughts on *Jane Eyre* meant more to her, she told her publisher, than any review. She was also amused that the curates she had satirized in *Shirley* had taken her treatment of them in such good humor. She was dismayed, however, to see that Lewes had emphasized her sex in his *Edinburgh Review* article. She sent him a note: "I can be on my guard against my enemies, but God deliver me from my friends!"

Outwardly, Charlotte's life had little changed. She still spent much time with her father, reading to him in the evening and caring for him when he became ill. She found it moving that he shared with her letters that her mother had written him, letters that suggested to Charlotte her mother had been a refined, modest, and gentle woman.

Charlotte's solitary existence was relieved on occasion by visitors who sought her out because of her books. Thus she received a call from her friends Sir James and Lady KAY SHUTTLEWORTH and was delighted to accept their invitation to stay with them at their residence in East Lancashire. She enjoyed their stately home, the drives in the country, and other opportunities for rest and relaxation.

Indeed, Charlotte was in much need of restoration, since the unhealthy atmosphere at Haworth continued to destroy her health. Her father's bronchitis, however, made her reluctant to accept the Kay Shuttleworths' invitation to accompany them to London. Her only regret was missing the Royal Literary Fund Society, where she would have seen famous figures such as Thackeray and Charles Dickens. She walked on the moors, remembering her days with Emily and Anne, taking solace in the thought that "Eternal life is theirs now."

By June Charlotte was able to travel to London to see her publisher. She did not meet many people on this trip, but she delighted in a glimpse of the duke of Wellington ("a real grand old man"), a visit to the House of Commons, and another meeting with Thackeray. She questioned him on certain weaknesses in his writing and reported that he defended himself "like a great Turk and heathen; that is to say, the excuses were often worse than the crime itself." They parted good friends. She also met George Henry Lewes, whose countenance reminded her of Emily's. Whatever their disagreements, she could not "hate him." She also made a brief visit to friends in Scotland and thought its capital city a romantic spot far superior to London in that respect.

By mid-July Charlotte was home. She found her father well and the house in good order. With her father's encouragement she set off in August on a one-week excursion with the Shuttleworths to the Lake District. She enjoyed a quiet time, with leisure to read books by John Ruskin and Cardinal Newman. She read Alfred, Lord Tennyson's *In Memoriam,* pronouncing it in a letter to Mrs. Gaskell to be beautiful, mournful, and monotonous. She also sent Mrs. Gaskell the first book she and her sisters had published, praising her sisters' poems but calling hers "juvenile."

Chapters 22–23
Near the end of 1850 *Agnes Grey* and *Wuthering Heights* were republished with an introduction by Charlotte. During this period she carried on a lively literary correspondence, commenting on her relationship with Lewes and declaring her preferences for writers like Sand, whom she found superior to Honoré de Balzac. An avid reader of biographies, she expressed particular interest in the *Life of Dr. Arnold,* the famous Victorian school headmaster and father of poet and critic Matthew Arnold. She confessed to some discontent with her solitary existence, which was now regularly invaded, however, by visitors who found Haworth rather dreary with its "rain-blackened tombstones." Mrs. Gaskell quotes a visitor's letter that suggested Charlotte enjoyed meeting new people who had come to speak with her about her writing. Her father always seemed to loom in the background, protective of his daughter but also keeping to himself. Charlotte had something of the manner and the looks of Jane Eyre, another visitor thought.

Immediately after the republication of her sisters' novels, Charlotte visited Harriet Martineau, whose company Charlotte hoped would relieve a "heavy burden of depression" she had been suffering for three months. Her hostess gave her the "most perfect liberty," so that Charlotte could breakfast whenever she liked and set her own schedule. In the mornings, both women worked, then met in the afternoon for conversation and a walk. Sometimes her hostess returned to work in the evening. Charlotte admired her apparently inexhaustible energy. A commanding personality, Martineau had her despotic side, Charlotte confessed in a letter to a friend. Martineau's atheism and materialism shocked her, but she spoke in confidence about such matters and regretted that Martineau had published views that brought on her so many attacks.

Charlotte had begun work on *Villette* and refused invitations to come to London, stating that she had not earned a trip so long as her book remained unfinished. There was, nonetheless, one London event she could not deny herself the pleasure of attending: the Great Exhibition of 1851. In early June she also attended Thackeray's series of lectures on the great English comic writers and met him afterward to discuss his performance. She delighted in the CRYSTAL PALACE, visiting it five times, until she had exhausted its wonders.

Chapters 24–25
When Charlotte returned home, she wrote to Mrs. Gaskell about her experiences in London, defending Thackeray from some of the criticisms made of his lectures and agreeing with Mrs. Gaskell's assessment of the Great Exhibition. The letter also reveals, as Mrs. Gaskell observes, how fond Charlotte had become of her friend's children: "They seem to me little wonders; their talk, their ways are all matter of half-admiring, half-puzzled speculation."

Charlotte also shared with her future biographer her reaction to John Stuart Mill's writings about women. She thought him excessively intellectual, not taking into account the feelings that tied women to their homes and families. She did not disagree with his main point—that women should be allowed to attempt any occupation that interested them—but his argument seemed too logical and too removed from the emotions women actually experienced when confronting choices open to them. When Mrs. Gaskell inquired about Charlotte herself, she replied that she was in good health and the household in good order. Yet by the autumn of 1851, her biographer reports, the return of "sick headaches" and influenza in the unhealthy atmosphere of Haworth again drove Charlotte to depression.

Miss Wooler's visit cheered Charlotte, but a sore throat, chest pains, and difficulty breathing made everyday life a misery. Her work on *Villette* stalled. She put the book away hoping that her inspiration would return. She had trouble sleeping and digesting her food and suffered from nausea. The death of Emily's dog, Keeper, saddened her. She wrote to Mrs. Gaskell, freely confessing all her troubles. She buoyed herself with reading favorite authors such as Thackeray and refused invitations from friends to convalesce at their homes. She kept up an active correspondence with her anxious publishers, but by the spring of 1852 she had made no further progress on the novel they were expecting. She took consolation in her father's good health during this time and in the success of his cataract operation.

By May 1852 Charlotte had overcome her writer's block and was beginning to feel better physically. By the autumn she had finished the first part of the novel and was anxious to obtain George Smith's evaluation. She pointed out that she was incapable of writing a book for its "moral," even though she greatly admired Harriet Beecher Stowe's attack on slavery in *Uncle Tom's Cabin.*

Charlotte responded well to her publisher's criticisms but also defended her strategy and explained why Lucy Snowe could not marry Dr. John but would rather be saved for her professor. She thought the third volume of her novel would "do away with some of the objections." When the publisher worried about the grief-stricken tone of the book and that its heroine was "morbid and weak," Charlotte replied: "I consider that she is both morbid and weak at times; her character set up no pretension to unmixed strength, and anybody living her life would necessarily become morbid." If this was not apparent, however, then Charlotte conceded "there must be a great fault somewhere." She alternated her work on *Villette* with avid reading of Thackeray's new novel, *The History of Henry Esmond,* which had much of the author's characteristic force, especially in his creation of the willful Beatrix.

By the end of the year Charlotte had completed her novel. She was disappointed in her publisher's response. All along Smith had been hoping for a happier ending. If the third volume did not satisfy him, "I must pronounce you right," she admitted. "It is not pleasant, and it will probably be found as unwelcome to the reader, as it was, in a sense, compulsory upon the writer."

Chapters 26–28
Mrs. Gaskell explains that when she undertook to write Charlotte's biography, her main purpose was

to show "what a noble, true, and tender woman" her subject was and to withhold nothing "though some things, from their very nature, could not be spoken of so fully as others." It is these considerations that lead her to discuss Charlotte's marriage to Arthur Bell Nicholls.

The biographer points out that Charlotte's husband had been in a position to observe her for several years and that his attraction to her had nothing whatsoever to do with her literary fame. Indeed, that aspect of her life, taken in itself, "would rather repel him," Mrs. Gaskell suggests. Rather his grateful observation of her life constituted a "great testimony to her character as a woman."

Mrs. Gaskell relates how Reverend Nicholls knocked on Charlotte's door one day in late December 1852 and how she suddenly intuited the nature of his proposal. In shock, Charlotte "half led, half put him out of the room," she later recalled, when she learned that he had not yet dared to speak to her father about the proposed marriage. Charlotte then told her father of Nicholls's visit, and her father immediately and vehemently opposed the idea of marriage. She honored his objections. Reverend Nicholls then resigned his Haworth curacy. Charlotte, in her biographer's words, felt pained at her father's criticisms of Nicholls.

To relieve her distress, Charlotte visited her publisher in London in early January 1853. She spent less time on social engagements and more on sightseeing, visiting Newgate Prison and many other London locations. By February, she was buoyed by the excellent reviews of *Villette*, marred only by Martineau's dislike of the novel. Charlotte felt bitter about her friend's response to her latest work and about continuing concerns by some reviewers that her work was "coarse," a charge Mrs. Gaskell refutes, citing the experience of Charlotte's own life and the thrust of her imagination.

In late February, Charlotte was pleased to report that she had hung Thackeray's portrait next to the duke of Wellington's, and she seemed cheered by its presence. Less favorable reviews of her novel followed, but Charlotte was cheered by a visit to Mrs. Gaskell. When Mrs. Gaskell's guests debated Thackeray's merits, a

heretofore taciturn Charlotte "threw herself warmly into the discussion." She did not always agree with her literary hero, especially in his criticisms of Fielding, but she did like to pay tribute to his "force, his penetration, his pithy simplicity, his eloquence."

In July 1853 Charlotte wrote Mrs. Gaskell thanking her for an account of Harriet Beecher Stowe and reporting that her father was recovering well from an illness. Mrs. Gaskell visited Haworth on a dull, gray late-September day, noting the "wavelike hills," the stone cottages, the "poor, hungry-looking fields," and the "crowded grave-yard" that surrounded the parsonage house.

The biographer found her subject at breakfast with her father. Tabby, now nearly 90, was still a member of the household. A refurnished parlor testified to Charlotte's literary success. They discussed Charlotte's books, and she told Mrs. Gaskell some of her family history. Patrick was a courteous host, and Charlotte a dutiful daughter, and the biographer believed that "I understood her life better for seeing the place where it had been spent—where she had loved and suffered." With Charlotte out of the room, Patrick listened intently and with much pleasure to Mrs. Gaskell's accounts of Charlotte's literary reputation. Charlotte wanted to know more about Harriet Beecher Stowe and seemed gratified to learn that she was "small and slight." They walked together and Mrs. Gaskell could see how much respect Charlotte's neighbors had for her.

The differences between the two women came out in their discussions about the nature of life, with Charlotte seeming more fatalistic and resigned than Mrs. Gaskell. The latter also sensed that the former was carrying a "great anxiety." Charlotte spent the winter of 1853–54 in a "solitary and anxious manner," her biography reports. Nevertheless, "by degrees Mr. Brontë became reconciled to the idea of his daughter's marriage."

Charlotte wrote letters to her publishers, to Miss Wooler, and to other friends describing her "uniform and retired life." By April she had announced to Miss Wooler that she was engaged. In part, Mr. Nicholls had won the day by corresponding with Charlotte and patiently hoping for her father's change of heart. Indeed, Charlotte suggested that her prospective husband would turn out to be a comfort in her father's declining years. Charlotte took several shopping trips to Leeds in preparation for her wedding, set for June 29, 1854.

Mrs. Gaskell does not describe the wedding, other than to say Miss Wooler gave the bride away and that the couple spent their honeymoon in Ireland. "Henceforward the sacred doors of home are closed upon her married life," the biographer states. Mrs. Gaskell quotes from letters suggesting that Charlotte was happily married.

Early in the new year Charlotte began to suffer from "new sensations of perpetual nausea." In her weakened state, she grieved over the loss of Tabby. By mid-February Charlotte was confined to bed and attended by her husband. She never wrote again, and by the third week in March she became delirious. In one of her lucid moments she whispered, "Oh. I am not going to die, am I? He will not separate us, we have been so happy." On Saturday morning, March 31, 1855, she died.

The funeral, Mrs. Gaskell reports, was a purely Haworth matter, with one representative of each family present as well as two village girls who had been touched by Charlotte's kindness to them. The biographer quotes a friend of Charlotte's who wrote "all her life was but labour and pain; and she never threw down the burden for the sake of present pleasure." Noting the harsh public criticism of Charlotte while she was alive, Mrs. Gaskell commemorates her book to "that larger and more solemn public, who know how to look with tender humility at faults and errors; how to admire generously extraordinary genius, and how to reverence with warm, full hearts all noble virtue. To that Public I commit the memory of Charlotte Brontë."

PUBLICATION HISTORY

The Life of Charlotte Brontë was published in two volumes by Smith, Elder on March 25, 1857. A first edition of 2,000 copies sold out and another 2,000 copies were in print by early May. The quick sales rivaled the initial response to *Jane Eyre,* and the biography emulated Charlotte's own fiction by making the female heroine a courageous figure struggling against the restraints her family imposed on her. Periodicals such as *FRASER'S MAGAZINE* and *North American Review,* which had deplored the crudity of Charlotte's work, now embraced her as a genius in conflict with the provinciality of her upbringing. Mrs. Gaskell received letters from many writers who recanted their earlier hostility to Charlotte's "coarseness," as the repentant novelist Charles Kingsley put it. Few critics observed that Mrs. Gaskell had transformed and simplified Charlotte into a fictional heroine. Henceforth, it would become difficult to divorce not only Charlotte's but all the Brontës' lives from their work.

The critic George Henry Lewes rightly observed that Mrs. Gaskell had succeeded brilliantly in her work of vindication. Later commentators have regretted, however, that in building Charlotte up, Mrs. Gaskell also tore down the reputations of other family members. Yet even Charlotte's wounded husband, Arthur Bell Nicholls, regarded Mrs. Gaskell's account as inevitable, if painful. Patrick, on the other hand, requested changes in the second edition. He objected to the account of eccentricities attributed in error to him, but his response—like Nicholls's—was measured and later highly approving: "My opinion, and the reading world's opinion of the 'Memoir,' is that it is every way worthy of what one Great Woman, should have written of Another, and that it ought to stand, and will stand in the first rank, of Biographies, till the end of time."

More troublesome to Mrs. Gaskell were two libel suits threatened by Mrs. Robinson, now Lady Scott, and the son of William Carus WILSON. Mrs. Gaskell had described the former as the "bed woman" who had corrupted Branwell Brontë. The latter alleged that the biography had unfairly portrayed his father's school, Cowan Bridge, and libeled his father. Lady Scott's suit was settled out of court, and although Wilson's charges were aired in the press, no legal action was actually taken. Subsequent biographers have exonerated Mrs. Gaskell in both cases.

Mrs. Gaskell's biography was published in several editions. Her corrections did not materially change the thrust of the book. Perhaps more than any other biography in the English language, it contributed to making Charlotte Brontë a major canonical author as well as stimulating large sales of her sisters' books and the publication of Charlotte's abandoned novel, *The Professor*. The Brontë home became a literary pilgrimage site. Brontë souvenirs were sold in local shops. Not surprisingly, Patrick Brontë and Nicholls reacted to this new attention with considerable pride and irritation, since one of their own had become a world figure, but their peaceful lives were irrevocably disturbed by visitors seeking interviews.

Linden-Car Place in *THE TENANT OF WILDFELL HALL*. This is the home of the novel's narrator and protagonist, Gilbert MARKHAM. Following the English custom, Linden-Car is also used as the name for the countryside, much of it given over to farming, around the rural Markham home.

Lindenhope Place in *THE TENANT OF WILDFELL HALL*. This is the nearest village to Gilbert MARKHAM's home, LINDEN-CAR, and to the desolate WILDFELL HALL, where Helen HUNTINGDON resides under the assumed name Helen Graham. Rev. Michael MILLWARD, the vicar of Lindenhope, is the village elder.

Linton, Catherine (Cathy) Character in *WUTHERING HEIGHTS*. The only offspring of Catherine EARNSHAW and Edgar LINTON, she is born prematurely on the night her mother dies. Pampered and protected by her widowed father, young Cathy is 13 before she leaves the grounds of her home at THRUSHCROSS GRANGE. When she finally does so, alone and without permission, Cathy gravitates to the nearest house on the moor, WUTHERING HEIGHTS, where she encounters one of her male cousins, Hareton EARNSHAW. The other cousin, Linton HEATHCLIFF, she first meets when her father brings the motherless boy to the Grange. Cathy does not see Linton again for several years, by which time they are of sufficient age to become sweethearts. Their little romance would have been short lived

had not Linton's father, HEATHCLIFF, forced the two to marry so that he could gain control of both Wuthering Heights and Thrushcross Grange. Almost as soon as she becomes a wife, however, young Cathy is widowed, which permits her to fall in love with the heir to Wuthering Heights and the last of the ancient Earnshaw clan, Hareton.

Linton, Catherine Earnshaw *See* EARNSHAW, CATHERINE.

Linton, Edgar Character in *WUTHERING HEIGHTS*. During the bulk of the action of the novel, Edgar Linton is the master of THRUSHCROSS GRANGE. Blond, gentle, almost epicene, Edgar is HEATHCLIFF's rival for Catherine EARNSHAW's affections. Cathy marries Edgar, but she never abjures her bond with Heathcliff. Unable to forsake either man, she ultimately dies, leaving Edgar the widowed father of a premature infant girl, Catherine LINTON. Edgar guards his daughter closely, taking special pains to keep her from any contact with Heathcliff—who had power not only over his wife, but also over his sister, Isabella LINTON, whom Heathcliff married. The product of that union, Linton HEATHCLIFF, eventually becomes the instrument by which Heathcliff manages to steal young Cathy away as well, when he forces the cousins to marry. When Edgar dies shortly thereafter, he does so with the knowledge that his rival has gained control over all his property. Even after death Edgar is forced to share with Heathcliff that which is most dear to him: Edgar is laid to rest beside his wife, but Heathcliff is later buried on the other side of his lost Cathy.

Linton, Isabella Character in *WUTHERING HEIGHTS*. Edgar LINTON's sister, Isabella is exposed to HEATHCLIFF at an early age when her brother courts Catherine EARNSHAW at WUTHERING HEIGHTS. After Edgar and Cathy marry, Isabella proclaims herself in love with Heathcliff, who has become handsome and somewhat more refined during a few years' absence. Catherine warns her against acting on her feelings: "'I'd as soon put that little canary into the park on a winter's day as recommend you to bestow your heart on him!'" Isabella ignores this warning, as well as one given by Heathcliff himself, who hangs her little dog by the neck as the couple elope together. Edgar, who has other reasons for hating Heathcliff, declares his sister dead upon her elopement with Heathcliff. When Isabella finally manages to escape from her husband and Wuthering Heights, she is obliged to reside away from Thrushcross Grange. Edgar sees her again only some 12 years later when, as she is dying, she asks her brother to take charge of her son, Linton HEATHCLIFF.

Linton, Mr. Minor character in *WUTHERING HEIGHTS*. Old Mr. Linton is father to Edgar and Isabella LINTON and makes a brief appearance at the beginning of the novel. He and his wife both die of the fever Catherine EARNSHAW carries with her when she goes to THRUSHCROSS GRANGE to convalesce.

Linton, Mrs. Minor character in *WUTHERING HEIGHTS*. Old Mrs. Linton is the mother of Edgar and Isabella LINTON. She makes a brief appearance early in the novel, after which she dies from a fever she apparently catches from the ailing Catherine EARNSHAW, whom Mrs. Linton has brought to THRUSHCROSS GRANGE to convalesce.

Little Dick HAWORTH PARSONAGE canary, acquired in 1841.

living Term for an income that a clergyman could draw upon to support himself. It consisted of rents paid to a landholder and other interest accruing from real estate investments. In *THE PROFESSOR*, the Hon. John SEACOMBE offers William CRIMSWORTH the living at Seacombe. In this case John Seacombe owns land (including a village) that has been given his family name. Thus Crimsworth's aristocratic uncle is setting him up for life—in the sense that if Crimsworth accepts the offer he can be assured of a comfortable home and income. Instead of accepting an income, however, Crimsworth decides to secure

his own through TRADE and later as a teacher and owner of a school.

Lloyd, Mr. Character in *JANE EYRE*. He is a doctor summoned to treat Jane EYRE after her fainting fit in Mr. REED's room, where Jane became terrified at the prospect of seeing his ghost. The kindly Mr. Lloyd listens to Jane's account of her miserable existence, and later he helps her leave the Reed estate. She relies on him still later to provide a good recommendation when she leaves LOWOOD for employment as a governess.

Lockwood, Mr. Character and one of the narrators of *WUTHERING HEIGHTS*. Lockwood's first-person narration opens and closes the novel, providing it with a frame. In between he speaks periodically in his own voice, mostly through diary entries memorializing Nelly DEAN's retrospective storytelling, and also appears from time to time as a character. Lockwood is an outsider, a city dweller who has sought out the barren northern moors as an escape from his own chilly nature, which has cost him the affections of a young woman he loved. As HEATHCLIFF's tenant at THRUSHCROSS GRANGE, he is in a position not only to observe but sometimes also to affect events as they unfold at nearby WUTHERING HEIGHTS. In the end, the bleakness of the landscape and of his landlord's soul drives Lockwood away, but he cannot resist returning the next year to discover the end of the story. It is he who pronounces a kind of benediction over the graves of the tormented love triangle that once was Catherine EARNSHAW, Edgar LINTON, and Heathcliff.

Lothersdale Village near Skipton and site of the home of Mrs. SIDGWICK and her family, who employed Charlotte as a governess in 1839.

Lowborough, Lady Annabella *See* WILMOT, ANNABELLA.

Lowborough, Lord Character in *THE TENANT OF WILDFELL HALL*. Lord Lowborough is one of Arthur, Lord HUNTINGDON's cronies, but a reluctant one. An alcoholic, drug addict, and gambler, Lowborough marries Annabella WILMOT. He subsequently loses his fortune and then his wife. Naturally depressive, he is almost undone when he discovers his wife's adulterous betrayal, but he summons up enough internal strength to divorce her, reform his ways, and find another wife who ultimately makes him a happy man.

Lowood   Jane EYRE is sent to this charity school by her guardian Mrs. REED. It is presided over by the EVANGELICAL clergyman Mr. BROCKLEHURST, who believes in putting the girls on a strict diet and denying them any pleasures. The diet of the school is so poor, and the living conditions so unhealthy, that several of the girls die of typhoid. The ensuing

scandal stimulates an investigation and reform, which makes Jane's later years at the school far more tolerable. The Lowood episode is based on Charlotte Brontë's own experience at COWAN BRIDGE, a grim school graphically described in Mrs. GASKELL's *THE LIFE OF CHARLOTTE BRONTË*.

Luddite   In 1811 and 1812, the name given to mill workers in Yorkshire and in other parts of northern England who destroyed the new machinery they believed would put them out of work. The term came from the surname of their leader, Ned Ludd. The term is now used to refer to anyone opposed to technological innovation. Luddites appear in *Shirley,* when they break the frames at Robert MOORE's factory.

Lowood, the school where Jane Eyre spends eight years as a student and teacher. (*Life and Works of Charlotte Brontë and Her Sisters* [1872–73], illustrations by E. M. Wimperis)

Lynn, Frederick   Minor character in JANE EYRE. He accompanies his parents, Lady and Sir George LYNN, and his brother to THORNFIELD for a party. He is described as a dashing "spark."

Lynn, Henry   Minor character in JANE EYRE. He and his brother accompany their parents, Lady and Sir George LYNN, to THORNFIELD for a party. Like his brother, he is described as a dashing "spark."

Lynn, Lady   Minor character in JANE EYRE. She arrives at THORNFIELD with her husband, Sir George LYNN. Jane EYRE describes her as haughty and handsomely dressed.

Lynn, Sir George   Minor character in JANE EYRE. He is one of the group of neighbors Mr. Rochester brings to THORNFIELD for a party. Jane EYRE describes him as a "big, fresh-looking country gentleman."

Luddites (frame brakers) smashed machinery that they feared would put them out of work in the woolen mills. Charlotte Brontë writes about them in Shirley. (Life and Works of Charlotte Brontë and Her Sisters [1872–73], illustrations by E. M. Wimperis)

M—— Place in *THE TENANT OF WILDFELL HALL*. M—— is the coach stop closest to GRASSDALE MANOR.

MacTurk, Dr. Physician who attended Charlotte Brontë during her last illness. Charlotte's husband, Arthur Bell NICHOLLS, sent for this doctor from BRADFORD because he feared no HAWORTH physician was capable of caring for his wife in her deteriorating condition.

MacTurk, Mr. Minor character in *SHIRLEY*. He is a doctor who attends Robert MOORE after Moore has been shot.

Maid of Killarney, or Albion and Flora: a modern tale; in which are interwoven some cursory remarks on religion and politics Novella published anonymously by Patrick BRONTË in 1818. Set in contemporary Ireland and featuring an English hero, Albion, the tale evokes beautiful Irish lakes and mountains. Patrick clearly draws on his personal experience of Irish poverty, and perhaps for this reason, as well as that the love story tends to overwhelm the religious lesson, he chose not to acknowledge his authorship. Albion, in love with Flora, undergoes a religious conversion experience which formed such a keen part of the SERMONS OF PATRICK BRONTË.

Patrick also shows a prejudice against Roman Catholicism, arguing that Catholics should not be allowed into Parliament because of their loyalty to the pope, that would also appear in his daughter Charlotte's novels *THE PROFESSOR* and *VILLETTE*. Patrick's TORY politics and his praise of the duke of WELLINGTON would influence all his children in both their juvenilia and their mature work.

Malone, Peter Augustus Minor character in *SHIRLEY*. The curate of Briarfield, he is one of three curates satirized in the novel. An Irishman with a hot temper, he is the only curate on whom Matthewson HELSTONE believes he can rely in a confrontation with the LUDDITES.

Manchester Situated in northwest England, this city was the center of the cotton industry during the Brontës' lifetime. Charlotte accompanied her father to Manchester for his cataract operation in 1846.

Mann, Miss Minor character in *SHIRLEY*. Caroline HELSTONE visits Miss Mann, a formidable spinster, who subjects Caroline to a detailed recounting of the old woman's life.

Marchmount, Miss Character in *VILLETTE*. Miss Marchmount employs Lucy SNOWE as her companion. Lucy finds the elderly, ailing lady irritable and demanding, but she is also a proper person who respects Lucy and learns to confide in her about the lost love of her youth. In time, Lucy is able to admire Miss Marchmount as an "original character." When Miss Marchmount dies of a stroke, Lucy has to set out again to make a life for herself.

Markham, Fergus Minor character in *THE TENANT OF WILDFELL HALL*. Gilbert MARKHAM's younger, less refined brother, Fergus is a country bumpkin whose presence serves to accentuate Gilbert's gentlemanly qualities.

Markham, Gilbert Major character in *THE TENANT OF WILDFELL HALL*. Gilbert Markham is the narrator of the novel and also its protagonist. The eldest son of a prosperous gentleman farmer, Gilbert falls in love with Helen HUNTINGDON while she is residing at WILDFELL HALL under the alias Helen Graham. Initially Gilbert knows nothing of Helen's past, but he cherishes her beauty and forthright character, which contrast markedly with the attributes of the fey Eliza MILLWARD, his first love. He is offended when local gossip suggests Helen is the paramour of her landlord, Frederick LAWRENCE. When Gilbert sees what he believes is proof of their illicit relationship, he is quick to take Helen's part. Believing that Lawrence is taking advantage of a poor widow, Markham beats him savagely, an act he soon regrets when Helen reveals that Lawrence is actually her brother.

Markham loves Helen, and he also wants to save her, but when Helen resists his offer of marriage, Markham faithfully adheres to his promise not to press her. The two are separated for a period, during which Helen returns to care for her dying husband, Arthur, Lord HUNTINGDON. After he dies and Helen inherits her uncle's estate, Markham is initially embarrassed by his own lesser estate. Once again he rallies, however, proving himself more than worthy of her love. The two marry at the end of the novel.

Markham, Mrs. Minor character in *THE TENANT OF WILDFELL HALL*. Mrs. Markham is the doting mother of Gilbert, Fergus, and Rose MARKHAM. Mistress of LINDEN-CAR, she was married to a successful gentleman farmer who has died by the time the novel opens.

Markham, Rose Minor character in *THE TENANT OF WILDFELL HALL*. Rose is Gilbert MARKHAM's younger sister. A pretty, gossipy woman, she marries Gilbert's friend J. HALFORD, Esq.

Marmion Poem by Sir Walter SCOTT published in 1808. It tells the story of Lord Marmion, who rejects his betrothed, Constance, and fails to secure the wealthy Lady Clare in marriage. In *JANE EYRE*, Jane EYRE is reading the poem when St. John RIVERS observes the drawing she has made of Rosamond OLIVER, the young woman he is in love with.

Martineau, Harriet (1802–1876) English writer. Privately educated, Martineau became a prominent literary figure, befriended by writers such as George Eliot, Thomas CARLYLE, and Charlotte Brontë. She wrote on an impressive range of subjects, from economics to philosophy, politics, and literature. She also wrote novels and fiction for children. Her review of *VILLETTE*, which called the novel a very painful book to read and deplored its

attacks on Catholicism, upset Charlotte. The two writers remained friends, however, and Charlotte paid several visits to Martineau.

Mary Minor character in *JANE EYRE*. She is married to Edward ROCHESTER's servant JOHN. Both Mary and John look after Mr. Rochester at FERN-DEAN, the manor house he lives in after the fire at THORNFIELD.

Mason, Bertha Character in *JANE EYRE*. She is Mr. ROCHESTER's first wife, whom he wed in Spanish Town, Jamaica. She is the daughter of a wealthy Creole family whom Rochester's father arranged for him to marry, thinking that his second son would gain a fortune of 30,000 pounds while his elder son would inherit the family seat, THORN-FIELD. The young Edward Rochester was bewitched by Bertha Mason's charms, not realizing that her family suffered from a history of insanity. After marrying her, he discovered they had nothing in common and that he could not carry on a civilized conversation with her. Her behavior grew increasingly erratic until she became, except for brief periods, completely mad. After four years of marriage he decided to take her home to Thornfield, seclude her there, and travel in Europe. Only Grace POOLE, Bertha's caretaker, understands the true relationship between Bertha Mason and Edward Rochester.

When Jane EYRE comes to Thornfield, she is not told of Bertha's existence. Bertha attacks her own brother, Richard MASON, when he visits Thornfield. She also appears to Jane on the night before Jane's wedding and tears her bridal veil. Only after Richard Mason makes a public objection to Jane's marriage does Mr. Rochester tell Jane how he came to marry Bertha and why he shut her up in Thornfield. Bertha eventually perishes after she sets fire to the house.

Mason, Richard Character in *JANE EYRE*. He arrives during Mr. ROCHESTER's party. At first put off by this mysterious stranger who calls himself an old friend, Rochester regains his confidence and entertains his new guest, who is eventually revealed to be the brother of Rochester's wife. Bertha MASON. Bertha, who is insane, later attacks Mason, and Carter, a doctor, is fetched to THORN-

FIELD. When Jane EYRE is to be married to her master, Mason turns up at the church, and his lawyer declares the marriage cannot take place because the bridegroom is already married, unbeknownst to Jane. Rochester confronts the timid Mason but cannot deny the allegations, and so Mason becomes the instrument of thwarting Rochester's first attempt to marry Jane.

materialist Term applied to anyone who denies the world of the spirit. Materialists believe in the substance of this world, relying on the human senses for their understanding of the nature of things. In *VILLETTE*, Lucy SNOWE calls Dr. John Graham BRETTON a materialist because he seems unmoved by the demonic force of the actress he and Lucy watch on stage.

Mathilde Character mentioned in *VILLETTE*. She is one of the students who has difficulty translating a passage from *THE VICAR OF WAKEFIELD*.

Matou, Rosine Minor character in *VILLETTE*. The portress, a "pretty but fickle young woman," she delivers messages to the school faculty and is often the first to know about any news.

Maxwell, Mrs. Peggy Minor character in *THE TENANT OF WILDFELL HALL*. Mistress of the country estate STANINGLEY, Mrs. Maxwell is Helen HUNTINGDON's aunt. Because she has reared Helen, Aunt Maxwell feels it her duty to counsel her niece, whom she strongly advises not to marry Arthur, Lord HUNTINGDON. Later, after both Huntingdon and Mr. Maxwell have died, Aunt Maxwell lives on with Helen and her new husband, Gilbert MARKHAM, at Staningley.

Meltham, Sir Hugh Minor character in *AGNES GREY*. He is one of the "old codgers" who courts Rosalie MURRAY.

Methodist Member of a Christian denomination founded in 1739 by John Wesley, who traveled on horseback spreading his message to enthusiastic worshipers. Methodism is an EVANGELICAL religion, that is, it emphasizes intense personal conversions. In *VILLETTE*, Lucy SNOWE describes Polly HOME praying like a "CATHOLIC or Methodist enthusiast." To Lucy, Catholics and Methodists are extremists, fanatics who would usurp reason by appealing to sentimentality and other emotions. Methodists are portrayed as extremists in *SHIRLEY* as well.

Miller, Lucasta In *The Brontë Myth* (2001), Lucasta Miller provides an exceptionally well-informed account of how the Brontës became not merely a part of the canon of English literature but also characters in their own right, who now rival their own creations for the public's attention. Miller begins her story with how Charlotte, later abetted by Elizabeth GASKELL, provided the first dramatic accounts of the family that intrigued readers. Miller's account of the different biographical, psychological, and artistic approaches to the story of the Brontës and of their work is especially valuable, providing a historiography of both Brontë scholarship and of an evolving popular fascination with the family.

Miller, Miss Minor character in *JANE EYRE*. She is a teacher at LOWOOD and is the first to meet Jane EYRE when she arrives.

Millward, Eliza Character in *THE TENANT OF WILDFELL HALL*. Eliza is the younger, prettier daughter of the vicar of LINDENHOPE, Rev. Michael MILLWARD. At the outset of the novel, Gilbert MARKHAM thinks he is in love with her, but after Helen HUNTINGDON steals his heart, Eliza jealously spreads rumors about Helen and her solitary life in the derelict WILDFELL HALL.

Millward, Mary Character in *THE TENANT OF WILDFELL HALL*. Mary is the older, less attractive daughter of the vicar of LINDENHOPE, Rev. Michael MILLWARD. After her mother's death Mary was obliged to become the family housekeeper, a role she escapes by marrying Richard WILSON when he becomes her father's curate.

Millward, Rev. Michael Character in *THE TENANT OF WILDFELL HALL*. Vicar of the village of LINDENHOPE, Rev. Millward is an opinionated, strict disciplinarian whose disapproval fixes on the alien Helen HUNTINGDON.

Milton, John (1608–1674) English poet. He is most famous for his epic poem *Paradise Lost* (1665), in which he sets out to explain God's ways to man. His work follows very closely the account of the Bible. In SHIRLEY, Shirley KEELDAR takes issue with Milton's conception of Eve as inferior; she charges the poet with portraying a woman as a servant instead of a complete, independent human being.

Minny Horse in *WUTHERING HEIGHTS*. Minny is Catherine LINTON's pony, one of the small, hardy breed known as galloways, named for the district of southwestern Scotland where they originated.

Miret, M. Minor character in *VILLETTE*. He is a bookseller who does business with Madame BECK's school.

Moore, Hortense Major character in *SHIRLEY*. She is the devoted sister of Robert MOORE. Hortense supervises Robert's home and helps educate his distant cousin, Caroline HELSTONE, who has become deeply attached to both Robert and his sister. Although Hortense tends to be bossy, she means well and Caroline profits from her instruction. Hortense and Caroline miss each other greatly when Matthewson Helstone, Caroline's uncle, forbids her to visit the Moores because of their WHIGgish political views. Later Hortense and Caroline are reunited after Caroline recovers from her illness and marries Robert.

Moore, Louis Character in *SHIRLEY*. Louis is Robert MOORE's brother. Unlike Robert, Louis is a tutor, not a man of business. His quiet ways do not reveal his determined spirit and worldly abilities. His employers looked down on him as a servant, but his pupil, the wealthy and high-strung Shirley KEELDAR, perceives Louis's strengths and falls in love with him. She does not show her emotions, however, and finds it difficult to deal with Louis because of his subordinate position. But when Shirley's uncle Henry SYMPSON goads her into accepting a marriage proposal from Sir Philip NUNNELY, Shirley resists and declares her love for Louis, who proves equal to opposing Sympson in spite of Sympson's sneering allusions to Louis's lowly position. Shirley marries Louis at the same time as Caroline HELSTONE marries his brother Robert.

Moore, Robert Major character in *SHIRLEY*. Moore, the local mill employer, confronts violence from his workers who believe Moore's introduction of new machinery will deprive them of their jobs. This "thin, dark, sallow" man is determined to protect his property and make his mill a thriving business. He is half-Belgian and comes from a long line of cloth merchants from Antwerp, as well as a Yorkshire family that did business in warehouses and seaports. His ingrained commercial sensibility contributes to his desire to use the latest inventions. But he is also stymied by the Napoleonic wars, which have made it difficult to conduct trade with the Continent.

For much of the novel Moore is taken up with this threat to his livelihood and apparently does not notice that Caroline HELSTONE is in love with him. Indeed, he seems attracted to the wealthy, independent Shirley KEELDAR and even proposes to her. But Caroline eventually learns that while Moore finds Keeldar attractive, he has proposed largely because of her fortune, a deed he is deeply ashamed to admit and which he realizes is unworthy of him. Caroline is his true love, and the couple are united after she suffers a long, life-threatening illness (the result of a broken heart) and he recovers from a serious gunshot wound from one of the workers attacking his mill.

Morgan, Reverend William A close friend of Patrick Brontë's, he baptized Charlotte, Emily, and Anne; officiated at Maria's funeral; and attended the funerals of Emily and Anne. He also helped Branwell set up a studio in Bradford and officiated at Branwell's funeral. According to the biographer Juliet BARKER, he might have had a romantic interest in Charlotte.

Muller, Heinrich Minor character in *VILLETTE*. He becomes jealous when he sees Paul EMMANUEL kiss the hand of Justine Marie SAVEUR (2), M. Paul's goddaughter.

Murgatroyd, Fred Minor character in *SHIRLEY*. He is one of Robert MOORE's servants.

Murray, Charles Major character in *AGNES GREY*. Although he is his mother's pride, he proves a special trial for Agnes GREY, who is employed as his governess. Charles is the spoiled, oldest son of the family. He has almost no capacity or incentive to learn his lessons.

Murray, John Minor character in *AGNES GREY*. At 11, John is the youngest of the Murray children to whom Agnes GREY is a governess. He is poorly behaved and is sent away to school, which is a great relief to Agnes.

Murray, Matilda Character in *AGNES GREY*. One of the Murray children for whom Agnes GREY is a governess, she is 14, with the high-spirited, spontaneous nature of an animal. She has no interest in her schoolwork and would rather ride her horse.

Murray, Mr. Major character in *AGNES GREY*. Agnes GREY's employer at Horton Lodge. She takes up her position as governess in Mr. Murray's household after she is dismissed from the Bloomfield residence at Wellwood House. In more ample surroundings, she looks forward to her role with renewed enthusiasm. Mr. Murray is a typical country gentleman with a bluff manner.

Murray, Mrs. Major character in *AGNES GREY*. Agnes GREY's employer, she seems gruff. She is aware that as a governess Agnes will have some problems with her children, and she counsels Agnes to have patience.

Murray, Rosalie Major character in *AGNES GREY*. At 16, she is the oldest of the Murray children in Agnes GREY's care, and she treats Agnes no better than a servant. Rosalie is vain about her looks and makes every effort to entice men. Mr. HATFIELD, the rector, feels particularly aggrieved against her, because she has led him to expect that she would accept his proposal of marriage. She instead marries Sir Thomas ASHBY, whom she discovers to be an unimaginative man with little interest in her. Later she calls on Agnes to confide that she is suffering through a bad marriage.

Myers, Alice Minor character in *THE TENANT OF WILDFELL HALL*. After Arthur, Lord HUNTINGDON and Annabella WILMOT cease to be lovers, Alice Myers is brought to the Huntingdon residence at GRASSDALE MANOR as tutor to young Arthur. Helen HUNTINGDON, who finds Alice to be possessed of an inferior intellect, rightly guesses that the young woman will serve less as her son's governess than as her husband's mistress.

Nasmyth, Rev. Mr. Character mentioned in *JANE EYRE*. Miss TEMPLE marries Rev. Nasmyth and leaves LOWOOD, prompting Jane EYRE to also think of departing.

Newby, T. C. The publisher of *WUTHERING HEIGHTS* and *AGNES GREY*. Elizabeth GASKELL presented a negative portrait of him in *THE LIFE OF CHARLOTTE BRONTË*, which caused the latter book's publisher, George SMITH, some concern.

Nicholls, Arthur Bell (1819–1905) Husband of Charlotte Brontë. Reverend Arthur Bell Nicholls arrived at HAWORTH in May 1845 to serve as Patrick Brontë's curate. Charlotte first considered him a well-read and respectable young man. Not until nearly seven years later is there any extant evidence that she took a special interest in him, singling him out for attention in one of her letters. Evidently Nicholls had shown signs of interest in her, because Patrick reacted to his curate with increasing sarcasm and Nicholls himself talked of returning to his native Ireland. When he came to tea on a Monday evening, December 13, 1852, Charlotte became uncomfortable under his intense scrutiny. Heretofore she had not thought of him as a sensitive man, and when she heard him make a proposal and saw him shake with nerves, she, in turn, was shocked. She consulted her father, who reacted with rage, and she gave her word that she would refuse Nicholls the next day. But the refusal cost her greatly, because she had begun to think of Nicholls differently: She was moved by his devotion and feared that her father would deem any man unacceptable as a husband for her.

As Nicholls's health declined, and Patrick proved even more hostile, Charlotte felt herself drawn to the curate. On the day of his departure, she found him sobbing. When he asked her if he could hope for an engagement, she said no, but that she was aware of how much he suffered. He then began writing to her. She made no reply until his sixth letter, when she reiterated that he would have to submit to his lot. He wrote again, accepting her advice but asking if he might continue the correspondence. She agreed, and then finding it intolerable that her father should be deceived, she confessed to Patrick that she was writing to Nicholls, and Patrick did not object.

Nicholls then took the initiative, proposing a meeting with Charlotte in autumn 1853. Again she consulted her father, who allowed the meeting after she expressed her desire to know Nicholls better. When they met, she informed the curate that her father was still very opposed to their match. Nicholls reacted mildly and evidently decreased Charlotte's tension. The rendezvous also apparently helped her stand up to her father: She pointed out that she was not likely to get another proposal (she was 37 years old), that Nicholls was her choice, and that she meant for him to live in the house with them. An angry Patrick did not speak to his daughter for a week.

In spite of Charlotte's firmness with her father, she had doubts about Nicholls and the marriage. Both she and Patrick had hoped she would one day make a very good match, and Nicholls seemed far below their expectations. But Charlotte had been won over by his dogged persistence, and surprisingly, Patrick gave his consent. They were married on June 29, 1854.

The marriage proved to be a happy one. Nicholls was a practical, diplomatic, and conscientious husband and did all that could be expected to mollify Patrick. Indeed, Charlotte seems to have become absorbed in her marriage and in the life of a curate's wife. Friends observed a mellow, contented woman who did not resemble the ambitious, driven personality they had known.

Charlotte's health deteriorated suddenly, apparently the result of a difficult pregnancy, although the specific cause of her death has been debated by scholars. Nicholls and Patrick continued to live at Haworth until Patrick's death six years later. Patrick's will left everything to Nicholls, who returned to Ireland and married a cousin, Mary Bell. He died in 1905.

"No coward soul is mine" Poem by Emily BRONTË. This seven-stanza work is Emily's last great poem, written January 25, 1846. Although it does not reflect conventional religious notions about death and the afterlife, the poem is nevertheless a declaration of faith that opens on a memorably triumphant note:

No coward soul is mine
No trembler in the world's storm-drenched sphere
I see Heaven's glories shine
And Faith shines equal arming me from Fear

This was the last poem Emily transcribed into the fair copy notebooks she first created in February 1844. It was not, however, the last poem she ever wrote, as Charlotte indicated when she published it as part of a selection of previously unpublished poems in her 1850 dual edition of WUTHERING HEIGHTS and AGNES GREY. That designation belongs to a long GONDAL poem written in September 1846 and revised just months before Emily's death in December 1848. "No coward soul is mine" may itself be a Gondal poem. Certainly it was written during the same period when Emily was composing her novel, which itself reflects many aspects of Gondal and draws on other poetry that clearly falls under the Gondal rubric. But in 1850 Charlotte, grief-stricken and eager to correct previous misperceptions, was determined to present her sisters to the public in the most favorable light possible. She edited the poem to make it more conventional and pious, changing the last lines from "Since thou art Being and Breath / And what thou art may never be destroyed" to "Thou— THOU art Being and Breath, / And what THOU art may never be destroyed." By repeating and emphasizing *thou,* Charlotte transformed Emily's poem from the merely spiritual into praise for the Christian god. Her readers would have recognized the capitalized *THOU* as a clear reference to the Lord they worshiped each Sunday in church.

Northangerland, earl of *See* ANGRIA.

Norton Conyers Charlotte Brontë visited this home, which is near Ripon. The home's oak panelling, portraits, long gallery, and association with tales of a madwoman all suggest it as a source for THORNFIELD in *JANE EYRE.*

Nunnely Place in *SHIRLEY.* A village with an old church, a forest, and monastic ruins, it is the home of Sir Philip NUNNELY.

Nunnely, Lady Minor character in *SHIRLEY.* The mother of Sir Philip NUNNELY, she disapproves of his proposal to marry Shirley KEELDAR.

Nunnely, Sir Moncton Minor character in *SHIRLEY.* The father of Sir Philip NUNNELY, he seems to have little interest in his son's courtship of Shirley KEELDAR.

Nunnely, Sir Philip Character in *SHIRLEY.* He courts Shirley KEELDAR. Although he loves literature, Shirley finds his constant quoting of his own bad verse tiresome. He seems completely unaware of how unappealing his words are to her, but he is kind, and Shirley sometimes enjoys his company, even if she has no intention of accepting his proposal.

Nussey, Ellen A close friend of Charlotte Brontë's who visited HAWORTH several times. Nussey came from a family of cloth manufacturers. Some critics believe she was the model for Caroline HELSTONE in *SHIRLEY.* Ellen and Charlotte met in 1831 at Miss WOOLER's school, and Charlotte visited Ellen several times at her home. They corresponded freely, and Elizabeth GASKELL and other biographers have relied on these letters for many facts about the Brontës: Charlotte confided in Ellen about the marriage proposals she received, including the courtship of Arthur Bell NICHOLLS; her plans to set up a school with her sisters; Branwell's plans to enter the Royal Academy; Charlotte's experiences as a governess; her periods in Brussels; her worries about Branwell; the writing of *Jane Eyre, Shirley,* and *Villette;* her literary success; her sisters' illnesses and deaths; her visits to London; her view of George Henry LEWES; her relationship with George SMITH; and James TAYLOR's interest in her. After Charlotte's death, Ellen became part of the Brontë myth by engaging in "little chats" with the numerous biographers, reporters, and fans who made pilgrimages to Haworth and its surroundings.

O

"Oh, thy bright eyes must answer now" Poem by Emily BRONTË. Written October 14, 1844, and published under the title "Plead for Me" in the Brontës' 1846 *POEMS*, "Oh, thy bright eyes" appears to be a personal credo in which the speaker asks that her "radiant angel" plead her case with "Stern Reason." She has, she says, "persevered to shun / The common paths that others run," choosing instead "to worship where / Faith cannot doubt nor Hope despair." That place is her own soul, where the "God of Visions" dwells. Critics have interpreted the poem as Emily's own declaration of a heterodox religion combining self-reliance and an ultimate faith in her own artistic gifts.

Oldfield, Mr. Minor character in *THE TENANT OF WILDFELL HALL*. Mr. Oldfield is one of Esther HARGRAVE's suitors. Esther thinks he is too old for her and resists her family's efforts to force her to marry him. Helen HUNTINGDON, recalling her own revulsion at her elderly suitor, Mr. BOARHAM, supports Esther in her decision.

Oliver, Mr. Minor character in *JANE EYRE*. Mr. Oliver thinks highly of St. John RIVERS, praising his work and his family. His only regret is that St. John will waste his life on missionary work. Jane EYRE wonders why St. John doesn't give up his missionary plans and marry Mr. Oliver's daughter, Rosamond, with whom he is obviously in love.

Oliver, Rosamond Character in *JANE EYRE*. The beautiful daughter of a wealthy man, she has captivated St. John RIVERS. Jane EYRE can see that St. John is disconcerted in Rosamond's company and

encourages him to express his love to her. But Rivers balks, saying that although he is drawn to Rosamond, he realizes that she would not make a proper wife for a missionary. Jane disagrees with him, but as she gets to know him better, she concludes that he is right.

"On Conversion" Short story by Patrick BRONTË published in *The Pastoral Visitor* (1815). In this story a sinner full of remorse turns to the Scriptures for solace, recognizing that he is about to engage in a spiritual struggle: "The conflict may be long and severe; but I hope through Christ Jesus to obtain the victory and the prize." His conversion is an arduous process with many setbacks, But he triumphs—as much because of his joy in salvation as his fear of damnation. Although Juliet BARKER terms this a rather typical evangelical story, she also notes that Patrick shows some skill at maintaining suspense by dividing the tale into three self-contained episodes, each of which leaves readers wanting more.

orders in council Laws made in England by the monarch and recognized but not passed by Parliament. In *SHIRLEY*, orders in council prohibit neutral powers from trading with France, which was at war with England during Napoléon's rule. The laws interfered with U.S. trading activities, and the United States retaliated by refusing to buy textiles from Yorkshire mills. Robert MOORE and other mill operators face financial ruin so long as they are unable to sell their goods to America.

Panache, Madame   Character mentioned in *VILLETTE*. A history teacher at Madame BECK's pensionnat, she comes into conflict with Professor Paul EMMANUEL. Lucy SNOWE compares the conflict to one between Napoléon BONAPARTE and Madame Germaine de STAEL. Like Madame de Stael, Madame Panache staunchly holds her ground.

Parrysland   The name Emily and Anne Brontë invented for their fictional world. *See YOUNG MEN'S MAGAZINE, THE.*

Paul et Virginie   In *VILLETTE*, the ship Paul EMMANUEL sails on to the West Indies.

Path, Louise   Minor character in *THE PROFESSOR*. William CRIMSWORTH describes her as his most pleasant student.

Pearson, Anne   Minor character in *SHIRLEY*. The daughter of the mill owner Mr. PEARSON, she reports that her father has been shot at by the LUDDITES.

Pearson, Mr.   Minor character in *SHIRLEY*. A mill owner, Pearson is shot at by the LUDDITES.

Pelagie   Minor character in *THE PROFESSOR*. She is one of Mademoiselle Zoraide REUTER's French teachers.

Pelet, M.   Major character in *THE PROFESSOR*. The proprietor of a private school, Pelet employs William CRIMSWORTH as a teacher. Crimsworth is at first impressed with Pelet's interest in him. But when Crimsworth discovers that M. Pelet and Mademoiselle Zoraide REUTER are conspiring to manipulate him into an affection for her, he becomes much more circumspect and cool toward Pelet. Eventually he gives Pelet notice and finds employment at another school. Pelet later marries Mademoiselle Reuter.

Pelet, Madame   Minor character in *THE PROFESSOR*. She is M. PELET's mother and "an incessant and indiscreet talker." She maintains her own circle of friends.

Penistone Crags (Penistow Crag)   Location in *WUTHERING HEIGHTS*. The Penistone Crags are a rocky outcropping about four miles from THRUSHCROSS GRANGE and about a mile beyond WUTHERING HEIGHTS. Young Catherine LINTON longs to visit them. Her unauthorized trip there at age 13 marks both the first time she has left the precincts of her home and her first encounter with the inhabitants of Wuthering Heights, who will shape her destiny. Emily Brontë probably modeled the Penistone Crags on Ponden Kirk, a rocky promontory that rises above HAWORTH MOOR.

Pensionnat Heger   The Belgian school in Brussels that served as the model for the schools in *THE PROFESSOR* and *VILLETTE*. Although Emily Brontë traveled with her sister Charlotte to Brussels in February 1842, only Charlotte put the experience to significant use in fiction. The boarding school, dedicated to the education of young women, was situated in the oldest part of the city near a central park. Like the schools in *The Professor* and *Villette*, the Pensionnat Heger had a beautiful garden. Madame Clair Zoe HEGER lived on the premises with her three daughters, just as Madame BECK does in *Villette*. Madame Heger's husband, Constantin Georges Romain HEGER, had a distinguished reputation as a teacher there. Although the Hegers were Catholics and catered to Belgian Roman Catholic students, the Brontë sisters were permitted to excuse themselves from mass and other forms of worship. Nevertheless, the sisters' adjustment to the school proved to be a trial. Like Lucy SNOWE in *Villette*, neither Charlotte nor Emily was fluent in French, yet all the students were expected to do their lessons in the language. In addition, Charlotte (25) and Emily (24) were considerably older than their fellow students and found it difficult to achieve a rapport with them, as does Lucy. Despite these obstacles, Charlotte's and Emily's writing improved under the regimen of their brilliant teacher, Professor Heger, and they both became teachers at the school: Emily conducted classes in music, and Charlotte taught English. Charlotte won praise from Professor Heger for her mastery of French; she also made progress in German.

Eventually, however, school routines became monotonous. Emily never really made friends, and Charlotte sought only to please Professor Heger. Feeling distraught at her loneliness and guilty over her passion for Professor Heger, Charlotte was driven, as fictionalized through Lucy in *Villette*, to confess to a Catholic priest. By the end of 1843, Charlotte left the school with a diploma, still in love with Monsieur Heger but realizing that her feelings could not be reciprocated. The biographer Juliet BARKER speculates that this incident—when Charlotte almost forsook her Protestantism—accounts for the anti-Catholic sentiments in her fiction. Certainly Charlotte treats CATHOLICISM as an insidious religion that attempts to subvert her heroine's deepest convictions.

Perceval, Spencer (1762–1812)   British statesman and prime minister from 1809 to 1812. In *SHIRLEY*, Mr. Hiram YORKE, a WHIG, attacks Perceval as part of the TORY Party, which supports a corrupt monarchy and the Church of England.

Percy, Alexander   *See* ANGRIA.

"Philosopher, The"   Poem by Emily BRONTË. Composed on February 3, 1845, "The Philosopher" is a dialogue poem in which the Philosopher explains his melancholy to Man by pointing to an inner struggle: "Three Gods within this little frame / Are warring night and day." Once the Philosopher had a vision of a Spirit, who pierced the gloom of his own existence with a white light, but although the Philosopher has searched for

this Spirit in "Heaven, Hell, Earth, and Air," he has never found the elusive one or experienced this light himself. Therefore, like HEATHCLIFF, his only hope for an end to his torment is death. Anne Brontë's poem "THE THREE GUIDES" is in all likelihood a response to what she must have seen as Emily's nihilism.

Philosopher's Island   *See* GLASS TOWN.

Phoenix   Dog in *WUTHERING HEIGHTS*. Phoenix is one of two pointers that accompany Catherine LINTON on her first visit to WUTHERING HEIGHTS, where both dogs are apparently attacked by the resident canines.

Pierrot, Madame   Minor character in *JANE EYRE*. She teaches French at LOWOOD.

Pilgrim's Progress, The   An allegory by John Bunyan (1628–88). Published in two parts in 1678 and 1684, the book is presented as a dream the author has had: a vision of a character named Christian bearing a burden on his back and reading a book. The book tells Christian that his family and city will be destroyed in a fire. He goes through many trials on his way through the Slough of Despond, the Valley of the Shadow of Death, and Vanity Fair and is joined by another character, Hopeful, on the way to the Celestial City. In *VILLETTE*, Lucy SNOWE compares her visits to Mrs. Louisa BRETTON to the journey of Christian and Hopeful beside a "pleasant stream." She evidently identifies with the story of a man alone seeking his salvation, for Lucy is alone and longs for a deliverer.

Pillule, Dr.   Character mentioned in *VILLETTE*. Dr. John Graham BRETTON replaces Dr. Pillule, who previously had attended to the health of the students and faculty at Madame BECK's school.

Pilot   Mr. ROCHESTER's faithful dog in *JANE EYRE*. Pilot goes to Jane EYRE for help after his master falls from his horse. At FERNDEAN, where Rochester withdraws after the devastating fire at THORNFIELD, Pilot remains at his master's side.

Pitt, William (1759–1806)   British prime minister from 1783 to 1801 and from 1804 to 1806. At home he instituted many reforms, and abroad he negotiated several alliances against revolutionary France. In SHIRLEY, Mr. Hiram YORKE, a WHIG, attacks Pitt for his support of the king and the established church.

Poems First publication of Charlotte, Emily, and Anne BRONTË under the pseudonyms Currer, Ellis, and Acton BELL. This slender collection of 61 poems, printed in 1846, had its genesis the year before, when Charlotte discovered a cache of poems written by Emily. Deeply impressed by the quality of the work, Charlotte quickly seized on the notion that the three sisters should combine their penchant for writing with their need for income. First, however, Charlotte had to overcome Emily's apparent rage at her older sister's intrusion into her private world; most if not all of Emily's poems grew out of the GONDAL saga Emily and Anne had continued long after Charlotte and Branwell were obliged to end their corresponding tales of ANGRIA. Anne smoothed the way for reconciliation by offering her own verses for the proposed publication. Both she and Emily, however, had conditions: The Gondal origins of the poems had to be disguised, and the verses could be published only if the sisters assumed pseudonyms.

Charlotte acquiesced, ultimately seeing the wisdom of posing as male authors. The three chose pen names that retained their own initials, then set about choosing verses for their volume. Charlotte chose 19, only three of which appear to have been recent compositions. The bulk of her contribution, the other 16 poems, seems to have been written as early as 1837, when she was immersed in Angria, although three are known to have been composed in 1838, 1839, and 1841. Emily contributed 21 poems, all but two—dating from 1839—written in 1844 and 1845. She was scrupulous about editing out references to Gondal, most notably in one of her most celebrated works, "THE PRISONER," which she created by combining two sections of a lengthy poem and adding a final verse. She also included her last great poem, "NO COWARD SOUL IS MINE." A fair copy dated January 25, 1846, shows that, in contrast to Charlotte, Emily was then working at the height of her poetic powers. Anne, like Emily, contributed 21

poems, most of recent vintage and all dating from 1840 or later, and bearing few signs of their Gondal origins.

Charlotte began writing inquiry letters to publishers. Evidently she suffered a number of rejections before her January 28, 1846, letter to AYLOTT & JONES—offering to underwrite publication costs and signed simply "C. Brontë"—met with success. On February 6 she forwarded the manuscript, and on March 3 she sent a banker's draft for £31 10s. Less than a week later Aylott & Jones had sent out proof sheets, which the sisters corrected. On May 7 three copies of the 165-page book arrived at HAWORTH PARSONAGE. Its contents were as follows:

"Pilate's Wife's Dream" (CB)
"Faith and Despondency" (EB)
"A Reminiscence" (AB)
"Mementos" (CB)
"Stars" (EB)
"The Philosopher" (EB)
"The Arbour" (AB)
"Home" (AB)
"The Wife's Will" (CB)
"Remembrance" (EB)
"Vanitas Vanitatum, Omnia Vanitas" (AB)
"The Wood" (CB)
"A Death Scene" (EB)
"Song" (EB)
"The Penitent" (AB)
"Music on Christmas Morning" (AB)
"Frances" (CB)
"Anticipation" (EB)
"Stanzas" (AB)
"Gilbert" (CB)
"The Prisoner" (EB)
"If this be all" (AB)
"Life" (CB)
"Hope" (EB)
"Memory" (AB)
"The Letter" (CB)
"A Day-Dream" (EB)
"To Cowper" (AB)
"Regret" (CB)
"To Imagination" (EB)
"The Doubter's Prayer" (AB)
"Presentiment" (CB)
"How clear she shines" (EB)
"A Word to the Elect" (AB)

"The Teacher's Monologue" (CB)
"Sympathy" (EB)
"Past Days" (AB)
"Passion" (CB)
"Preference" (CB)
"Plead for Me" (EB)
"The Consolation" (AB)
"Evening Solace" (CB)
"Self-Interrogation" (EB)
"Lines composed in a Wood on a Windy Day" (AB)
"Stanzas" (CB)
"Death" (EB)
"Views of Life" (AB)
"Parting" (CB)
"Stanzas to" (EB)
"Appeal" (AB)
"Honour's Martyr" (EB)
"The Student's Life" (AB)
"Apostasy" (CB)
"Stanzas" (EB)
"The Captive Dove" (AB)
"Winter Stores" (CB)
"My Comforter" (EB)
"Self-Congratulation" (AB)
"The Missionary" (CB)
"The Old Stoic" (EB)
"Fluctuations" (AB)

PUBLICATION HISTORY

The same day that the advance copies of their poetry collection were in the Brontë sisters' hands, Charlotte wrote to Aylott & Jones requesting that review copies be sent to leading periodicals. She agreed to pay for advertisements but cautioned that she would spend no more than two pounds. Two months later the first reviews appeared. Frustratingly, many reviewers seemed far more interested in the identity of the authors than in their work. A laudatory review in the *Critic*, however, impelled Charlotte to authorize Aylott & Jones to spend 10 pounds more on advertising. It was a wasted investment. Three months elapsed before the press took any further notice of *Poems*, and then two notices consisted entirely of reprintings of selected verses. A year after publication, *Poems* had sold only two copies.

After the success of the Brontë sisters' novels, Aylott & Jones saw an opportunity to dispose of the many copies of *Poems* still sitting unsold on its shelves. The publisher asked Charlotte, who in turn inquired of her current publisher, Smith, Elder & Co., if there was any interest in reissuing the poetry collection. Smith, Elder purchased the unsold copies of *Poems* from Aylott & Jones and reissued them with new covers in November 1848. Despite the Bells' notoriety, however, the volume again had disappointing sales.

poems of Anne Brontë   What is known of Anne Brontë's poetic output, some 59 poems, comes mainly from a series of fair copy books she began in 1836 and continued until 1848. The only exceptions are the draft GONDAL poem that begins, "A prisoner in a dungeon deep"—which critic Edward Chitham suggests Anne kept simply for its catalog of Gondal names—and a final poem, "A dreadful darkness closes in," composed January 7 and 28, 1849, which Anne did not have time to transcribe before she died. Like her sister Emily, with whom she shared a very close bond, a "twinship," Anne wrote poems in two categories: Gondal and non-Gondal.

The early years of her poetic endeavors were taken up entirely with fleshing out the Gondal story, but as early as 1840, Anne began composing verses unrelated to this joint fantasy. The year 1840 was a watershed for Anne, as it marked the time she left the fold of HAWORTH PARSONAGE for employment in the outside world. During the five years Anne worked as a governess at THORP GREEN, the majority of her poetic output consisted of non-Gondal works, with the exception of four poems, written during or just following holiday visits home. But Gondal was really Emily's creation and obsession, and away from her older sister's influence and insistence, Anne addressed other themes in her poetry. Isolated at Thorp Green, she began writing about her inner life, producing both love poems and meditations on faith.

Many readers theorize that the eight love poems Anne wrote, starting with one written January 1, 1840, and signed by a Gondal figure, concern Anne's attraction to her father's curate William WEIGHTMAN, who arrived at HAWORTH in late summer 1839 and died there in September 1842. Charlotte's letters provide evidence of her own infatuation with Weightman and hint at Anne's similar feelings. Indeed, Anne's poems contain evidence that Patrick's curate—whom she does not name—was of more than passing interest to her. In the seven non-Gondal love poems, the male subject is consistently characterized as having a bright smile, a light touch, and an attractive voice. In addition, beginning with a poem dated December 1842, the young man is consistently described as having died and been laid to rest in the church, as Weightman was. This poem, "To ———," bears every sign, from its standard title to its restrained emotion, of being an exercise following the 19th-century model of a love poem. The date of the poem, as well as internal references to the dead man's "angel smile" and musical voice, point to Weightman as the subject. "Severed and gone, so many years!" written in April 1847, refers to the corner where the loved one lies entombed, a "dreary place of rest" from which, like Weightman's burial place in the walls of Haworth Church, "[t]he charnel moisture never dries."

During his brief tenure at Haworth, William Weightman flirted with many of the local girls, including Charlotte and Anne, but he let it be known that he was in love with a young lady named Agnes Walton, a resident of Appleby, the Westmorland town that was his home. The restrained air of most of Anne's love poems reflects not only her own innate reticence, but also her awareness that Weightman did not truly return her affection. In "To ———" the dead young man is referred to as "our darling." In "Severed and gone," although the speaker declares that after death the loved one lives on in her heart, he does so "not in mine alone." In Anne's masterful late poem "SELF-COMMUNION," written between November 1847 and April 17, 1848, she confesses that she has known romantic rapture "only in my dreams."

Despite its title, "Self-Communion" is not confessional. It is, instead, the culmination of Anne's attempt to reconcile in verse the conflicting demands of feeling and reason. Many of her poetic works take the form of a dialogue between these two, but even from an early age she seems to have been predisposed toward a rational approach to life. We can see this inner debate

taking shape in the lengthy poem "Views of Life," written in June 1845, where the polarities are labeled hope and experience. In "Views of Life," to which Emily seems to have contributed, Anne gives youthful hope its due. But by the time Anne wrote "THE THREE GUIDES" in the summer of 1847, her views had been tempered by her experiences at Thorp Green, which gave her some perspective on Emily's emotional extremes and on Branwell's irresponsible self-indulgence. While the first of the three guides, the "Spirit of Earth," is easily dismissed as representing untempered rationalism, Anne devotes much more time to the wild and passionate "Spirit of Pride," capable of ecstasy and dreams but also "false and destructive." It is hard not to see this spirit as an embodiment of Emily's embrace of emotional extremes, which shaped such singular works as *Wuthering Heights* and "No coward soul is mine," but which also contributed to an estrangement between Emily and her younger sister. While Emily was never willing to leave Gondal or Haworth behind, Anne had experienced the wider world and concluded that her guide there would be the "Spirit of Faith."

Anne's "Self-Communion," a lengthy autobiographical poem, contains the strongest statement of her religious beliefs in her work. The poet links the discovery of herself and her faith with her disillusionment with another, reflecting Anne's feelings toward Emily:

And as my love the warmer glowed
The deeper would that anguish sink,
That this dark stream between us flowed,
Though both stood bending o'er its brink.
Until, at last, I learned to bear
A colder heart within my breast;
To share such thoughts as I could share,
    And calmly keep the rest.
I saw that they were sundered now,
The trees that at the root were one;
They yet might mingle leaf and bough,
But still the stems must stand alone.

Anne learned to stand alone, separated from the rest of her family by temperament and religious belief. When she writes in "Self-Communion" that because of a child's own reading of the Bible, it "wiser than its teacher grows," she is perhaps alluding to her own early acceptance of the doctrine of universal salvation, which went far beyond the opposition to predestination embraced by the other Brontës. Certainly her insistence on finding God in the here and now was at odds with Emily's insistence on the presence of the supernatural within the natural world. Anne did not embrace the transcendental, insisting on a kind of plainspokenness in which art was made to serve the Lord. It hardly comes as a surprise that some of her poems labeled "hymns"—the best known is "Believe not those who say," published as "The Narrow Way"—have been incorporated into the standard hymnbooks of Methodists, Baptists, and Anglicans.

Anne's poems appeared in print on five occasions during her lifetime. After Charlotte discovered one of Emily's fair copy books in 1845, Anne proffered her own private work, perhaps as a means of easing the tension that resulted from Charlotte's invasion of Emily's privacy. Anne ultimately contributed 21 poems to the 1846 POEMS by Currer, Ellis, and Acton Bell. The next year she included one of her own poems in AGNES GREY and in 1848 did the same with THE TENANT OF WILDFELL HALL. On August 11, 1848, Anne's "The Three Guides" appeared in FRASER'S MAGAZINE, which also published "The Narrow Way" that December. After Anne's death, Charlotte chose seven of her sister's poems for publication with the second, combined edition of Wuthering Heights and Agnes Grey. Charlotte seems deliberately to have chosen religious works in order to combat the heavy criticism directed at Acton Bell over the controversial subject matter of Wildfell Hall, and even these poems she edited in such a fashion as to present Anne as a conventionally pious soul.

A few years after Charlotte and her father died, Arthur Bell Nicholls, Charlotte's widower, returned to his native Ireland, taking the remaining Brontë manuscripts with him. Most of these he sold in 1895 to the collector T. J. WISE, who mistakenly attributed some of Emily's poems to Anne and vice versa. By the time an authoritative text of Anne Brontë's poems was published by Edward Chitham in 1979, questions about Anne's authorship had been resolved with respect to all but three poems.

poems of Branwell Brontë   More than 150 extant Brontë poems have been attributed to Branwell Brontë. Most of these were written in youth and are related to the GLASS TOWN saga or to Branwell and Charlotte's ANGRIA epic. Although Branwell, unlike his sisters, did not use these products of childhood as the foundation for more mature works, in 1837, between two abortive attempts to become a professional portrait painter, Branwell appears to have made a concerted effort to convert his juvenile poetry into publishable form. Of the 33 poems he heavily revised and copied into a notebook that year, all but two are assigned titles. Many of these poems, such as "Sound the Loud Trumpet" and "The Angrian Hymn," declare their Angrian origins, while others, such as "THE DOUBTER'S HYMN" and "Upon that dreary winter's night," seem more closely related to the events of Branwell's life than to the imaginary Angria.

During this period Branwell seemed bent on redeeming himself, after his failure to enroll at art school in London, by making a living as a literary man. In addition to producing a fair number of new poems, he barraged BLACKWOOD'S MAGAZINE with letters offering his services as an editor or a contributor and sent some of his best poetic efforts to both the august magazine and the celebrated poet William WORDSWORTH. Neither effort was acknowledged. Branwell's hopes, never realistic, were easily dashed, and in 1838 he returned to art. With his father's help he set up a modest studio in BRADFORD. That endeavor, too, ended in failure.

Branwell's year in Bradford resulted in few portrait commissions, but it did inspire a significant and lengthy narrative poem, known alternatively as "SIR HENRY TUNSTALL" and "The Wanderer." Plainly, Branwell's poetic impulse was still alive. After Branwell returned to Haworth, he resumed his reading of the classics with his father. This activity had formed the core of his formal education as a boy; now it not only helped Branwell prepare for another career as a tutor but also stimulated him to translate the first book of Horace's Odes in 1840.

Dismissed in June 1840 from his post as tutor to the Posthlethwaite family, Branwell next found work as a railway clerk. That job, too, was short lived, but Branwell came away with several poems he had composed during 18 months of what he regarded as menial labor. Publication of a few poems in the *Leeds Intelligencer* and the HALIFAX GUARDIAN in 1842 helped soothe his wounded pride but benefited him little otherwise. Branwell's next job, as tutor to the ROBINSON FAMILY children, would be his last. He wrote little during the two and a half years he worked at THORP GREEN, and his employment ended abruptly when he was fired in June 1845 for "behavior bad beyond expression" (i.e., having an affair with his employer's wife, Lydia ROBINSON).

Thereafter, Branwell seemed to succumb to the trilogy of vices—drink, drugs, and debt—that had characterized his entire adulthood, undermining both his professional aspirations and his health. He did, however, continue to write, occasionally expressing his despair over the end of his affair with Lydia Robinson and over life itself. In the last poem he is believed to have written, "Percy Hall," Branwell once again assumes the persona of his fictitious alter ego, Percy, Earl of Northangerland.

The publication history of Branwell's poetry, like that of his sisters', is muddled. Only a handful of his poems was published during his lifetime, and although Charlotte edited and posthumously published selections from Emily's and Anne's poetry, she did not do the same for Branwell. When Charlotte's widower, Arthur Bell Nicholls, removed to his native Ireland after Patrick Brontë's death in 1861, he took with him all of the Brontë manuscripts he could find, including Branwell's. The bulk of these were purchased from Nicholls in 1895 by Thomas James WISE, who went on to coedit with J. A. Symington three volumes of the so-called Shakespeare Head edition of Brontëana, devoted to the work of Charlotte and Branwell. After Wise died, some of his Brontë material was shown to have been forged, but the efforts of the Brontë scholar C. W. Hatfield helped sort out those sections of the Shakespeare Head devoted to Branwell's poetic works.

Still, no definitive edition of Branwell's poetry exists. A scholarly edition, *The Poems of Patrick Branwell Brontë*, appeared in 1983, edited by Tom Winifrith, but this edition is likewise a selection, leaving out such substantial items as the blank verse drama "The Revenge," which Branwell wrote in 1830 and which remains unpublished. Although Winifrith concluded that Branwell's poems are probably not worth the effort and expense of a full scholarly edition, as he admits, Branwell's poems "are part of the evidence we use to write the Brontë story, and it is important that this evidence should be as fully and accurately transcribed as possible."

poems of Charlotte Brontë   Charlotte Brontë wrote more than 200 poems, and her output exceeds that of her sisters, Emily and Anne, combined. It is nevertheless true that her poetry is generally considered weaker than that of her sisters; Charlotte herself acknowledged that her poetic gifts were not of the highest order. In part the explanation for her shortcomings in this genre can be found in her poetry's ANGRIA origins: Most of them were youthful compositions. Her earliest known poem is "O when shall our brave land be free," dated July 24, 1829, at which time she was 13 years old. The following year, 1830, was the most productive of her entire poetic career: She wrote (sometimes in conjunction with Branwell) more than 60 poems, many of them "published" in the homemade literary periodical first titled BRANWELL'S BLACKWOOD'S MAGAZINE and later called by Charlotte THE YOUNG MEN'S MAGAZINE, which she edited from July 1829 until she left in January 1831 for MISS WOOLER's school at Roe Head. Charlotte's (and Branwell's) main source of inspiration during this period was the GLASS TOWN Confederacy and its story, although she also composed non–Glass Town works that apparently served primarily as experiments with poetic form.

During her tenure as a student at Roe Head, January 1831–May 1832, Charlotte wrote only three poems, all of them composed while she was home for the holidays and all of them concerning Glass Town. In the meantime, Emily and Anne had seceded from Glass Town, creating their own GONDAL kingdom. After Charlotte left Roe Head in 1832, she and Branwell developed Glass Town and transformed it into Angria. This endeavor gave rise to Charlotte's second period of intense poetic output. During 1833 and 1834, she wrote more than 30 poems, only one of which was not connected with Angria. This work, "Richard

Coeur de Lion & Rondel," appeared first in a bound manuscript of poems that bore the legend "1833 All that is written in this book, must be in a good, plain *and legible hand*. P.B." Patrick, apparently suspicious of what his children were scribbling in minuscule handwriting on tiny sheets of paper, had put his foot down. The clergyman had reason to be suspicious, for Charlotte had recently been engaged in spinning out stories of the Angrian king's political intrigues and marital infidelities. Charlotte would include four more "presentable" poems in this manuscript.

Two of these poems, however, marked a departure in the young poet's career. The melancholy "Memory," dated October 2, 1835, and especially the November–December 1835 composition "Morning was in its freshness still," with its lamentation "'Tis bitter sometimes to recall / Illusions once deemed fair," seem deeply felt, hinting at Charlotte's unhappiness at Roe Head and her conflicted feelings about her Angrian obsession. Another, more famous poem, "WE WOVE A WEB IN CHILDHOOD," composed in December 1835, further explores these feelings, vividly describing the disparity between her fantasy world and the drudgery of her teaching duties. Charlotte's inner turmoil would deepen into a crisis of religious faith that she described in a January 1836 poem:

Long since as I remember well
My childish eyes would weep
To read how calmly Stephen fell
    In Jesus' arms asleep
Oh! Could I feel the holy glow
    That brightened death for him
I'd cease to weep that all below
    Is grown so drear & dim

By the end of that year, however, she was once again deeply immersed in Angria and poetic creation, turning out her longest, most ambitious narrative poem, the highly Byronic "And when you left me what thought had I then." Emboldened by ambition, in December 1836 she wrote to the poet laureate (and Byron antagonist) Robert SOUTHEY, inquiring about her prospects. Southey was not encouraging. A subsequent inquiry from Charlotte brought an even more withering response, which Charlotte, perhaps jokingly, labeled: "Southey's advice to be kept

forever. My twenty-first birthday. Roe Head. April 21, 1837." She then embarked on her third and final period of concentrated poetic composition.

Between January 1837 and July 1838 Charlotte wrote some 60 poems, most of them long narratives related to Angria but many others shorter, fragmentary lyrics and meditations. By the time of summer vacation in 1838, Charlotte seems to have realized that her gifts lay in prose, not poetry. Between that time and her departure for Brussels in February 1842, she composed only six more poems, four of them integrated in Angrian narratives.

In Brussels Charlotte did write a poem on the death of her friend Martha TAYLOR, and she continued to revise old poems and to translate French and German verse. After her return from Brussels in January 1844, the failure of her scheme to set up herself and her sisters as teachers, and her rejection by her professor Constantin George Romain HEGER, Charlotte was provoked into a flurry of poetic activity. Most of the verse written in 1845 speaks of love and betrayal and has a rushed, headlong quality. That autumn she made the now famous discovery of Emily's private cache of poetry that led to the publication of Currer, Ellis, and Acton BELL's *POEMS* in 1846.

Charlotte's poetic career had essentially ended. She wrote only another handful of verses, some of which were incorporated into *THE PROFESSOR* and *JANE EYRE*. "He saw my heart's woe," composed December 1847, was her final word on Monsieur Heger. In 1848, she wrote two poems to commemorate Emily's death, and in 1849 she wrote one about Anne's death.

Twenty-two of Charlotte's poems saw publication during her lifetime. Nineteen of these appeared in *Poems* and two in *Jane Eyre*. The remaining one, "The Orphans," a translation of the French poet Louis Belmontet's (1798–1879) "Les Orphelins," was published in the *Manchester Athenaeum Album* in 1850. After Charlotte's death in 1855, her husband, Arthur Bell NICHOLLS, transcribed 24 of her poems from her minutely printed script, introducing both errors and intentional changes that were perpetuated in subsequent publications by him and by Thomas James WISE, who purchased a large cache of Brontë manuscripts from Nicholls in 1895. Charlotte had composed largely on loose sheets of paper, and Nicholls added to the confusion surrounding her poetic output by giving away bits and pieces of manuscript before the Wise purchase. Some of these pieces were actually works by Anne and by Branwell mistakenly attributed to Charlotte. Wise compounded Nicholls's piecemeal treatment of Charlotte's poetry by further breaking up manuscripts and selling their components to the highest bidder. The result was that when the Shakespeare Head edition of Charlotte's poetry was published between 1931 and 1938, it included only 141 of the 206 poems that were attributed to her in the 1985 collection edited by Victor A. Neufeldt.

poems of Emily Brontë Emily Brontë's poetic canon consists of nearly 200 poems and poetic fragments that she composed at least from the time she was a teenager up until just months before her death at age 30. More than half of her surviving poetic works, including the last lines of verse she wrote, are related in some way to the GONDAL saga she created with her sister Anne. In February 1844 Emily had begun the process of making "fair copies," transcribing a selection of her poetry in her tiny hand into two notebooks and noting the dates of composition or completion of each poem. One of these notebooks—labeled "Emily Jane Brontë. Transcribed February 1844. Gondal Poems"—contains transcripts of 45 poems concerning Gondal, while the other—labeled "E.J.B. Transcribed February, 1844"—comprises 31 poems that include no overt references to her fantasy saga.

Emily's copying exercise coincided with a period of intense poetic creation in which she wrote some of her most memorable verses, including the Gondal-related poem "COLD IN THE EARTH—AND THE DEEP SNOW PILED ABOVE THEE," dated March 3, 1845, and a number of deeply personal poems about her spiritual life, such as the October 14, 1844, "OH, THY BRIGHT EYES MUST ANSWER NOW." In the "Biographical Notice" Charlotte later wrote for a combined second edition of Emily's *WUTHERING HEIGHTS* and Anne's *Agnes Grey,* Charlotte describes the advent of the sisters' literary career by deferring to her discovery in autumn 1845 of "a MS. Volume of verse in my sister Emily's handwriting." The volume to which she refers was

in all likelihood Emily's more personal collection; Emily's reaction to her sister's invasion of her privacy was pronounced and long lived. Charlotte's published account relates how it took hours to "reconcile [Emily] to the discovery" she had made and days to "persuade her that such poems merited publication." The version Charlotte told a friend, however, is decidedly more negative: After she had "wrung out" of Emily a "reluctant consent to have the 'rhymes' as they were contemptuously termed, published," Emily referred to her poetry only "with scorn"—or not at all. Emily would write only two more poems over the next three years: the unquestionably great and triumphant "NO COWARD SOUL IS MINE," on January 2, 1846, and a long, rambling poetic fragment written September 14, 1846, related to Gondal, "Why ask to know the date—the clime?" which she would reduce to a bitter four-stanza indictment of humanity in May 1848, months before her death.

Charlotte was not mistaken in her belief that her sister probably harbored "some spark of honourable ambition." Emily did finally agree to publish some of her poems, ultimately contributing 21, most of them accomplished verses written between 1844 and 1845. Emily published them, however, only on her own terms, pseudonymously as Ellis BELL and with all traces of Gondal erased. Such concern on Emily's part to hide her fantasy life resulted in the radical revision of "THE PRISONER," originally a much longer epic, begun as recently as October 1845, for the 1846 compendium *POEMS.*

Emily next channeled her literary efforts into prose. *Wuthering Heights* seemed to burst from her almost without precedent or premeditation. One can see traces of Gondal, however, not only in HEATHCLIFF and Cathy EARNSHAW's passionate relationship but also in the resemblance between the novel and some of Emily's earlier poetic efforts. One example is the apparently Gondal-related "I see around me tombstones grey," written July 17, 1841, which concludes:

We would not leave our native home
For *any* world beyond the Tomb.
No—rather on thy kindly breast
Let us be laid in lasting rest;
Or waken but to share with thee
A mutual immortality.

Echoes of these sentiments plainly inform one of Cathy's most memorable speeches, when she tells the servant Nelly DEAN:

> "I dreamt, once, that I was [in heaven]. . . . heaven did not seem to be my home; and I broke my heart with weeping to come back to earth; and the angels were so angry that they flung me out, into the middle of the heath on top of Wuthering Heights; where I woke sobbing for joy."

There is evidence that after Emily's death Charlotte attempted to sanitize her memory by destroying some of her sister's manuscripts. Certainly Charlotte edited not only the 1850 edition of *Wuthering Heights* but also the selection of Emily's unpublished poems that were included in the same volume, altering lines and adding titles. In addition, Charlotte added lines of her own composition to four of these 17 poems and may have written in its entirety the 18th poem in this selection, "Stanzas." As C. W. Hatfield, the editor of *The 1941 Complete Poems of Emily Brontë*, has remarked, lines such as "I'll walk where my own nature would be leading: / It vexes me to choose another guide" seem better to express what Charlotte hoped would be the public perception of her sister than Emily's own thoughts about herself.

After Charlotte died in 1855, her husband, Arthur Bell Nicholls, seems to have transcribed some of Emily's poems, introducing alterations and errors of his own. In May 1860, Emily's "A Farewell to Alexander" was published in *Cornhill Magazine* under the title "The Outcast Mother." After Patrick Brontë died in 1861, Nicholls returned to his native Ireland, taking with him all of Emily's surviving manuscripts. He did not publish any more of Emily's poems, and in 1895, he sold all her manuscripts (except the "Gondal poems" notebook, which was sold at auction after his death) to Thomas James WISE. Wise had also purchased manuscripts belonging to the other Brontë children, and in attempting to sort them out, he mistakenly attributed to Emily some of her siblings' poems. The canon of Emily Brontë poetry remained muddled for nearly half a century, and it was not until Hatfield's 1941 edition that all of the misattributions were sorted out and the contents of the missing "Gondal poems" notebook added. Even this edition left something to be desired, however: Manuscript versions of 14 minor poems or poetical fragments were still missing, and Hatfield was obliged to depend on transcriptions in these instances.

poems of Patrick Brontë As the biographer Juliet BARKER explains, Patrick Brontë was part of a generation of EVANGELICALS who believed in the power of literature to reach an audience far greater than their congregations. Also like his fellow clergymen, he sought to instruct and entertain in the service of his religion. *Winter Evening Thoughts* (1810), his earliest identifiable poem, ranges in subject matter from patriotic expressions of support for England in its battle against France during the Napoleonic Wars and sympathetic portraits of poor villagers to the temptations of the flesh (a young girl seduced into prostitution) and stirring depictions of adventures at sea. Sin, he warns could bring his country defeat: "Nor hostile arms, nor hostile wiles / Could ever shake thy solid throne, / But for thy sins—thy sins alone."

Cottage Poems (1811), written in a simple and plain style, was aimed at the lower classes: The poems praise the austere life of the poor ("The Happy Cottagers!"), especially when it is strengthened by religious belief. Patrick did not address the grim conditions of factory workers or their protests, which would shortly break out in the LUDDITE riots. Instead, the poet sought to express an ideal—a pure faith that would sustain his readers in their poverty. Thus on the Bible he writes that it is the "Book of Books . . . in which the wisest may learn that they know nothing, and fools be made wise." He exhorts the poor to "shine . . . with a peculiar degree of gospel simplicity . . . wonderfully calculated to disarm prejudice, and to silence, and put infidelity to the blush." These poems are pedestrian and show none of the flair that would mark his daughters' work, although Barker points out that his verses are "no worse than most clerical productions of the time."

The Rural Minstrel: A Miscellany of Descriptive Poems (1813), as the subtitle suggests, is a more concrete picture of country life. Its realism—depictions of poverty and illness—mark a growth in Patrick's literary powers as well his compassion for the poor. He also includes personal verses addressed to his wife: "Maria, let us walk, and breathe, the morning air, / And hear the cuckoo sing,— / And every tuneful bird, that woos the gentle spring. . . . How much enhance is all this bliss to me, / Since it is shared, in mutual joy with thee!" Even this kind of poem, however, closes with a conventional invocation to God for his blessing.

Finally, Patrick's love of nature is evident in this volume. Enthusiasm for the elemental life that he conveyed to his children can be found in given lines: "The finny tribe that glance across the lake, / The timid hare, that rustles through the brake, / The squirrel blithe, that frisks on yonder spray, / The wily fox, that prowls about for prey."

Poetaster, The *See* YOUNG MEN'S MAGAZINE, THE.

Poole, Grace Minor character in *JANE EYRE*. When Jane EYRE hears a "preternatural" laugh at THORN-FIELD, Mrs. FAIRFAX attributes it to Grace, a servant whose behavior is sometimes unruly. In fact, the laugh belongs to Bertha MASON, Mr. ROCHESTER's insane first wife for whom Grace cares.

popish Term meaning "Catholic" and used by PROTESTANTS to emphasize their disapproval of CATHOLICISM, which Protestants believe is too much dominated by the role of the pope.

prince regent In *SHIRLEY*, Caroline HELSTONE is delighted with Jessy YORKE's criticism of the scheming prince regent, George Augustus Frederick, later crowned George IV. The dissolute prince was George III's eldest son, and he caused nothing but trouble for his father. He also intrigued against his father, enlisting the aid of the WHIGS, an automatic mark against him in Caroline's book, because she shares her uncle's TORY politics.

"Prisoner, The" Poem by Emily BRONTË. Composed on October 9, 1845, and given the title "Julian M. and A. G. Rochelle," this lengthy poem was later truncated and given a new concluding verse so that Emily could mask its GONDAL origins when it was published in the 1846 POEMS collection. The original consisted of 38 stanzas about

Rochelle, an orphaned, imprisoned fair-haired girl, and her caretaker and former playmate, a boy named Julian. Rochelle tells Julian that although she is forced to dwell in a dungeon, she is visited nightly by visions that offer "'for short life, eternal liberty.'" The freedom she experiences when her "'outward sense is gone'" and "'inward essence feels'" turns into agony when, with daylight, she begins again to hear and see and "'feel the chain.'" The poem goes on to describe Julian's efforts to save Rochelle, first freeing her from her fetters, then guarding her when she refuses to leave him. The heart of the matter, however, is the distinction Rochelle makes between "outward sense" and "inward vision," a belief shared by Emily, who clearly preferred the world within to that without. The poem thus lost little when Emily cut out the longer story line, publishing this allegory of poetic vision as "The Prisoner: A Fragment."

Professor, The Charlotte BRONTË wrote her first novel based on her experience in BRUSSELS, where along with her sister Emily she attended a Belgian school, the PENSIONNAT HEGER, to improve her French and her general education. She and Emily hoped to establish their own school, which would allow them to support themselves while remaining reclusive. They disliked the idea of leaving home to work as governesses, a form of employment they had tried and found wanting—as sister Anne would make clear in *AGNES GREY*.

In 1842, at age 27, Charlotte began her employment as a pupil-teacher under the direction of Madame Clair Zoe HEGER. Two years later Charlotte returned home grief stricken: She had fallen in love with Madame Heger's husband, Constantin George Romain HEGER, a charismatic professor who had broadened her vision of the world and stirred her imagination. Unlike Frances Evans HENRI, however, the heroine of *The Professor*, Charlotte could not win the love of her teacher, and her novel reflects her effort to cope with a painful obsession.

Charlotte Brontë completed *The Professor* on June 27, 1846, having shown her sisters parts of the novel. They had, in turn, confided in her the knowledge of their compositions. All three sisters exchanged manuscripts and commented on

Brussels, Belgium, the setting of The Professor. *Charlotte based her first novel on her experience at the Pensionnat Heger, where she fell in love with the director's husband, Professor Constantin Heger.* (*Life and Works of Charlotte Brontë and Her Sisters* [1872–73], illustrations by E. M. Wimperis)

each other's work. In *The Professor*, Charlotte sought to jettison the fairy tale elements of her juvenilia—the reliance on coincidence, on providing happy turns of fortune for her characters, and other beneficial developments. She determined, instead, to create a character who would thrive on his own resources. Indeed, she would show a man rising by dint of his own efforts, a strenuous journey that resulted not in tremendous rewards but in modest contentment. Nevertheless, the life of her main character and narrator, William CRIMSWORTH, was not without melodramatic incidents, suggesting Charlotte could not quite relinquish the habits of her youthful writing. Not only did that early style infect *The Professor*, but specific characters and events in the novel hearken back to her juvenilia. By contrast, Anne's novel *Agnes Grey* seems far more successful in portraying the world of work and adulthood. *The Professor*'s best passages draw on Charlotte's experience in Belgium, where her firsthand observation and participation in school life enabled her to give her masculine narrator an authentic voice and command of his subject matter—how a man makes his way in the world.

SYNOPSIS

Chapter 1: Introductory

The novel begins with a letter from William Crimsworth to Charles, an old friend at ETON COLLEGE, explaining what happened to him after he left school. He recounts that he met with his maternal uncles, Lord TYNEDALE and the Hon. John SEACOMBE. The latter proposed that Crimsworth pursue a career in the church and even offered his nephew the gift of a LIVING at Seacombe. As a RECTOR at Seacombe, William could expect to marry one of his cousins, his uncle suggested. William rejected his uncle's suggestions. "I should be a bad husband, under such circumstances, as well as a bad clergyman," William reports to Charles. Startled, both uncles asked William how he expected to proceed, since he had no other family members he could count on to support him. Lord Tynedale asked whether William expected to follow his father's example and become a tradesman. The question was put with such contempt for the idea of TRADE that William, who had no great confidence that he could be a good tradesman, answered that he could not do better than to adopt his father's occupation. William and his uncles parted in "mutual disgust."

William next wrote to his brother Edward CRIMSWORTH, 10 years older and married to a wealthy mill owner's daughter. Through William's letter to Charles the reader learns that the mill had been run by the brothers' father, who had driven the business into bankruptcy and died shortly thereafter. Edward and William's mother was left destitute, as she had severed connections with her aristocratic brothers, Lord Tynedale and Seacombe, when they had condemned her match with a tradesman. Six months after William's birth, his mother died. Edward and William were cared for by their father's family.

Later when John Seacombe decided to run for Parliament, one of William's paternal uncles threatened to raise a public issue of Seacombe's refusal to support his sister's orphaned children. Seacombe responded by funding William's education at Eton. He was separated from his older brother, Edward, now 30, reputed to be fast making a fortune.

Determined to remain his own man, William explained in his letter to his older brother that there had been a breach with their maternal uncles. William asked Edward for a job, and Edward replied that he could come to where Edward lives and works. William arrived in the mill town (which the novel does not name) and in the smoky, industrialized environment found his way to Crimsworth Hall, his brother's residence.

Edward's huge mansion disturbed William, who wondered if his brother would be as indifferent to him as his uncles were. Having been separated for so long from Edward, William did not know what to expect. Edward was brief and abrupt at their first meeting. At dinner, William met Edward's wife, vivacious and vain. He retired on his first night, bringing the reader to the present and the close of his letter to his friend Charles. William wonders what encouragement he will receive and gazes at the portraits of his parents, who seem to evoke a sense of seriousness, gentleness, and kindness.

Chapters 2–6

William wakes up in the industrial landscape of the mill town. The sooty buildings and machinery deprive the land of its romance. He doubts that he is fit for trade, and calls himself a "rebel against circumstances."

At breakfast, Edward resumes his abrupt manner, and William wonders whether he has the strength to stand up for himself. Edward informs him that they will shortly depart for work. In his office Edward examines William's qualifications. When told that William can read and write German and French, Edward gives him a letter to translate. Finding this a useful skill Edward announces that he will employ William as a second clerk to deal with foreign correspondence.

Edward informs William that he can expect no special favors at work, and he will have to find his own place to live. William replies that he would not think of doing otherwise. Edward leaves, handing over William to his first clerk, Timothy STEIGHTON.

Steighton's job is to watch William closely and to detect errors. But William works diligently and arrives at work punctually, giving his brother no cause for complaint. William has no other contact with his brother-employer. He is invited to a dance at Crimsworth Hall, but he is offered no introduction to society and finds himself isolated at this event. He encounters Mr. HUNSDEN, a mill owner and manufacturer who watches William admire the portraits of his parents. The outspoken Hunsden criticizes Edward for paying William shabby wages. Hunsden implies that William is not suited for such employment, then abruptly strides away when he recognizes a group of friends.

Acknowledging Hunsden's judgment and aware of his brother's antipathy, William realizes that he has chosen the wrong profession. He finds his place intolerable but does not know what to do about it. On a country walk he encounters Hunsden, who suggests they have coffee together. Hunsden berates William for living in dismal lodgings and working as a drone for his brother. William asks what he should do instead, and Hunsden replies that it depends on William's motives and his nature. Hunsden finds William's air of aristocratic superiority infuriating. Although Hunsden receives no satisfaction from William, he succeeds in provoking in William a searching inquiry into his own purposes and prospects.

At work the next day William is upset with himself. Although he has performed well, he knows that his brother does not approve of him and is looking for an excuse to dismiss him. Edward appears and commands William to stop work, accusing him of disloyalty and of blackening Edward's reputation in the community. William quits his job on the spot, but his brother, determined to have a confrontation, threatens him with a carriage whip and calls him a liar. Edward mentions that Hunsden has been spreading stories of Edward's ill treatment of William, and although William denies any part in Hunsden's campaign, he does tell Edward that he has been a hard master and a brutal brother. When Edward raises his whip as if to strike, William says that he will seek redress from a magistrate, and Edward desists. As William walks away from his job, he feels as if a great weight has been lifted from him.

Reentering town, William is accosted by Hunsden, who affirms that he has been spreading the story of Edward's cruel treatment. William is not grateful for Hunsden's interference in his affairs. He disabuses Hunsden of the idea that he cannot

seek help from his aristocratic uncles. An incredulous Hunsden asks William if he is through with trade and speculates that William will go into the church after all. He advises William to go to the Continent, where he can put to use his knowledge of German and French. He even offers William a letter of introduction, which William accepts, but then Hunsden is astonished when William refuses to extend a word of thanks. "The lad is a heathen," Hunsden remarks, vowing that they shall meet again one day.

Chapters 7–18
In Belgium, William meets with Mr. BROWN, a friend of Hunsden's. Brown, in turn, refers William to M. PELET, the head of a private school, who is impressed with William's command of French. William is hired to teach English and Latin to male pupils and quickly demonstrates his ability to keep order in the classroom. He asks about a boarded-up window in his school apartment and M. Pelet explains that it looks out on the garden of a girls' school; the view has been obstructed out of propriety. William learns that the girls' school is headed by Mademoiselle Zoraide REUTER.

William's impression of Pelet is initially very favorable. Madame PELET, the schoolmaster's mother, keeps house and introduces William to Madame REUTER, the mother of Mademoiselle Reuter. He agrees to give lessons to the young women students, welcoming the change in his routine and satisfying his curiosity about the garden and the school next door.

Expecting to meet a middle-aged woman, William is somewhat surprised at Mademoiselle Reuter's fresh complexion and youthful appearance. She engages him to teach, although she has some reservations because he is very young and the children's parents might object. William is impressed by her business acumen.

During his first lesson, William is enchanted with this new experience of teaching young women. They take advantage of him—especially three giddy girls, EULALIE, HORTENSE, and CAROLINE. Soon he realizes that he must discipline these three "queens of the school." He reasserts his authority by directing the students to take down his dictation, severely correcting the most troublesome ones. After the lesson, which Mademoiselle Reuter admires, William spends a good deal of time speaking with her, returning to Pelet's school when dinner is already half over.

Pelet asks William about his talk with Mademoiselle Reuter. William agrees with Pelet that Reuter was "sounding out" his character. Pelet jests that William might wish to take her for his wife, and William replies that she is too old for him. She is attractive but her mouth is a "little harsh," William observes. Pelet insists that Mademoiselle Reuter will eventually capture William's heart. Then after more talk of the female pupils, Pelet startles William by suggesting that one of them might be a suitable match for William, especially since they come from wealthy families.

William describes the assortment of pupils in Mademoiselle Reuter's school, which includes French, English, Belgians, Austrians, and Prussians. Many come from the BOURGEOIS class; others are children of the military and of government officials. They dress alike and have similar manners. They are rather self-centered and think nothing of misleading others in order to live comfortably. They engage in a good deal of "backbiting and talebearing." William ascribes much of the lying and their "mentally deprived" state to their Roman Catholicism even while asserting he is no "bigot in matters of theology." He describes how one student, Aurelia KOSLOW, tries to monopolize his attention by giving him provoking, leering, and laughing looks. Another, Adele DRONSART, is suspicious and sullen and shunned by her other classmates. Juanna TRISTA has a "fibrous and bilious" temperament. Louise PATH is the most pleasing student, agreeable and even tempered. SYLVIE (1) is, however, the most intelligent and gentle. In general he notes two types of English student: the "continental," who are the product of adventurers, and the "British English," who are rather austere and say very little. William also mentions the three French teachers: Mademoiselles ZEPHYRINE, PELAGIE, and SUZETTE. Mademoiselle Reuter is the "star" of this group; she is sensible, sagacious, and affable. Her staff obeys her as a superior, although they do not love her.

When Mademoiselle Reuter asks William to accompany her to the garden, he realizes that he is "on the brink" of falling in love with her. But then sometime later he happens to see her in the garden with M. Pelet. Overhearing their conversation, William realizes that the two are courting and that he has been merely part of their sport (they joke about William falling in love with her). William is angry and has trouble sleeping.

William rises the next morning determined to recover his composure. He is cool but correct with M. Pelet, and when he arrives at Mademoiselle Reuter's school, he casually mentions that he saw her in the garden taking a late walk, thus implying that he is aware of her relationship with M. Pelet. She pales but quickly recovers her equilibrium, and William admires her stalwart character. Any shared confidence between them, however, has been destroyed.

Mademoiselle Reuter introduces William to a new pupil, Mademoiselle Henri, who is teaching lace mending to the students but who wishes, as well, to improve her English. At first, William is stern with her, not allowing her to take a lesson when she arrives late for the class. The next day, after dealing with his pupils at Mademoiselle Reuter's, William focuses more clearly on Mademoiselle Henri. She seems older than the other students and more earnest. Although she is disconcerted by his abrupt teaching style, she proves to be an excellent student, if not yet capable of performing her exercises perfectly.

At the next day's lesson William is startled to discover that Mademoiselle Henri can recite in nearly perfect English. He questions her about her background. She replies that she has not had English lessons before and has not had the opportunity to consort with English families. Noting her full name, Frances Evans Henri, William is about to ask her about her own family when Mademoiselle Reuter interrupts to ask Mademoiselle Henri to help her with the other students. Then Mademoiselle Reuter questions William about his new pupil. Will she be able to make progress in English? William assures the persistent schoolmistress that Mademoiselle Henri certainly has at least an average ability to learn and already has an excellent accent. Mademoiselle Reuter urges William to advise Mademoiselle Henri, who has little family and is not yet settled on her plans. A man's advice, Mademoiselle Reuter emphasizes, is likely to be taken more seriously by Mademoiselle

Henri. William is struck by Mademoiselle's Reuter's careful, virtually subservient attitude. The more correct and cold he becomes with her, the more intent she seems to please him and consult him.

In two weeks' time, William concludes that Mademoiselle Henri has at least two good points: She is persistent, and she has a well-developed sense of duty. Frances (the name William now uses for her) "toiled for and with her pupils like a drudge." He is impressed when Frances excels in a lesson that calls upon the students to make up a story based on William's anecdote about Anglo-Saxon peasants. He finds that Frances has an impressive imagination and an ability to evoke the past. His curiosity piqued, he summons Frances to an interview about her story. When he compliments her on her work, she smiles in an almost triumphant fashion, leading William to suppose that she has a mature sense of herself and the world.

This encounter stimulates William to plan other meetings so that he can learn more about his fascinating pupil. Eventually he learns that she is not Belgian: She was born in Geneva to a Swiss father and an English mother. Her parents are dead, and she lives with an aunt. She is 19 years old. Her fervent wish is to live in England, and that is why it so important for her to perfect her English. Then she adds in a burst of confidence in her teacher: "I love to live among Protestants; they are more honest than Catholics; a Romish school is a building with porous walls, a hollow floor, a false ceiling; every room in this house, Monsieur, has eye-holes and ear-holes, and what the house is, the inhabitants are, very treacherous; they all think it is lawful to tell lies; they all call it politeness to profess friendship where they feel hatred." Although he does not say so, this is exactly the kind of duplicity that William himself has experienced with Mademoiselle Reuter and M. Pelet.

William has fallen in love. At his lessons with Frances he bends near her head, placing his hand next to hers. Frances responds to his attention and begins to appear more confident at school. An alarmed Mademoiselle Reuter abruptly dismisses Frances from the school, although she tells William that Frances has left voluntarily and has left no address. William vows to find her.

Chapter 19

William reflects that in novels, human emotions and events tend to be exaggerated: Novels rarely reflect how life goes on, day by day, a steady stream of small events rather than the drama of conflict. In his own case, for example, he notes that he does not despair at Frances's departure. It is a staggering blow, but like most human beings he "mitigates" his regret and pain. William admits that he now regards Frances as his "treasure," but that does not mean he gives way to "resentment, disappointment, and grief." He allows a week to pass and then once again asks Mademoiselle Reuter for Frances's address. Taken aback, Mademoiselle Reuter asks him if he thinks she is lying, but he does not answer her directly and instead simply repeats his request, adding that he wants to know if she will "oblige" him in this matter. When she says she cannot because she does not know the address, William replies: "Very well; I understand you perfectly." He announces that he will resign his position in a month's time. Rather than wait for her reply, he bows and leaves her presence.

That evening William receives a letter from Frances. She explains that she has been to the school to speak with him, but that Mademoiselle Reuter said he was not available. She includes 20 francs in the note to pay him for her lessons and admits that she is "heartbroken to be quite separated from you." She ends by asking, "What claim have I on your sympathy? None: I will then say no more.—Farewell, Monsieur."

The note has no return address, and William can find out little about the manner in which it was delivered. After a month of futile efforts to find Frances, William encounters her by chance in a Protestant cemetery, at the grave of her English mother, Julienne HENRI. Of their reunion William observes: "I hate boldness—that boldness which is the brassy brow and insensate nerves; but I love the courage of the strong heart, the fervour of the generous blood; I loved with passion the light of Frances Evans' clear hazel eye when it did not fear to look straight into mine; I loved the tones with which she uttered the words: 'Mon maitre! mon maitre!'" Her master, indeed, William confesses, "I love the movement with which she confided her hand to my hand; I loved her as she stood there, penniless and parentless."

He learns that Frances's aunt has died. She explains that a week after her aunt's death, Mademoiselle Reuter visited her to say her services would no longer be needed at the school. Since she had taught the students so well, they were not able to get on without her. William follows her home and observes that she has been reading John MILTON's *Paradise Lost,* probably for its religious character, he speculates. Frances relies on her lace mending, although she dreams of a better position and of living in England. William vows to himself that his goal now is to make Frances his wife.

Chapter 20–25

William returns to M. Pelet's school determined to work out a plan for new employment and marriage. He is surprised when M. Pelet arrives drunk and in a foul mood, loudly attacking Mademoiselle Reuter because he mistakenly believes that William has won her heart. William takes some satisfaction in Pelet's suffering and surrender of self-control. He attributes some of Pelet's fury to the natural ferocity of Frenchmen. Nevertheless, Mademoiselle Reuter succeeds in calming Pelet, and it is announced that the couple are to be married.

William renews his determination to leave lest his life turn into a "modern French novel," by which he seems to mean a ménage à trois involving Pelet, Reuter, and himself. To William the very idea is "loathsome" and "depraved." He resolves to leave Pelet's school in a week, even though he has not yet provided a future for him and Frances.

Part of William's problem is resolved when Frances writes to tell him that one of her lace-mending clients, an English lady, Mrs. WHARTON, has recommended her to another woman who runs an English school in Brussels. Frances is hired to teach geography, history, grammar, and composition in French. The good salary will allow Frances to support herself. At nearly the same time, William receives a note that Hunsden is about to make a visit. Although William is still unsure about his future, he has a powerful friend in Victor VANDEN-HUTEN, whose son, a pupil at Pelet's, William saved on an outing from drowning. William pays a call on Monsieur Vandenhuten but is disappointed to discover that he has gone abroad.

Hunsden shows up to cross-examine William about his life and his reasons for leaving Pelet's school. Hunsden is skeptical of William's behavior and of his attachment to Frances. William changes the subject, inquiring about news from home. He learns that his brother Edward has become bankrupt and that Crimsworth Hall has been sold. William's reaction to this news is to worry about the family portraits. Hunsden professes not to know whether they have been sold.

William visits Vandenhuten's residence once again and this time his friend is home. William asks him for help, and Victor refers him to several associates who might be able to offer him employment. The reticent William confesses: "I forgot fastidiousness, conquered reserve, thrust pride from me: I asked, I persevered, I remonstrated, I dunned." In short, he finds a good position as a teacher with a handsome salary at one of the colleges in Brussels.

With his future secure, William proposes to Frances, pointing out that it is no longer necessary for her to work. Although she loves William, Frances firmly explains that she could not think of marrying him if it means she would have to forsake her own work: "How dull my days would be!" She wonders how she would occupy herself while William was away teaching: "I must act in some way, and act with you," she insists. William agrees, remembering that it was her active mind that first attracted her to him.

Before the couple are married and begin their life together, Hunsden visits them. William's gruff benefactor enjoys arguing with Frances and teasing her about her extravagant love of the English. When Frances stands up to Hunsden, William observes that Hunsden likes her all the more: "He liked something strong, whether in man or woman; he liked whatever dared to clear conventional limits."

Two months after Frances's period of mourning for her aunt, William and Frances are married. After a year and a half, Frances proposes that the couple start their own school. Her idea is that in 10 years' time they will have accumulated sufficient capital to retire to England. Summing up their lives together, William observes that while Frances continues to call him her master and to defer to him, she is her own person and capable of vexing, teasing, and piquing him for his "bizarreries anglaises" and his "caprices insulaires." A "wild" and "witty" woman, she is an ardent reader: "BYRON excited her; SCOTT she loved; WORDSWORTH only she puzzled at, wondered over, and hesitated to pronounce an opinion upon."

The couple have a son, Victor, named in honor of Monsieur Vandenhuten. After 10 years of marriage, William reports they are about to embark for England. They plan to send their son to Eton, although Hunsden worries that they are spoiling him and turning him into a "milksop." The novel ends with a family scene: Hunsden is visiting, and young Victor is calling his parents to the table to have tea.

PUBLICATION HISTORY

On July 4, 1846, Charlotte Brontë offered her book, along with Emily's *Wuthering Heights* and Anne's *Agnes Grey,* to Henry COLBURN, a prominent London publisher. But Colburn did not publish Charlotte's novel, and although other publishers showed some interest in it, the novel remained unpublished during her lifetime, in part because no publisher seemed willing to offer acceptable terms of payment. Reader William Smith WILLIAMS at Smith, Elder & Co. acknowledged that *The Professor* had literary power but did not think it would sell. Even after the success of *JANE EYRE,* Charlotte's publisher rejected her proposal to revise *The Professor* for publication. Biographer Juliet BARKER implies that the novel's lack of acceptance had to do with the weak, hardly credible male narrator and that Charlotte achieved publishing success only when she made the narrators of her novels women. With the assistance of Elizabeth GASKELL, Charlotte's biographer, and the consent of Charlotte's husband, Arthur Bell NICHOLLS, the novel was finally published in 1857, with slight revisions. Although no publication figures are available, Barker reports that two-thirds of the first edition were sold out within a month of publication, and a cheap edition was produced in 1860.

Protestant   Term applied to those believers who broke away from the Roman Catholic Church, inspired by reformers such as Martin Luther (1483–1546), who argued that the church had become corrupt and placed too much emphasis on the central place of Rome, dominated by the pope and the priesthood. Protestantism, in turn, emphasized the individual conscience and the direct encounter of the believer with the holy word of the Bible. In *VILLETTE,* Lucy SNOWE is a vehement Protestant who rejects attempts to convert her to CATHOLICISM, which she also calls "Romanism" and describes as "POPISH."

Pryce, Reverend David   This curate proposed to Charlotte Brontë during a brief visit to HAWORTH PARSONAGE. Charlotte, who had met the young Irish clergyman only once, turned him down, writing her friend Ellen NUSSEY, "I've heard of love at first sight, but this beats all."

Pryor, Mrs.   Character in *SHIRLEY.* Mrs. Pryor is Shirley KEELDAR's former governess, who serves her as a companion. When Caroline HELSTONE becomes gravely ill, Mrs. Pryor nurses her and reveals that she is Caroline's long-lost mother. Overjoyed by this unexpected revelation, Caroline recovers her health and when she marries, makes her mother a part of her household.

Quashie   *See* GLASS TOWN.

Quaximina Square   *See* GLASS TOWN.

Rachel   Character in *THE TENANT OF WILDFELL HALL*. As Helen HUNTINGDON's lady's maid at GRASSDALE MANOR, Rachel is in sympathy with her mistress and disapproves of the manner in which Arthur, Lord HUNTINGDON treats his wife. When Helen decides to leave Grassdale, she takes Rachel into her confidence but tells her that she cannot take a servant along because she will not be able to pay her. Rachel declares that she does not need to be paid and leaves with Helen and young Arthur HUNTINGDON when they flee to WILDFELL HALL.

Raphael (1483–1520)   Italian Renaissance painter renowned for his tender portraits of Madonnas. In *SHIRLEY*, Caroline HELSTONE's "delicate beauty" is compared to a Raphael painting.

Rasselas   A long poem by Samuel Johnson (1709–84) about the youngest son of an Asian despot. The poem, published in 1759, dramatizes Rasselas's desire to escape to a freer world. Helen BURNS reads the poem in *JANE EYRE*, probably because it appeals to her belief in a flawed human nature and that individuals can easily secure their happiness. Having the opposite beliefs, the assertive Jane EYRE finds the poem does not excite her interest.

Rawdon   A town near BRADFORD, where Charlotte Brontë worked as governess for the WHITE FAMILY. Rawdon was also the site of the Woodhouse Grove School, where Patrick Brontë and Maria Branwell first met in 1812.

rector   In the CHURCH OF ENGLAND (Anglican Church), the rector is the parish priest who receives the tithes (contributions) of his parishioners.

Reed, Eliza   Minor character in *JANE EYRE*. She is one of Mrs. REED's two daughters. Jane EYRE calls Eliza "headstrong and selfish."

Reed, Georgiana   Minor character in *JANE EYRE*. Noted for her beauty, Georgiana is one of Mrs. REED's two daughters. The "spoiled" Georgiana takes little notice of Jane.

Reed, John   Character in *JANE EYRE*. Mrs. REED's son, he torments Jane EYRE, striking her and constantly getting her into trouble. He leaves her alone, however, after she strikes back and frightens him.

Reed, Mr.   Character mentioned in *JANE EYRE*. He is the deceased husband of Mrs. REED and the brother of Jane EYRE's mother. Mr. Reed promised his sister, disowned by the family for marrying below her station, to take care of Jane. As a punishment, Mrs. Reed sends Jane to a chilly red room where the girl fears she will encounter Mr. Reed's ghost.

Reed, Mrs.   Character in *JANE EYRE*. Upon the death of Jane EYRE's mother, the sister of Mr. REED, Jane is taken into the Reed household. After her husband's death, Mrs. Reed continues to care for Jane but treats her harshly. When Jane rebels, Mrs. Reed sends her away to the LOWOOD school. On her deathbed, Mrs. Reed repents, realizing she has treated Jane unjustly, and tells Jane that an uncle, John EYRE, once searched her out. Yet Mrs. Reed finds it impossible, in the end, not to reject Jane as having a "bad disposition."

Reform Bill of 1832   This act of Parliament extended the vote to almost all male members of the middle class in Britain. Working men and all women were still excluded from the franchise, but leaseholders of even modest properties, such as shopkeepers, were included. The WHIGS supported the bill and thereafter became known as the Liberal Party. Charlotte Brontë, a stout supporter of the duke of WELLINGTON and the TORY Party, opposed the reform act.

Reuter, Madame   Minor character in *THE PROFESSOR*. She is Mademoiselle Zoraide REUTER's mother.

Reuter, Mademoiselle Zoraide   Character in *THE PROFESSOR*. The headmistress of a private school for girls, she hires William CRIMSWORTH to teach her students. At the same time she conspires with M. PELET, Crimsworth's main employer at the nearby boys' school, to stimulate in Crimsworth romantic feelings for her. Although she is older than Crimsworth and somewhat plump, Crimsworth finds her attractive and charming. Then he overhears her plotting with M. Pelet, and his affection for her is destroyed. Afterward he behaves formally toward her, and she loses her power over him. When he falls in love with Frances Evans HENRI, a pupil-teacher in the school, Mademoiselle Reuter ends Henri's employment and refuses to tell Crimsworth where the young woman lives. Crimsworth quits his position at both schools as soon as he is able to find Frances.

Richard   Minor character in *THE TENANT OF WILDFELL HALL*. Richard is Arthur, Lord HUNTINGDON's coachman at GRASSDALE MANOR.

Richardson, Samuel (1689–1761)   Sometimes identified as the first English novelist, Richardson was a printer whose literary career began when he published a series of letters, purportedly written by a young woman, giving advice about how young women should conduct themselves in society. These letters formed the basis of his first epistolary novel, *Pamela* (1740), in which a young servant girl defends her chastity and eventually wins the love of her master, Mr. B, who marries her. Richardson's masterpiece, *Clarissa* (1748), also an epistolary novel, added a tragic dimension to his realistic and vivid psychological portrayal of the self and society: Clarissa wins the love of her pursuer, Lovelace, but is broken and eventually dies from his assault on her mental and physical being. In *AGNES GREY*, Anne Brontë is close in spirit to Richardson, for she creates a heroine whose trials, like Pamela's, are redeemed by her steadfast virtue. The darker, melodramatic side of Richardson is reflected in Emily's and Charlotte's ROMANTIC novels. All three sisters, however, built upon and extended Richardson's exploration of the female psyche.

Rivers, Diana   Character in *JANE EYRE*. Diana and her sister and brother provide Jane EYRE a refuge after she leaves THORNFIELD. Jane is struck by Diana's beauty and sensitivity. Later Jane discovers that she is the Rivers siblings' cousin, since the Reverend Mr. Rivers was the brother of Jane's mother. When Jane inherits 20,000 pounds from her uncle, she shares it equally with Diana, Mary RIVERS, and St. John RIVERS.

Rivers, Mary   Character in *JANE EYRE*. She is the sister of Diana and St. John RIVERS. Like her siblings, Mary welcomes Jane EYRE into her house and is later the recipient of Jane's generosity when Jane inherits her uncle's fortune.

Rivers, St. John   Character in *JANE EYRE*. He invites Jane EYRE into his house after she is turned away by his servant, Hannah. He provides Jane with a refuge, and later he asks her to marry him and join his plan to become a missionary. While she respects his piety and good works, she does not love him and rejects his proposal, in part because she sees that he values her for the work she can perform and not for herself.

Robertson, Reverend Hammond.   A friend of Patrick Brontë's, he was involved in the LUDDITE riots and became a model for Matthewson HELSTONE in *SHIRLEY*.

Robinson, Lydia (Lady Scott)   Mrs. Lydia Robinson was the mistress of THORP GREEN, where Anne had already served as governess to the Robinson children for two years when Branwell was invited to join the household in December 1842 as a tutor for young Edmund Robinson, but he was dismissed after only 18 months in that role. It is likely that he had engaged in an adulterous affair with Lydia Robinson and been dismissed by her husband. It is certain that Branwell was in love with her. Mrs. Robinson went on to become Lady Scott, marrying Sir Edward Scott after her first husband died. Branwell went into decline after his involvement with Lydia Robinson, consumed by heartache and the alcohol, opium, and gambling in which he sought comfort.

Robinson family In *AGNES GREY*, Anne Brontë drew on her experience as a governess from 1840 to 1845 for the family of Reverend Edmund Robinson, a well-to-do clergyman residing at Thorp Green near York. This was by far the best position she could have hoped for, since the Robinson family occupied an estate twice as large as BLAKE HALL, where she had taught the Ingham children in 1839. She had pleasing surroundings, a large agricultural area with parkland. Reverend Robinson was an invalid who rarely performed his clerical duties. He had a lively wife, Lydia ROBINSON, and five children, four of whom were entrusted to Anne's care. The children were rather spoiled but were old enough to be educable. Anne was able to draw on this improvement in her environment and status in describing Agnes GREY's change from Mr. and Mrs. BLOOMFIELD's employ to Mr. and Mrs. MURRAY's household. Like Agnes, Anne did not like the second family much better than the first, and by the end of July 1841 she wrote that she hoped to find a more satisfying position. Like Agnes, however, Anne remained with her second employers for a considerable time, not leaving the Robinsons until June 1845.

Rochemort, M. Minor character in *VILLETTE*. He is one of two examiners invited by Paul EMMANUEL to test Lucy SNOWE's command of French. He is quite hostile and determined to conclude that she is an idiot. During the exam, Lucy realizes that he is one of two men who harassed her as she was trying to find her way to Madame BECK's school.

Rochester, Mr. Edward Fairfax Major character in *JANE EYRE*. The owner of THORNFIELD, he employs Jane EYRE as a governess for his ward, Adèle VARENS. Jane's patient, loving nature wins his admiration and then his love. Although still married to a wife, Bertha MASON, who has become insane and whom he keeps secluded at Thornfield, Rochester attempts to marry Jane. Thwarted at the last minute by one of his wife's relatives, he retreats into brooding isolation, which is overcome only when he is blinded in a fire that destroys Thornfield, kills his wife, and results eventually in his marriage to Jane.

Roe Head   *See* WOOLER, MISS.

Rogue, Alexander Branwell Brontë's Byronic hero (see BYRON, GEORGE GORDON), who appears in the GLASS TOWN saga and in *Letters from an Englishman, The Pirate,* and *Real Life in Verdopolis.* When Branwell had Rogue corrupt Charlotte's hero, the marquis of Douro, she retaliated with *THE GREEN DWARF*, which she placed in Branwell's *THE YOUNG MEN'S MAGAZINE.*

romantic Term applied to works of European and American literature that emphasize intense feelings and conflicts, with heroes who seem divorced from everyday reality and live by their own standards and convictions. Romantic literature emphasizes states of mind rather than accurate depictions of society. The romantic hero is, in other words, a law unto himself and can seem a force of nature, as in the example of HEATHCLIFF, or a man of extreme will determined to shape the world to his desires, as is Mr. ROCHESTER. The term *romantic* derives from romanticism, a literary movement of the late 18th and early 19th centuries that rejected the rationalism of the 18th century and sought to explore the irrational and volatile aspects of human nature.

Romanism   *See* CATHOLICISM.

Rousseau, Jean-Jacques (1712–1778) French philosopher and novelist. He wrote about the foundations of society in *The Social Contract* (1762), arguing that in a state of nature man was innocent and only in society did he become corrupt. His novel, *Emile,* set forth his ideas about education. His autobiography, *Confessions* (1782), is a minutely detailed description of how he experienced the world. His work is part of the foundation of romanticism. Above all, Rousseau was concerned with the shaping of the individual's life. He is one of Shirley KEELDAR's favorite authors in *SHIRLEY*.

Rover Dog in *THE TENANT OF WILDFELL HALL*. Rover is the name young Arthur HUNTINGDON gives his puppy, which is a gift from Gilbert MARKHAM and the offspring of Markham's setter, SANCHO.

Rue d'Isabelle Street where the PENSIONNAT HEGER was located in BRUSSELS.

Rue Royale In BRUSSELS, the street where Charlotte Brontë caught sight of Queen Victoria "flashing through" in 1843.

Rural Minstrel, The: A Miscellany of Descriptive Poems *See* POEMS OF PATRICK BRONTË.

Rydings In Birstall, near Leeds, the home of Ellen NUSSEY and her family. Charlotte drew on the house's thorn bushes, rookery, and oak struck by lightning in her portrait of THORNFIELD in *JANE EYRE*.

Ryecote Farm Place in *THE TENANT OF WILDFELL HALL*. Ryecote is the property of Robert WILSON, one of Gilbert MARKHAM's neighbors in the countryside around LINDENHOPE.

Ste. Gudule A Catholic cathedral in BRUSSELS where, in September 1843, a desperate Charlotte Brontë, tormented by her love for Monsieur HEGER, made her confession to a priest. She would later draw on the incident for *VILLETTE*, when Lucy SNOWE confesses to a priest.

St. George's Chapel Charlotte Brontë attended this Anglican church in BRUSSELS.

St. Paul's Cathedral The famous London church built by the renowned architect Sir Christopher Wren, it is still one of the great features of the London skyline. In *VILLETTE*, Lucy SNOWE includes the cathedral on her tour of London.

St. Pierre, Mademoiselle Minor character in *VILLETTE*. She is one of the teachers at Madame BECK's school. She keeps excellent order in the classroom and organizes the annual fete for Professor Paul EMMANUEL, who she still hopes will marry her.

Samuel The Bible contains two books of Samuel, the first prophet, who presides over the election of Saul, Israel's first king. In *VILLETTE*, Lucy SNOWE enjoys reading about the calling of Samuel to his prophetic office.

Sancho Dog in *THE TENANT OF WILDFELL HALL*. Sancho is Gilbert MARKHAM's black-and-white setter, who helps ease his introduction to Helen HUNTINGDON at WILDFELL HALL.

Sand, George (Amandine-Aurore-Lucile, Baronne Dudevant) (1804–1876) Sand was one of the great novelists of the French ROMANTIC movement, but her flamboyant life, her decision to dress like a man, and her many love affairs brought her as much fame as her writing. In novels such as *Indiana* (1832) and *Lélia* (1833), she attacks the conventions of society and presents bold portraits of women, probably one reason that Charlotte preferred Sand's work to that of the seemingly more conventional Jane AUSTEN when she wrote to critic George Henry LEWES, an Austen advocate.

Sara, Lady Character mentioned in *VILLETTE*. She is one of Ginevra FANSHAWE's chaperons.

Sarah (1) Minor character in *JANE EYRE*. She is a servant who helps take care of Jane EYRE during her illness at GATESHEAD HALL.

Sarah (2) Minor character in *THE TENANT OF WILDFELL HALL*. She is a maid to Rev. MILLWARD and his family at the vicarage in LINDENHOPE.

Saveur, Justine Marie (1) Character mentioned in *VILLETTE*. She is the young woman Paul EMMANUEL fell in love with. When she could not secure her family's approval of her marriage to M. Paul, she retired to a convent, where she died shortly afterward. Devoted to her memory, M. Paul honors her by serving her family, even though they had opposed him as Justine Marie's suitor.

Saveur, Justine Marie (2) Minor character in *VILLETTE*. She is Paul EMMANUEL's goddaughter. Lucy SNOWE mistakenly thinks that M. Paul is in love with Justine Marie, but as he tells Lucy later, he thinks of Justine Marie only as his daughter.

Scarborough England's oldest spa town, situated in North Yorkshire. Anne Brontë loved the area, and Charlotte took her there in an effort to improve her health, but Anne died during her visit and was buried there in St. Mary's churchyard in 1849.

Scatcherd, Miss   Character in *JANE EYRE*. She teaches history and grammar at LOWOOD. Helen BURNS calls Miss Scatcherd "hasty."

Schiller, (Johan Christoph) Friedrich von (1759–1805)   German dramatist, poet, philosopher, and historian. His early plays, such as *Don Carlos* (1787), reflect his intense commitment to human liberty. While continuing to write drama, he later devoted himself to philosophy and poetry as well while teaching as a history professor at the University of Jena, beginning in 1790. In *VILLETTE*, Polly HOME reads Schiller's love ballads with her German teacher, Anna BRAUN.

Scott, Joe   Minor character in *SHIRLEY*. One of Robert MOORE's employees, he helps Moore combat the workers who want to destroy the mill because the new machinery will put them out of work. He has a son named Henry.

Scott, Lady   *See* ROBINSON, LYDIA.

Scott, Sir Walter (1771–1832)   The Scottish-born writer first made his mark as a composer of ballads that emphasized the ROMANTIC pleasures of country life. His work was popular. *The Lay of the Last Minstrel*, his first major poem, appeared in 1805. *Marmion* (1808) and *The Lady of the Lake* (1810) increased his audience. But feeling challenged by other romantic poets, he turned to historical novels, bringing to the genre a love of dialect and regionalisms combined with a dedication to the idea of a united British Isles. Charlotte Brontë was an avid reader of Scott and considered him superior to nearly all the writers of his day. She visited his home in Scotland and other sites of his novels. In her novel *THE PROFESSOR*, William CRIMSWORTH mentions that Frances Evans HENRI loves Scott.

Seacombe, the Hon. John   Minor character in *THE PROFESSOR*. The aristocratic uncle of William CRIMSWORTH, he offers his nephew the LIVING at Seacombe and is alienated when Crimsworth rejects the offer. By refusing his uncle's help, Crimsworth is declaring his independence and his rejection of blue blood values, which hold no gentlemen should engage in commercial enterprises.

Sir Walter Scott. Charlotte Brontë was an avid reader of Scott's poetry and novels, and Francis Henri reads Scott in The Professor. *(Library of Congress)*

"Self-Communion"   Poem by Anne BRONTË. Anne undertook the writing of this lengthy poem in November 1847, around the time she was working on her second novel. Like *THE TENANT OF WILDFELL HALL*, the content of "Self-Communion" is closely related to events in Anne's life. Anne worked on the poem until April 1848, approximately a year before she died, turning it into a kind of spiritual autobiography. Like many of her poetical works, "Self-Communion" takes the form of a dialogue, in this case seemingly an earnest conversation between her earthbound self and her eternal soul that attempts to sum up the poet's own life. Even at a young age, Anne is spurred on by the sense, as Helen HUNTINGDON tells her ill husband in *Wildfell Hall*, that death can come at any time and one must prepare for it today rather than tomorrow:

... Time keeps working still
And moving on for good or ill:
   He will not rest nor stay.
In pain or ease, in smiles or tears,
   He still keeps adding to my years
   And stealing life away.
His footsteps in the ceaseless sound
   Of yonder clock, I seem to hear,
That through this stillness so profound
   Distinctly strikes the vacant ear.

Looking backward, she can see how transitory are the relationships that once seemed to mean most to her. She confesses to having known "speechless raptures" of love—perhaps centered on her father's curate, William WEIGHTMAN—but then adds ruefully that these have been realized "only in my dreams." Her most intense personal involvement, with her sister Emily, was perhaps most disappointing of all:

... there was a jarring bitterness
When jarring discords grew between;
And sometimes it was grief to know
My fondness was but half returned.
But this was nothing to the woe
With which another truth was learned:—
That I must check, or nurse apart
Full many an impulse of the heart

The source of "discord" between Anne and Emily was Anne's faith in God. From this hard lesson Anne learned, as she says, that her goal must be to strive eternally to subdue spiritual foes and vanquish doubt.

Sellars, Jane *See* ALEXANDER, CHRISTINE, AND JANE SELLARS.

sermons of Patrick Brontë Only two of Patrick Brontë's sermons survive in manuscript. Both are typical of the EVANGELICAL obsession with conversion. He counsels his parishioners not to consider the inner meaning of baptism simply as a kind of spiritual therapy. The formalities of the church, its ceremonies and functions, are founded on receiving the Holy Ghost into one's heart. There should be an "inward radical change," he says, a forsaking of worldly desires in favor of "godly zeal." This spiritual renewal also has to be expressed in "outward conduct," the practice of "faith, hope, and charity." Thus Patrick describes baptism as a kind of "victory over the world," an evading of its "snares" and temptations. Compared to his poetry, the sermons seem less routine and conventional and more the product of personal conviction.

In general, Patrick advocates a congruence between faith and action: "Faith and works," he emphasizes, are "inseparable." The believer will show his faith by attending church regularly and conforming to its rites. In his views of baptism, Patrick constantly refers to St. Paul, who is, for Patrick, the very embodiment of the converted man.

Seventy Times Seven, and the First of the Seventy-First. A Pious Discourse delivered by the Reverend Jabes Branderham, in the Chapel of Gimmerden Sough Fictitious book title in *WUTHERING HEIGHTS*. On his second visit to WUTHERING HEIGHTS, Mr. LOCKWOOD is forced to spend the night there. Closeted in a paneled bed that once belonged to Catherine EARNSHAW, he discovers her books, including this one. Falling into a fitful sleep over *Seventy Times Seven*, Lockwood dreams that he is in a chapel where he is forced to listen to an interminable 499-part sermon delivered by Reverend Branderham. Emily BRONTË, a clergyman's daughter, was probably having some fun with memories of extra-long sermons she had been obliged to sit through.

Sheffield A large industrial city in south Yorkshire mentioned in both *JANE EYRE* and *SHIRLEY*.

Shielders Character mentioned in *WUTHERING HEIGHTS*. Shielders, a curate, or assistant minister, is named by Old Mr. LINTON as the source of his information that the orphaned Catherine EARNSHAW is being permitted to grow up a heathen.

Shirley Novel by Charlotte BRONTË. More than any of her other works, this novel, Charlotte's third, addresses the question of a woman's place in society and her entitlement to an education. Similarly, Charlotte's treatment of the downtrodden mill workers and their fears about the new machines replacing them, strikes a note seldom heard in novels that deal intensely with family life and the strivings of individuals. *Shirley* explores a whole class of workers, as well as the conflict between owners/employers and employees.

At the same time, no matter how engaged Charlotte may seem to be with social and political issues, the plot of her novel resolves itself in conventional terms with the marriages of her two heroines. As in all of Charlotte's other fiction, *Shirley* reveals an inordinate admiration of male power and the wish of even the most independent and intelligent women to succumb to it.

Set in Yorkshire, the novel reflects Charlotte's abiding love of the landscape and its people. Biographers have discussed Shirley KEELDAR as an idealized portrait of Emily Brontë. Shirley apparently has some of the same assertiveness that the elusive Emily exhibited, although detailed comparisons between the fictional character and her real-life inspiration are difficult because so little is known about Emily.

A more accomplished work than THE PROFESSOR, especially in Charlotte's ability to create a range of characters, *Shirley* does not have the ROMANTIC intensity of JANE EYRE or the structural sophistication of VILLETTE. Nevertheless, it creates a deeply imagined world and a vivid portrait of England on the verge of the Industrial Revolution.

SYNOPSIS

Chapter 1: Levitical

Set in the north of England during the years 1811–12 and the Napoleonic Wars, the novel presents a satirical portrait of the "abundant shower of curates" this part of the country had experi-

Child laborers (as young as nine years old) worked in the woolen mills described in Shirley, *a novel that explores, among other themes, the conflicts surrounding the working class.* (Life and Works of Charlotte Brontë and Her Sisters [1872–73], illustrations by E. M. Wimperis)

enced in recent years. The narrator describes three clergyman: Joseph DONNE, curate of Whinbury; Peter Augustus MALONE, curate of Briarfield; and David SWEETING, curate of Nunnely. They are visiting John GALE, "a small clothier." The narrator calls them three young "Levites," poking ironic fun at their less than diligent attendance to duties. (Levites are the descendants of the biblical Levi, son of Jacob, and are supposed to be dedicated to the reestablishment of the temple in Jerusalem.) The curates are well tended by their landladies, Mrs. GALE, Mrs. HOGG, and Mrs. WHIPP, and enjoy hearty meals. They have no interest in politics, philosophy, or literature, not even in religion. Instead they dispute "minute points of ecclesiastical discipline." The Irishman Malone is the most aggressive of the group whereas Mr. Donne assumes an air of "self-complacency," and Mr. Sweeting, one of "indifference."

This group's comfortable repast is disturbed by Matthewson HELSTONE, an arrogant-looking man who is informed that the men have had an argument about DISSENTERS. Mr. Helstone notes that the three clergyman have been making as much noise as Moses BARRACLOUGH, the "preaching tailor, and all his hearers . . . in the METHODIST chapel." Mr. Helstone has come to tell the clergymen that Robert MOORE, who owns the local Hollows Mill, has been threatened with violence because he has introduced new machinery, which the workmen suspect will deprive them of employment. There has been talk against Moore by men such as Mike HARTLEY, a weaver who is called an ANTINOMIAN, JACOBIN, and LEVELLER. Only Malone (armed with pistols) agrees to accompany Helstone on the ride back to Moore's mill.

Chapter 2: The Waggons

Helstone and Malone meet Moore at his mill as preparations are made to thwart its attackers. They discuss with Moore the likelihood of violence. The narrator explains that Moore, the descendent of Belgian and English businessmen and traders, has been hard hit by Britain's ORDERS IN COUNCIL, which stipulate that neutral powers cannot trade with France—a decree that has outraged the United States. Consequently, Americans no longer purchase cloth from Yorkshire, and mills like Moore's face financial ruin. Moore's plight is complicated by the fact that his workers regard him as a "semi-foreigner" and despise his progressive views.

Joe SCOTT then reports that Moore's new frames and shears have been wrecked by the workers. Scott also delivers a message from the workers, who threaten to destroy any new machinery Moore attempts to introduce into the manufacturing process.

Chapters 3–4: Mr. Yorke, Mr. Yorke (continued)

The narrator describes the differences between Helstone and Moore, the former a high TORY and the latter a WHIG. Although both men have vigorous and even militant natures, they disagree on politics. Moore champions the invincibility of Napoléon BONAPARTE and likens him to a Moses who will liberate the captive peoples of Europe suffering under autocratic regimes. Helstone argues that aristocratic, imperial France was certainly no worse than "bloody republican France."

This argument is interrupted by Mr. Hiram YORKE, who has brought with him Joe Scott. Mr. Yorke found him groaning and tied up after an assault by the workers who have broken Moore's new frames. Moore and Helstone accompany Yorke and Scott to Yorke's home. Next the narrator describes Yorke as a rather narrow-minded man with a limited imagination, although he is honest and respected by his neighbors. Yorke likes Moore because of his "anti-Yorkshire outlook" and his Belgian-accented English, both of which remind Yorke of his traveling days on the Continent. Yorke has also done business with Moore's father and realizes that the son is a "sharp man of business." By temperament and politics, then, Yorke feels more akin to Moore than to the conservative Helstone.

Helstone and Yorke loved the same woman, Mary Cave, who chose the former because of his position in the community. Her decision resulted in her attachment to an unresponsive husband, and it is rumored that she died of a broken heart. A passionate man, Yorke cannot forgive Helstone for marrying Mary and then not cherishing her, although Helstone is unaware of his rival's feelings.

Like Moore, Yorke attacks the Tory administration, singling out William PITT, Robert Stewart CASTLEREAGH, and Spencer PERCEVAL and decrying a "king-ridden, priest-ridden, and peer-ridden" land. Moore cuts short this attack and Helstone's reply by observing he has to do something about his broken frames. In surprisingly good spirits, he announces his departure, for he "dare not stay a night with a rebel and blasphemer like you, Yorke; and I hardly dare ride home with a cruel and tyrannical ecclesiastic, like Mr. Helstone."

Chapter 5: Hollow's Cottage

Joe Scott and Robert Moore spend a night at Moore's mill and the next morning talk about the rough manners of the region. Moore expresses his appreciation for plain speaking and forthrightness. His sister, Hortense MOORE, serves him breakfast. She is proud of both her brothers, Robert and Louis MOORE, although the latter seems the quieter and less ambitious sibling.

Conversation over breakfast focuses on Robert's unpopularity as a mill owner. Caroline HELSTONE, who lives with her uncle, visits and notes that one mill owner, Mr. PEARSON, has already been shot at. She expresses her desire to have an occupation and frets that she cannot make her own way in life. Moore breaks off their talk, announcing that he must visit the Sykes wool warehouse.

Chapter 6: Coriolanus

Caroline Helstone's background is explained. She is the daughter of parents who separated shortly after her birth "in consequence of disagreement of disposition." Caroline's mother was the half sister of Robert Moore's mother, so Caroline is a distant cousin of Robert, Louis, and Hortense. Her father was Mr. Helstone's brother, James HELSTONE. Caroline has been brought up by Mr. Helstone, who has told her very little about her parents. Her mother is apparently alive but has not been heard from for several years. Caroline finds her true home among the Moores; indeed, she has fallen in love with Robert and tells him, "You were made to be great." He rejects her compliment, saying he does not regard himself as any better than other men, and he seems unaware of her attraction to him, although he treats her tenderly.

Caroline studies with Hortense, who urges her to read Shakespeare's play *Coriolanus* to discover "how low and how high you are." But the real point of reading the play is to demonstrate how like CORIOLANUS Robert is. Mr. Helstone himself has pointed out that Robert is proud, determined, scornful of his enemies, and contemptuous of the "mob"—exactly the attributes of Coriolanus, as Caroline observes. Caroline cautions Moore not to include all working people under the catchall term of *mob*, and he calls her a "little democrat."

Chapter 7: The Curates at Tea

The narrator notes that at 18 Caroline is just entering the "school of Experience." She returns home and her uncle, after a perfunctory inquiry about her time at the Moores', bids her go to bed.

At breakfast, Caroline attempts to draw out her uncle on the subject of her parents and why they separated, but he calls her questions "stupid and babyish" and refuses to say much. Caroline is troubled by stories that her father was not a good man and treated her mother badly.

When the three curates, Malone, Donne, and Sweeting, call for tea, Caroline reflects on how little they interest her even though they are educated men like Robert Moore. She is spared their company when she is visited by Mrs. SYKES and her three daughters. The mother is described as tall and "bilious." Her daughter Mary SYKES is good looking, sincere, and complacent. Harriet SYKES is the beauty, if also rather cold and arrogant. Hannah SYKES is "dashing," but also "conceited" and "pushing." Caroline cares little for these women or the visit but is polite, listening to their conversation about attending a religious service on Sunday (Caroline stayed home reading a novel Robert had given her).

Dinner is announced and Caroline is again in the company of the three curates. Mr. Helstone is charmed by the Sykes sisters because he likes women who have little sense; he sees them as "toys" to play with. Hannah is his favorite. She is lively but without Harriet's egotism. Mr. Sweeting, on the other hand, likes all the Sykes sisters and hopes to marry one of them. Caroline plays the piano, then Harriet. Mr. Sweeting next produces his flute. Malone, not to be outdone, tries to impress Caroline with his attentions but succeeds only in occupying several sofa cushions at once as he tries to dominate the company. The whole affair seems to depress Caroline.

Caroline perks up when Robert Moore visits. He has come to tell Helstone that he believes he has found out who damaged his frames. Caroline tries to dissuade Moore from prosecuting the culprits, fearing that he will only become more unpopular and excite revenge. But Moore is intent on protecting his property and punishing those who threaten it. Caroline tells him she understands his position and that it won't do to be "romantic," but she still fears for his safety. He kisses her goodnight.

Chapter 8: Noah and Moses

SUGDEN shows up at Robert Moore's mill with a warrant to arrest Moses Barraclough, one of the instigators of the attack on Moore's equipment. Christopher SYKES, a mill owner, arrives but appears diffident and unwilling to support Moore in his prosecution of Barraclough. Moore points out that another mill owner, Pearson, tried to win his men with concessions and was shot at anyway. When Barraclough confronts Moore and argues for the dignity of hand labor, Moore responds that new methods of manufacturing are inevitable and will come even if his mill is destroyed. One of Barraclough's associates, William FARREN, remarks that "invention may be all right, but I know it isn't right for poor folks to starve." An exasperated Moore observes he is hardly the only clothier in Yorkshire and cannot bear responsibility for the plight of workmen. Farren points out that Moore is responsible for himself. Moore insists that he cannot solve the economic problems that have threatened the livelihood of workmen. Moore's seeming harshness, however, belies the favorable impression Farren makes upon him. Not realizing that he has moved Moore, Farren despairs that he will be able to find work and support his family.

Chapter 9: Briarmains

The scene shifts to BRIARMAINS, the home of Mr. Yorke and Mrs. YORKE, a "strong-minded woman" skeptical of human nature and a brooder over human failings. The couple have two daughters, Rose and Jessy YORKE. The former is deemed "stubborn" and like her mother; the latter is her father's pet, with her "engaging prattle" and "winning ways." The girls have three brothers: Matthew YORKE, the eldest, a high-handed lad that the other brothers do their best to avoid; Mark YORKE, "a bonnie-looking boy" who is calm and shrewd;

and Martin YORKE, the plainest of the three but with a keen intelligence that may make him the most remarkable.

Moore discusses with Mr. Yorke his lack of capital for his business. Yorke suggests Moore can remedy his problem by finding a wife who will have the funds to invest in his enterprise. Moore expresses his ambivalence about marriage. It would depend, he concludes, on the circumstances that would lead him to take an interest in a particular woman.

Chapters 10–13: Old Maids, Fieldhead, Shirley and Caroline, Further Communications on Business

Moore and Helstone quarrel at a public meeting about politics. Helstone calls Moore a Jacobin and enjoins his niece Caroline no longer to frequent Moore's household, where she has been learning French from Hortense. Caroline is devastated but obeys her uncle. She grows pale and loses some of her attractiveness.

Caroline occupies her time with visits to local acquaintances such as Miss MANN, a rather formidable old maid who subjects her visitor to a detailed recounting of her unimpeachable life. She also visits Miss AINLEY, who is lively and sensible but not much more. Caroline agrees to help her with her charity work.

Caroline is largely isolated and struggling with her feelings alone. Her only hope is to escape somehow from her dull home life. Her goal is to become a governess, and she considers how she can bring up the subject with her uncle. Meanwhile, out on a walk, she observes Robert Moore and Mr. Yorke walking near Fieldhead, a small mansion that Mr. Yorke owns. The very sight of Robert arouses Caroline, and she yearns for contact with him. She resolves to confront her uncle, who proves uncooperative. He sees no need for his niece to go out into the world, since he plans to provide for her. Consequently, Caroline's health continues to deteriorate, and women attribute her condition to having been "disappointed" in love, although they do not know the object of her affections.

The other topic of conversation is Miss Shirley Keeldar, who has just arrived in the neighborhood. She is a young woman who owns considerable property in the area. Caroline and her uncle call on Miss Keeldar at FIELDHEAD. Shirley greets them, thanking Mr. Helstone for coming to see her even though Mr. Yorke has turned her into a Jacobin. Mr. Helstone assures her that he will disabuse her of such opinions. The Helstones also meet Mrs. PRYOR, Shirley's former governess and now companion.

Shirley is very attractive, outspoken, and intelligent. She seeks out Caroline's company and suspects that Caroline needs someone to take care of her. The two women discuss men and how they treat women in their everyday lives. Shirley expresses a horror of giving up her independence, and Caroline wonders if they should remain single since her uncle speaks of marriage as such a "burden." But not all men are like Caroline's uncle, Shirley asserts. Even so, Shirley longs to find her superior in a man, a man worthy of her subordination to him.

Shirley discusses such writers as William COWPER and Jean-Jacques ROUSSEAU, who desperately sought but never really found their loves. Caroline believes these men were not made to be loved by women. Shirley asks how Caroline knows this—had she discussed such subjects with Robert Moore? Caroline says no: "The voice we hear in solitude told me all I know on these subjects."

Shirley asks Caroline if she wishes she had a trade or profession. Certainly, Caroline answers. But then what if such work made women less feminine? Shirley wonders. That does not matter, Caroline counters. It is only important that a woman be neat and decent.

Shirley and Caroline become fast friends. The next day Caroline asks Shirley why she is crying. Shirley alludes to someone she loves but will not say more. Caroline infers that Shirley's love is Robert Moore, for he has benefited from Shirley's generosity (she has provided the capital that has allowed Moore to stay in business after his new frames were destroyed), and Caroline has seen him walking at night with Shirley the way he used to walk with her. Caroline resolves to give him up for Shirley's sake.

Still searching for some way to live at least a semi-independent life, Caroline solicits Mrs. Pryor's aid. The former governess, however, tries to dissuade Caroline because governesses lead a rather "desolate" life.

Robert Moore visits Shirley while Caroline is there, and he falls into conversation with his cousin.

He walks Caroline home, observing that he has two natures, one for business and one for home (and presumably a family). Although he does not wish to leave her company—even when she tells him her uncle is coming and will be angry to see them together—Caroline still presumes it is Shirley he loves.

Chapters 14–15: Shirley Seeks to be Saved by Works, Mr. Donne's Exodus

Shirley expresses irritation that Caroline's affection for Robert is interfering with their friendship. Caroline protests, but Shirley is certain that Robert's presence makes her own seem superfluous. A troubled Shirley also vows to set out on a program of good works to somehow absolve her landowner conscience. She has heard that there are starving families in the area, and she wants to help them. She provides Miss Ainley with 300 pounds to carry out a charitable program.

Meanwhile Caroline attracts the attention of Cyril HALL, a bald middle-aged man who does not interest her much but who is preferable to the three curates. But he does not seem to be looking for a wife since he is devoted to his sister, Margaret HALL.

Shirley notices how intently Caroline watches Robert, and how Robert just as intently observes Caroline. Yet Caroline seems unaware of the implications of Shirley's statement. Meanwhile the narrator comments that Mr. Donne ("a frontless, arrogant, decorous slip of the commonplace") has the nerve to court an unresponsive Shirley. To Mr. Hall's remarks on Caroline's eventual marriage, she replies that she intends to "live single" like his sister, Margaret.

Chapters 16–17: Whitsuntide, The School-Feast

Robert Moore expresses his gratitude for being "rescued" financially by Shirley. Although he does not condone the violence that interfered with his work, he also realizes that the workers are responding to genuine grievances—even if, as a mill owner, he feels it is beyond his power to provide them with relief. Although suffering under her uncle's injunction not to fraternize with Robert Moore and his sister, Caroline is consoled by Shirley's lively and sympathetic company. Caroline also finds comfort in meetings with Cyril and Margaret Hall. They gather together at WHITSUNTIDE for the annual procession of the local school, with its three classes of 400 each and their bands a "day of happiness for rich and poor," the narrator comments.

The school feast is interrupted by the approach of a group of dissenters, "Baptists, Independents, and Wesleyans, joined in an unholy alliance." Shirley declares that they must be taught a lesson for their "bad manners." Mr. Helstone takes the lead in marching on the nonconformists, and this show of strength is enough to disperse them. When Robert appears, Caroline is struck by the "painful brightness" of his presence. She is impressed by how confident he looks beside Shirley, despite the problems at the mill. Caroline also sees Hortense, who is rather cool because she does not understand why Caroline has obeyed her uncle so slavishly.

While Caroline is observing the Moores, Shirley is observing Caroline. She tells her friend that she may not be as beautiful as Harriet Sykes, but Caroline has a more reflective and more "interesting" look, to which Caroline says that Shirley is merely flattering her. Both look on as Moore approaches Helstone. Evidently the two have reconciled and become part of a "war council" dedicated to thwarting attacks on the mill owners and operators. These men—along with Malone, the one curate deemed strong enough to be of help—seem to be preparing for some great event.

Chapter 18: Which the Genteel Reader is Recommended to Skip, Low Persons Being Here Introduced
Shirley discusses John MILTON's creation of Eve in *Paradise Lost*. In Shirley's opinion, he saw Eve as a servant, someone like Shirley's cook, Mrs. GILL. Shirley believes Eve must have been a "woman-Titan," not the subservient character of Milton's epic. To Caroline, on the other hand, Eve represents a "gentle human form—the form she ascribed to her own mother; unknown, unloved, but not unlonged for."

The two women then encounter William Farren, the man Robert Moore had argued with about the use of machinery in the mills. Shirley likes his good sense and humor, none of which he has revealed in Moore's presence. Shirley teases William about being proud. He responds, "Ay, I *am* proud, and so are *ye*," but he suggests

that their pride is "Yorkshire clean." He argues with Caroline about Moore. Caroline takes offense at his claim that Moore has a "cold, unfeeling heart." She counters that if Moore were put out of business, it would only mean that men like William would have even less work. He agrees but says the men are desperate and have to assert themselves.

William's companion, Joe Scott, engages Shirley in an argument about women and politics. He would sooner be an old woman than a Tory, he declares, for the Tories carry on wars that ruin trade. He does not think women should be concerned with politics. Shirley asks him whether he really believes that "all the wisdom in the world is lodged in male skulls." Joe answers by referring to St. Paul's view of women as inferior. Caroline tries to mediate by suggesting that St. Paul shaped his words for the particular audience he was addressing and some of his words may have been mistranslated. Joe does not think such an answer will "wash."

Chapters 19–20: A Summer Night, To-morrow
Shirley and Caroline observe Helstone and Moore preparing for an attack on the mill. Caroline wants to join Moore, but Shirley tells her she can do nothing to help him. "Don't be sentimental; Robert is not so," Shirley adds. Caroline fears that her cousin will be outnumbered, but Shirley is certain he has armed himself with plenty of help. Indeed, the narrator reports "he was prepared for [the attack] at every point." Nevertheless, Caroline, in an agony of frustration, asks, "Am I always to be curbed and kept down?" Shirley, Caroline asserts, does not know "what I have in my heart."

Shirley comments that men think they can conceal danger from women as if they were children. To them a good woman is "half doll, half angel," and they would be amazed to discover what a real woman is like. Women understand men much better than men understand women, Shirley concludes. When Moore visits, he tells Shirley that she has sent over too much food for the men involved in the fight over the mill, and they have a conversation about Caroline, whom, Shirley suggests, Moore does not understand as well as he thinks he does.

Chapter 21: Mrs. Pryor

Mr. Helstone visits Shirley and tells her that Robert Moore has won his admiration for the cool way he has dealt with his opposition. As Helstone leaves, he predicts that the "tide will turn" and Moore will eventually become a popular figure. Mr. Yorke, who is also visiting Shirley, asks her when she will marry Moore. She neither confirms nor denies that she intends to marry, but she asks Yorke whether he will give her away.

Mrs. Pryor and Caroline have a long conversation. Caroline reveals that she longs for love, although she does not confide that Moore is her beloved. Mrs. Pryor wants to make sure that Caroline has not been influenced by romances, which show only the "green tempting surface of the marsh." Caroline assures her that she does not do such reading, although she insists that there are happy marriages.

Chapter 22: Two Lives

Moore now concentrates on prosecuting the men who conspired to attack his mill. This local violence is paralleled by the war taking place on the Continent. Shirley and Caroline see less of each other because of the visit of Shirley's relatives, her aunt and uncle Mr. and Mrs. SYMPSON and two female cousins. Caroline goes off to visit Miss Ainley, who observes that "single women should have more to do—better chances of interesting and profitable occupation than they possess now." The chapter ends with a plea by the narrator to the men of England not to make of their daughters' lives a "desert."

Chapter 23: An Evening Out

Caroline walks toward Hollow's Cottage, not intending to meet Robert but simply to relieve the "nightmare of her life." She visits Hortense and encounters a disagreeable Mrs. Yorke. Jessy, one of Mrs. Yorke's daughters, admits that her mother is treating Caroline badly and that her sister, Rose, is ignoring Caroline. Mrs. Yorke criticizes Caroline for being morbid and delicate and for treating life like a romance. Caroline objects. There is also an argument about politics and war. Caroline objects to Jessy's tirade against the duke of WELLINGTON but is delighted in another tirade against the PRINCE REGENT.

Robert Moore appears with his brother, Louis MOORE, a "grave, still, retiring man." Caroline does not consider Louis as handsome as Robert, but she is impressed with his sensible presence.

Chapters 24–25: The Valley of the Shadow of Death, The West Wind Blows

Caroline succumbs to her despair over her love for Robert Moore. "I have no object in life," she says. As she weakens, Mrs. Pryor comes to nurse her and also reveals that she is Caroline's mother. This reunion with her longed-for mother inspires Caroline, and she makes a slow but steady recovery. Mrs. Pryor is as happy as her daughter, explaining how it was that they were separated all these years. She had feared that, like her father, Caroline's handsome form concealed a warped mind and spirit, and her mother could not bear to nurture such a creature.

William Farren comes often to wheel Caroline around on walks, and Caroline refuses to credit her mother's notion that she should not consort with a man of the laboring class. Caroline and William share a rapport, and she sees more of his true character than he wishes to reveal to those he realizes do not respect him.

Chapter 26: Old Copy-Books

Caroline, with Mrs. Pryor's permission, reveals to Shirley that her ex-governess is in fact Caroline's mother. To Charlotte's surprise, Shirley has already guessed as much. When pressed about how she could have formed such a conclusion, Shirley answers that all she had to do was observe the rapport between Mrs. Pryor and Caroline and their likenesses.

Caroline visits Shirley's relatives, the Sympsons, and discovers that Louis Moore was once Shirley's tutor. She questions young Henry SYMPSON about Shirley, who tells Caroline that she was a "wild, laughing thing" but also a quick study. Caroline is amazed that Shirley seems to treat Louis Moore with indifference, especially after Henry Sympson discovers that Moore has kept Shirley's old copy books of the lessons he gave her in French. Caroline is impressed with Louis, yet she cannot get Shirley to say a good word for him; indeed, Shirley's lack of interest in the tutor is so pronounced that it invites speculation and a sense of mystery that intrigues Caroline.

Chapter 27: The First Blue-Stocking

Shirley outrages her uncle, Mr. Sympson, by refusing to marry Samuel Fawthorpe WYNNE, a member of the local gentry whom Mr. Sympson considers a worthy husband. She announces that she will only marry whom she esteems, admires, and loves. Mr. Sympson calls Shirley's attitude "unladylike." Another suitor, Sir Philip NUNNELY, is fond of quoting his own bad poetry, and Shirley rejects his suit as well, although she finds Sir Philip a kind and sometimes comforting companion.

Although Shirley has shown indifference toward her former tutor Louis Moore, she tries to engage this aloof figure in conversation and clearly desires something from him. But the nature of their relationship and their attitudes toward each other remain a mystery.

Chapters 28–29: Phoebe, Louis Moore

In private, Shirley gives vent to her troubled feelings, even calling herself a fool and coward, although her reasons are not clear. Meanwhile Henry Sympson tells Louis that Shirley's will leaves her property to Henry and bequeaths money to Henry's sisters and to Caroline. She also leaves another sum, she has confessed to Henry, to a "good man, who would make the best use of it that any human being could do." Henry is afraid that Shirley will die. In private, Louis reveals his disturbed state of mind. He thinks of himself as more than Shirley's former tutor. His comparison of Caroline and Shirley leaves no doubt that he prefers the latter, even if he concedes that Caroline has a delicate beauty a RAPHAEL could have painted.

Phoebe, one of Samuel Wynne's dogs, runs away from home and snatches at Shirley's arm when she tries to pet it. The animal draws blood, and Shirley worries that she has been infected with rabies. It is an anxiety she conceals from others, and it is the reason why she had made her will. (When she later confesses her dread to Louis, he assures her that she has nothing to worry; the animal was surely not rabid.)

Chapter 30: Rushedge, a Confessional

Many people wonder why Robert Moore has stayed away from Fieldhead and its environs, especially since Shirley has been so helpful in supporting his business. Moore reveals the reason to Hiram Yorke. Although Robert does not love Shirley, he feels grateful to her and was influenced by others who said he should marry and ensure his financial security. Robert tells Yorke that he is ashamed to confess he proposed to Shirley even though he did not love her. She saw through his half-hearted, mercenary proposal and rejected him. "I stood to be scorned," Robert admits to Yorke, although Robert did believe that Shirley was in love with him.

He confesses that there are more important things in life than self-interest and that a man can only respect himself if he is concerned with justice for others. Just after this realization Moore is shot by someone avenging his prosecution of the LUDDITES.

Chapter 31: Uncle and Niece

Shirley visits Sir Philip Nunnely and receives a cold reception from his parents. When her uncle learns that Sir Philip has left without announcement of an engagement, he questions Shirley, who replies, "Bon voyage!" To her outraged uncle, she boldly says that although Sir Philip is a pleasant person, she does not love him and respect him as a wife should. Certainly she could not obey such a man. When he badgers her further, she tells him that she rejects his narrow principles and she denies that he has any authority over her.

Then Louis Moore announces that his brother has been shot. He tells Shirley that he is going to Briarmains, where Robert is being nursed by the Yorkes. There is a tender moment when Louis takes Shirley's hand. On his way to his brother he reflects that her touch "thrilled like lightning." Now that he has "possessed" her hand he vows that their fingers "must meet again."

Chapters 32–34: The Schoolboy and the Wood Nymph, Martin's Tactics, Case of Domestic Persecution— Remarkable Instance of Pious Perseverance in the Discharge of Religious Duties

Caroline worries over Robert Moore's recovery from the gunshot wound, but she cannot visit him because of her falling out with Mrs. Yorke, who has forbidden Caroline to enter the house. Walking on the Yorke property, however, Caroline encounters Martin Yorke, and persuades him to arrange a meeting between her and Robert. The clever boy is attracted to Caroline's beauty, and he works out a plot that lures Mrs. HORSFALL out of Robert's room during a hour when no one else will observe Caroline's visit. Reunited with her cousin, Caroline learns that he has missed her as much as she has longed to see him; indeed, he has wondered why she has not come, since he does not know that it has been forbidden.

Caroline tries to arrange a second meeting with Moore through Martin, but he proves somewhat more recalcitrant now that he has become smitten with Caroline and desirous of her company. She prevails on him, emphasizing how much Robert wants to see her, and Martin grudgingly agrees to help her again.

Chapter 35: *Wherin Matters Make Some Progress, but Not Much*

After his second meeting with Caroline, Robert decides he is fit enough to return home, where he is nursed by his sister, Hortense. Caroline visits, and Hortense is delighted to see that she has recovered her health. Robert too notices the transformation and asks her about it. She says that she is happy now that she has found her mother and that Robert is regaining his strength.

Worried that Caroline has too high an opinion of him, Robert is determined to confess that he has not always acted from the highest motives. She says she could not bear to "think ill" of him, But he replies that he cannot bear that she gives him credit for more than he deserves. Caroline adds that she already "half" knows what he would confess, for Shirley told Caroline that Robert had shocked her, although she did give any details. Caroline observes that Shirley has injured Robert's high opinion of himself. On the point of proposing to Caroline, he is interrupted by Cyril Hall.

Chapter 36: *Written in the Schoolroom*

Louis writes in his journal about his love for Shirley. He has never wanted to presume that he had a right to court her, But now that he is determined to leave Mr. Sympson's employ, he will hazard a scene between them that will establish how she truly feels about him. Shirley enters his schoolroom and comments on how self-contained both he and his brother are. In response, Louis announces that he stands before Shirley for the first time as *"myself"*—not, in other words, in the subservient role of tutor or family servant. He demands to know, "Am I to die without you, or am I to live for you?" She responds, "Die without me if you will. Live for me if you dare."

When Mr. Sympson enters the schoolroom, Shirley reveals that Louis will be her husband. Mr. Sympson utters words that Louis will not repeat because they would pollute his journal, then Mr. Sympson leaves "as if shot from a cannon."

Chapter 37: *The Winding-Up*

Mr. Sweeting marries Dora SYKES, the fourth daughter of Mrs. Sykes. Mr. Donne also marries, although his wife's name is not divulged. Malone simply vanishes, and the narrator does not explain his departure. Robert Moore learns that his attacker was Michael Hartley, a "half-crazed weaver" and "mad leveller in politics" who died afterward from "delirium tremens." Moore gives Hartley's widow a guinea to bury him.

The novel ends in June 1812, with Napoléon Bonaparte once again campaigning across Europe. With the orders in council repealed, Robert Moore and other mill owners profit anew from trade abroad. Robert now feels he can marry, and Caroline accepts his proposal. Her mother comes to live with them. Louis Moore marries Shirley and becomes a master of his land as well as a source of wise council and authority to his neighbors. With the story complete, the narrator bids the reader "God speed him in the quest!"

PUBLICATION HISTORY

The novel was published on October 26, 1846, under the pseudonym Currer Bell. Reviewers found the male characters unconvincing and speculated that the author was a woman, for the book revealed the "anatomy of the female heart." The novelist's handling of strong human emotions seemed vulgar to some reviewers and coarse to others. Even so, Charlotte received high marks for her vivid style and grasp of Yorkshire manners. In general reviewers found the book better written than its predecessor, *Jane Eyre,* although *Shirley* lacked the former's passion and originality.

Speculation increased about the true identity of Currer Bell, and Charlotte soon lost her anonymity. If *Shirley* did not mark an advance in her literary achievement, it enhanced the reading public's

A woolen mill of the type described in Shirley. *Charlotte Brontë's novel is a tribute to her love of the landscape and people of Yorkshire, where the story is set.* (Life and Works of Charlotte Brontë and Her Sisters [1872–1873], illustrations by E. M. Wimperis)

interest in the author and her growing body of work. A modest success when it first appeared, *Shirley* sold an impressive 20,000 copies in 1857 after the appearance of Elizabeth GASKELL's biography, THE LIFE OF CHARLOTTE BRONTË.

Shorter, Clement   Clement Shorter advanced scholarship on the Brontës and stirred public fascination with the family when he published a new collection of letters, *Charlotte Brontë and Her Circle* (1896). His entry for Charlotte in the

Encyclopaedia Britannica emphasized the drama of her life, as related by Elizabeth GASKELL. Like Gaskell, however, he tended to take a defensive position—denying Charlotte's infatuation with Constantin George Romain HEGER, for example—that obscured a full understanding of both the author and her work.

Sidgwick, Mrs. Charlotte Brontë worked as a governess in the Sidgwick household of Stonegappe, Lothersdale, near Skipton in 1839. She did not get along with Mrs. Sidgwick and had difficulty with the two unruly children in her charge.

Signs of the Times, The Pamphlet written by Patrick Brontë in 1835 defending the established church of England and Ireland. He also acknowledged the need for reform and argued in favor of tolerating other religions. DISSENTERS, he argued, should find their own sources of funding for schools and churches. He stoutly defended freedom of speech, for without it freedom itself could not prosper. Although Patrick was a conservative, it is clear that he did not oppose all forms of change.

Silas, Pere Character in *VILLETTE*. Lucy SNOWE confesses to this Roman Catholic priest when she is distraught over her unrequited love for Dr. John Graham BRETTON. Later she learns that Pere Silas is the spiritual guide of Paul EMMANUEL, whom Lucy grows to love after her hopes for Dr. John vanish. The kindly Pere Silas tries to convert Lucy to CATHOLICISM, but she staunchly remains a PROTESTANT. Eventually she earns the respect and love of both Pere Silas and Paul Emmanuel.

"Sir Henry Tunstall" Poem by Branwell BRONTË. This long (512-line) narrative poem was one of Branwell's more ambitious efforts. Bearing the alternative title "The Wanderer," the poem was begun in summer 1838, while Branwell was living in BRADFORD making a vain attempt to earn his living as a portrait painter. He completed his first version of the poem in 1840, then revised it two years later, when he apparently attempted to publish "Sir Henry Tunstall" in *BLACKWOOD'S MAGAZINE*. In a draft of a letter to the editor, Branwell wrote: "This piece endeavors, I fear feebly enough, to describe the harsh contrast between the mind changed by long absence from home, and the feelings kept flourishing in the hearts of those who have never wandered, and who vainly expect to find the heart returning as fresh as when they had bidden it farewell." Branwell signed one of the surviving versions of "Sir Henry Tunstall" with the name of his fictitious (ANGRIA) alter ego, Northangerland, but plainly he saw some resemblance between his poetic protagonist and himself. Branwell's adventures were not half so grand, but they were dramatic and certainly served to alienate him from his family.

Skulker Dog in *WUTHERING HEIGHTS*. Skulker is the bulldog who seizes hold of Catherine EARNSHAW's ankle during her and HEATHCLIFF's youthful trespass on the grounds of THRUSHCROSS GRANGE. The injury obliges Cathy to spend five weeks recuperating at the Grange, where she is introduced to a world of refinement she never before knew existed—and to Edgar LINTON.

Smith, George Head of the publishing firm Smith, Elder, which published Charlotte Brontë's novels *JANE EYRE*, *SHIRLEY*, and *VILLETTE*, as well as a reissued edition of the Brontë sisters' POEMS. Smith served as the model for Dr. John Graham BRETTON in *Villette*. Charlotte showed Smith her work on the novel after completing two of the three original volumes. He encouraged her to finish *Villette* and did not mention the resemblance between himself and Bretton. Charlotte might have been declaring her love for Smith when she had Lucy SNOWE fall in love with Dr. John, for Lucy shares many of her creator's characteristics. At any rate, Smith was disappointed when he read the final volume of the novel. Dr. John's role is greatly diminished, and Lucy does not marry him. To Charlotte, such an ending would have made the novel more romantic and perhaps pleasing to her readership, but she believed it would also have been unrealistic. Smith persisted in his opinion that Lucy and Dr. John should have married, but he accepted Charlotte's novel and published it.

Smith, Miss Minor character in *JANE EYRE*. She teaches the children at LOWOOD to make their own clothes.

Sneaky, John *See* GLASS TOWN.

Snowe, Lucy Major character in *VILLETTE*. Lucy Snowe is the narrator of the novel, which is based on Charlotte Brontë's experiences at the PENSION-NAT HEGER in BRUSSELS. Lucy is often the guest of her godmother, Mrs. Louisa BRETTON, who lives with her only son, John Graham BRETTON, a lively and charming young man to whom Lucy becomes greatly attached. The household is transformed by the arrival of another visitor, Paulina (Polly) HOME. She has lost her mother and awaits her father, who she hopes will take her away with him. Lucy observes that John Graham and Polly form a deep bond.

Eventually Polly is sent away to school and Lucy herself must make her own way in the world, becoming the companion of an older woman and later a teacher at a school in Villette, France. Lucy has reached the school with difficulty—aided, she later learns, by Dr. John Graham Bretton, a fact that eluded her on the dark night when the seeming stranger guided her.

Lucy is lonely at the school, but she is a shrewd observer of human nature and learns to live by her own resources. At the same time, it is clear that she falls in love with Dr. John, who is infatuated with one of the school's pupils, Ginevra FANSHAWE. Just as he seems to have overcome his fancy for this rather superficial and cruel young woman, Lucy's hopes of winning his love are dashed when Dr. John and Polly are reunited after several years of separation. Polly is now Miss de Bassompierre; her father, Mr. HOME, has inherited the French title.

Although Lucy is depressed by her failure to win Dr. John's love, she becomes increasingly attracted to her teacher and colleague, Paul EMMANUEL. This fitful, demanding professor is, by turns, tender and harsh, constantly testing Lucy's devotion to knowledge and to their friendship. Religion seems to separate them, since he is a devout Catholic and she is a staunch Protestant. But he learns to respect her religious principles, and eventually they fall in love.

Sophie Minor character in *JANE EYRE*. She is Adèle VARENS's French nurse at THORNFIELD.

Southey, Robert (1774–1843) English poet and biographer. One of the important writers of his day, Southey was part of the ROMANTIC school of poetry, but his biography of Admiral Nelson and his letters have proven more lasting contributions to literature. Charlotte Brontë wrote to Southey at the beginning of her career and received kind but cautious advice about writing and authorship.

Sowerby Bridge Small textile-manufacturing town north of HALIFAX. Branwell Brontë worked here as a railway clerk. Sowerby Bridge had a new railway station, the second to last on the Leeds and Manchester Railway line. Branwell's job involved monitoring the 24 trains that passed through the station daily, work for which he was well paid.

Stael, Madame Germaine de (1766–1817) Born in Paris, this French writer and intellectual became a fierce opponent of Napoléon BONAPARTE and was forced to leave Paris after her first novel, *Delphine* (1802), was published. Her subsequent work, such as the novel *Corinne* (1807), which celebrated the successful career of a woman in the arts and literature, also caused controversy. Madame de Stael became a model for ambitious women in the United States and Europe. In *VILLETTE*, Lucy SNOWE compares Professor Paul EMMANUEL's conflicts with female teachers to Napoléon's fights with Madame de Stael.

Staningley Place in *THE TENANT OF WILDFELL HALL*. Staningley is the home of Helen HUNTINGDON's aunt, Mrs. Peggy MAXWELL, and uncle. Helen lived at Staningley before her marriage to Arthur, Lord HUNTINGDON. After Huntingdon's death, Helen returns to Staningley, which she inherits upon her uncle's death. At the end of the novel, Helen and Aunt Maxwell stay on at Staningley with Gilbert MARKHAM, Helen's new husband.

Steighton, Timothy Character in *THE PROFESSOR*. Timothy Steighton is Edward CRIMSWORTH's first clerk. Edward assigns Steighton the task of spying on his brother, William CRIMSWORTH, in the expectation that William will be caught making an error. William successfully avoids making any mistakes.

Stonegappe   Residence near LOTHERDALE, four miles from Skipton. Charlotte Brontë worked there as governess for Mrs. SIDGWICK's family in the spring and summer of 1839. Stonegappe was and still is an imposing three-story manor surrounded by its own woodlands and overlooking the flood valley of the Aire River. Despite her description of her circumstances to her sister Emily as "divine," Charlotte was intensely unhappy during her brief tenure at Stonegappe.

Strand, the   Street in London that runs approximately parallel to the river Thames from the TEMPLE GARDENS to Trafalgar Square in WESTMINSTER. Lined with hotels, law courts, theaters, and office buildings, it connects the City and the WEST END. In *VILLETTE*, Lucy SNOWE walks the Strand in her tour of London.

Sugden   Minor character in *SHIRLEY*. He serves a warrant on Moses BARRACLOUGH for leading workmen to destroy Robert MOORE's mill machinery.

Suzette   Minor character in *THE PROFESSOR*. She is one of the French teachers at Mademoiselle Zoraide REUTER's school.

Sweeny, Mrs.   Minor character in *VILLETTE*. She is the drunken nurse-governess who is dismissed and replaced by Lucy SNOWE.

Sweeting, David   Minor character in *SHIRLEY*. One of three curates satirized in the novel, he serves Nunnely. He courts and marries Dora SYKES.

Swift, Jonathan (1667–1745)   Author of *Gulliver's Travels* (1726), a book that appeals to Jane EYRE in *JANE EYRE* because it describes wonderful worlds with magical possibilities as well as the voyage of a man who leaves England for long periods.

Sykes, Christopher   Minor character in *SHIRLEY*. He is a large landowner. Two of his daughters are courted by David SWEETING, one of the area's curates. His daughter Dora SYKES marries Sweeting. Sykes is timid and refuses to join Robert MOORE in his prosecution of the men who wrecked his machinery.

Sykes, Dora   Minor character in *SHIRLEY*. She is courted by David SWEETING, one of the curates, and marries him.

Sykes, Hannah   Minor character in *SHIRLEY*. She is lively and susceptible to flattery but without much intelligence, making her particularly appealing to Matthewson HELSTONE, who prefers trivial women.

Sykes, Harriet   Minor character in *SHIRLEY*. One of Mrs. SYKES's four daughters, Harriet is slim whereas Dora is stout.

Sykes, Mary   Minor character in *SHIRLEY*. She is one of Mrs. SYKES's daughters and described as "well-looked, well-meant, and . . . well-dispositioned."

Sykes, Mrs.   Minor character in *SHIRLEY*. She is the mother of Dora, Harriet, Hannah, and Mary SYKES and wife of Christopher SYKES. She is a rather lofty personage who displays her arrogance on a visit to Matthewson HELSTONE's household.

Sylvie (1)   Minor character in *THE PROFESSOR*. William CRIMSWORTH observes that she is his most gentle and intelligent student.

Sylvie (2)   Paul EMMANUEL's dog in *VILLETTE*. She often accompanies him when he gardens.

Sympson, Henry   Minor character in *SHIRLEY*. He is described as limp and pale. He is tutored by Louis MOORE. Henry finds in Louis's desk Shirley KEELDAR's copybook, the first hint that Louis takes an avid interest in his former pupil. Henry has a crush on Shirley.

Sympson, Mr.   Character in *SHIRLEY*. As Shirley KEELDAR's uncle, Mr. Sympson feels he has a right to question her about her matrimonial intentions. As an independent woman of means, Shirley rejects his inquiries and treats him brusquely. Later, to his pressing questions about Samuel Fawthorpe WYNNE, she tells her uncle she will not marry the wealthy landowner and aristocrat whom Mr. Sympson considers a splendid prospect. Asked to account for herself, Shirley replies that she can only marry a man whom she can esteem, admire, and love. Mr. Sympson finds her manner and her language "unladylike."

Sympson, Mrs.   Minor character in *SHIRLEY*. She is the pious, church-going wife of Mr. SYMPSON, Shirley KEELDAR's uncle.

T

Tabby *See* AYKROYD, TABITHA.

Tales of the Islanders, The Series of "plays," and stories begun by Charlotte Brontë in 1827. Charlotte composed these stories and put them together in handmade books. They are remarkable in that the Brontës appear as characters under their own names. The "first volume of tales" begins with an *ARABIAN NIGHTS* flavor. The children, "sitting round the warm blazing kitchen fire," choose an island and a hero each for possible settings and characters in an adventure story. The duke of WELLINGTON, Sir Walter SCOTT, and various islands such as Arran and Guernsey are proposed, but they later turn to ideas of their own "fictitious Island." The characters and places that appear in these tales become part of the GLASS TOWN and ANGRIA sagas. *See also* JUVENILIA.

Taylor, James (1817–1874) Manager and occasional reader at the publishing house of Smith, Elder. Charlotte Brontë met James Taylor during an 1848 visit to London, and afterward he became her frequent correspondent. Ellen NUSSEY noted James Taylor's romantic interest in Charlotte, but Charlotte quickly disabused her friend of any notion that his interest was returned: To Charlotte he seemed "rigid, despotic and self-willed." Taylor continued to pursue Charlotte, however, traveling to HAWORTH in April 1851 to propose marriage. Charlotte had entertained the notion previously, but coming face to face with Taylor (who she said reminded her of Branwell on that occasion) scotched any such thought. He was, she said, a "stern and abrupt little man." She refused him, and shortly thereafter Taylor left for India to oversee Smith, Elder's operations in Bombay.

Taylor, Martha A friend of Charlotte Brontë's at Miss WOOLER's school. Her sister was Mary TAYLOR.

Charlotte described Martha as lively and talkative. She died of cholera in Brussels in 1842.

Taylor, Mary A friend of Charlotte Brontë's at Miss WOOLER's school. Charlotte admired her discipline and independence. Mary visited Charlotte at HAWORTH, traveled to Brussels with her sister, Martha TAYLOR, and remained Charlotte's confidant even after she immigrated to New Zealand. She later destroyed Charlotte's letters. She died in 1893.

Temple, Miss Character in *JANE EYRE*. The superintendent of LOWOOD, Miss Temple is a compassionate mentor to Jane EYRE. Miss Temple softens the harsh discipline that Mr. BROCKLEHURST imposes and is willing to withstand his criticism of her lenient behavior. She feeds the children better food when their breakfast of burned porridge is inedible. She encourages Jane to become a good student, and she fosters Jane's friendship with Helen BURNS, a long-suffering child who dies of consumption (TUBERCULOSIS). When Miss Temple leaves Lowood to marry Rev. Mr. NASMYTH, Jane is stimulated to think of leaving also.

Temple Gardens These famous London gardens are in the Temple, or Inns of Court, a group of buildings dating back to the 12th century on land that includes Temple Church. The site was once owned by the Knights Templar. In *VILLETTE*, Lucy SNOWE visits the Temple Gardens on her tour of London.

Tenant of Wildfell Hall, The Anne BRONTË's second novel. Anne worked on the novel during summer 1847, following the visit that April of a Mrs. Collins, the wife of a former local curate, Reverend John Collins. As Charlotte would later write her friend Ellen NUSSEY, Mrs. Collins took nearly two hours to relate the story of how the "wretched and most criminal Mr Collins," after an "infamous career of vice," abandoned his wife, leaving her with a "hideous disease" and no funds to support her two children. Like the rest of the Brontës, Anne was horrified by Mrs. Collins's ordeal, but she seems to have been more impressed that this long-suffering woman managed, despite all odds, to regain both her health and her respectability—and to save her children from their father's contagion. Anne had found her heroine: In *The Tenant of Wildfell Hall,* Helen HUNTINGDON's fate would closely parallel that of Mrs. Collins, allowing Anne to write a startlingly advanced defense of women's rights.

If Mrs. Collins provided the model for Helen Huntingdon, Anne needed to look no further than her immediate family for a prototype of the dissolute Arthur, Lord HUNTINGDON. Although her portrait of Lord Huntingdon reflects some of the negative traits displayed by John Collins, Anne could find a surfeit of detail with which to flesh out her heroine's depraved husband in her brother Branwell's conspicuous decline and fall. After his dismissal from his position as a tutor at THORP GREEN in July 1845 for behavior that Charlotte labeled "bad beyond expression"—his love affair with the lady of the house, Mrs. Lydia ROBIN-SON—Branwell sank into a profound depression, unable to support himself and his increasing dependency on alcohol and opium. His self-destruction, like Arthur Huntingdon's, seemed self-willed, brought about by too much early indulgence and too much free time. The publication of Anne's novel was followed three months later by Branwell's death at age 31 from TUBERCULOSIS.

SYNOPSIS

Chapter 1: A Discovery

Possibly borrowing a page from sister Emily's *WUTHERING HEIGHTS*, Anne chose to relate her story of past events within a contemporary framework, employing a narrator who is an actor in his own tale. *The Tenant of Wildfell Hall* opens in 1847 with a letter from the narrator, a gentleman farmer named Gilbert MARKHAM, to his friend J. HALFORD, Esq. Relying on "a certain faded old journal," Markham offers to relate "a tale of many chapters" about some significant events that occurred to him many years earlier.

Markham begins his story in the autumn of 1827, when he was 24 years old. One damp October evening he and other members of his family are entertained by the news, delivered by his sister, Rose MARKHAM, that a stranger, a single lady, has taken up residence in the half-ruined local manor, WILDFELL HALL. The woman, who calls herself Mrs. Helen Graham (the alias of Helen Huntingdon) has declined to offer much information about herself, and her neighbors are left to wonder about the history of this young, handsome woman whose "slightish mourning" leads them to think she is a widow. Rose and her mother, Mrs. MARKHAM, visit Mrs. Graham the following day but fail to learn anything more about her. When Markham finally sees Mrs. Graham in church a few days later, he is somewhat put off by her apparent sternness and turns his attention to the "little creature" next to him, the plump and pretty Eliza MILLWARD, the vicar's younger daughter and the object of Markham's affections.

Chapters 2–3: An Interview, A Controversy

After his hunt in the vicinity of his home at LINDEN-CAR fails to flush out any game, Markham climbs the steep terrain about two miles away known as Wildfell. After killing a hawk and two crows, he comes within sight of the Elizabethan manor atop the hill, where he stops beside the garden wall. Here he and his setter, SANCHO, encounter a merry five-year-old boy, but as the boy begins to pet the dog, Mrs. Graham interrupts them and demands, "'Give me the child!'" After Markham declares that he has no intention of harming young Arthur HUNTINGDON, also going by the alias Graham, Helen calms down somewhat, but she quickly withdraws with her child in tow. Gilbert returns home feeling angry and abused, then leaves for the vicarage, where he seeks reassurance from Eliza Millward.

Two days later, Mrs. Graham calls at Linden-Car, bringing her young son Arthur with her. When Gilbert's mother mildly chastises her for spoiling the child, Helen responds with a defensiveness that reinforces Gilbert's negative impression of her. When Mrs. Markham invites Helen and her child to a small party, Helen begs off, citing the damp, dark evenings that might sicken the boy. When Arthur cringes at the very sight of the wine that Mrs. Markham presses upon her guests, his mother explains that she has done everything in her power to make him loathe alcoholic drink, hoping "to save him from one degrading vice at least."

Markham protests her overprotectiveness, but Helen responds that it is her duty to prevent her son from falling prey to the temptations that trap most men—including, she hints, Arthur's father. To Markham's and his own mother's argument that her excessive care will have the opposite result, Helen counters: "Would you use the same argument with regard to a girl?" Her assertion that children of both sexes should be equally protected from bad influences and that she would rather Arthur die tomorrow than become a "man of the world," leaves Gilbert nonplussed. His declaration that ladies must always have the last word, however, elicits an invitation for him to bring his sister to call on her at Wildfell Hall, where Helen promises to listen to all he has to say.

Chapters 4–5: The Party, The Studio
The Markhams' party is small but merry, attended by Rev. Michael MILLWARD and his daughters, Mary MILLWARD and Eliza, as well as the widow Mrs. WILSON, her daughter, Jane WILSON, and her sons, Robert and Richard WILSON. Also in attendance is Frederick LAWRENCE, the squire of the village of LINDENHOPE and owner of Wildfell Hall. When asked to supply information about his tenant, Lawrence declines to provide any, proclaiming himself the last person to know anything about Mrs. Graham. Markham, asked for his opinion of the newcomer, calls her "too hard, too sharp, too bitter for my taste," then turns his attentions to Eliza.

The next day, however, Markham accompanies his sister when she calls at Wildfell Hall, where the two are ushered into Mrs. Graham's studio, one of the only habitable rooms in the house. Markham, closely examining his hostess's current effort, a painting of Wildfell Hall itself, is surprised to find it labeled "Fernley Manor, Cumberland." When he asks about this, Helen Graham responds that she needs to keep her whereabouts secret from certain persons. Arthur pipes up that his mother sells her paintings through a London dealer. When Helen suddenly darts from the room at the appearance of a stranger, Markham takes the opportunity to examine a number of her canvases,

focusing on a portrait of a handsome young man. When he asks Helen about the portrait upon her return, she cuts him off abruptly, asking him to inquire no further. Then, seeing she has hurt his feelings, she apologizes. Markham responds with good grace.

Chapters 6–7: Progression, The Excursion
Over the next few months Markham's acquaintance with Helen Graham progresses, and the older woman begins to replace Eliza Millward's place in his affections. Markham contrives to meet Helen and Arthur during their frequent out-of-door ramblings, and one day, after she permits Markham to give Arthur a ride on his horse, she also permits him to walk her home. As he is returning to Linden-Car, Markham encounters Mr. Lawrence, who teases his friend about his change in attitude about Mrs. Graham. Markham responds by asking Lawrence if he is in love with Helen Graham, despite Lawrence's obvious interest in Jane Wilson. Frederick demurs, and the two part company.

A few days later, Markham joins his sister, Rose, and brother, Fergus MARKHAM, and Eliza Millward as they travel to Wildfell Hall. In an attempt to dodge Fergus's questions about her biography, Helen turns rather desperately to Markham, asking him to accompany her on the long trip to the sea so that she can have a new subject to paint. Rose insists that they must all go together, and two months later they do so. When Helen steals away from the group in order to be alone and sketch, Markham is not far behind her. Although Helen seems barely to suffer his presence, Markham spends the time admiring her. After they rejoin the others he cannot help but compare her with Eliza Millward, to the latter's detriment. He decides that he must break off his relationship with the vicar's daughter.

Chapters 8–10: The Present, A Snake in the Grass, A Contract and a Quarrel
When a book Markham had ordered arrives from London, he hastens to Wildfell Hall to make Helen a present of it. Having found Helen approachable but unwilling to tolerate even the mildest advances, Markham is determined to at least establish a friendship with her. Finding Helen unwilling to discuss any personal matters,

he has learned that she is almost eager to talk about such subjects as painting and philosophy. Arthur, too, provides a conduit to his mother. First Markham presents the boy with one of Sancho's offspring, then he gives the boy a book. Now, having heard Helen express a wish to read Sir Walter SCOTT's epic poem *MARMION*, he sees another opening. But Helen declares that she cannot accept the book unless Markham lets her pay for it, "Because I don't like to put myself under obligations I can never repay.'" After Markham assures her that he will never seek any kind of repayment, she relents, and he is sorely tempted to kiss her hand in gratitude. He restrains himself, however, knowing that by doing so he would undo all the progress he has made with Helen.

The next day Markham makes a visit to the vicarage as part of his plan to let Eliza down "easy." The girl greets him with the news of "'shocking reports about Mrs. Graham.'" Although Eliza refuses to tell him precisely what the gossip is, Markham leaves somewhat shaken. A few days later, when the Markhams host another party, he learns something of his neighbors' talk about the tenant of Wildfell Hall. Observing the slight greeting that passes between Helen Graham and Frederick Lawrence, Eliza whispers innuendo in Markham's ear. The burden of this is not clear to him, however, until the more sober Jane Wilson declines to sit beside Helen Graham, citing her lack of respectability. There is apparently speculation that Helen Graham is not only not a widow, but that she has never had a husband. Eliza, seeing an opportunity to alienate Markham further from her rival for his affections, intimates that Frederick Lawrence might be little Arthur's father.

A seed of doubt is thus planted in Markham's mind, although he continues to defend Helen Graham until he can escape the party. In search of solitude, he sits down on a bench in a secluded arbor, where he is unexpectedly joined by Helen and Arthur, who have likewise left the party in search of some peace. As they sit talking, they see Frederick Lawrence and Jane Wilson talking together, and Helen remarks that Jane seems rather a cold person. Markham responds that Jane may regard her as a rival. When Frederick Lawrence blushes as Jane Wilson points coldly at

the other pair, Markham takes his reaction as confirmation that Frederick has had designs on Helen. Helen, for her part, gets up abruptly to rejoin the party. When she declines Markham's offer to walk her home, he takes umbrage at Lawrence's warning not to harbor romantic hopes about Mrs. Graham, calling his erstwhile friend a hypocrite.

After the guests depart, Markham discovers that the slander about Helen has spread throughout the company. When he visits Wildfell Hall about a week later, he and Helen walk companionably through her garden, and she stops to pick a rose for Markham to take home to his sister. Almost overcome with feeling for Helen, Markham asks if he might not keep it for himself, and when Helen picks another just for him, he takes not only the flower, but also her hand. For a moment Helen's face reflects gladness, but then it darkens, and she tells him that if he cannot regard her as a "plain, cold, motherly, or sisterly friend," she will have to ask that he leave her alone. When Markham asks why this must be, Helen merely responds that she may tell him someday—but only if he never repeats the gesture he just made toward her.

The two part in a friendly fashion, but as Markham walks down the hill from Wildfell Hall, his suspicions are again raised when he encounters Lawrence riding up the hill. When Markham grabs hold of Lawrence's horse's bridle and demands that Lawrence explain his "perfidious duplicity," Lawrence declines to answer. The two almost come to blows but are interrupted by the vicar, who tells them not to fight over "that young widow."

Chapters 11–12: The Vicar Again, A Tête-à-Tête and a Discovery

Just after Rose has taken a turn berating her brother for consorting with the much-maligned Mrs. Graham, the vicar pays a visit to the Markhams, where he relates the story of his latest call on the tenant of Wildfell Hall. Rev. Mr. Millward, fulfilling what he sees as his pastoral duty, has just shared with Helen Graham the rumors about her circulating in Lindenhope and vicinity. To the vicar, Helen Graham's reaction was far from positive: After turning white in the face, she told him that his pastoral advice was unnecessary, and she declined to explain herself in any way. Markham leaves quickly and in anger.

Hastening to Wildfell Hall, Markham offers to redeem Helen's reputation by marrying her. Just as he is on the verge of declaring his love for her, Helen declares that more than her shady local reputation stands in the way of their union. Vainly, Markham reminds Helen that she once promised to tell him something of her former life, but she begs off, citing the stress of the day and the lateness of the hour. She promises that if he will meet her the next day on the moor she will tell him all. When she implores him to leave, however, Markham cannot restrain himself. He asks her if she loves him and presses her hand to his lips. This action elicits an anguished cry from her, and this time Markham does go, but not before he glances back to see her sobbing convulsively.

Unable to entirely leave Helen's orbit, Markham slowly walks back toward the hall, where he resolves to observe her from afar. He is taken aback, however, to hear Helen talking calmly to another about a walk in the moonlight. When two figures emerge from the house, one belongs to Frederick Lawrence. The conversation Markham overhears next confirms his worst fears, as Lawrence, walking with his arm around Helen's waist, declares that he cannot consent to lose her. Markham, unable to stand more, staggers home, where he spends a tortured night and wakes to a gloomy morning.

Chapters 13–14: A Return to Duty, An Assault

After several days of ill-tempered fretting, Markham decides to make a trip to RYECOTE FARM to consult with Robert Wilson about a business matter. While waiting for the absent Robert to return, Markham is forced to make conversation with Jane Wilson and the visiting Eliza Millward, who tease him about his attachment to Helen Graham. After he takes his leave of the Wilsons, Markham strides off to inspect a cornfield, only to take an abrupt detour when he spies Helen and Arthur approaching. Although Arthur runs after him, Markham turns his back and walks resolutely away from them.

The next day, on his way to town on business, Markham is overtaken by Frederick Lawrence, who greets him cordially. When Markham snubs

him, Lawrence asks why he should be so mean to his friends simply because he has been disappointed in love. Markham responds by cracking his whip handle over Lawrence's skull, causing the latter to fall from his horse. After determining that Lawrence is not dead, Markham remounts his own horse and gallops away. Soon, however, he comes to his senses and rides back. Lawrence, though bleeding profusely and obviously badly injured, refuses Markham's help. Markham then leaves the other man to his fate, rationalizing his abandonment.

Immediately upon his return home, however, Markham learns from Rose that Frederick Lawrence has been thrown from his horse and brought home dying. Urged by his mother to see the injured fellow, Markham demurs, sending his brother the next morning. When Fergus returns, it is clear that Lawrence has decided not to give out the true cause of his injury, instead letting others believe that he is suffering from his fall and the wet ground upon which he lay afterward.

Chapter 15: An Encounter and Its Consequences

The next day, as Markham stands in one of his fields, he is hailed by Arthur Graham, who tells him that Helen wants to see him. Even as Gilbert tries to dismiss the boy, Helen appears, insisting that she must speak with him. After she convinces Arthur to go off and gather bluebells, Helen turns on Markham, demanding to know why he did not come, as they had arranged, to hear her explanation of her circumstances. Markham responds that he did not come because in the interim he learned for himself what she had to tell him. Helen tells him that such a discovery is impossible, but that now she has no intention of explaining herself to him, as he is not the man she thought him to be.

The two part in mutual hostility, but Markham soon regrets his haste. He believes that Helen does in fact love him—perhaps, he reasons, she is simply tired of Mr. Lawrence—and he is at least curious to know how she will endeavor to explain herself. He goes to see her the next day.

Markham makes a bad start with Helen, quizzing her about her relationship with Lawrence. When she bridles, he begins to tell her how he overheard her conversation with Lawrence the last time he was at Wildfell Hall. While Markham describes the torment occasioned by his eavesdropping, Helen begins to smile subtly, confessing that she is pleased that he has more depth of soul than she feared—at least he has not dismissed her simply because of local gossip about her. Then she asks him if he would be pleased to learn that his conclusions about her are mistaken. When Markham responds passionately that he would, Helen hands him a thick manuscript, telling him to read however much of it he wishes, but to share its contents with no one and to return it to her when he finishes.

Chapters 16–17: The Warnings of Experience, Further Warnings

Here begins the narrative contained in Helen's journal, which takes up the majority of the novel. The journal is begun on June 1, 1821, at STANING-LEY, the country estate where Helen lives with her aunt, Mrs. Peggy MAXWELL, and uncle before her marriage. Helen is restive following several weeks in the city, where she has apparently met a man who caught her fancy. Perhaps coincidentally, shortly after the family's homecoming, Helen's aunt begins to quiz her about the possibility of marriage. Helen is, her aunt says, only 18 years old, possessed of a good name and a good fortune, as well as good looks. She should not be in a hurry to marry, and she should beware of unprincipled men. Although Helen assures her aunt that she will indeed be cautious, she wonders to herself if her aunt has ever herself been in love.

Helen goes on to recount some events from what her uncle jovially refers to as her "first campaign"—that is, her first season in London as a eligible female. She recalls with distaste an older gentleman named Mr. BOARHAM, a rich friend of her aunt who would not leave her alone. One evening Helen was saved from his unwanted attentions by a Mr. Arthur Huntingdon, the son of a late friend of her uncle. Arthur Huntingdon remained Helen's companion for the remainder of the evening. She finds him entertaining and attractive, but her aunt warns that he has a reputation for being "'wildish.'"

Huntingdon comes to call the next morning, and he is attentive to both Helen and her uncle. In comparison, Mr. Boarham looks even less invit-

ing, and Helen has no trouble refusing Boarham's marriage proposal, despite her aunt's caution to consider the offer carefully.

The next day Helen accompanies her aunt and uncle to a dinner party hosted by a Mr. WILMOT, where she meets Mr. Wilmot's niece, Annabella WILMOT, a flirtatious young heiress who seems bent on monopolizing the attentions of Arthur Huntingdon, who is also present. Huntingdon soon comes to Helen's side, however, and she has just begun to enjoy his company when her aunt intervenes. Helen leaves them alone, only to be accosted by Mr. Wilmot, whom she finds unbearable. Once again she is saved from the unwanted attention of an older man by Huntingdon, who presses her to tell him how she feels about him. Nonplussed, Helen turns the question around and is pleased and astonished to hear him reply, "Sweet angel, I adore you!"

Seeing Helen's visceral reaction to Huntingdon, her aunt again interrupts. Shortly thereafter, they leave the party. Back home, Aunt Maxwell subjects Helen to a barrage of questions about her attitude toward Huntingdon, whom the older woman clearly regards as a bad character. Helen in turn defends him, stating that if he is not the ideal mate, she would be happy to make it her goal to reform him. Shortly thereafter, the family leaves London, owing both to Helen's uncle's gout and to her aunt's concern about Helen's future.

Chapter 18–20: The Miniature, An Incident, Persistence

In her next diary entry, dated August 25, Helen confesses her eagerness to return to London and see Arthur Huntingdon, who is always in her thoughts and dreams. She says, however, that if he should wish to marry her, she will make a point of ascertaining the goodness of his character before saying yes or no.

Two weeks later, Helen's uncle hosts a party to which Arthur Huntingdon has been invited. After dinner the first night, Helen is called upon to exhibit her drawings as part of the entertainment. She is horribly embarrassed when Huntingdon discovers a likeness of himself she sketched on the reverse of one of her drawings and absentmindedly forgot to erase. As he searches through her other drawings, Huntingdon is able to perceive that this portrait is not her only attempt to render his likeness, as her pencil has left an impression of other portraits of him on the backs of several other cardboard canvases. Then he leaves to join Annabella Wilmot.

Concluding that Huntingdon now despises her because he knows she loves him, Helen quits the party. After she believes the others have retired for the night, she ventures out to find a candle, only to find Huntingdon at the bottom of the stairs. Seizing her hand, he demands to know if she is jealous of Annabella. When Helen refuses to answer him, he puts his arm around her neck and kisses her. In a state of utter confusion, Helen breaks free and flees upstairs.

At breakfast the next morning Huntingdon speaks to Helen with a familiarity and kindliness that she finds irresistible. When he discovers her painting in the library later in the day, he looks through her portfolio, where he retrieves a completed miniature of himself. He teases Helen with it for a time but eventually gives it back to her, whereupon she tears it in half and throws it into the fire. Her decisive action has the effect of driving him away. Later, he tells Helen that if she does not value him, he will be forced to turn his attention to Annabella Wilmot. Helen berates herself for allowing her pride to win out over her heart. As for Huntingdon, she decides he could never have truly loved her, or he would not have given her up so easily.

Her fears seem confirmed the next evening, when she is interrupted in the middle of a song by the entrance of Huntingdon, who asks Annabella to sing. Deeply hurt by this snub, Helen escapes from the drawing room to the library, where Huntingdon seeks her out. Insisting that she tell him if she was crying over him, Huntingdon embraces her, telling her he cannot live without her. In rapid succession, he asks her to marry him, demands that she tell him she loves him, and showers her with kisses. This whirlwind wooing is interrupted by the entrance of Aunt Maxwell, with whom Huntingdon pleads for consent to marry Helen. Disapprovingly, Helen's aunt sends him back to the party and Helen to her room.

The next morning finds Helen filled with excitement, although when she is accosted early by Arthur Huntingdon, she cautions him against presumptuousness, knowing how profoundly her aunt dislikes him. Arthur, for his part, dismisses this impediment, saying he will be whatever she wants him to be. Helen in turn defends him to her aunt, saying Huntingdon is a better man than Mrs. Maxwell thinks he is and that if he is far from perfect, as his wife she will devote herself to reforming him. When the time comes for an interview with her uncle, Helen tells him she has made up her mind to marry Huntingdon. Uncle Maxwell, who is Helen's guardian, agrees, telling her he will write immediately to her father, a man Helen has never known. Mr. Maxwell does, however, warn Helen that her future husband has squandered much of his inheritance. Although she is no heiress, her father can settle a fair amount of money on her, so she and Arthur should be able to live comfortably.

Chapters 21–22: Opinions, Traits of Friendship
With the wedding date set for Christmas, Helen feels free to tell others of her engagement. Much to Helen's surprise, her best friend, Milicent HARGRAVE, expresses disappointment in the match, saying that Helen is superior to Arthur in every way. Annabella Wilmot adds her voice to the chorus of disapproval, adding that Helen should envy her because Annabella will probably wed Huntingdon's friend Lord LOWBOROUGH, whose wealth and position Arthur cannot begin to rival.

Arthur's friends likewise disapprove of the upcoming marriage, albeit for different reasons. Marriage to Helen—to anyone, for that matter—means for them the end of their glorious days of drunken carousing, as Huntingdon was "the very life and prop of the community." While Helen gives him leave to keep up his friendships, Huntingdon cavalierly declares that he is done with them. Helen is grateful. When Arthur leaves for a day of shooting with her uncle, she does not know what to do without him.

A few days later, though, Helen begins to have doubts about Arthur when he tells her with relish the story of his participation in the undoing of his supposed friend Lowborough. Lowborough was once a serious gambler, one who continued to gamble long after he had lost his fortune and his future wife. Despite his knowledge of Lowborough's circumstances, Huntingdon conspires with his friend Mr. GRIMSBY to prolong Lowborough's career of dissipation by encouraging his alcoholism and abetting his addiction to laudanum. One day Lowborough confesses to Huntingdon that the only way to entirely reform is to find a woman to love and to quit the gentleman's club that had been the scene of so many revels. Lowborough finally finds what he thinks is his salvation in Annabella Wilmot, who confesses to her intimate, Huntingdon, how little affection she bears the man she has decided to marry.

Helen upbraids Arthur for his failure to warn his erstwhile friend that Annabella is interested only in Lowborough's title and family seat. She goes on to criticize his conduct toward Lowborough, whereupon Arthur glibly promises to reform his behavior to her liking. Helen so wants to believe him that she disregards the hints that her trusted servant, RACHEL, drops about Huntingdon's improprieties. Helen's own unease about her impending marriage refuses to recede, however, fueled by her fiancé's apparent inability to approach life with the same seriousness she does, as evidenced by the short, frivolous notes he sends her during the weeks leading up to their marriage.

Chapters 23–24: First Weeks of Matrimony, First Quarrel
Helen resumes her journal in February 1822, four months after her last entry. At this point she has been Mrs. Huntingdon of GRASSDALE MANOR for eight weeks, and already she knows that Arthur is not the man she previously thought him to be. Still, she declines to torture herself with thoughts that she would not have married him had she known his true character, opting instead to love him. Plainly, Arthur is fond of her—almost *too* fond, she confesses to her diary. But his affection for her is almost always relegated to second place, for he is, above all things, supremely selfish. When they travel to the Continent on their honeymoon, Arthur rushes their tour; he wants to get back to Grassdale, where he can, he says, have Helen all to himself. Once there, he complains of her devotion to God, which he feels detracts from the attention she should be giving him. After expressing the wish that Arthur would give more of himself to God, Helen drops the subject, fearing that she will alienate her new husband.

A little more than a month later, Helen reports in her diary that she senses Arthur growing restive. Confined indoors during the inclement weather, he can think of nothing better to do than loll on the sofa beside his new bride and regale her with stories of his past loves. One day in early April Helen objects to Arthur's tale of his dalliance with an older married woman, proclaiming she would not have married him if she had known he had engaged in such affairs. Her objection leads to a quarrel that lasts several days, at the end of which Arthur prepares to leave for London. Helen, determined to prevent him from going, approaches him just before his departure. The two reconcile, and Arthur agrees not to leave without her. Grateful for her husband's apologetic attitude—and for his love—Helen consents to go with him the following week.

Chapter 25: First Absence
Helen stays in London with her husband for exactly a month, during which time, against her better judgment, she permits Arthur to dress her in finery and show her off to his city acquaintances. At the end of four weeks, Helen has grown tired of the hubbub but is reluctant to follow her husband's request that she return to Grassdale alone, leaving him in London. Finally she acquiesces, and Arthur remains behind to conduct, he says, a little business with his lawyer that should not take more than two weeks.

Nearly three months pass before Arthur returns. In the interim, Helen writes him increasingly angry letters, to which he replies in his usual lighthearted fashion, always promising to return soon. One letter mentions that his dissolute friend Ralph HATTERSLEY is courting Helen's friend Milicent. Helen tells herself that her friend will never consent to marry a man of such poor qualities. But Milicent, lacking a fortune, is cowed by her ambitious mother and the overbearing Hattersley into accepting, or at least acquiescing to, his proposal. She begs Helen for advice about how she can learn to love such a man, one who seems to have so much in common with Helen's own husband. Helen finds it impossible to offer her friend any encouragement.

When Arthur finally comes home at the end of July, Helen hardly recognizes him. He is ill and listless, the beauty that she had fallen in love with diminished. For the next month, Helen nurses him tenderly. Once recovered, however, Arthur is eager to pick up where he left off, proposing that they host a shooting party at Grassdale.

Chapters 26–27: The Guests, A Misdemeanour

The Huntingdons' shooting party lasts for weeks. The guests who figure most prominently in Helen's mind are Lord Lowborough and his wife of eight months, the former Annabella Wilmot. Lowborough's temperament seems much changed to Helen: Marriage seems to have helped him cast off his customary gloominess. Still, he is not always cheerful, for Annabella is not always attentive or kind. One of her chief amusements, in fact, seems to be flirting with Helen's husband, who willingly reciprocates.

Helen believes that Arthur is engaging in this flirtation solely to excite her jealousy, but one day she witnesses something that indicates otherwise. After tea Annabella is entertaining the guests by singing and playing at the piano, while Arthur leans attentively over the back of her chair. Seeing Lord Lowborough's irritation with this tableau, Helen starts to interrupt Milicent and Arthur's tête-à-tête, but she stops when she sees Arthur surreptitiously press Annabella's hand to his lips. Upon seeing his wife, Arthur drops his eyes. Later, when the guests have withdrawn, he drops to his knees before Helen in mock supplication.

Helen severely tells her husband not to test her further. Arthur apologizes, but he seems not to take her seriously, blaming his lapse on too much drink—another habit for which Helen reprimands him. Arthur at first responds like a sulky child, then cajoles Helen into forgiving him for an act he vows never to repeat.

The next morning Helen has occasion to upbraid Annabella when the latter raises the question of Huntingdon's "merry" behavior the night before. Annabella shows no shame for her own behavior, but she is brutally frank about Huntingdon, asking Helen if he deserves the love she gives her husband.

Chapter 28: Parental Feelings

A year after her marriage, Helen assesses her feelings and finds that her hope for the future, although not gone, is certainly diminished. What matters most to her now, however, is not her hus-

band but her infant son, also named Arthur. Huntingdon, who seems to view his son as a rival for Helen's affections, calls the child an "oyster" and asks, "[W]hat is there to love?" Helen expresses the hope that as the child grows, his father may learn to care more for him.

Chapters 29–30: The Neighbor, Domestic Scenes

Entering the third year of her marriage, Helen gives thanks for her son, as she finds little consolation in her husband, who once again has left her alone in the country for much of the previous year. During her long solitary spring, Helen learns from the brother of her friend Milicent, Walter HARGRAVE, who has recently seen Huntingdon in London, that her husband is once again devoting himself to dissipation, not to business. Helen bridles, not wanting to hear such news. But she receives more news of her husband, again from Hargrave, who tells her that Huntingdon has written to him of his intention to return home the next week. Hargrave goes on to say that Huntingdon had always told him it was his intention to stay away four months, and this announcement strikes Helen like a blow. To her Huntingdon had kept up a steady stream of promises of imminent return.

The next day Helen receives a letter from Huntingdon announcing his return the following week. This time he does come home, but he is in even worse condition than after his previous trip to London. Ill and ill tempered, Huntingdon complains about the servants and is jealous of Helen's attentions to their son. Reduced to tears, Helen implores her husband to repent his ways. Unable to convert him to her faith in God, she is, with Hargrave's help, at least able to prevent Huntingdon from complete dependence on alcohol. But Helen, still loyal to her husband, is concerned about the tender feelings Hargrave seems to bear her.

Gradually Huntingdon regains his strength, and in late August, he leaves without Helen to join his friends on a hunting party in Scotland. Helen and her son go to Staningley, where Helen, conscious of her aunt's and uncle's concern, glosses over Huntingdon's shortcomings. When Huntingdon returns from his Scottish holiday, Helen is relieved to find him cheerful and restored to good health.

Chapters 31–33: Social Virtues, Comparisons:
Information Rejected, Two Evenings

With the return of spring, however, Huntingdon prepares once more to leave for London. Helen had planned to go with him this time, but shortly before their scheduled departure, Huntingdon uncharacteristically urges her to visit her sick father and worried brother. When she returns to Grassdale, she finds her husband gone, having left behind a note containing a transparent excuse about an unexpected emergency having called him to London early. Since it was to be such a short visit, the note goes on to say, there is no point in Helen troubling herself to join him. Helen, still hopeful of reviving her marriage, takes comfort in her husband's promises that he will observe moderation during all future trips to London or Paris.

Three months later Huntingdon is back home, better in health but worse in temper. When Helen's father dies, her husband refuses to allow her to attend the funeral, insisting that he needs her at home. After three weeks, Huntingdon has returned to his old habits. Helen humors him, finally agreeing to act as hostess to his invited house guests.

Among the guests are Lord and Lady Lowborough. Annabella taunts her husband for refusing to join with the other men in their drinking games. When Helen chides her, Annabella coolly responds that she would be happy for her husband to return to alcoholism, for then she would be rid of him sooner. Helen also finds the unwanted attentions of Walter Hargrave more than a little unpleasant. When Hargrave tells Helen how much he detests Huntingdon, Helen tartly tells him to air such opinions out of her hearing. The other guests are little better. When the party of drunken men joins the women, they attempt to drag Lowborough back into their brawl. A fight breaks out between Hattersley and Hargrave over the former's rough treatment of his wife. When Hattersley next attacks Huntingdon for mocking him, Helen leaves the party.

A few days later Milicent Hattersley, protesting that she loves her husband and that he will improve as he grows older, provides Helen with some perspective on her own lot. Like her friend, Helen has been protecting herself and her friends

from a frank acknowledgment of Huntingdon's shortcomings. She sees clearly, though, that while there may be some hope for Milicent's marriage, she cannot be so sanguine about her own. At that moment Hattersley enters, delighting his wife and his young daughter. When Milicent leaves briefly, Helen takes the opportunity to chastise Hattersley for taking advantage of his wife's good nature. He listens without rancor to her lecture, but then asserts that Huntingdon, who is far worse than he, is afraid of his own wife, wishing her to be more compliant. Hargrave, who enters in the middle of the conversation, agrees that Huntingdon is a bad character, then attempts to expand on this judgment by speaking to Helen privately. Helen brushes him off, not wanting to hear ill tidings.

Two evenings later, Helen overhears Grimsby and Hattersley complaining of their host's temperance, which they blame on Helen. Helen is amused by their discussion and goes off in search of Huntingdon to tell him what his guests are saying about him. Coming up behind him on a shadowy walkway, Helen springs on her husband, throwing her arms around him from behind. Huntingdon responds with, "Bless you, darling!" Then starting, he exclaims in horror, "Helen!—what the devil is this!"

Helen, preferring to acknowledge what she considers the more instinctive of Huntingdon's greetings, remarks on his nervousness. Huntingdon tries repeatedly to shoo Helen away. Helen is so full of hope at this apparent renewal of her husband's love that she does leave, even as Huntingdon continues to gaze anxiously toward a group of nearby shrubs.

Helen's good mood continues. The next evening, when Rachel comes to help her dress, she is astonished to see that her maid has been crying and even more astonished when, after some urging, Rachel declares that she does not like the way the master is going on. Rachel bursts out with, "'Well, if I was you, I wouldn't have that Lady Lowborough in the house another minute . . . !'"

At dinner, Helen closely watches her husband and Annabella but sees nothing suspicious pass between them. Afterward, Hargrave entices Helen to play chess with him while Milicent looks on. When, as expected, Hargrave bests her, he attempts to console her for being "Beaten—beaten!" and Helen is both alarmed and insulted by his unwanted sympathy. When she goes into the next room he follows and again entreats her to hear him out. Then Hargrave tells her of a scheme whereby Grimsby will distract Lord Lowborough while Annabella escapes into the shrubbery to meet another man.

Having heard enough, Helen rushes outside, determined to know the truth for herself. Stopping by the shrubbery she hears her husband and Annabella exchanging words of affection. When Annabella asks Huntingdon if he still loves his wife, he answers, "'Not *one bit*, by all that's sacred!'" Helen falls to her knees, crushed by this confirmation of her worst fears.

When Helen confronts Huntingdon later that night, he at first denies all, then looks on coolly as Helen demands to know if he will let her leave him, taking their child and what remains of her money. When Huntingdon denies this request, she asks to take only the boy, but Huntingdon rages that she will not. Helen then tells him that henceforth they shall be husband and wife in name only.

Chapters 34–35: Concealment, Provocations
Helen, having found that her love for her husband has turned to hate, must still keep up appearances. She finds, however, that both Hargrave's insinuating tenderness and Annabella's dissimulating familiarity are unbearable. When Helen lets Annabella know that she is aware of Huntingdon's affair, Annabella begs her not to reveal the liaison to Lowborough. Helen agrees, not out of kindness to Annabella but to protect Annabella's cousin Milicent and Lowborough. Once Annabella knows she has nothing to fear from Helen she behaves more outrageously, going so far as to tell Helen she loves Huntingdon more than Helen ever could.

Chapter 36–38: Dual Solitude, The Neighbor Again, The Injured Man
Helen and Huntingdon continue their loveless marriage. Huntingdon turns back to drink. When he receives a love letter from Annabella, he shows it to Helen, who responds by snatching up her child and leaving the room. Her actions frighten young Arthur, who remains attached to

his father. Although she understands the child's emotions, Helen fears that her boy will take after his father, who indulges the child more than is good for him.

While Huntingdon is away on another jaunt with his friends, Hargrave once again takes the opportunity to profess his love for Helen, who again repulses him. By her fifth wedding anniversary, Helen writes in her journal that she has formulated a plan of action and sets forth her reasons for this decision. The previous fall, she was obliged to host yet another house party for Huntingdon's friends, including Lady Lowborough. Taking her aside one day, Helen plainly told Annabella that if she saw any evidence of Annabella's "criminal connection" to Huntingdon, she would inform Lord Lowborough of the illicit union.

Helen has no need to do this, however, for Lowborough already knows about his wife's infidelity. One day he asks Helen why she did not tell him what he has only just discovered. He is distraught when Helen says the affair has been going on for about two years. Then Hattersley bursts into the room and proposes that Lowborough challenge Huntingdon to a duel; Lowborough declines. Lowborough and Annabella leave the next morning and soon thereafter separate.

Chapters 39–40: A Scheme of Escape, A Misadventure
Concerned that Huntingdon and his friends are corrupting her son by encouraging the child to drink and to have contempt for Helen's sobriety, Helen resolves to get young Arthur away from his father. She decides that she will raise enough money by selling her jewels while working to improve her painting skills so that she will be able to support herself and her child. Her resolve is strengthened when Hargrave recounts a recent conversation in which Huntingdon declared that any of his friends who wanted to have Helen could do so, with his blessing.

Helen then tells Hargrave about her determination to leave Huntingdon and to take young Arthur with her. Hargrave drops on one knee before her, begging her to let him help her. Helen refuses, but she is too late. The pair has been seen by Grimsby, who will doubtless report what he has seen to Huntingdon. Hargrave presses himself on

Helen, forcing her to defend herself with a palette knife. As they exchange angry words, Huntingdon and Hattersley enter the room.

Huntingdon corners his wife and berates her. Hattersley, too, seems to think that something illicit has happened between Helen and Hargrave, and Helen insists that Hargrave speak up in her defense. Reluctantly, he does so, which only causes Huntingdon to sneer. Hargrave takes his leave. Helen notes in her diary that she has not seen him since.

While she is recording all this, Huntingdon interrupts her, seizing the book from her. He then reads her entries avidly, discovering Helen's plan of escape. He responds by demanding that she hand over all her keys, then he orders that all her canvases and painting materials be burned. When Huntingdon returns her keys, he tells her she will find that he has taken her money and her jewels. From now on, he says, he will give her a small allowance, and he will hire a steward to keep the household accounts. This, he says, will keep her from temptation and prevent her from running away and disgracing him.

The next morning Helen awakens to the knowledge that she is a slave and a prisoner. Only her faith will sustain her.

Chapters 41–42: "Hope Springs Eternal in the Human Breast," A Reformation

Helen is roused from her despondency by the knowledge that she must save young Arthur. If she cannot yet spirit him away, she can work to save him from the vices inculcated in him by his father, vices that include a fondness for the taste of alcohol. Helen is so opposed to drink that she adds an emetic to her child's wine, causing him inevitably to associate the taste of it with nausea.

Helen is also at work on another escape plan: She intends to ask her brother to help her move to the abandoned, tumbledown old hall where they were born and where she hopes to live with young Arthur under an assumed name. She will have to ask her brother, Frederick, for a loan, and this she intends to do soon, as he is coming for a visit.

In Huntingdon's absence, Frederick stays two weeks, during which Helen explains her plight. Although he deems Helen's plan wildly impractical, he agrees to help her.

Esther HARGRAVE returns from a season in London, where her mother has found a potential husband for her. Esther confesses to Helen that she finds the fellow too old and unattractive, and Helen backs her decision not to marry a man she dislikes. Helen's seriousness causes Esther to ask her if she is happy. Although Helen refuses to answer her young friend, it is as plain to Esther as to everyone else that Helen suffers in her marriage.

Milicent Hattersley and her husband come to visit Helen, and Hattersley tells her that it is his intention to reform, swearing off drink and living a Christian life. Helen tells him that it is never too late to do so, but that he should change his ways before his wife and children come to hate him.

Chapters 43–44: The Boundary Past, The Retreat

Huntingdon returns from his long absence, announcing his intention to hire a governess for Arthur. Helen protests, but her husband tells her she is not fit to teach children. Alice MYERS soon appears on the scene, and Helen finds her suspiciously lacking in both intellect and attainments, though she is attentive to Huntingdon. When Rachel expresses a similar reaction to Miss Myers, Helen tells her maid about her escape plan, and Rachel offers to come with her. Helen protests that she cannot pay Rachel, but Rachel insists that she does not need to be paid, as she has some savings put away. She wants, like Helen, only to "get shut of this wicked house."

Helen prepares to leave, writing letters to Frederick, Milicent, and her aunt, explaining her plans. With the help of Rachel and BENSON, the butler, Helen has packed up her things and sent them secretly away, addressed to Mrs. Graham, her mother's maiden name and henceforth Helen's alias.

The next morning Helen makes her escape, with Rachel and young Arthur by her side. Hoping to pass herself off as a widow, she wears black, with a veil over her face to hide her identity until she is far away from Grassdale. When the small party finally reaches the desolate Wildfell Hall, they are greeted by the old woman who acts as caretaker.

Helen quickly sets up housekeeping as the widow Graham, the tenant of Wildfell Hall, owned by Frederick Lawrence. She learns that Huntingdon is making every effort to find her so that he can recover his son—even telling Helen's relatives that he is willing to pay Helen for the boy. Concerned that her true identity not be discovered, Helen does her best to remain a hermit, but her neighbors will not leave her alone. A final, incomplete entry in her journal notes that she has made the acquaintance of the "beau of the parish."

Chapter 45: Reconciliation
Addressing his friend Halford, Markham confesses that reading Helen's journal has filled him with a sense of loathing for Huntingdon; more than that, however, it has relieved a great emotional burden from his shoulders, for he now understands what Helen has been through and why she has behaved as she has. The journal has also made him ashamed of his own conduct.

The morning after reading Helen's lengthy account of her marriage, Markham rushes over to Wildfell Hall to see her. Rachel tells him at first that Helen is poorly, but then Arthur brings word that Helen wishes to see him. Tentatively, she asks Markham if he has read her journal. He says he has and asks for her forgiveness for his bad behavior. Helen asks the same of him. Then, struggling for composure, she tells him that they must never meet again. Markham protests that he loves her more than ever, but Helen says it is for that very reason they must part forever. He is young and should find a wife, and she—in spite of everything—remains married to Huntingdon. She will not hold out even the promise of some future meeting or accept Markham's proposal that they exchange messages through her brother. She does agree, however, to "keeping up a spiritual intercourse" through letters after she leaves Wildfell Hall, as she intends to do shortly. Gilbert seizes this slender strand of hope with the desperateness of a drowning man. After speaking of love that will survive death, the two spontaneously embrace.

Tearing himself away from Helen, Gilbert hurriedly leaves Wildfell Hall. After a period of disconsolation, he goes to see Frederick Lawrence, intending to apologize for assaulting him. Lawrence declines to see him, but Markham boldly pushes past the butler, determined to make things right with Helen's brother. He finds Lawrence in bad condition but nonetheless plunges ahead with his explanation. He did not know that Lawrence was Helen's brother; he had

mistaken Lawrence for a rival for Helen's affections. Lawrence, to Markham's relief, offers his hand, at the same time telling Markham that he has told Helen nothing of the matter. He has not even told her he is ill.

Lawrence asks if Markham will mail a letter to his sister, explaining that he is unable to see her owing to illness. Finally, he asks Markham to visit from time to time.

Chapters 46–49: Friendly Counsels, Startling Intelligence, Further Intelligence, "The rain descended, and the floods came, and the winds blew, and beat upon the house, and it fell: and great was the fall of it"
The only news Markham receives about Helen comes through Frederick Lawrence, on whom he frequently calls. Markham finds he cannot resist asking if Helen mentions him, but Lawrence says she does not discuss him much.

Nonetheless, Markham is grateful to Lawrence, and when it seems that the latter is falling into the marital trap being laid by Jane Wilson, Markham feels it is his duty to disabuse Lawrence of some misconceptions about her. He tells his friend that Jane Wilson and Eliza Millward are responsible for the vicious gossip about Helen, including the presumption that she was having an affair with her landlord, Lawrence. Although at the time Lawrence does not welcome the news, it has its desired effect of ending any further courtship of Jane Wilson.

Some time later, Eliza Millward calls on the Markhams, bearing word of Helen. Not only is Helen's husband not dead, Eliza says, she had run away from him. What is more, Helen has now returned to him, and the two have effected a "'perfect reconciliation.'" Shocked by this news, Markham hurries to see Lawrence, demanding to know if it is true. He had not even known that Helen was gone from Wildfell Hall, but Lawrence now tells him that she has indeed left, returning to Grassdale and Huntingdon. Markham, who feels that her whereabouts must have been revealed by someone who betrayed her, is doubly shocked to learn that Helen returned of her own free will. Huntingdon is alone and gravely ill, and Helen, out of a sense of duty, has returned to nurse him.

Lawrence hands Markham the letter in which Helen explains the circumstances in which she now finds herself. When she first arrived at Grassdale Huntingdon was half delirious, mistaking Helen for Alice Myers. When he finally accepts the fact that Helen has returned, he bitterly remarks that she has done so only to increase her store in heaven and ensure that he goes to hell. Helen calmly tells him that her goal is to tend to his physical needs, but that she will gladly benefit his soul, too, if she can.

Huntingdon proves to be a difficult patient. He demands to see his son, but having forfeited Helen's trust, he is obliged first to sign a written agreement that he will make no effort to take young Arthur from her. When the boy seems fearful of him, Huntingdon accuses Helen of turning their son against him. When Helen attempts to make Huntingdon more comfortable, he throws her courtesy back in her face. Still, he is concerned with his mortality and with his soul. Ever patient, ever committed to God and to duty, Helen tells him that he may not be in mortal danger now, but he should prepare himself for the inevitable. For her part, Helen tells her brother, she is doing what she perceives God requires of her.

Having read her letter, Markham asks if he may keep it. Lawrence grants this desire, as well as Markham's request that he ask Helen to permit him to tell his mother and sister of Helen's true history.

A few days later, Lawrence shows Markham another letter from Helen, which gives Markham authority to reveal her identity but asks him not to think of her. The letter goes on to detail Huntingdon's recovery. Now that he is better, he has become an impossibly demanding patient, inclined to pursue the old bad habits of excessive drinking and eating that nearly killed him. Markham finds little comfort in Helen's news, but he is heartened by his ability to clear Helen's name.

Helen's subsequent letters to her brother carry news of Huntingdon's relapse and renewed fear of death. His one remaining friend, Hattersley, comes to Grassdale with Milicent to comfort Huntingdon and try to relieve Helen. But the sicker Huntingdon becomes, the more he leans on Helen for comfort and support. When Hattersley suggests that it is time to call for a clergyman,

Huntingdon refuses, saying only Helen can help him now. In extremis he begs her pardon but still refuses to repent of his sins or ask God's forgiveness. A few days later he is gone.

Chapter 50: Doubts and Disappointments
Markham cannot help but feel overjoyed that Helen is at last released. Restlessly, he waits for Lawrence to return from Huntingdon's funeral at Grassdale. When Lawrence does return, all he tells Markham is that Helen is exhausted. Markham is left with no alternative but to honor his promise not to try to contact Helen for six months after their parting. In another 10 weeks he can write to her himself.

Just when the waiting period is up, Helen's uncle dies. When Lawrence returns from the uncle's funeral at Staningley, he tells Markham that Helen is still there, but he does not volunteer her address. Five months pass, during which Markham keeps his distance from Lawrence. Lawrence then comes to see him, telling him he is off to join Helen, who is recovering at the seaside. Markham, too proud to ask for more information, is obliged to wait more than two more months before Lawrence comes home.

Markham interrupts his narrative here to explain that Annabella has met a bad end, having run off with another man. When the two inevitably parted, she sank into misery and disgrace, ultimately dying from neglect and penury. Lord Lowborough, after divorcing her, remarried. Another of Huntingdon's former friends, Grimsby, died as he lived, murdered in a drunken brawl. Hattersley, by contrast, kept to the road of reform, living in the country and making a name for himself as a horse breeder.

Chapters 51–53: An Unexpected Occurrence, Fluctuations, Conclusion
One cold winter day some months later, Markham encounters Eliza Millward while out walking. Eliza stuns him with the news that Frederick Lawrence is about to leave again, this time to attend Helen's wedding to Hargrave. In a state of shock, Markham rushes to Lawrence's house, where he learns that Lawrence has already left for Grassdale. Markham follows him, telling himself there is a slim chance that he can save Helen from what surely will be another bad marriage.

Anne Brontë found inspiration for The Tenant of Wildfell Hall, *her second novel, in the story of Mrs. Collins, a local woman whose husband abandoned her without means to support their two young children. She modeled the heroine's husband on her brother Branwell and his reckless behavior.* (*Life and Works of Charlotte Brontë and Her Sisters* [1872–73], illustrations by E. M. Wimperis)

After traveling all night through a snowstorm, Markham arrives at Grassdale. As he approaches a little rural church there, he sees a newlywed couple emerging from the building. To his great surprise and relief it is the former Esther Hargrave and Lawrence, who explains that Markham must not have received his letter announcing his marriage.

Markham travels on to Grassdale Manor, where he is disappointed to learn that Helen is at Staningley. Stopping only to eat and wash, he continues on his long journey toward the woman he loves. Riding on a stagecoach, he overhears two other passengers discussing Helen, who has inherited her uncle's estate. Once arrived, Markham is assailed by doubts about his suitability now that Helen's status has so increased. As he stands gloomily on the drive, he hears young Arthur call his name. A coach bearing the boy, his mother,

and his great aunt stops briefly, then travels on to the manor. When Markham enters there, he finds Helen looking very much herself. She asks first for news of Lindenhope, then asks why Markham seems so little pleased to see her.

Markham tells her of his feelings of inferiority, and Helen is obliged to draw him out. Offering him a winter-blooming rose that is "'not so fragrant as a summer flower,'" she asks if he will take it. When he hesitates to take it from her, Helen snatches it back and throws it out into the snow. Markham retrieves it, telling Helen that she has misconstrued him. Helen has offered herself to him, and he has been waiting so long that he cannot believe his good fortune. Even now she says that they must wait another year to prepare themselves and their friends for the union. Satisfied at last, Markham reacquaints himself with Arthur and gets to know Aunt Maxwell.

Markham brings his narrative to a close by telling Halford how he and Helen married the following summer, taking up residence at Staningley with Aunt Maxwell and young Arthur.

PUBLICATION HISTORY

Published during the last week of June 1848, Anne's second novel was presented as another work by Acton BELL, one of the group of three scandalous authors of *JANE EYRE*, *Wuthering Heights*, and *AGNES GREY*. Many critics speculated that Acton, Currer, and Ellis Bell not only were male but also were the same person. Although Emily refused to leave home, Charlotte and Anne went to London in person on July 7 to prove to their publisher that these novels were the work of more than one person. On meeting them, George SMITH proposed to use these two "rather quaintly dressed little ladies, rather pale-faced and anxious-looking" to publicize the new book. Anne and Charlotte declined, having achieved their mission and desirous to continue writing under their pseudonyms.

Reviewers criticized Acton Bell, or Anne, once more for exhibiting a "morbid love for the coarse," as stated by the *Spectator*, but despite such harsh judgments—or perhaps because of them—her novel sold well, with a second edition appearing just a month after initial publication. This gave Anne an opportunity to answer her critics, and she took the unusual step of writing a preface for this second edition, defending her decision to depict vice in graphic detail. She also addressed the speculation about her gender, stating categorically, ". . . I am at a loss to conceive . . . why a woman should be censured for writing anything that would be proper and becoming for a man."

Nine months later Anne was dead, and Charlotte, who felt the subject matter of *The Tenant of Wildfell Hall* to have been an "entire mistake," suppressed any subsequent editions of the novel. In the "Biographical Notice" to the 1850 edition of *Wuthering Heights* and *Agnes Grey*, Charlotte explained that the "terrible effects of talents abused and faculties abused" as depicted in Anne's second novel were taken from life, observed "close at hand and for a long time." For Charlotte, Anne's contemplation of Branwell's sad end made her sister believe it "to be her duty to reproduce every detail . . . as a warning to others." Charlotte thought, on the other hand, that it was a bad business, and consequently no other edition of Anne's last work appeared until after Charlotte's death in 1855.

Thackeray,   William   Makepeace   (1811–1863) English novelist and satirist. He first came to public attention with his amusing sketches for *FRASER'S MAGAZINE* and then as a satirist, publishing his work in the humor magazine *Punch*. His literary fame rests on two novels, *Vanity Fair* (1847–48) and *The History of Henry Esmond* (1852). Both reflect Thackeray's deep cynicism about society but also his keen interest in history and in public events—also evinced in his celebrated lectures, *The Four Georges* (1855). Charlotte Brontë attended these lectures and met Thackeray, who showed keen interest in her and visited her on several occasions when she was in London. Charlotte kept a portrait of Thackeray on the wall in HAWORTH PARSONAGE. She admired the way he could capture the whole canvas of society, but she also criticized his tendency to favor editorial commentary over dramatic narrative and his obsession with history

William Makepeace Thackeray. Charlotte Brontë admired the great Victorian novelist and attended his lectures in London. He supported her work as well. (Library of Congress)

Thornfield, Mr. Rochester's estate in Jane Eyre   (*Life and Works of Charlotte Brontë and Her Sisters* [1872–73], illustrations by E. M. Wimperis)

to the detriment of his stories. Elizabeth GASKELL's biography first described the friendship between Thackeray and Charlotte.

Thomas   Character in *THE TENANT OF WILDFELL HALL*. Thomas is a manservant at STANINGLEY, home of Helen HUNTINGDON's aunt, Mrs. Peggy MAXWELL, and uncle.

Thornfield   The estate of Edward Fairfax ROCHESTER, Jane EYRE's employer and eventual husband, in *JANE EYRE*. It is a substantial building, three stories high—more of a manor house than a nobleman's estate. Upon her arrival Jane admires the "mighty old thorn trees," as broad and knotty as oaks, and its secluded atmosphere in the hills. The grounds are extensive and reflect the major role the Rochester family has played in

this part of the country. Thornfield is destroyed in a fire that blinds Mr. Rochester and kills his first wife, Bertha MASON.

Thornton   From 1815 to 1820 Patrick Brontë was minister in this town (three miles from BRADFORD and six from HAWORTH), where Charlotte, Branwell, Emily, and Anne were born.

Thorp Green   Manor at Little Ouseburn, near York. Set in the center of a vast estate, Thorp Green was home to Reverend Edmund Robinson, his wife, Lydia ROBINSON, and their five children. The manor was the second largest of its kind in the area, also housing three male and seven female servants, as well as a governess. Between May 1840 and June 1845, Anne Brontë was the governess, charged with oversight of the Robinson's three eldest daughters. In December 1842, Branwell joined his sister at Thorp Green, where he acted as tutor to young Edmund Robinson until he was dismissed in July 1845 for his alleged love affair with Mrs. Robinson.

Thousand and One Nights   *See* ARABIAN NIGHTS.

"Three Guides, The"   Poem by Anne BRONTË. Anne finished composing this 27-stanza poem on August 11, 1847. As the critic Muriel Spark first noted in 1953, "The Three Guides" seems to be in some respects a response to her sister Emily and, in particular, to Emily's *Wuthering Heights* and "THE PHILOSOPHER." Anne's poem concerns three spirits—Earth, Pride, and Faith—who can serve as exemplars. The poet rejects the first of these, the Spirit of Earth, for its "heartless, cold grey eye" and inability to heed the "still small voice of Heaven." Even more pernicious is the Spirit of Pride, with its "ecstatic joys" and eyes like "lightning," that are also ruthless, scoffing, and overproud. Anne, not surprisingly, chooses for her guide the Spirit of Faith.

The Spirit of Pride shares many of HEATHCLIFF's characteristics, good and bad. Anne clearly saw this character as the embodiment of Emily's own refusal to accept the kind of religious faith that Anne deemed essential. "The Three Guides" is in a sense Anne's answer to the "three Gods" warring within the poet in "The Philosopher." Their conflicting demands lead the philosopher to opt for oblivion. Plainly this was not a conclusion that Anne could in any way support.

Throttler   Dog in *WUTHERING HEIGHTS*. Throttler is the son of SKULKER, given by old Mr. LINTON as a gift to Hindley EARNSHAW. When Isabella LINTON arrives at WUTHERING HEIGHTS as HEATHCLIFF's wife, Throttler proves to be the only friendly inhabitant she finds in her new home.

Thrushcross Grange (the Grange)   Location in *WUTHERING HEIGHTS*. This isolated but stately home, surrounded by apparently vast parklands, is the ancestral home of the Linton family. HEATHCLIFF takes revenge on Edgar LINTON for having married Catherine EARNSHAW by gaining control of the estate. The location of the Grange was prob-ably based on that of Ponden Hall, a manor house near the village of Stanbury and a few miles from the Brontë home in HAWORTH. As children, the Brontës apparently borrowed books from the private library at Ponden Hall.

Tiger   HAWORTH PARSONAGE cat. Tiger died in March 1844.

Top Withens   A farmhouse on HAWORTH MOOR, now a deserted ruin atop a rise, it was occupied during the Brontës' lifetimes and is thought to have suggested the location of WUTHERING HEIGHTS.

Tory   Political party associated with the landed gentry and the CHURCH OF ENGLAND. It was the establishment party between 1630 and 1830 and later came to be known as the Conservative Party. In *SHIRLEY*, Matthewson HELSTONE is called a "high Tory," meaning that as a rector he is in the upper strata of the party, one of its most privileged and staunchest members.

Tower of All Nations   *See* GLASS TOWN.

"Tract for the Times, A"   Article by Patrick BRONTË appearing in the *Leeds Intelligencer* in 1850. In it Patrick defends the established church against attacks by Catholics and DISSENTERS. He predicts chaos and cataclysmic events akin to the French Revolution if the CHURCH OF ENGLAND were overthrown.

trade   Term used in *THE PROFESSOR* and in many other English novels to describe the traffic in goods for sale and exchange. Among the aristocratic class trade traditionally was considered a middle-class occupation. An aristocrat or noble had inherited wealth, much of it coming from land holdings, so work, as defined by the aristocracy, meant the supervision of land. Other kinds of work, such as trade or factory ownership, were considered "common"—that is, vulgar and not fit for a gentleman. William CRIMSWORTH declares his independence from such snobbish distinctions when he announces that he intends to pursue a career in trade, even though he has been educated as a gentleman at ETON COLLEGE. Such distinctions between what was fitting for the upper and middle classes were beginning to break down in 19th-century England. In *The Professor*, for example, HUNSDEN comes from an old, distinguished family, but he is also an investor and involved in the world of trade.

Tree, Captain Andrew   *See GREEN DWARF, THE.*

Trista, Juanna   Minor character in *THE PROFESSOR*. William CRIMSWORTH describes her as a rebellious student.

Trollope, Anthony (1815–1882)   English novelist born in London. He worked as a civil servant for the post office while turning out a remarkable number of novels of consistently high standard. He is perhaps best known for his Barsetshire series, which began with *The Warden* (1855) and was succeeded by the immensely popular *Barsetshire Towers* (1857). Trollope's masterpiece is considered to be *The Way We Live Now* (1875), a comprehensive canvas of Victorian society. Anne Brontë's novels prefigure Trollope's insofar as they conduct a sustained, cumulative view of society, worked out in plots that emphasize a painstaking examination of human character. As Anne tends to avoid flashy characters and melodrama, her works stand in relation to her sisters Emily's and Charlotte's as Trollope's stand in relation to the rather GOTHIC and ROMANTIC work of Charles Dickens (1812–70).

tuberculosis   A disease more commonly called "consumption" in the 19th century. In 1825, the two eldest Brontë girls, Maria and Elizabeth, died at ages 11 and 10, respectively, less than six weeks apart of tuberculosis, the 19th-century plague. Interestingly, consumption was thought to strike figures of literary genius with particular frequency. The sisters seem to have contracted the disease during their year at the Clergy Daughters School, COWAN BRIDGE. Charlotte would later use the school as the model for the infamous LOWOOD in *JANE EYRE*. Tuberculosis struck the Brontës again in 1848 and 1849, when Branwell, Emily, and Anne all succumbed to the disease within an eight-month period.

Turner, Miss   Character mentioned in *VILLETTE*. Lucy SNOWE refers to "poor Miss Turner," an English teacher who did not know how to discipline her students.

Tynedale, Lord   One of William CRIMSWORTH's aristocratic uncles in *THE PROFESSOR*. Tynedale is surprised that Crimsworth rejects the offer of his other uncle, the Hon. John SEACOMBE, of a LIVING as a clergyman at Seacombe. Tynedale asks Crimsworth if he means to go into TRADE like his father. Crimsworth shocks Tynedale by saying he does. Crimsworth's reply effectively severs his connection with his uncles, who disapprove of what they see as a vulgar choice.

V

Vandenhuten, Victor In *THE PROFESSOR*, William CRIMSWORTH saves Victor Vandenhuten's son from drowning. The grateful father vows to help William, who later applies to him when William seeks a new teaching position. With Vandenhuten's assistance William finds the teaching position that provides him with enough income to fulfill his desire to marry Frances Evans HENRI.

Varens, Adèle Character in *JANE EYRE*. Edward Fairfax ROCHESTER's ward and Jane EYRE's pupil, Adèle is the young daughter of Céline VARENS, a French opera singer who betrayed Mr. Rochester after he had made her his mistress. He took pity on Adèle when her mother abandoned her as well. Adèle is a willing pupil. She and Jane become devoted to each other and, in turn, to Mr. Rochester.

Varens, Céline Character mentioned in *JANE EYRE*. She is a French opera singer who exploits Edward Fairfax ROCHESTER's obsession with her. Although he installs her in a Paris apartment and decks her with jewels, she is unfaithful and even ridicules him by taking another lover—as Rochester learns one night when he sees her with the other man. He overhears her conversation and realizes that she is unworthy of his love. He spurns her, then fights a duel with his rival, wounding the man and thus ending his infatuation. Céline's young daughter, Adèle VARENS, becomes Mr. Rochester's ward and Jane EYRE's pupil after her mother abandons her.

Verdopolis *See* ANGRIA.

Vernet *See* GLASS TOWN.

Vicar of Wakefield, The Published in 1766, this classic novel by Oliver Goldsmith (1730–1774) is about an unworldly, kindly, and generous vicar. In *VILLETTE*, Lucy SNOWE's students have trouble translating a passage from the novel into French.

Villette The town modeled on BRUSSELS in *VILLETTE*.

Villette Novel by Charlotte BRONTË. Charlotte began writing *Villette* in early 1852, and by March 29 she had completed the first volume of her three-volume novel. The story drew on details of her own life, particularly her studies and stay at the PENSIONNAT HEGER in BRUSSELS in 1843. Like her heroine Lucy SNOWE, she made a confession at a Catholic Church, and like Lucy, she felt keenly the "solitude of her existence," as biographer Juliet BARKER puts it.

Charlotte put off traveling to London and other activities to keep working on her novel. She had trouble keeping to a regular writing schedule, however, and this failure to be productive apparently brought on a period of depression and ill health reminiscent of Lucy Snowe's period of physical and mental debilitation in *Villette*.

Two holiday excursions improved Charlotte's health considerably, although it was not until late June 1852 that she was able to resume writing the novel, which even then was interrupted when her father Patrick had a stroke. Even worse, Charlotte began to suffer headaches as she made slow progress on the second volume of *Villette*. She faced the problem of how to resolve Lucy Snowe's life: Should she win over Dr. John Graham BRETTON, who was smitten with two women far more beautiful than Lucy? Complicating her decision, the novel's Dr. John was based on her publisher George SMITH, whom Charlotte loved, and Mrs. Louisa BRETTON was based on Smith's mother. To have the astringent Lucy conquer her rivals was tantamount to declaring Charlotte's own hopes for herself. In the end, she decided that fiction should not reflect her wishes and that it was not meant for Lucy to win over the handsome doctor.

By sending off the second volume to George Smith, Charlotte was asking for confirmation of her decision, and his approval of her narrative helped fill her with the confidence to attempt the third, concluding volume. As Charlotte wrote to Smith, "if Lucy married anybody—it must be the Professor." She was referring to M. Paul EMMANUEL, a fitful, formidable character expressly designed to challenge and to win over Lucy's rather austere, if passionate temperament. By November 20, Charlotte had completed the novel and wrote Smith, "Now that 'Villette' is off my hands I mean to try to wait the result with calm. Conscience—if she be just—will not reproach me, for I have tried to do my best."

Although Smith accepted the novel, he lamented that Dr. John played so small a role in the third volume, and he wished that Lucy had married him. Charlotte replied to Smith that the ending seemed "compulsory upon the writer" even if it disappointed her readers. "The spirit of Romance would have indicated another course, far more flowery and inviting . . . but this would have been unlike Real Life, inconsistent with Truth—as variance with Probability."

SYNOPSIS

Volume One

Chapter 1: Bretton
The novel begins with a description of the narrator's godmother, Mrs. Bretton, a widow. She lives in the ancient town of Bretton (named after her family). The narrator, identified in the second chapter as Lucy Snowe, visits Mrs. Bretton often and is made much of because she is the only child in the household, as Mrs. Bretton's son, John Graham, is away at school. So satisfying are Lucy's visits that she compares them to the sojourns of Christian and Hopeful, characters in John Bunyan's THE PILGRIM'S PROGRESS, "beside a pleasant stream." This self-contained world is suddenly disrupted when Lucy learns of a child related to Dr. Bretton, Mrs. Bretton's dead husband. The child is the young daughter of a Mrs. HOME, a silly person and a careless mother,

according to Mrs. Bretton, who has died. Mr. HOME, the distraught girl's father and an impractical man, in Mrs. Bretton's opinion, has been advised to restore himself through travel. Mrs. Bretton has offered to attend to his daughter, although she worries lest the daughter turn out like the mother.

The girl arrives on a rainy night, and Mrs. Bretton fusses over her. Her name is Paulina HOME, but she is called Polly and says she will be happy to stay with Mrs. Bretton until her father comes for her. Polly is a commanding figure, demanding that Mrs. Bretton allow her to get down off her lap and ordering her nurse HARRIET to prepare her bed. Polly and Lucy share a room, although Polly barely acknowledges her roommate's existence. She refers to Lucy as "the girl." Polly tells her nurse Harriet to neaten up Polly's clothing. Polly misses her father and does not like the idea of staying with strangers.

Chapter 2: Paulina
Days go by and Lucy Snowe sees no evidence that Polly is adjusting to her new home. On moonlit nights Lucy watches Polly sitting upright in bed, praying like some "Catholic or Methodist enthusiast." Lucy can make out few words of these prayers, except for the word *father,* and Lucy concludes that Polly's father is the one fixed thought she has.

Polly's glum features light up one day when she spots her father advancing toward her home. Mrs. Bretton tells Mr. Home, who is on his way out of the country, that he will only upset his daughter, but Polly is overjoyed. Lucy witnesses the intense reunion of father and child, observing that Mr. Home looks Scottish and speaks with a northern accent. A man with proud yet homely features, he remains subdued, although Lucy can tell he is moved by seeing his daughter again. Polly resumes her commanding behavior at tea, making certain that she is the one to serve her father even though she is hardly big enough to handle the tea items. Mr. Home is gratified and calls his daughter his comfort.

Later in the day Mrs. Bretton's son John Graham returns home, and he and Mr. Home meet as old friends. Graham is 16, with handsome Celtic looks. Lucy finds him spoiled and whimsical, a "faithless boy." Graham teases Polly, introducing himself as "your slave." Polly responds formally by curtseying and saying "How do you do?" Engaging her in conversation, he elicits from Polly her determination to accompany her father in his travels. Even when Graham promises her a pony ride, Polly persists in declaring she does not like him and that she does not want to stay in his home. She also finds his long red hair "queer," and he responds by saying he finds her just as strange. They continue to tease each other until Graham suddenly takes hold of her and lifts her up. She protests, telling him he would not like it if she could do the same to him.

Chapter 3: The Playmates
Mr. Home stays at Mrs. Bretton's for two days. Graham tries to engage Polly's attention, but she puts him off, saying she has "business" to attend to. He tries to entice her by opening up his desk and displaying various brightly colored items he has collected. Lucy notes that Polly seems to take a "furtive" interest in Graham's teasing. Finally he manages to secure her complete attention with a picture of a Blenham spaniel, which he gives to her. When she refuses to take it, he threatens to tear the picture into pieces. When she relents and says she will accept his offer, he says he requires the payment of a kiss. She then snatches the picture and goes to her father for refuge. Graham pursues her, and she slaps him. He retreats, groaning that she has injured his eye and that a doctor should be sent for. As soon as Polly begins to feel sorry for him, Graham, who has been pretending all along, snatches her up, again angering her. She calls him the "naughtiest" and "rudest" person "that ever was."

Polly pleads with her father to take her with him, but he tells her she is too young for such travel and that she will please him best by not sorrowing over his departure. After Mr. Home leaves, Lucy says that Polly was in agony and Mrs. Bretton shed a tear. Graham merely gazes at Polly, while Lucy herself remains "calm."

After Mr. Home's departure, Graham treats Polly tenderly, and she warms to him. Soon they form a bond, with Polly acting almost as his servant, bringing him his breakfast and joining Mrs. Bretton in doting on him. Indeed, Polly seems to merge her identity with Graham's, learning the names of his friends and catering to his interests.

But when Graham shuts her out from his parties with school friends, Polly rejects him, telling Lucy that she likes Graham best on Sundays when he is quiet and engaged in his studies or in the little pleasures of life at home. She enjoys reading the Bible with Graham, especially the stories about DANIEL in the Lion's Den, JOSEPH (2) cast in the pit and his father Jacob's mourning over him, and the calling of SAMUEL. In her affectionate moments, she embraces Graham, and he says she is almost like his little sister.

Two months later, Mr. Home writes to say he wishes Polly to join him since he has no intention of returning to England for several years. Lucy wonders how Polly will take this turn of events. When Lucy mentions the idea of travel with Mr. Home, Polly becomes cross, pointing out that she has just learned to accustom herself to life without her father. When Lucy tells Polly about her father's letter, Polly says "of course" she will enjoy returning to her father.

Polly asks Lucy to tell Graham about her departure. Graham's reacts with dismay, saying he will miss his "mousie," but then he becomes absorbed in his study and ignores Polly, who has come to nestle beside him. Later that evening Polly dramatically announces she cannot sleep and cannot live. Lucy tries to calm her by taking her to bid Graham good night. Polly is pacified, and Lucy tries to explain that a 16-year-old boy cannot possibly be as passionately attached to a six-year-old girl as she is to him. Polly is disappointed but also buoyed by Lucy's comment that Polly is Graham's "favorite." Going to bed, Polly questions Lucy about how much she likes Graham. Lucy answers "a little," and Polly explains that Graham, like all boys, is "full of faults." Lucy warms the shivering Polly in her bed, wondering how this capricious child will fare in the world. Polly leaves Bretton the next day.

Chapter 4: Miss Marchmount
Lucy returns home after a six-month stay at Bretton, not expecting to see Polly again; indeed, Lucy never does return to Bretton, later learning that Mrs. Bretton and her son have moved to London, since she could no longer afford to maintain her property. In the city Graham takes up an occupation, although about this development and her own experience during the next eight years Lucy

says very little, except that she has learned to be self-reliant.

Lucy's life changes when Miss MARCHMOUNT, a maiden lady, calls for her. An invalid, Miss Marchmount requires constant care. She has a reputation for being irritable and demanding. Lucy's heart sinks to think of spending her youth in service to this cranky woman. Without other prospects, however, Lucy agrees to attend Miss Marchmount and finds that while her employer can be trying, she is basically a good person who copes with her infirmities with fortitude and patience. If Miss Marchmount is sometimes a scold, she does not humiliate Lucy, and Lucy is able to form an affectionate bond with her.

After a short time, Lucy finds herself devoted to Miss Marchmount, an "original character," and does not seem to miss the life of nature or the world outside of her employment. "All within me narrowed to my lot," Lucy observes. Then, on a stormy night, the kind that has agitated Lucy's feelings before, Miss Marchmount awakes and announces that she feels as though she has recovered her youth, and she tells Lucy about FRANK, the love of her youth. She grieves that she had only "twelve months of bliss" with him followed by "thirty years of sorrow." At Lucy's importunate request, Miss Marchmount recalls the night she lost her lover, a dreadful scene in which Frank was fatally injured in a riding accident and dragged by his horse. Miss Marchmount asks Lucy why she had to endure such an event, holding her lover in her arms as he said he was dying in paradise. Lucy cannot answer, and the next morning she discovers Miss Marchmount dead of a stroke.

Chapters 5–6: Turning a New Leaf, London
At 23, Lucy finds herself alone again, with only 15 pounds, the rest of her salary. She consults Mrs. BARRETT, a housekeeper friend, but she is given no satisfactory advice. Then she goes out for a long walk at night and is stimulated by the AURORA BOREALIS. It is as if a voice calls to her, urging her to begin a new life in London, which is only 50 miles away, a day's journey.

With Mrs. Barrett's recommendation of a small inn in London, Lucy sets off, perhaps having it in mind to become something like the nurse she observes in the LEIGH HOUSEHOLD, where Mrs.

Barrett lives. The nurse attends Mrs. Leigh's children, converses with them in French, and is treated very well, Lucy observes.

On a wet February night Lucy arrives in London. She is struck by the way Londoners speak, and she is critical of a glib and arrogant chambermaid. Finding herself alone in the strange city and retiring for the night, Lucy gives way to grief, but she quiets herself, realizing that she has no choice but to go "forward."

The next morning, on the first of March, Lucy awakes to find herself revived, absorbing the spirit of a great city. She engages a waiter in conversation and learns that he remembers her two uncles, CHARLES and WILMOT, who often stayed at the inn. She enjoys touring the city, buying a book in a bookshop, visiting ST. PAUL'S CATHEDRAL, "antique WESTMINSTER," TEMPLE GARDENS, the STRAND, CORNHILL, and the WEST END.

Returning to the inn, Lucy resolves to take a bold step: She will sail to the Continent. With the waiter's help, she books passage that night and is dropped off by a coachman. Two waterman row her out to her ship, the *VIVID*, and demand 6 shillings from her. Aboard the ship, the steward tells her she has been cheated, and Lucy agrees, without much sign of emotion. Lucy is firm with a rude stewardess who shows her to her cabin. The stewardess keeps her up all night talking about the WATSONS, a family who will board tomorrow and pay profitable fees for the voyage.

The next morning a great fuss is made over the Watsons, two males and two females who are obviously used to being treated as wealthy people. Lucy finds the males fat, plain, and vulgar, and the females, handsome and colorfully dressed. Lucy is startled to learn that the most beautiful of the Watson women is married to the ugliest and coarsest man and yet seems not to mind. Lucy interprets the woman's laughter as a hysterical reaction to her plight. Ginevra FANSHAWE, another young woman passenger, is escorted onto the boat by her father, who gives Lucy a disapproving look. Ginevra approaches Lucy and engages her in conversation. Ginevra is delighted to learn that this is Lucy's first sea voyage. She asks Lucy about her plans, and Lucy confesses she has none. Then Ginevra chatters on about her desultory education and how little she has learned. She is now in a school in VILLETTE, she tells Lucy. Asked about her plans again, Lucy says she must find work for she is as "poor as JOB." Ginevra tells Lucy about her large family (eight brothers and sisters), many of whom are not well off and have had to marry for money.

Lucy manages to enjoy the air before succumbing to seasickness. She finds the queasy Ginevra a trial, for the young girl is much more fretful than any of the Watsons, who are also ill. A storm stimulates Ginevra to say she is going to die, but a calm brings the ship into port. Lucy is again overcome with the enormity of finding her place in a foreign land. In this weakened state, she makes her way to an inn for the night.

Chapters 7–8: Villette, Madame Beck

The next morning Lucy rises, her confidence renewed. She is accosted by a strange man who demands the keys to her room; he has been sent from the Custom House to deliver her luggage. As she leaves her room, she realizes her inn is a large hotel, and as she enters its great hall, she is again overwhelmed by her effort to make her own way in the world.

Lucy is confronted by an array of tables, at which many men (there are no women present) are eating breakfast. After her meal, an "inner voice" prompts Lucy to set off for Villette, where Madame BECK, according to Miss Fanshawe, runs a school. It is 40 miles away, and Lucy does not even have an address, yet she feels she has left a "desert" and has no place to return to. It is raining, and on the dreary trip Lucy alternates between fanciful dreams of her success and anxieties over what she will find.

Upon arrival, Lucy discovers that her luggage has not been put on her coach, but through the intervention of an Englishman who speaks French

Lucy Snowe arrives at the Pensionnat de Demoiselles in Villette. (*Life and Works of Charlotte Brontë and Her Sisters* [1872–73], illustrations by E. M. Wimperis)

she finds out that it will be delivered the next day. The Englishman notes the anxiety in her voice and inquires whether she has friends nearby. He is handsome—even princely looking—and he recommends a local inn. Harassed by two men who follow her, Lucy loses her way, only to come across a sign for a "Pensionnat de Demoiselles," and beneath it the name Madame Beck. Lucy decides to knock on the door and to ask for Madame Beck, who turns out to be a "dumpy little woman," looking motherly but otherwise noncommittal as Lucy relates how she came to knock on Madame Beck's door. Dreading a return to the street, she promises to serve faithfully in any capacity. A hesitant Madame Beck consults her cousin, M. Paul Emmanuel, who has just arrived. She has faith that he can study a countenance and judge Lucy's character, since Lucy has no references. M. Paul is somewhat noncommittal, but in the end he advises Madame Beck to hire Lucy if the school needs another person on its staff. Thus a relieved Lucy is hired.

Lucy is given a meal in the kitchen and a bed in a room with three students. In the middle of the night Lucy is awakened by the noise of Madame Beck carefully going through her possessions, perhaps trying to form some estimate of the woman she has hired. Lucy appreciates her employer's caution but deplores the invasion of her privacy.

The next day Lucy meets Mrs. SWEENY, who has been employed as a nurse and governess at the school. Although Mrs. Sweeny has told Madame Beck that she is a native of Middlesex, Lucy can tell that in fact she is Irish. Lucy suspects that with her suspiciously expensive and flamboyant wardrobe, Mrs. Sweeny has led an adventurous life. The night before, Lucy saw Mrs. Sweeny dozing with a liquor bottle by her side. Now Mrs. Sweeny tries to intimidate both Lucy and Madame Beck, but Madame Beck calmly calls the police and has Mrs. Sweeny removed.

All of this is accomplished by breakfast, and by noon Lucy is acting as Madame Beck's lady's maid, helping her to dress. The casualness of Madame Beck's dress—she stays in her slippers until noon—surprises Lucy, who comments that no female head of an English school would behave in such a manner. Still, Lucy admires Madame's

figure and her dress, which she calls "BOURGEOIS." Madame Beck is a charitable woman who rules with a firm hand. Like the King Minos of Greek mythology, she is renowned for the just use of her power.

Lucy learns that the school has 100 day students and 20 who board. The staff includes four teachers, eight masters, and six servants. As Lucy acquires French she is able to answer Madame's questions about England and the English, a people Madame Beck finds superior to her neighbors on the Continent.

Madame Beck governs through "espionage," that is, she has her spies and is aware of everything of consequence in her school. She is "rationally benevolent"; she finds it a good policy to be generous with those in need, but Lucy notes that when someone tries to appeal to her feelings, Madame Beck withdraws her sympathy.

Lucy extols the school's garden, where classes are held in warm weather. Teachers deliver lectures, and students learn by taking notes. Meanwhile Madame studies Lucy's habits and behavior with children who recite their English lessons to her. When Mr. WILSON, the English instructor, fails to show up for work, Madame tells Lucy to substitute. Thus Lucy is forced to forsake her sewing and enter the classroom. Although she fears her French is not good enough, Lucy assures Madame Beck that she will not let her rebellious French pupils master her. Madame Beck says that Lucy will be on her own; if she requires assistance, then she will have failed. The students BLANCHE, VIRGINIE, and ANGELIQUE quickly form a plot against Lucy, hoping to quickly oust her. They titter and whisper as Lucy begins the lesson.

Lucy's first act is to take Blanche's composition book to the estrade (the raised platform on which the teacher lectures) and tear out the pages of "stupid" composition. This act silences the students, except for DOLORES, an unruly Catalonian, whom Lucy handles by suddenly ejecting her from the classroom and locking her in a closet. This proves to be a popular decision, because Dolores is heartily disliked by her classmates. The lesson continues, and the students perform with great industry.

After the lesson, Madame Beck (who has been spying on Lucy) congratulates her new teacher and fires Mr. Wilson. Lucy's days as a nurse-governess are over.

Chapter 9: Isidore

Lucy enjoys teaching at the school, impressed with how the middle-class students mingle easily with their aristocratic schoolmates. The school benefits from the cosmopolitan atmosphere of Villette and the multinational character of its student body. Lucy notices that the bourgeoisie tends to be better mannered, without the insolence and deceit of the upper classes.

Approaching her job with firmness and good humor, Lucy wins the loyalty of her students, especially the older ones. Nevertheless, Lucy has to contend with Madame Beck's continual spying on her and the Catholic teachers' monitoring of her PROTESTANT opinions.

Lucy is reunited with Ginevra Fanshawe, who returns to the school. Ginevra proves to be sensible, if highly critical and selfish. Ginevra goes into hysterics when Lucy refuses to mend Ginevra's clothes. Yet she remains a charming companion to Lucy, who hears about Ginevra's suitor, a young man she calls "Isidore." She does not think her uncle would approve of Isidore, and she does not love him or care that she will break his heart. Lucy tells Ginevra that Isidore is too good for her. A poor student, except for her performance in music, singing, and dancing, Ginevra leaves her lessons undone or gets others to do them for her. Mrs. CHOLMODELEY, Ginevra's chaperone, takes her to parties and other events in the city. As with Lucy, Ginevra tries to take advantage of this fashionable lady, who eventually refuses her charge's constant requests for dresses and other presents.

Lucy and Ginevra quarrel when Lucy refuses to praise Ginevra's *"parure"* (finery), and Ginevra deplores Lucy's "puritanical tastes." Later, when Ginevra tells Lucy that her new clothing has been supplied by Isidore, Lucy chastises Ginevra for taking advantage of a man she has no intention of marrying. Ginevra responds that Isidore is not a suitable match for he understands nothing of her faults; she is more comfortable with Lucy's criticism than with Isidore's adoration. Appreciating Ginevra's candor, Lucy nevertheless insists that her pupil return Isidore's gifts. Ginevra counters that Isidore gains great pleasure from seeing her well dressed. But to Lucy, Ginevra is merely practicing deceit. Ginevra points out that she had taken up with Isidore because she had thought he would help her enjoy her youth, but now he has turned serious. The exasperated Lucy tells Ginevra to leave her room.

Chapter 10: Dr. John

Lucy observes that while Madame Beck worries about her students' futures and takes good care of them, she expresses no tenderness. Even with very young children she never caresses them or allows them to express their affection for her physically. Yet Madame Beck is extraordinarily tolerant. Her eldest girl DESIREE, a destructive student, smashes items in the kitchen and tries to put the blame on the servant, yet Madame Beck does not confront Desiree. Even when Desiree resorts to stealing, Madame Beck rationalizes Desiree's behavior and restores stolen property while sending Desiree out for walks.

Madame Beck's stalwart nature is evident, however, when she calmly helps Dr. John set the broken arm of Madame Beck's second daughter, FIFENE. The young doctor appears to have an English complexion, and he speaks English perfectly. Suddenly Lucy realizes that he is the courteous gentleman who helped her when she first landed in Villette. She does not expect to see him again, however, since Madame Beck usually relies on Dr. PILLULE, who happened to be out of town when Fifene broke her arm.

Desiree exploits Dr. John's visit by claiming an illness, and both Madame Beck and Dr. John join in her "farce," treating her seriously even though it is apparent that she is shamming. The doctor's tolerance puzzles Lucy, especially since he returns periodically to treat Desiree for her nonexistent sickness.

Lucy does not think Dr. John notices her or remembers their meeting, but one day he catches her looking at him. He says that such close scrutiny must result from her detecting a fault in him, and he asks her to tell him what it is. Confounded by his question, she remains silent and goes about her work.

Chapter 11: The Portresse's Cabinet

Lucy sees more of Dr. John when he treats GEORGETTE, Madame Beck's youngest child, for a fever.

His visit creates a stir in the school as Madame Beck introduces him to the "proud and handsome Blanche de Melcy" and to the "vain, flirting Angelique." Gossip spreads even to the town itself, but Madame Beck is firm with protesting parents, telling them she uses the doctor to treat her own children, too. Her pupils praise the doctor for his treatment of them and the uproar soon subsides, even though it is rumored that Madame Beck is to marry Dr. John. Lucy doubts it was ever Madame Beck's intention to woo the doctor.

Lucy wonders what the doctor has made of this fuss. At 40, Madame Beck is perhaps 14 years his senior, but he seems to have derived amusement from his visits to her. Lucy's bafflement increases when she hears the doctor enter the school and speak with a woman who may be the portress, Rosine MATOU, a pretty but fickle young woman. Next she hears and then sees the doctor attending to Georgette as Madame Beck lectures him about taking better care of his health and not working so hard. The doctor shrugs off her concern, and she appeals to Lucy for a judgment. Lucy observes that something may have momentarily upset him, and the doctor is startled to hear her speak in English, for up to now they have had no conversation together. The doctor apparently wanted to speak to her but then thought better of it. After the doctor leaves, Madame Beck seems to lapse into depression while Lucy makes a study of Rosine and wonders if or how she has captured the doctor's heart.

Chapters 12–13: The Casket, a Sneeze Out of Season
Lucy describes the legend associated with Madame Beck's school and garden: It was once a convent and is haunted by the ghost of a young girl. Dismissing the story as "romantic rubbish," Lucy explains how she loved to walk in the beautiful garden. One summer evening, enjoying the coolness, fragrance, and solitude, Lucy sits on a bench in a secluded, shady part of the garden that is shunned by most of the teachers and forbidden to the students. She thinks of her childhood and then of the future. Suddenly an object falls from one of the casement windows overlooking the garden. It is a casket containing a message for her, since it mentions the gray dress she is wearing. Although she has never dreamed of receiving love letters, she cannot help but wonder if this message

is a *billet doux*. But it is not for her after all, as several girls and teachers wear gray dresses. Lucy sees Rosine admit Dr. John to her apartment. Lucy cannot believe the note is his since it does not seem to be his style. He asks her not to betray him, and she replies that she cannot betray what she does not know. She spots Rosine, who is also wearing a gray dress. The doctor fears a scandal, but Lucy thinks to herself that Madame Beck would surely not allow this incident to be gossiped about. Before the matter can be resolved, Lucy sees Madame Beck entering the garden. Although Dr. John escapes, Lucy is sure that Madame has caught at least a glimpse of him and must be wondering what has happened. Madame Beck does not, however, question Lucy about the incident.

Lucy turns her attention to explaining how each evening students gather to hear a lesson read from an ancient volume relating the lives of the saints. She finds the tales, with their emphasis on human corruption, nearly intolerable. To her Protestant sensibility, the stories seems too "POPISH." She leaves these "lectures" as soon as possible and takes refuge in her own "still shadow world." Although she finds Madame Beck's constant surveillance trying (Lucy spies on her employer meticulously examining all of Lucy's possessions), she withdraws from the scene, not wanting to provoke a confrontation. Madame Beck is, after all, a tolerant employer who imposes few restrictions, and Lucy cannot be sure of finding another like her. With no secrets to hide, Lucy can put up with Madame's snooping, stimulated no doubt by the sight of Lucy and Dr. John in the garden. For all her protestations of calm, however, Lucy gives way one evening to a torrent of tears, although she recovers the next day.

Although Georgette has recovered from her fever, Madame Beck insists on calling for Dr. John, and Lucy suspects that her employer has some sort of plan in mind since Madame announces she will not be home when the doctor calls. When Dr. John arrives, Rosine asks him the question Lucy has wanted to put to him: How did he happen to be so quickly on the spot when the casket was dropped from the casement window? Dr. John explains he had been attending a patient, GUS-TAVE, and saw the casket thrown from the window. Rosine asks who threw it; Dr. John replies that it is

The garden in the Rue Fossette in Villette   (*Life and Works of Charlotte Brontë and Her Sisters* [1872–73], illustrations by E. M. Wimperis)

a secret. Later, after Rosine leaves, both Lucy and Dr. John see a note fall from a casement window, and the doctor asks Lucy to fetch it. When she does, he rips it up without reading it. The doctor does not tell her who is dropping these messages, but he implies that a young woman is being courted by someone whom the doctor does not trust. He appears to be about to confide in Lucy when Madame Beck's sneeze alerts them that she is approaching.

Chapter 14: The Fete

Lucy describes her life at school as enjoyable yet solitary. Although many of the teachers try to befriend her and Lucy welcomes their attention, she finds them to be without principle, and she would rather remain solitary than become complicit in their corruption. One is avaricious, another prodigal. To Lucy, Madame acknowledges the faults of one of these teachers, Mademoiselle ST. PIERRE, but says she is valuable because she is so good at keeping order in the classroom. To Lucy's Protestant mind, the school represents the "essence of Romanism." While there is a pretense of freedom, the children are in fact enslaved to a dogma—CATHOLICISM.

Lucy is enchanted with preparations for the "fete," the summer party organized by Mademoiselle St. Pierre. The highlight is the presentation of a play. M. Paul Emmanuel, an austere and formidable professor of literature, rehearses the students for their parts. Both the teachers and the students are cowed by his authority. A *coiffeur* comes to the school to dress the girls' hair. The school is scoured and decorated for the great event.

Lucy is taken aback by M. Paul's request that she take a part in the vaudeville play. Louise Vanderkelkov has fallen ill, he explains, and he needs a replacement. Unable to resist his mixture of menace and pleading she consents, although she finds the role difficult to master and retires to a garret to learn her lines (bedeviled by a large rat and beetles). The school is surprised when M. Paul presents Lucy as a player in the vaudeville. An argument ensues when Lucy objects to her masculine costume (she is playing a man's part). She negotiates a compromise with M. Paul, accepting certain garments, rejecting others. In performance, Lucy gains confidence and relishes her role. Surprised at her liking for drama, Lucy nonetheless resolves never to take part in such a performance again, because she prefers to be an observer than an actor. An overjoyed M. Paul forsakes his forbidding manner and compliments Lucy on her performance, asking her to take part in a ball, although Lucy informs him that she cannot dance. She is content to see Ginevra Fanshawe

star in the ball as she did in the play. The vain Ginevra attempts to coax Lucy into praising her beauty and to admitting that she envies her friend. Lucy refuses to indulge Ginevra, who brags that she has just broken the hearts of two young men (Isidore and Alfred de HAMAL). She cruelly says that at 23 Lucy has experienced nothing of love and never will (Ginevra is 18); she is not beautiful and no one cares for her cleverness. Despite such talk, Lucy agrees to accompany Ginevra to observe the two young men. Lucy calls Dr. Hamal a handsome, charming dandy. Ginevra refuses to point out Isidore, saying she is ashamed of his orange whiskers. Lucy fixes on Dr. John, who has no equal in the room. His manly figure and demeanor obviously attract Lucy, who had her eye on him during her performance in the vaudeville. Lucy suddenly realizes that "Isidore" is Dr. John, and that the note in the casket was from Ginevra—facts that Dr. John confirms when Lucy confronts him with them. The doctor asks Lucy how she thinks he stands with Ginevra, and Lucy answers that Ginevra's emotions are constantly changing. Soliciting a good opinion of Ginevra the doctor is put off by Lucy's implied criticism of his beloved and asks Lucy if she is not being too "severe." Not as severe as she is with Ginevra, Lucy answers. When she tries to get Dr. John to praise his rival, the doctor explodes with criticism of the flighty Hamal. Lucy then asks if he is not being too "severe." But then Lucy softens and assures the melancholy doctor that if Ginevra is worthy of his affection, then she cannot help but return it. A surprised Dr. John does not seem pleased, and he retires for the evening.

Chapter 15: The Long Vacation

With the early summer fete over, students and teachers devote themselves to two months of arduous work, preparing for examinations. M. Paul is in charge of this period, although he must relinquish supervision of the English examination to the English teacher, which he does rather petulantly. He accuses Lucy of precisely his own concern, being in control and earning the prizes that would show him off to advantage in the school. If anything, he cares too much about such honors and Lucy too little, Lucy confesses. When Lucy says she will support abandoning the English examination if Madame Beck agrees, M. Paul changes his mood and declares that the examinations should go ahead and he will no longer act as Lucy's rival. He is as good as his word. The examination goes ahead as scheduled, and the students leave to enjoy their long vacation.

The September days are lonely and depressing for Lucy, who has no place to go. It only makes Lucy more miserable when she is put in charge of a Marie Broc, a *cretin* (idiot), and she is not relieved of this duty until the end of the month. She consoles herself with long walks through town and country. Brooding about Madame Beck's being at the seashore and Ginevra's holidays, Lucy begins to fear that she is making herself permanently unhappy. Succumbing to a fever, she retires to her bed during an Indian summer. She loses sleep. Her servant, GOTON, urges her to see a doctor, but Lucy refuses, believing that no physician can cure her malady.

Racked with nightmares and regarding the school now as her tomb, Lucy wanders one night into the fields and then enters a church, seeking solace from a priest hearing confession. Since she tells him she is a Protestant, he asks why she has come to him. She replies that she needs help to relieve the pressure of an afflicted mind. When the priest also learns that she is not troubled by a crime or a sin, he admits that he does not know how to help her, although her case has touched him. That alone is enough to make Lucy feel better, even though the priest goes on to say that her troubled mind may be the result of a "dry" Protestantism that cannot deal with her passions. He gives her his home address, saying it will be better to see her there than in the cold church, which is not good for her weakened constitution. Lucy rejects his "Popish superstition" but still appreciates his kindness, comparing him to the theologian François FENELON.

Lucy ends the first volume of her story as she had begun in Villette, feeling lost and not knowing who to turn to. Leaving the church, she faints.

Volume Two

Chapters 16–18: Auld Lang Syne, La Terrasse, We Quarrel

Lucy treats her "swoon" as the wandering of her soul. She awakes in the parlor of an "unknown house," yet the furnishings in the room seem familiar to her. She is attended by a *bonne* (maid) who speaks neither French nor English. Lucy thinks she must be dreaming of her godmother's drawing room in Bretton when she was 14. She drifts off to sleep, thinking when she awakes she will be in her right mind in Madame Beck's school. But the "illusion" of Bretton persists: She sees a portrait of John Graham Bretton, and then Mrs. Bretton enters the room. She tells Lucy that Graham found her on the street and that she has been ill for nine days. Mrs. Bretton does not seem to recognize Lucy.

When Graham enters the room, Lucy realizes that he is Dr. John. She tells the reader that she has known this for some time, but that she had enjoyed observing him without his realizing she was Lucy Snowe. Announcing herself as such would have immediately changed their relationship. But when Mrs. Bretton remarks on how closely Graham's patient resembles Lucy Snowe, Lucy confesses her identity. An astonished Graham admits to having stupidly not realized who she was.

Lucy and Graham tell each other what has happened to them in the last 10 years. Graham, now a successful doctor, has bought a house and installed his mother (with some of the furnishings Lucy recognized) in it. He says that the next day he will explore the reasons for Lucy's poor health, and as she goes to sleep, she feels comforted—but she also cautions herself not to invest too much feeling in her friends and to expect only an "occasional, amiable intercourse." Lucy calls this effort to remain tranquil "struggles with the natural character," an effort that can make a difference in the "general tenor of life."

Mrs. Bretton insists that her son has ordered Lucy to remain in bed. He thinks Lucy suffers from a "nervous fever." Lucy finds her godmother's presence as soothing as when she was a child. She says little about her illness, not wanting to upset her godmother's placid nature.

After a quiet, lonely, but also dreamy day, Lucy receives a visit from Dr. John, as she calls Graham. He explains she is in a chateau called La Terrasse, because it juts out from a "broad turfed walk" like a terrace. It is a romantic moonlit night, and Lucy knows that Ginevra Fanshawe is on Dr. John's mind, a truth he confirms when she mentions Ginevra's name. As they discuss her condition, Lucy confesses that her illness stems from low spirits. Dr. John explains how she was put into his protection by the priest to whom she had confessed, who had followed her out of concern for her condition. Lucy corrects Dr. John's impression that she is Catholic, telling him that she sought out the priest—whom Dr. John tells her was Pere SILAS—to overcome her sense of desolation.

Observing the loving, teasing conversations between Mrs. Bretton and her son, Lucy wonders what Graham's mother would think of Ginevra Fanshawe, whose wayward, arbitrary conduct has made the doctor suffer. Sensing that Lucy does not approve of Ginevra, Dr. John begs her to forgive Ginevra for her youthful attraction to fashion. Losing her temper, Lucy tells him that his doting on Ginevra has caused Lucy to lose some of her respect for him, and she abruptly leaves his company. Later Lucy apologizes for her hasty words, blaming her illness and her perception that Dr. John could not grasp Ginevra's deficiencies unless they were pointed out to him. He kindly forgives her. Dr. John continues to praise Ginevra, and Lucy thinks to herself that his idea of his beloved is "nonsense," although she suspects he has some awareness of Ginevra's true character.

Chapter 19: The Cleopatra
With Dr. John's assistance, Lucy prolongs her vacation by another two weeks so that she can regain her strength. She is visited by Madame Beck, who extravagantly praises Dr. John's chateau and Mrs. Bretton. Dr. John devotes much time to Lucy, taking her on so many excursions around Villette that she declares she has seen more of it during her convalescence than in her eight months of teaching. In Basseville, a poor section, she witnesses his tender care of the indigent and their appreciation of his work. Lucy is impressed with his knowledge of the city, especially its galleries and museums.

At one of the galleries Lucy is attracted to the portrait of Cleopatra, portrayed as a huge, full-figured woman, and calls it a remarkable piece of "claptrap." M. Paul observes her and is shocked that she should be left alone to look at such a painting. He recommends several other paintings,

which Lucy finds dull and uninspired, while a group gathers around the Cleopatra. M. Paul questions Lucy closely about her vacation and her illness, criticizing her for not having more patience with the *cretin*, Marie Broc, and marveling that as a Protestant Lucy can look at the painting of Cleopatra without feeling corrupted by it. She then spots the Colonel de Hamal admiring the Cleopatra. Dr. John approaches the portrait but does not appear to find it pleasing. He returns to Lucy, who expresses her pleasure in walking around the gallery with Graham, as she now calls him (he is known as Dr. John formally but is called Graham by those close to him, including Lucy). He seems so much more fresh and direct than the foppish Hamal, and Graham confirms Lucy's suspicion that the Cleopatra is not to his taste.

Chapters 20–22: The Concert, Reaction, The Letter
Lucy describes her surprise at her godmother's decision to buy her a pink dress and send her to a concert with Graham. Lucy worries that the dress will seem outlandish and that Graham will take it as a bid to attract him. But he seems to take her new dress in stride, and Lucy describes her delight as all three drive in a carriage through the most stylish part of town to the orchestra hall. Attending her first performance in a public place, Lucy is stunned by the blaze of crimson and gold, the majestic staircase, the grandeur of the setting. Surrounded by elegant women, Lucy and her godmother comment on Graham's penchant for being dazzled by stylish women. He takes their criticism in good humor, joking that his mother wishes him to remain a bachelor.

Lucy notices Paul Emmanuel and his brother, Josef EMMANUEL, and is curious to see the melancholy king and thoughtful and kind-looking queen, accompanied by their son, the Duc de DINDONNEAU. She also spots MATHILDE and Angelique, two pupils from Madame Beck's school; Lucy remembers that they had not done well when she assigned them to translate a page from *THE VICAR OF WAKEFIELD*. Then Graham and Lucy see Ginevra Fanshawe, who only glances at the doctor. The musical performances—the female pianists, a singer, a chorus—seem to engage Lucy less than her observation of the audience. The doctor confirms he has seen Ginevra and tells Lucy that his "lady-love" is with Lady SARA, whose mother he had treated professionally. He admits that he has idealized Ginevra in spite of her faults, but that now he is no longer under her spell. Indeed, he considers her a harmful person and is aggrieved that Ginevra has laughed at his mother's appearance at the concert. Then the doctor notices that Lucy has attracted the sardonic eye of M. Paul, who seems to disapprove of her pink dress.

The concert ends with a lottery, at which Dr. John wins a lady's headdress and Lucy a cigar case, which she treasures in memory of that evening. Lucy and the doctor discuss Ginevra's irregular upbringing, which accounts, Lucy suggests, for the young woman's erratic behavior. They return happily to the Bretton household.

Recovered from her illness, Lucy returns to Madame Beck's. She is accompanied by Dr. John, whom she recalls first showed her the way to the school, although neither recognized the other. She is moved to tears by his gallant heart as he promises that he and his mother will look in on her. Lucy struggles with her feelings, hoping that the doctor will continue his interest in her, yet trying to prepare herself to accept that he may not. Her "Reason" tells her that she may never express what she feels. "Imagination," on the other hand, spurs her to "hope."

Lucy awakens the next morning in despair. Through a window Professor Emmanuel observes her crying, and he tries to provoke her into telling him about her sadness. She maintains her silence, requesting that he leave her alone. At breakfast she finds Ginevra Fanshawe, exuberant and healthy looking, taunting her about her appearance at the concert. Ginevra exults in her own insulting behavior at the event and wants to know if the doctor noticed it. Lucy responds with such a fanciful description of how distraught Dr. John became, that Ginevra doubts Lucy's words.

Two weeks pass as Lucy accustoms herself to the routines of the school. Then Professor Emmanuel delivers a letter from Dr. John, which Lucy does not read immediately. In her class Professor Emmanuel criticizes Lucy for her teaching methods but suddenly softens and asks her about the letter. She tells him she has not read it yet and accepts his offer of a handkerchief to wipe her agitated face.

The school day at an end, Lucy retires to read the doctor's letter. She is comforted by Dr. John's good-natured recollection of their time together. In her solitary room Lucy suddenly sees what looks like the apparition of a nun. She rushes into Madame Beck's room in a fright; when she returns, followed by Madame's guests, she discovers Dr. John's letter is missing. As one of the guests who has accompanied her to her room, Dr. John comforts the hysterical Lucy and promises her to write 20 more letters to replace the stolen one. When she cannot be consoled, he produces the letter, which he has found on the floor. When he questions her about the intruder, she at first refuses to give a description lest he and others think she has imagined the incident. But he coaxes the details out of her and diagnoses her case as one of "spectral illusion" arising out of a long "mental conflict." He tells her that "happiness is the cure" and a "cheerful mind" the preventative. Lucy asks how easy it is to cultivate happiness, teasing the doctor about his infatuation with Ginevra. He assures Lucy that he has mastered his passion and Ginevra no longer appeals to him. Much calmer, Lucy tells the doctor she does not think she will be bothered again that night.

Chapters 23–25: Vashti, M. de Bassompierre, The Little Countess
Lucy enjoys many more letters from Dr. John and outings with him to "keep away the nun," as he puts it. One afternoon he arrives at Madame Beck's and requests that Lucy dress for the theater; his mother cannot attend and he has decided that Lucy must go with him. They are both excited at the appearance of a renowned actress, who appears as a "royal Vashti," a queen grown old and "wasted like a wax in flame." The actress seems to embody a demonic force, an evil spirit, that defies the "MATERIALIST" conception of the world apparently exemplified by Dr. John, who is intensely curious about the performance but not disturbed by it.

At the cry of fire in the theater, Dr. John calmly takes charge, preventing a woman from being trampled and helping to clear a path out of the theater. Dr. John and Lucy take the injured woman in their carriage to her hotel, and Lucy and the doctor retire for the evening.

Lucy then describes a period of seven weeks in which her life seems to stand still; she works on various projects and yet finds no fulfillment. In this state of mind Lucy is approached by Ginevra Fanshawe, who announces that her uncle M. de Bassompierre has arrived. As Ginevra describes a visit to her uncle and his daughter at the hotel, Lucy realizes they are the people she met at the concert after the fire. Ginevra also mentions that Dr. John and his mother were at the hotel, and Lucy realizes that Ginevra is upset because the doctor paid more attention to his new friends than to her. Lucy is elated when a letter arrives and then is let down when she discovers it is from his mother. Mrs. Bretton sings her busy son's praises and invites Lucy to spend her holiday with her and Graham.

Mrs. Bretton notices that Lucy is thinner than when she last saw her almost two months ago. Lucy discovers that Miss de Bassompierre is also staying with the Brettons. To her surprise, the young woman announces that she is Polly Home, whom Lucy did not recognize at the concert or afterward at the hotel. Indeed, Polly explains that her father and Graham did not recognize each other and only realized their connection when they exchanged business cards. Mr. Home has taken the title of count from dead French relatives who left their estates to him.

It has been 10 years since they lived in the Bretton household, and the two young women compare their memories, with Lucy remembering that Graham and Polly were playmates, and Polly remembering that Graham seemed far more interested in his male friends.

The Brettons, Lucy, and the Bassompierres spend a snowy, jolly Christmas together at La Terrasse. Lucy observes a "baffled" Graham trying to come to terms with Polly, the "little countess," who seems not to enjoy his teasing even though she has courted his attention. She seems poised between a "dancing fairy and a delicate dame."

The next day the Bassompierres discover that Lucy is a teacher. A shocked Polly asks her why she does such a job, and Lucy replies that she needs the money and shelter that the school provides. The outspoken Polly says she pities Lucy, but M. de Bassompierre remarks that he should like his daughter to behave as independently as

Lucy if Polly should find herself in need of similar support. M. de Bassompierre asks Lucy whether Polly might be admitted as a pupil, and Lucy suggests that Madame Beck would receive him promptly to enroll Polly. Polly protests that at a previous school, her father proved such a nuisance on his visits that the headmistress, Madame Aigredoux, expelled both pupil and parent. When her father does not refute Polly's story, plans for her to attend the school are dropped.

Gradually Graham and Polly resume the rapport they shared in the Bretton cottage 10 years earlier. When Polly's father goes out for the day, she makes him promise to return with Graham, who is in town doing his professional rounds.

Chapters 26–27: A Burial, The Hôtel Crécy
Lucy returns to Madame Beck's. She is treated well, even better now that Madame Beck sees that Lucy has found favor with Dr. John and his mother. The doctor continues to send Lucy letters, which Madame Beck steals, reads, and returns to Lucy's room. Lucy wonders what the madame makes of the doctor's energetic and genial style. But Lucy is also sad because she believes the doctor will no longer write to her; she does not say why. When she finds that someone else has been "borrowing" her letters, she puts them in a jar and buries it, along with her "grief," near a pear tree. She is startled when she again sees the apparition of a nun; this time Lucy tries to speak to it and touch it, but it only recedes.

On a visit to La Terrasse, Polly pleads with Lucy to leave the school and live with her. Lucy declines M. de Bassompierre's offer of three times her school salary, observing that it is not in her nature to be employed as a young woman's companion and that she would rather do housework than submit to the role of a "bright lady's shadow." Working for Madame Beck makes Lucy feel independent, not the appendage of someone else.

Lucy's visits to La Terrasse continue, and she notices that Polly is shy with Graham. Her father teases her about it. Although Lucy will not serve as Polly's paid companion, she agrees to accompany Polly to German lessons at Fraulein Anna BRAUN's. In the meantime, Professor Emmanuel taunts Lucy about her social engagements and tells her that teachers are not supposed to go on so many outings. Lucy calmly replies that she is better for the change in her habits.

Together Lucy and Polly read Friedrich von SCHILLER's ballads, and Polly becomes adept at translation. Close to the age of 19, Polly objects to Lucy's comment that she can know little about the love Schiller writes about. When Lucy refuses to talk about love, Polly reveals that Ginevra, her cousin, often visits and talks about love. Polly calls Ginevra's comments "insolent" and "false." Nevertheless, Ginevra's unkind opinions about Mrs. Bretton and her son have contributed to Polly's reserve around Graham. Polly accepts Lucy's proposal that they contrive a meeting at which they can test whether Graham retains any strong romantic feelings for Ginevra.

Polly arranges for Ginevra to meet her and Lucy at a holiday event in honor of the Duc de Dindonneau. On their meeting, observing that Lucy now travels in the highest company, enjoying a position of respect considerably beyond that accorded to a teacher, Ginevra asks her pointedly: "Who *are* you?" Lucy deflects the question, saying only that perhaps she is a person "in disguise" and is offended when Ginevra says she used to think of Lucy as a "nobody." To Ginevra's persistent questioning, Lucy finally replies: "I am a rising character." Lucy realizes that Ginevra cannot conceive of anyone attaining importance without wealth or high status in society.

The holiday event turns out to be a lecture by M. Paul Emmanuel in the Tribune, or great hall. The charismatic teacher delivers an inspiring talk about France, its role in the world, and the part the younger generation must play. Lucy notices that Polly's French is better than Ginevra's, even though Ginevra has spent half her life on the Continent. Dr. John is seated between Ginevra and Polly, and Lucy observes that he treats Ginevra courteously but without any special show of affection. Polly distinguishes herself as the better conversationalist, better schooled and poised than Ginevra. Dr. John engages Lucy in their first conversation in three months, asking her what she thinks of the company, including Ginevra. He then reminisces about Polly's first visit to the Bretton household and asks Lucy to recount her memories of that time. She is shocked when he asks her to remind Polly that as children he and Polly were

quite close. Lucy concludes that the doctor has no idea of Lucy's own intense feeling for him. She refuses to play a part in what she calls a "love drama." Their conversation is interrupted when M. Paul hisses in French to Lucy that she is a "coquette" and that she is revealing her passionate soul. She answers in French that she has a right to her passion, and Dr. John laughs at her spirit as the Frenchman departs. Later, Lucy rebuffs M. Paul's offer to escort her back to the school, and Dr. John leaves Lucy to speak with Polly. M. Paul persists in questioning Lucy, asking whether he or Dr. John has upset her. When Lucy refuses to acknowledge that either man has disturbed her, the professor apologizes anyway. When she relents and forgives him, she sees his face lighten in a way she has never noticed before. The evening ends with Ginevra upset that she has not been able to excite the doctor's passions.

Chapter 28: The Watchguard

Lucy is charged with delivering an urgent message to M. Paul, a task the portress, Rosine, refuses because she has interrupted him five times that day and is afraid to face his wrath another time. With some anxiety, Lucy delivers the message to the protesting professor. In urging him to read the message Lucy disturbs his desk. His eyeglasses fall to the lecture platform and break, yet when she looks up at him, she finds him smiling. He departs on his errand to the Athenée, a society of higher learning, to greet an official visitor.

Later that evening Lucy encounters the professor, who is again in a disagreeable mood and commands Lucy to sit at the end of a long table. When he observes her making a watchguard (a chain for a man's watch), he accuses her of deliberately irritating him and of wearing "giddy" colors. Lucy manages to tease the professor and they part on a friendly note. She marvels that the professor should find her so flamboyant when others have commented on her sober behavior.

Volume Three

Chapters 29–30: Monsieur's Fete, M. Paul

Lucy describes the tribute the school arranges each year for Professor Emmanuel. One of the teachers, Mademoiselle Zelie de St. Pierre, dresses in her finest clothes, has her hair done, and perfumes her handkerchief in order, it is rumored, to capture M. Paul's eye. He seems to reciprocate her efforts by constantly gazing at her. The honored man greets his well-wishers cordially, as if to "make amends" for his often abrupt and sharp behavior during the rest of the year. His pupils and colleagues then present him with bouquets of flowers, that is, all except Lucy, who does not like cut flowers because they represent to her a sham imitation of life. Lucy delays giving him the jewel box she has made instead, and he launches into his customary lecture. After Lucy drops her thimble and hits her head on the corner of a desk as she picks it up, M. Paul launches into a tirade against the personalities and habits of English women. When he turns to attacking England's men and the country itself, Lucy cries out in French her loyalty to England and its history. The professor smiles into his handkerchief, taking a malicious satisfaction in provoking Lucy. Her outburst, in fact, changes his mood so that he returns to the subject of flowers and their pleasant associations, complimenting Mademoiselle Zelie, in particular, on her bouquet.

After the fete, Lucy discovers M. Paul ransacking her desk. She knows he has done this before but has never caught him at it. He shows no shame at being caught this time. He accuses her of spoiling his day, and she replies that this was not her intention. She then places her gift in his hand. He is gratified by her gift, and Lucy thinks they are friends until the next time they quarrel.

Lucy observes that nothing can change M. Paul's mercurial temperament. He respects no one without testing them. He devises lessons for Lucy, which she completes, sometimes spurred on by his interest in her, sometimes deflated by his scornful treatment of her lack of ambition to learn. Although he accuses her of plagiarism and calls her a "*faible*" (weak) student, when he loses patience he reasserts his desire that she should learn.

Lucy resists his plan for her and other pupils to participate in an examination in which they would write an impromptu composition in French. Lucy declares she has no talent for such spontaneous exercises and that she has always needed time to form her thoughts. He criticizes her for the "obsti-

nacy" of her sex and argues that she fears failure. She counters that she will not make a public display of herself. When he goes to fetch a glass of water for her, she escapes.

Chapter 31: *The Dryad*

Lucy walks in the garden, musing about her life and her feelings for Dr. John, when she is startled to hear a male voice. It is M. Paul, and she learns that it was he who covered her with a shawl when she slept at her desk. He tells her she needs "watching over"; in fact, he confesses that he has taken a room that gives him a view of the garden and the school so that he can study her and the students. Whatever he learns by this means is dishonorable, Lucy tells him. But he asserts there is no dogma that forbids his spying. Lucy tells the professor he has diminished his own dignity—a charge he rejects, pointedly noting that he has seen other strange events in the garden. His tone chills Lucy, and he asks why she is upset. She says she is cold, but he senses that she is drawn to the supernatural, and he provokes from her an admission that she has had certain disturbing experiences since she came to the school. Professor Emmanuel remarks that they share a rapport in such matters; in fact, he says, they share many of the same mannerisms, looks, and expressions and are born under the same star. Then they both admit to having seen the ghostly nun. They hear a rustling in a tree, and Lucy thinks a dryad may appear, but it is the nun herself—more clearly visible than ever before until she vanishes in the wind.

Chapter 32: *The First Letter*

When Polly returns after travels with her father, she asks Lucy her opinion of Dr. John. Taking Lucy into her confidence, she admits that the doctor has sent her a declaration of his love. Neither Polly nor the doctor is prepared yet to approach her father, and Polly solicits Lucy's advice. Lucy approves of Polly's decision not to write to Graham until her father is made aware of Graham's feelings. The lovers fear that Polly's father still regards her as a child and is not prepared for the thought of her marrying. Lucy counsels Polly to "leave the revelation to Time and your kind Fate." Indeed, Lucy believes that Polly and Graham are destined to be married and to live happily.

Chapter 33: M. Paul Keeps His Promise

On the first day of May, a cheerful M. Paul Emmanuel fulfills his promise of taking everyone in the school to a country breakfast. He tells them a delightful story, and they sit down to a meal at a farmhouse. Lucy is struck by the professor's good humor and then by his sincere faith: He crosses himself and reveals a devout side that most of his freethinking colleagues do not share. After the meal, the students frolic in the meadow. Lucy and the professor sit quietly, reading and talking. She is impressed with his gentleness and his questions: If he were her brother, would she stay with him? If he left Villette, would she miss him? Hiding her tears in a book, she wonders why he asks such questions, and he changes the subject. After returning to the school, Lucy hears the professor approaching and takes sanctuary in the school oratory. He asks for her, and Mademoiselle St. Pierre tells him that Lucy has gone to bed. Madame Beck chides him out the door. Lucy wonders why she did not go to the professor.

Chapters 34–36: Malevola, Fraternity, The Apple of Discord

Madame Beck asks Lucy if she would mind doing a few errands for her, including taking a basket of fruit to Madame WALRAVENS, who is having a fete. When Lucy meets Madame Walravens, she is struck by a figure who looks like Malevola, an evil fairy, and who stares at her in a malign fashion. Presented with the basket, Madame Walravens tells Lucy to tell Madame Beck that she can buy her own fruit. Lucy wonders why Madame Beck sent her on this strange mission. At Madame Walraven's house she meets a priest who reminds her of Pere Silas. She also sees a picture of a young, pale woman, grief stricken, in a nun's habit. The priest tells Lucy that the woman is Justine Marie SAVEUR (1), who died young and is still mourned by her "affianced lover." The priest explains that the lover was a former pupil of his and now his benefactor. When Justine Marie's parents forbade her to marry the son of a failed banker, she withdrew to a convent and died. Madame Walravens, Justine Marie's grandmother, had also opposed the marriage, but when Justine Marie's father died after a scandal had ruined his name and fortune, Justine Marie's lover took pity on her family and installed them in

the house Lucy now visits. The priest, the lover's old tutor, and an old servant, AGNES, have also become part of the household. When the priest learns that Lucy has come from Madame Beck's school, he tells her that M. Paul Emmanuel is the lover of whom he speaks. Then the priest reveals that he is indeed Pere Silas, the priest to whom Lucy once confessed. While Lucy continues to have reservations about Roman Catholicism, she admits there are "good Romanists."

When Lucy returns home, Madame Beck is entertained by her account of Madame Walravens, and she tells Lucy that M. Paul will never marry because of his devotion to Justine Marie. Madame Beck then tells Lucy to forget the professor, but Lucy cannot forget. Indeed, she begin to reevaluate the professor's behavior—his kindness, his attentions to her, his jealousy and suspicion, and her own narrow view of him. She had never imagined him capable of such great love. Lucy declares that he has become "my Christian hero."

Lucy is startled when M. Paul calls on her to demonstrate to Messieurs BOISSEC and ROCHEMORT that she can write a composition in French. These two professors have accused M. Paul of writing compositions and signing his students' names to them. Lucy, never good at impromptu tests, fails this one and even tells the professors that they should stop examining her because she is an idiot. Lucy had laboriously worked on compositions, but composition was not a spontaneous part of her learning, and the matter was simply not in her head. Unable to explain her plight, she angrily bursts into tears. When the two men direct Lucy to write on the subject of human justice, she is about to refuse when she realizes these are the two men who hounded her the first night she arrived in Villette. Seized with an inspiration, the image of an old, good woman defending her home and hearth, Lucy writes her composition and excuses herself.

Later Lucy and the professor quarrel about the exam, but then they meet again and he half apologizes for his fitful behavior. He says he is a solitary man with few connections to the world. Lucy objects, saying she knows that he is more than that. She describes Madame Walravens, Pere Silas, and Agnes, "the mistress, the chaplain, the servant." When he asks her to tell him how she knows his story, she reveals the details of the errand Madame Beck sent her on. Since she knows his story, M. Paul wants to know if he and Lucy can be close friends and share a bond like that of a brother and sister. Lucy does not answer, but her sympathetic attitude is clear to him. He asks her if she has connected the apparition of the nun with the portrait of the nun in his house. She has, she replies. He then cautions her not to be superstitious, saying, surely a heavenly presence would not interfere with human affairs. Madame Beck's daughter Fifene interrupts their conversation before Lucy has a chance to ask the professor if he has morbid feelings about the nun who has appeared to Lucy.

The next day Lucy is disappointed because the professor does not resume their talk; indeed, he keeps his distance for several days. His silence only makes her more passive, even though he had encouraged her to seek him out. She tries to approach him at sunset in his garden, but a bell rings for the last class and no meeting occurs. Instead she picks up a book left on her desk aimed at converting the reader to Catholicism, a book that she finds "sentimental" and "shallow." When she turns to the front page of the book she finds it was given to M. Paul by Pere Silas.

Lucy follows M. Paul's barking dog, Sylvie, into the garden. M. Paul asks her if she has read the "brochure." When she denies that she was moved by the book, he abruptly asks her what she has thought of him for the past few days. She does not answer. He questions her "self-reliant religion," which seems to be an obstacle in their friendship, as his friends have pointed out to him. Lucy responds that it is well for him to be cautious. Yet she also notes that they both believe in "God and Christ and the Bible." In a long discussion she explains her creed and defends it against "JESUIT slanders." She believes that she has made M. Paul realize that Protestants are not pagans; in turn, she respects the purity of M. Paul's Catholic convictions.

Pere Silas visits Madame Beck and secures permission to become Lucy's tutor in religion. Lucy accepts his book, although it does not sway her. To her Rome remains a tyrant power, not the seat of Christianity. "God is not with Rome," she vows. Taken to churches, she finds "papal pomp" and "ceremony" tawdry, "grossly material, not poetically spiritual." She informs the kindly Pere Silas that she does not wish to visit any more churches. Undoubtedly, she admits, every church makes errors, but she does not think her Protestant beliefs are as mistaken as those of the Roman church. Lucy is reconciled to her own religion, although M. Paul observes that they do believe in the same God. "God guide us all! God bless you Lucy!" he concludes.

Chapter 37: Sunshine
Lucy describes the growing love between Paulina (Polly) and Graham. Paulina confides in Lucy, but Lucy does not want to play a large part in the lovers' lives; she wants her own life. Paulina's father consults Lucy about the couple. M. de Bassompierre thinks of his daughter as still very young, although Lucy tells him she is almost 19 and grown up. He worries about losing his daughter. Lucy makes clear that Graham and Paulina are in love and that they wish for his consent to their engagement, but Graham is afraid to address M. de Bassompierre, realizing how much the father dotes on the daughter. The father claims Graham is not Paulina's equal, but Lucy suggests that even men of greater position and fortune would not appeal to M. de Bassompierre, and he agrees. Other suitors will come, Lucy points out, and they will please the father less than Graham.

Polly enters with a letter she wishes Lucy to give to Graham. When she sees her father, she is embarrassed. But when he questions her about the letter, she resolves to tell him the truth about her love for Graham. She also declares she would never do anything to hurt her father, but she protests when her father criticizes Graham and calls him a "scamp" who should be exiled to Siberia. As father and daughter struggle to understand each other, Graham appears and asks Lucy about his fate. Lucy takes him to M. de Bassompierre, and Graham asks him "What is my sentence?" M. de Bassompierre, formerly Mr. Home, teases Graham about his HIGHLANDER heritage. After more jibing, M. de Bassompierre invites Graham into his study for an interview. When the men emerge, M. de Bassompierre says to Graham, "take her." In fact, father and prospective son-in-law are well matched, as are Paulina and Graham, prompting Lucy to remark that some lives on earth do approach the happiness of heaven.

Chapters 38–39: Cloud, Old and New Acquaintance
Awaiting M. Paul's usual lesson in English, Lucy and the other students are informed by Madame Beck that the professor has answered the call of duty and is about to depart from Europe. Madame Beck asks Lucy to teach the lesson. Later Madame Beck tells Lucy that M. Paul will depart for GUADELOUPE in the West Indies by the end of the week. Lucy has difficulty sleeping and awakes with the name of M. Paul's destination in mind. In the month since they settled their "theological difference," they have become better friends, Lucy thinks. That he should now leave seems "incredible" to Lucy. On the day before his departure M. Paul has a child deliver a note to Lucy saying he cannot tell her the purpose of his voyage.

Late at night, Madame Beck visits Lucy and urges her to bed. Lucy objects and tells Madame Beck not to interfere in her life, prompting Madame Beck to caution her that she must not marry M. Paul. An outraged Lucy thinks of Madame as her "rival," for she has always supposed that Madame wanted to marry M. Paul. Madame Beck retreats, leaving Lucy to spend a long, sleepless night alone.

During a second sleepless night, Lucy is visited first by Ginevra Fanshawe and then by Goton, a servant who gives Lucy a sleeping potion. Both are emissaries from Madame Beck, but they learn nothing from Lucy. Excited rather than sedated by the drug, Lucy leaves the school the second night, passing a carriage occupied by Graham, Polly, M. de Bassompierre, and Mrs. Bretton on their way to a fete in a park. M. MIRET, a bookseller who does business with the school, spots Lucy and offers her a more comfortable seat at the fete, which Lucy has wandered into. She can hear Graham, Polly, M. de Bassompierre and Mrs. Bretton speaking fondly of her. Graham notices her, but she signals that she does not want to be recognized, and he leaves her alone.

As she wanders away from the fete, Lucy encounters Madame Beck and her child Desiree. Madame Beck is with her brother, M. Victor KINT, Josef Emmanuel, Pere Silas, and Madame Magliore Walravens. As she watches this group

Lucy learns that M. Paul's trip to Guadeloupe concerns an estate that belonged to Madame Walravens's late husband, and she is expected to inherit the property. Pere Silas had recommended that M. Paul travel to handle the disposition of the house to prevent his succumbing to the charms of a "heretic" (Lucy). Madame Beck concurs, since if she cannot marry M. Paul, she is happy to prevent Lucy from doing so. All three prevail on M. Paul to undertake a mission he could not spurn because of the trust invested in him.

Overhearing this group talking, Lucy is startled when the arrival of Justine Marie is announced. The healthy young girl who appears is nothing like the nun in the picture Lucy has seen. Even more strange is the fact that the ANTIGUA, the ship M. Paul was to sail on leaves, but he remains ashore. Justine Marie SAVEUR (2), Lucy realizes, is related to Madame Walravens, and M. Paul is her guardian. Now the plans are for him to sail in a fortnight on the PAUL ET VIRGINIE. Another member of the party, Heinrich MULLER, seems agitated when M. Paul kisses Justine Marie's hand. Lucy infers that the young girl is to be M. Paul's bride, although she admits that she does not have proof. It is past midnight now and Lucy leaves the scene, finding it unbearable to watch what she regards as a love scene.

Returning to the school, she is shocked to see the nun in her own bed. After Lucy throws herself at this apparition, she finds it is a "bolster dressed in a long black stole, and artfully vested with a white veil." Lucy finds a note that the nun has given her clothes to Lucy Snowe and will visit the school no more. Thrusting the clothes under her pillows, Lucy waits until she hears Madame Beck's carriage and falls into a deep sleep.

Chapter 40: The Happy Pair
The next day Lucy wakes to find that Ginevra Fanshawe is missing. She has apparently left the school with all her possessions, a shocking blow to Madame Beck. Remembering that one of the school doors had been left ajar the evening before, Lucy speculates that Ginevra eloped with M. de Hamal. A letter from Ginevra later confirms Lucy's suspicions. Ginevra also confesses that the Comte de Hamal was the "nun" haunting Lucy's chambers, a disguise he used on his visits to

Ginevra, and had gained entrance to the school by climbing the garden wall. Ginevra describes how she and de Hamal planned her escape from the school. She is delighted to be a countess, not the wife of a doctor, she concludes. Lucy explains that Ginevra later visited her, claiming to be very happy and to have made Dr. John jealous while reconciling her uncle, M. de Bassompierre, to her marriage. A subdued Lucy gives Ginevra only the "crust and rind of my nature." But Ginevra continues to send letters to her, rejoicing in the upbringing of her son, Alfred Fanshawe de Bassompierre de Hamal. Still later Ginevra's husband falls into debt and has to appeal to M. de Bassompierre. But Ginevra goes on, suffering as little as any human being Lucy has ever known.

Chapter 41: Faubourg Clotilde
Confessing that she is jealous, Lucy wonders if perhaps she has made too much of what she witnessed the previous night. She worries herself with speculations on whether M. Paul will come to see her before he departs. When he does appear in what she takes to be traveling clothes, she wonders if he is in a "bridegroom mood" since he is so kind and cheerful. She expects their meeting to be brief, a friendly farewell. When Madame Beck tries to intervene, interrupting M. Paul's visit, Lucy cries out, "My heart will break!" He whispers to her, "Trust me." A persistent Madame Beck calls to M. Paul, but he firmly and repeatedly asks her to leave the room. She counters that he is a man of unstable imagination and irresolute character, and she will call Pere Silas. He responds that "the event" will show her how resolute he is. Finally at his firm reply, Madame Beck departs. When Lucy expresses her sorrow at being forgotten, M. Paul says she still does not know him. He has come to fetch her, and now he asks her to walk into town with him. He asks her about her plans during his three-year stay in the West Indies. She confirms that she hopes to establish her own school.

M. Paul then takes her to a house and to a salon, showing her various rooms. He then takes her into another part of the house, which turns out to be a schoolroom. He next presents her with papers that show she is to be the directress of this school. He has bought and arranged everything for her. It has been his preoccupation with the new school that has kept him from Lucy, for she might have pried the secret out of him with her questions about his activities. He asks only that she think of him during his three-year stay in Guadeloupe. Lucy calls him her "king."

He assures her that he has told no one about the school. It is to be their secret. Her first pupils are to be the three daughters of M. Miret, the landlord of the school, as well as his goddaughter, Justine Marie Sauveur. This last revelation provokes Lucy to confess what she has witnessed the previous night. To her confession he replies, "Lucy, take my love. One day share my life." Preferring him to "all humanity," Lucy walks back to the school, the professor explaining that he has always thought of Justine Marie as his daughter.

Chapter 42: Finis
Lucy spends three happy years at her school. She receives many loving letters from M. Paul, expressing his respect for her Protestantism. Now Lucy writes in anticipation of M. Paul's return. She has prepared a library for him. The day of his return arrives, and she asks the reader to imagine "a happy succeeding life."

PUBLICATION HISTORY

Villette was published on January 28, 1853. Critics greeted it as a worthy successor to *JANE EYRE* and *SHIRLEY*, with charm and freshness. Some reviews complained about the last volume's shift of attention from Polly to Lucy, and others disliked the lack of plot. Charlotte's friend, Harriet MARTINEAU, wrote a review that condemned the book's anti-Catholicism and argued that too much talk of love overshadowed every other aspect of the book. William Makepeace THACKERAY, another of Charlotte's contemporaries, made a similar complaint. Such criticisms, while warranted, do not do justice to the author's superb re-creation of a mature woman's mind and feelings. Since *THE PROFESSOR* had not yet been published, reviewers had no opportunity to study how *Villette* constituted a rewriting of and vast improvement over the earlier novel. If not as romantically intense as *Jane Eyre*, *Villette* has been deemed by many critics Charlotte's most mature work.

Virginie Minor character in *VILLETTE*. Along with ANGELIQUE and BLANCHE she attempts to thwart Lucy SNOWE's lesson. But like William CRIMSWORTH in *THE PROFESSOR*, Lucy deals with these rebel students quickly and firmly.

Vivid, The The ship in *VILLETTE* that takes Lucy SNOWE to France.

W

Walravens, Madame Character in *VILLETTE*. Madame BECK asks Lucy SNOWE to take a gift basket to Madame Walravens. At Madame Walravens's house Lucy learns from Pere SILAS that Paul EMMANUEL was in love with Justine Marie SAVEUR (1), whose parents opposed her marriage to M. Paul. Justine Marie entered a convent and died there. Lucy sees a picture of her at Madame Walravens's house. After a reversal of fortune M. Paul has cared for Madame Walravens, Justine Marie's grandmother, and all those closely connected to his beloved, even though they opposed his plan to marry. Madame Walravens is disagreeable, but M. Paul is devoted to her nonetheless. Indeed, he travels to GUADELOUPE in the West Indies to oversee the disposition of property that she has lately inherited after the death of her husband.

"Wanderer, The" *See* "SIR HENRY TUNSTALL."

Waterloo Palace *See* GLASS TOWN.

Watsons, the Minor characters in *VILLETTE*. The family consists of two males and two females, all wealthy and vulgar, whom Lucy SNOWE meets aboard *THE VIVID* en route to Belgium.

Weightman, William (1814?–1842) Patrick Brontë's curate at HAWORTH. A native of the Westmorland town of Appleby, Weightman studied two years at the University of Durham before being appointed to his first curacy, at Haworth, in August 1839. The charming, outgoing curate became friendly with all the Brontës. Although he was engaged to a young woman in Appleby, he was apparently flirtatious, sending Charlotte, Emily, and Anne each a Valentine's Day card in 1840. Charlotte was at first smitten with Weightman; she drew a portrait of him in pencil before she became disenchanted with him. What Emily thought of the curate is not clear, but it is altogether possible that Anne fell in love with Weightman, who might have been the subject of a series of love poems she began after his arrival (*see* POEMS OF ANNE BRONTË). In 1842, Weightman contracted cholera while visiting sick parishioners. Cholera at that time was invariably fatal, and after lingering for a few weeks, on September 6, Weightman died at 28. Patrick preached his curate's funeral sermon, and the young man was interred at Haworth Church.

Wellesley, Lord Charles *See* GLASS TOWN; *YOUNG MEN'S MAGAZINE, THE.*

Wellington, duke of (Arthur Wellesley) (1769–1852) British general, statesman, and prime minister. He had a distinguished military career that climaxed with his defeat of Napoléon BONAPARTE at Waterloo. He was a member of the TORY Party and one of Charlotte Brontë's heroes, whom she incorporated as a pivotal character in her juvenile production of the GLASS TOWN saga. In *SHIRLEY*, Caroline HELSTONE objects to Jessy YORKE's tirade against the duke.

West End, the A section of London known primarily for its theaters. In *VILLETTE*, Lucy SNOWE visits the West End on her tour of London.

Westminster Borough of the city of London. The administrative center of the city, it is north of the river Thames. The borough includes Westminster Abbey, Buckingham Palace, and the Houses of Parliament. In *VILLETTE*, Lucy SNOWE tours Westminster when she comes to London.

Weston, Mr. Major character in *AGNES GREY*. Mr. HATFIELD's curate, Mr. Weston is a kind, generous man who cares for the humblest of his parishioners. Rosalie MURRAY tries to captivate him with her flirting and thinks she has succeeded, but in fact Mr. Weston's heart is captured by the quieter

The duke of Wellington, whom Robert Home painted in 1804, was the British victor over Napoléon, champion of the Tory Party, and one of Charlotte Brontë's heroes. (National Portrait Gallery, London)

and principled Agnes GREY. Later, when she leaves the employ of Mr. and Mrs. MURRAY, he seeks her out. After several visits to the Grey household, he proposes and Agnes accepts.

"We wove a web in childhood"   Poem by Charlotte BRONTË. Written on December 19, 1835, during Charlotte's Christmas holiday from her teaching duties during her first term at Roe Head, this is perhaps Charlotte's most famous, most frequently anthologized poem. It describes a series of visions of ANGRIA, Charlotte's only consolation during the grinding, lonely days among strangers. The poem ends with a long prose coda that poignantly illustrates both her solitude and her recognition of how transitory a consolation such visions are:

> Never shall I Charlotte Brontë forget what a voice of wild & wailing music now came thrillingly to my mind's almost to my body's ear, nor how distinctly I sitting in the school-room at Roe-head

saw the Duke of Zamorna. . . . "Miss Brontë what are you thinking about?" said a voice that dissipated all the charm & Miss Lister thrust her little rough black head into my face, "Sic transit" & c.

Wharton, Mrs.   Character mentioned in *THE PROFESSOR.* Frances Evans HENRI says Mrs. Wharton has offered her a teaching position.

Wheelwright family   The five daughters of Dr. Thomas Wheelwright attended the PENSIONNAT HEGER, where Emily Brontë taught the younger children music. The eldest daughter, Laetitia Wheelwright, disliked Emily but befriended Charlotte. After one of the younger girls, Julia Wheelwright, died of cholera in Brussels in 1842, the family left the city the next year.

Whig   Political party in power in England from 1714 to 1760. The Whig Party was made up of DISSENTERS and tradesmen. The Whigs were instrumental in establishing the Hanoverian succession, which put an end to the rule of the Stuart family in England. After the REFORM BILL OF 1832, the Whigs became known as Liberals. In *SHIRLEY,* set in 1811–12, Robert MOORE, a mill operator is called a Whig. He has arguments with his political opposite, Matthewson HELSTONE, a high TORY.

Whipp, Mrs.   Minor character in *SHIRLEY.* She is Mr. SWEETING's landlady.

Whitcross   Place in *JANE EYRE.* A coachman sets Jane EYRE at this "stone pillar set up where four roads meet" when she leaves THORNFIELD after her marriage plans to Edward ROCHESTER have been destroyed.

White family   Charlotte Brontë worked as governess to this family from March 1841 to the end of the year. The Whites lived at Upperwood House, Rawdon, near BRADFORD, and had three children, including an eight-year-old girl, Sarah, and a six-year-old boy, Jasper, who were Charlotte's pupils. Charlotte was poorly paid and overworked, and although her employers were happy with her, she longed for escape.

Whitsuntide   English holy day. Also called Whit-sunday, it is the seventh Sunday after Easter, commemorating the Pentecost. *Whit*, or *white*, derives from the white robes worn by those baptized on this day. One of the chapters in *SHIRLEY* is devoted to Whitsuntide celebrations.

"Why ask to know the date—the clime?"   Poem by Emily BRONTË. Begun on September 14, 1846, this unfinished poem was the last Emily ever wrote—and one of only two she would compose after the publication of the 1846 *POEMS*. While Charlotte preferred to think of "NO COWARD SOUL IS MINE" as Emily's final word on the human condition and the supremacy of faith, this longer, rambling spinoff of the GONDAL saga is Emily's last known creative endeavor. In the end she left this poetic fragment, about an unnamed Gondal warrior fighting abroad in a meaningless war, incomplete. In May 1848, just six months before she died, she revisited her final work, reducing it to a five-stanza indictment of "our own humanity / Foot-kissers of triumphant crime" that bitterly concludes, "I, doubly cursed on foreign sod, / Fought neither for my home nor God."

Wilcox, Miss   *See EMMA.*

Wildfell Hall   Place in *THE TENANT OF WILDFELL HALL.* Wildfell Hall is the ancestral home of Helen HUNTINGDON and Frederick LAWRENCE. Although Frederick still owns the nearly derelict property when Helen decides to take up residence there after fleeing her husband, the hall has not been occupied for 15 years. The once grand manor house, described as having been built in Elizabethan times of dark gray stone, sits upon a hill and is thought to have been modeled, like THRUSHCROSS GRANGE in *WUTHERING HEIGHTS*, on Ponden Hall, a manor house above HAWORTH MOOR. Clearly Anne Brontë's imaginary house is located elsewhere, however, for her Wildfell is within walking distance of the sea, to which Helen and Gilbert MARKHAM make a memorable journey.

Williams, William Smith   Reader for the publishing house Smith, Elder. He rejected Charlotte Brontë's novel *THE PROFESSOR* but was enthusiastic about *JANE EYRE*. Charlotte corresponded with him

and sought his advice. She and Anne later met him in London. Charlotte wrote to him about Emily's and Anne's illnesses and their deaths. He encouraged Charlotte to reveal her identity to the public (she had published under the pseudonym Currer Bell), and he entertained her during her other visits to London. He sent Charlotte books and advised her on the reprinting of her sister's works. He later allowed Charlotte's biographer Mrs. GASKELL to read the correspondence between himself and Charlotte. *See also* SMITH, GEORGE.

Wilmot   Character mentioned in *VILLETTE*. A waiter recalls Wilmot, one of Lucy Snowe's uncles who frequented the inn at which she is staying.

Wilmot, Annabella (Lady Lowborough)   Character in *THE TENANT OF WILDFELL HALL*. Annabella is the beautiful socialite niece of Helen HUNTINGDON's uncle's old friend. Helen first meets Annabella in London in the company of her cousin Milicent HARGRAVE, with whom Helen becomes fast friends. The three women are all present at a dinner party at which Helen first meets her future husband. At first Arthur, Lord HUNTINGDON seems bent on flirting with Annabella; later, however, he turns his attention to Helen, although his focus does not stray long from Annabella: Even after Huntingdon marries Helen and Annabella marries Lord LOWBOROUGH for his title, Huntingdon and Annabella continue an affair. When Helen sees irrefutable proof of their liaison, it kills her love for her husband and causes Lowborough to divorce his wife. The affair inevitably ends when Annabella elopes with yet another man. When Helen last hears of her, Annabella has died of poverty and neglect.

Wilmot, Mr.   Minor character in *THE TENANT OF WILDFELL HALL*. Mr. Wilmot is an old friend of Helen HUNTINGDON's uncle. Before Helen marries, he makes unwelcome advances to her during her first London season. His niece is Annabella WILMOT, who later has an affair with Helen's husband.

Wilson, Jane   Character in *THE TENANT OF WILDFELL WALL*. Jane Wilson is the socially ambitious daughter of one of Gilbert MARKHAM's neighbors.

She sets her sights on Frederick LAWRENCE, Helen HUNTINGDON's brother and the local squire, and she almost wins him. Frederick sees her true nature only after Gilbert points out Jane's hatred for Helen, whom she has maliciously slandered.

Wilson, Mary Ann (Ann)   Minor character in *JANE EYRE*. At LOWOOD Jane EYRE becomes friends with the witty student Mary Ann during Helen BURNS's illness.

Wilson, Mr.   Character mentioned in *VILLETTE*. When Mr. Wilson, an English teacher, fails to show up for his lesson, Madame BECK presses Lucy SNOWE into service.

Wilson, Mrs.   Minor character in *THE TENANT OF WILDFELL HALL*. Mrs. Wilson is the widow of an affluent farmer whose lands lie near those of Gilbert MARKHAM in LINDEN-CAR. Her daughter, Jane WILSON, has her sights set on Frederick LAWRENCE, the owner of WILDFELL HALL.

Wilson, Richard   Minor character in *THE TENANT OF WILDFELL HALL*. He is the younger son of Mrs. WILSON and her husband, a deceased farmer in the LINDEN-CAR area. Since he has not inherited his father's lands, Richard pursues another vocation, succeeding the Rev. Michael MILLWARD as vicar of LINDENHOPE and marrying the vicar's younger daughter, Mary MILLWARD, while still serving as curate.

Wilson, Robert   Minor character in *THE TENANT OF WILDFELL HALL*. He is the son and heir of an affluent farmer and the widow Mrs. WILSON. Robert works his lands in the neighborhood of LINDEN-CAR, the home of gentleman farmer Gilbert MARKHAM.

Wilson, Sir Broadly   Minor character in *AGNES GREY*. He is one of the "old codgers" who courts Rosalie MURRAY.

Wilson, William Carus   Wilson served as the model for the tyrannical Mr. BROCKLEHURST in Charlotte Brontë's *JANE EYRE*. He was head of the Clergy Daughters School at COWAN BRIDGE. Friends of Wilson later protested his portrait in

the novel and in Elizabeth GASKELL's biography of Charlotte.

Winter Evening Thoughts   *See* POEMS OF PATRICK BRONTË.

Wise, Thomas James   An American collector of Brontë manuscripts and memorabilia, Wise purchased the bulk of the Brontë manuscripts that Charlotte's husband, Arthur Bell NICHOLLS, had taken with him when he returned to Ireland in 1861. Wise employed the American journalist and critic Clement SHORTER as his go-between in this 1895 transaction, and between them the two men managed to muddle Brontë scholarship for nearly a century. Although Wise did publish many of the Brontës' previously unpublished works, his principal motivation seems to have been financial. He misattributed some works, broke others up, and distributed them in parts—perhaps even forging signatures—in an effort to cash in on the celebrity generated by Elizabeth GASKELL's biography of Charlotte. Wise's transcriptions of the Brontë juvenilia and poetry introduced errors into the canon that took decades to correct. Nonetheless, he was responsible, at least in name, for the 1934 Shakespeare Head edition of *The Poems of Charlotte and Patrick Branwell Brontë,* the collection upon which much future Brontë scholarship was based.

Wolf   Dog in *WUTHERING HEIGHTS*. Wolf is one of two dogs at WUTHERING HEIGHTS who attack Mr. LOCKWOOD upon JOSEPH (1)'s command, when the manservant thinks the visitor is making off with the house lantern.

Wood, Mark   Minor character in *AGNES GREY*. He is a poor laborer who suffers from CONSUMPTION. Rosalie MURRAY, who is supposed to attend to the poor and suffering in her community, cannot find time for Wood and sends Agnes GREY instead to comfort him.

Wood, Mr.   Minor character in *JANE EYRE*. His effort as a clergyman to marry Jane EYRE and Mr. ROCHESTER is interrupted by Richard MASON's attorney, who declares there is an "impediment" to the marriage.

Woodford   Place in *THE TENANT OF WILDFELL HALL.* Woodford is the village home of Frederick LAWRENCE, the squire of the lands around LINDEN-HOPE. The Lawrence family estate, WILDFELL HALL, has become nearly uninhabitable, having stood empty for 15 years before Lawrence's sister, Helen HUNTINGDON, takes up residence there.

Wooler, Miss   The headmistress and owner of the school at Roe Head, which Charlotte, Emily, and Anne Brontë attended. Miss Wooler became fond of Charlotte and engaged her as a teacher at the school. Neither Emily nor Anne adjusted well to the school in spite of Miss Wooler's sympathetic treatment; they fell gravely ill and had to be sent home. Miss Wooler and Charlotte remained life-long friends.

Wordsworth, William (1770–1850)   English poet. Perhaps the most famous ROMANTIC poet, Wordsworth is renowned for his love of nature and for the sublimity of his poetry. His bond with nature verges on mysticism, but many of his poems also celebrate human character in country settings. Although he was inspired by the French Revolution to write many of his earliest poems and announced a radical new approach to writing poetry in *Lyrical Ballads,* his first book (coauthored with Samuel Taylor Coleridge [1772–1834]), Wordsworth later became a rather conservative poet, dedicated more to preserving the values of the past than to overturning the precepts of the present. In Charlotte Brontë's novel *THE PROFESSOR,* Wordsworth is mentioned as the only poet that seems to puzzle Frances Evans HENRI. The character William CRIMSWORTH notes that Frances hesitates to express an opinion of Wordsworth's verse. Wordsworth's ecstatic but earthbound "Snowdon" vision in *The Prelude* greatly influenced Emily Brontë. Cathy EARNSHAW's vision of earth as paradise owes much to Wordsworth's elaboration of romantic aesthetics.

Wuthering Heights (the Heights)   Place in *WUTHERING HEIGHTS.* Like William Shakespeare's *Romeo and Juliet, Wuthering Heights* is the story of star-crossed lovers from two very different families. Wuthering Heights is the seat of the ancient Earnshaw clan. The estate received its name, the novel says, from "a significant provincial adjective, descriptive of the atmospheric tumult to which its station is exposed in stormy weather." When the novel opens, Wuthering Heights is indeed a storm-tossed place, its foundations rocked not only by the weather but also by the passions stirred by the arrival of a dark stranger, HEATHCLIFF. Heathcliff gradually gains control over the Heights, turning it into more of a prison than a home. He also briefly gains control of the nearby Linton family home, THRUSHCROSS GRANGE, which, surrounded by expansive parklands, has managed to survive as an outpost of civility amidst the wild moor. Emily Brontë might have based her rendition of Wuthering Heights in part on High Sunderland (or Sutherland) Hall near the town of HALIFAX, but its location probably owes more to Top Withens, an isolated farmhouse on HAWORTH MOOR.

Wuthering Heights   Novel by Emily BRONTË. In the fall of 1835, when the Brontë children were still involved with their imaginary worlds (see ANGRIA and GONDAL), Branwell produced the second volume of "The Life of Alexander Percy," in which he explored the relationship between his imaginary character, the earl of Northangerland, and Northangerland's first wife, Augusta Romana di Segovia. The couple is portrayed as having an intuitive and complete understanding of each other, and they are so absorbed in each other that their love becomes both destructive and death defying. Emily would later borrow elements of Branwell's characterization for her novel. During the winter and spring of 1845–46, Emily labored alongside her sisters to create a novel that, unlike the ill-fated *POEMS,* would help the family earn a living. But while Charlotte made an attempt to break with her juvenile forays into narrative fiction, Emily simply transplanted elements of the imaginary worlds of Gondal and Angria to the Yorkshire moors, thereby creating a work that, while grounded in a particular place and time, transcends its boundaries.

SYNOPSIS

Chapters 1–2

The novel opens—apparently with a diary entry—in 1801 with a retrospective narration delivered by a stranger, Mr. LOCKWOOD, who has rented THRUSHCROSS GRANGE from HEATHCLIFF. Lockwood describes having paid an introductory social call on his landlord at WUTHERING HEIGHTS, Heathcliff's home and the dwelling closest to the Grange.

Wuthering Heights and its master present a puzzling picture to the credulous Lockwood: Both are isolated and somewhat forbidding. Entering the house, Lockwood notes the date "1500" and the name "Hareton Earnshaw" carved over the threshold, but Heathcliff's abrupt manner keeps the visitor from asking questions about the history these words represent. Still, Lockwood feels a kinship with Heathcliff, for reasons he does not fully fathom. Despite his host's obvious indifference to him and the outright hostility of Heathcliff's dogs, Lockwood resolves to return.

After his midday dinner the next day, Lockwood walks the four miles to Wuthering Heights. In addition to the manservant, JOSEPH (1), a beautiful but morose young woman called Mrs. Heathcliff and a rough young man are at home when Lockwood arrives. All are so unwelcoming that Lockwood is relieved when Heathcliff enters. His relief quickly turns to confusion, however, when he discovers that young Mrs. Heathcliff is not the master's wife, but rather his daughter-in-law, Catherine LINTON. Next Lockwood is dumbfounded to discover that the rude youth he presumes to be Heathcliff's son is actually named

Wuthering Heights *by Emily Brontë is a haunting story of love, passion, and cruelty. William Wyler's 1939 film featured Laurence Olivier as Heathcliff and Merle Oberon as Catherine Earnshaw.* (Movie Star News)

Hareton EARNSHAW. Heathcliff treats both of these young people like servants.

He does not treat his guest much better. Lockwood, eager to escape the hostile atmosphere of Wuthering Heights despite a threatening storm, asks if someone can help guide him back to the Grange. Heathcliff rebuffs him, offering him only a bed with Hareton or Joseph. When Lockwood's rash attempt to walk home alone is foiled by two of the household dogs, the maid ZILLAH leads him up to a bed.

Chapter 3

Heathcliff's assertion that there is no spare bed in the house proves to have been inaccurate, but as Zillah ushers Lockwood into a room with a paneled bedchamber, she cautions him to take care that the master does not discover him there. Once inside, Lockwood finds some mysterious graffiti scratched into the paint: three variations on a name, repeated over and over again: "Catherine EARNSHAW," "Catherine Heathcliff," and "Catherine Linton." He also finds a musty book bearing the inscription "Catherine Earnshaw, her book," and a date nearly a quarter century past. Other books are similarly inscribed, and one of them includes an extra page that has been filled with the young Catherine's private musings on Heathcliff, Joseph, and a couple named Hindley EARNSHAW and Frances EARNSHAW.

After perusing Catherine's diary entries, Lockwood falls asleep while contemplating a volume with the title, *Seventy Times Seven, and the First of the Seventy-First. A Pious Discourse delivered by the Reverend Jabes Branderham, in the Chapel of Gimmerton Sough.* Lockwood dreams that he is walking through the snow with Joseph to the chapel at GIMMERTON, where one of them, or the preacher, is to be exposed and excommunicated for having committed the "First of the Seventy-First." After an interminable sermon, Rev. Jabes BRANDERHAM publicly denounces Lockwood, and members of the congregation begin to fight.

Lockwood then wakens to discover that the sound of blows in his dream is really that of a tree branch beating against his window. He falls back into a fitful sleep, from which he thinks he wakens and gets up to put a stop to the rapping on his window. Finding it impossible to open the casement, he puts his hand through the glass and reaches for the offending branch, only to find his fingers grasped by a tiny, ice-cold hand. Struggling to wrench free of its grasp, he hears a melancholy voice beg to be let in. He asks the speaker to identify herself, and she answers that she is Catherine LINTON, who has come home after losing her way on the moor. Lockwood vaguely discerns a child's face, but fear makes him snatch his hand back inside, and when the hand will not release its hold on him, he rubs it back and forth on the broken glass until blood runs down the panes and onto the bedclothes. Even after Lockwood manages to get free, the voice wails on, claiming, "'Twenty years, I've been a waif for twenty years!'" When it seems the specter is about to enter the room, Lockwood screams, waking Heathcliff.

Lockwood relates his dream to Heathcliff, who breaks down into an uncontrollable fit of sobbing as he opens the window and calls out to Cathy. When Lockwood next sees Heathcliff downstairs, the master is abusing his servants and his relatives alike, stopping only to accompany his tenant home to Thrushcross.

Chapters 4–6

Mystified by what he has experienced at Wuthering Heights, that evening Lockwood questions his housekeeper, Nelly DEAN, about the history of the place and its denizens. Mrs. Dean provides her version of the origins of the troubled household at the Heights.

Heathcliff's background is shrouded in mystery, but his stormy nature and dark complexion mark him, for Nelly Dean, as a gypsy. Her sympathies clearly lie with young Hareton and Catherine, the last of the Earnshaw and Linton families and the rightful owners of Wuthering Heights and Thrushcross Grange. Heathcliff, it seems, was first brought to Wuthering Heights by Hareton's grandfather, old Mr. EARNSHAW, after a trip to Liverpool, where he had discovered the starving little boy abandoned in the street. All of the Earnshaws, except for the master, who names the boy after a son who died in childhood, at first spurn the child. The name Heathcliff, Nelly says, "'has served him ever since, both for Christian and surname.'" The old man's indulgence toward the foundling fosters resentment in his only son, Hindley, who finally is sent away to school.

When Mr. Earnshaw dies, however, Hindley returns to Wuthering Heights, bringing a bride, Frances EARNSHAW, with him. In short order, Heathcliff is deprived of his lessons and sent to live with the servants. Hindley's younger sister, Cathy, who is as headstrong and willful as Heathcliff, is often banished as well. She and Heathcliff have grown inseparable. One day, the pair decide to go to Thrushcross Grange to spy on the Linton family and are caught. When the Grange bulldog grabs Cathy by the ankle, she is carried inside, while Heathcliff is ordered to leave. They remain separated for the next five weeks while Cathy stays on at the Grange to recuperate from her injury.

Chapter 7

During her convalescence at the Grange, Cathy is transformed from a "hatless little savage" into a beautiful, well-dressed young woman. Upon her return to Wuthering Heights, she looks for Heathcliff. He hangs back, aware that a breach has opened between them now that Cathy has been exposed to the civilizing influence of the Lintons. While Cathy greets Heathcliff affectionately, for the first time she also notices and points out how dirty and unkempt he is. Initially insulted and rebuffed by Cathy's remarks, Heathcliff asks Nelly to make him presentable.

Unfortunately, as a clean and cheerful Heathcliff is about to join Cathy and her visitors, young Edgar LINTON and his sister, Isabella LINTON, Hindley banishes him from the downstairs living quarters—but not before Heathcliff can fling a tureen of hot applesauce at Edgar for making insulting remarks about his appearance. Heathcliff's absence from the Christmas party grieves Cathy, who eventually sneaks off to join him. By now, however, nothing can console Heathcliff, who tells Nelly, "'I'm trying to settle how I shall repay Hindley back. I don't care how long I wait, if I can only do it, at last. I hope he will not die before I do!'"

Chapters 8–9

Nelly picks up the tale the following summer, in 1778, with the birth of Hareton Earnshaw, followed soon thereafter by the death of his mother, Frances. His wife's premature death throws Hindley into a fit of anger and dissipation from which

he never recovers. Eventually the only visitor to the Heights is Edgar Linton.

At 15, Cathy finds herself torn between Edgar's attentions and her long-term attachment to Heathcliff. One night she tells Nelly that Edgar has asked her to marry him and that she has accepted. She loves Edgar because he is handsome, rich, good tempered, and in love with her. Still, her heart and soul tell her she has done something wrong:

> "I've no more business to marry Edgar Linton than I have to be in heaven; and if the wicked man in there had not brought Heathcliff so low, I shouldn't have thought of it. It would degrade me to marry Heathcliff now; so he shall never know how I love him; and that, not because he's handsome, Nelly, but because he's more myself than I am."

Heathcliff, unbeknownst to the two women, has been seated nearby and has overheard their conversation. Once Cathy says that it would degrade her to marry him, he has heard enough and leaves the room—in fact, he quits Wuthering Heights altogether. When he cannot be found, Nelly, who saw him leave the room, tells Cathy that Heathcliff overheard the first part of her confession. In despair, Cathy stays up all night, even staying outside during a thunderstorm, fruitlessly waiting for him to return.

The next morning Cathy is pronounced dangerously ill with a fever. Old Mrs. Linton later takes her to Thrushcross Grange to convalesce, but she passes her illness on to her hostess and her husband, both of whom die in short order. A few months later, Catherine returns to the Grange permanently after marrying Edgar, who has inherited the property. Nelly is persuaded to follow her mistress there, leaving her former charge, five-year-old Hareton, to Hindley's indifferent care.

Chapter 10

After four weeks of illness, Lockwood is restless and eager to have Nelly continue her tale. She obliges, picking up where she left off.

Peace reigns at the Grange for six months after Catherine and Edgar are married, then Heathcliff appears one day in the garden, demanding to see Cathy. She is wild with excitement about his return and assumes her new husband will share the feeling. Edgar, however, warns her not to be "absurd": "'The whole household need not witness the sight of your welcoming a runaway servant as a brother.'" But Heathcliff has returned a changed man. Although he retains his ferocious demeanor, he also looks intelligent, mature, and prosperous. He makes clear that he has returned only to see Cathy and to be near her—at Wuthering Heights.

Edgar eventually resigns himself to visits between Cathy and Heathcliff, sometimes at the Grange and sometimes at the Heights, often with Isabella accompanying her sister-in-law. Soon Isabella declares herself to be in love with Heathcliff, a declaration Cathy refuses to take seriously: "'I'd as soon put out that little canary into the park on a winter's day as recommend you to bestow your heart on him!'"

Proof that what Cathy calls Heathcliff's "fierce, pitiless, wolfish" nature has not changed comes swiftly. On a trip into Gimmerton, the local village, Joseph learns that Heathcliff and Hindley stay up night after night drinking and gambling, with Hindley borrowing against his property and becoming more and more indebted to Heathcliff. Clearly Heathcliff has come back not only to see Cathy but also to avenge himself on her brother.

One day in Isabella's presence Cathy informs Heathcliff that her sister-in-law is pining away for him. Isabella, pained and embarrassed, runs off. Heathcliff expresses his dislike of Isabella, but then asks Cathy if Isabella is Edgar's heir. Cathy replies that Isabella must get in line behind "half-a-dozen nephews"—presumably, the children she will have with Edgar.

Chapter 11

Nelly visits the Heights, where she discovers that Hareton, deprived of parental care, has become almost a wild child. Nelly blames his lack of civility on Heathcliff and determines that she will prevent any spread of his influence at the Grange.

Consequently, when one day she spies Heathcliff surreptitiously embracing Isabella, Nelly feels it her duty to inform on him to Cathy. When Cathy confronts him, Heathcliff claims that she has treated him "infernally" and that his courtship of Isabella is his revenge. His plan, he says, is not to avenge himself on her—she is "wel-

come to torture [him] to death for [her] own amusement"—but like the slave who revolts, to "crush those beneath" him.

Nelly withdraws and immediately tells Edgar what has happened. Edgar summons three servants, directing them to wait in the passage while he confronts Cathy and Heathcliff. Both Cathy and Heathcliff sneer at what they view as Edgar's interruption, but then, discerning her husband's intentions, Cathy locks the door on Edgar's enforcers. When Edgar tries to wrest the key from her, she throws it into the fire and taunts her husband: "'We are vanquished! We are vanquished! Heathcliff would as soon lift a finger at you as the king would march his army against a colony of mice.'" Heathcliff pushes Edgar's chair, but then Edgar surprises them both by striking his enemy in the throat. Heathcliff, reluctant to fight Edgar as well as his reinforcements, breaks the lock and escapes.

Torn between the two, Cathy tells Nelly that she will try to break the two men's hearts by breaking her own. Nelly, who later confesses to Lockwood her dislike of Cathy, discounts this talk as an idle threat. Edgar, too, refuses to take Cathy's distress seriously and presses her to say she will see no more of Heathcliff. When Cathy responds by having a fit, Nelly tells him it is all an act.

Chapter 12

Cathy takes to her room and for two days refuses to unlock it. On the third day she finally opens the door and eagerly consumes the tea and toast Nelly brings her. She rails at Nelly about Edgar's failure to come to her bedside, his refusal to take her seriously. Nelly, for her part, begins to believe that Cathy can indeed make herself ill after she witnesses her mistress apparently experiencing hallucinations. When Cathy, wishing she were back home at Wuthering Heights, begs to feel the wind from the moor, Nelly complies by opening the window briefly. When she refuses to open it a second time, Cathy herself throws the casement open and begins deliriously to address Heathcliff, vowing, "'[T]hey may bury me twelve feet deep . . . but I won't rest till you are with me.'"

At this point Edgar enters the room and, seeing his wife's condition, blames Nelly for not telling him about Cathy's illness. Cathy threatens to jump from the window if Edgar so much as mentions Heathcliff. She is, she declares, past wanting Edgar.

Rushing out to get the doctor, Nelly discovers Isabella's nearly lifeless dog, FANNY (1), hanging from a bridle hook in the garden. She rescues the animal. When Nelly arrives at the doctor's house, Mr. KENNETH queries her about Cathy's illness, then tells her he has heard of Isabella's plans to run away with Heathcliff. Running back to the Grange, Nelly finds Isabella's room empty but feels constrained to tell Edgar while another, more serious crisis is already unfolding. The doctor tells Edgar that Cathy can recover if she is kept quiet. The next morning, when Isabella's absence is finally discovered, Edgar declares, "'Hereafter she is only my sister in name. . . .'" He will not speak to her again.

Chapter 13
Isabella and Heathcliff are not heard from for the next two months. During that time, Edgar tenderly nurses Cathy through a "brain fever." At about the time Cathy recovers enough to move about the Grange somewhat, Edgar receives a letter from Isabella telling him of her marriage to Heathcliff. When her brother fails to respond, Isabella then writes to Nelly, telling her that she and Heathcliff have returned to Wuthering Heights and that she already has grave doubts about her marriage. "'Is Mr. Heathcliff a man? If so, is he mad? And if not, is he a devil?'" she asks.

Isabella describes her reception at the Heights by the churlish Joseph and the actively hostile Hareton and Hindley Earnshaw. Hindley's hostility, she soon discovers, is directed at her husband: When he directs her upstairs to Heathcliff's chamber, he warns her to bolt the door behind her, as he plans to kill Heathcliff if ever he finds the door unlocked. Isabella turns to Joseph, who first shows her to an upstairs storeroom. When she protests that she wants to be shown to Heathcliff's room, he shows her to Hindley's bedroom. Exhausted and exasperated, Isabella finally takes shelter in a chair before the fire in Hareton's room. Later, when Heathcliff demands to know what she is doing there, Isabella explains that she could not get into their room because he has the key in his pocket. Heathcliff, swearing that they will never

share a room, rages on about Edgar being the cause of Cathy's illness. He swears that he will take his anger against Edgar out on Isabella until he manages to get his hands on her brother. More or less imprisoned in a house full of hate and with no one else to turn to, Isabella begs Nelly to visit her.

Chapter 14
Nelly tells Edgar of Isabella's letter and begs him to write—if not to forgive—Isabella. He refuses, claiming that he has nothing to forgive, but that he and his sister are now eternally divided.

When Nelly goes to Wuthering Heights later that day, she finds Isabella depressed and disheveled and Heathcliff hale and handsome: "So much had circumstances altered their positions, that he would certainly have struck a stranger as a born and bred gentleman, and his wife as a thorough little slattern!" Heathcliff questions Nelly about Cathy, taking umbrage at her suggestion that his feelings for Cathy in any way resemble Edgar's. He insists that Cathy's feelings for her husband pale beside her love for him. Isabella, he declares, is a fool for having married him:

> "She cannot accuse me of showing one bit of deceitful softness. The first thing she saw me do, on coming out of the Grange, was to hang up her little dog; and when she pleaded for it the first words I uttered were a wish that I had the hanging of every being belonging to her, except one."

He will do nothing to give Isabella the right to sue for separation, but he would be glad if she left. Meanwhile, he is her legal guardian and her jailer.

Heathcliff then tells Nelly his real reason for permitting her to come to the Heights: He wants her to arrange for him to see Cathy at the Grange. Nelly at first refuses, but after being badgered and threatened, she finally agrees to take a letter back to her mistress and to inform Heathcliff the next time Edgar is away. She justifies her actions to Mr. Lockwood as an attempt to avoid another explosion with Edgar Linton and to "create a favorable crisis in Catherine's mental illness."

Chapter 15
Four days later, while the others are at church, Nelly gives Cathy Heathcliff's letter. But Cathy

Heathcliff (Laurence Olivier) torments his wife, Isabella Linton (Geraldine Fitzgerald), as a means of revenge against her brother, Edgar.   (Movie Star News)

does not shake off her lethargy and disorientation until Nelly tells her that Heathcliff is in the garden, waiting to see her. Shortly thereafter, he appears in the room, where he takes Cathy in his arms and kisses her, crying out in despair over her condition. Cathy responds by telling him that he and Edgar have broken her heart.

On the verge of dying, Cathy exhibits so much savagery that Heathcliff asks if she is possessed by the devil. In a paroxysm of grief, Heathcliff turns his back on her, and she relents somewhat, calling him to her. Raising herself off the arm of her chair, she throws herself into Heathcliff's arms. When Nelly approaches to aid her, Heathcliff gnashes at her and foams "like a mad dog." As she

later tells Mr. Lockwood, "I did not feel as if I were in the company of a creature of my own species."

As the lovers cling to each other crying, alternately cursing and forgiving each other, Nelly sees Edgar and other members of the household returning from church and urges Heathcliff to leave. When he tries to do so, however, Cathy clings to him. Edgar enters the room, and finding them thus, springs at Heathcliff. Heathcliff, however, only hands over Cathy's apparently lifeless form, telling Edgar to look to her needs first.

Chapter 16
About midnight that night Cathy gives birth prematurely to a daughter, Catherine. Two hours

later Cathy dies, never having regained full consciousness. Leaving Edgar to sit with the body, Nelly goes out into the garden to find Heathcliff and tell him how his Cathy died. When Nelly describes a peaceful passing, Heathcliff thunders back, "'Catherine Earnshaw, may you not rest, as long as I am living! You said I killed you—haunt me then!'"

Cathy's body remains inside the Grange in an open casket for several days. Nelly, conscious of Heathcliff's vigil in the garden below, signals him when there is an opportunity to view his lost love. Nelly does not see him enter, but she discovers that Edgar's hair has been removed from a locket around Catherine's neck and replaced with a lock of Heathcliff's own. Nelly retrieves Edgar's golden curl and entwines it with Heathcliff's dark one inside Catherine's locket.

Neither Isabella, who was not invited, nor Hindley, who was, attends Catherine's funeral. She is buried with neither the Lintons nor the Earnshaws, but on a green slope in the corner of the churchyard under a simple headstone.

Chapter 17
The next evening, as Nelly sits rocking the motherless infant Cathy on her knee, she is interrupted by a breathless and nearly giddy Isabella, who has just run away from Wuthering Heights in the driving snow. Isabella recounts how the evening before, when Heathcliff returned from his vigil in the Grange park, Hindley locked him out, telling Isabella that he planned to murder their mutual tormenter. Isabella attempted to warn her husband, but Heathcliff managed to wrest Hindley's gun and knife from his grasp. Breaking a window, Heathcliff then sprang into the room, whereupon he beat Hindley severely.

The next morning, Isabella dared to confront her husband about his violence toward Hindley and blamed Heathcliff's evil nature for Cathy's death. Heathcliff, wretched with grief and anger, threw a knife at Isabella's head, wounding her beneath the ear. As she fled through the door, Heathcliff attempted to come after her and was checked by Hindley.

After relating the story of her escape, Isabella boards the coach for Gimmerton, never to return. Nelly hears that she eventually made a home for herself somewhere near London where, a few months after her escape, she gave birth to a boy named Linton HEATHCLIFF. Heathcliff learns of the child's existence and swears to Nelly that when it suits his purposes, he will take possession of his son. Twelve years later, when Isabella dies, Heathcliff apparently is not yet prepared to take in the sickly Linton.

But when, six months after Cathy's death, Hindley Earnshaw also dies, Heathcliff does, after a fashion, take over Hareton's care. When Nelly, who has arranged Hindley's funeral, tells Heathcliff to turn the boy over to Edgar Linton, Heathcliff responds: "'I have a fancy to try my hand at rearing a young one, so intimate to your master that I must supply the place of this with my own, if he attempt to remove it.'" Not wanting to engage with Heathcliff in a struggle over either of his nephews, Edgar backs off. Hareton, who should have inherited Wuthering Heights upon his father's death, instead lives on there virtually as a servant to the man who was Hindley's mortgagee and mortal enemy.

Chapters 18–20
Nelly Dean goes on to describe the next 12 years, relatively peaceful ones at Thrushcross Grange. During that period, she and Edgar raise young Cathy who, until she is 13, does not even leave the grounds around her home unescorted, and even then she is allowed to venture out only with her father.

Shortly before Isabella's death, however, the status quo ends. When Isabella writes to her brother, asking to see him one last time so that she can deliver her son to his care, Edgar immediately complies, leaving Cathy in Nelly Dean's care. During the time her father is away, Cathy cajoles Nelly into packing a picnic basket for her, then takes off alone on her pony, MINNY. Fearing that Cathy has left to explore the distant PENISTONE CRAGS, Nelly sets out to find her. As she is passing Wuthering Heights, Nelly notes that CHARLIE, one of the dogs that had accompanied Cathy that morning, lies cut and bleeding on the doorstep. Alarmed, Nelly stops to inquire about her charge, who is indeed inside.

Entering the house, Nelly finds Cathy happily chattering at Hareton, who Cathy is amazed and distressed to be told is her cousin. Her other cousin, Linton Heathcliff, soon arrives at Thrushcross Grange with Edgar. A pale, delicate, sickly boy, Linton is fretful and peevish, and no sooner has he arrived at the Grange than Joseph appears with the message that Heathcliff wants his son at Wuthering Heights. Edgar promises that Linton will go there the next day, after he has rested.

Informed that he is to join his father, Linton expresses amazement: His mother had never even told him he had a father. On the ride over with Nelly to Wuthering Heights, he questions her at length about Heathcliff and his new home. Upon their arrival at the Heights, Heathcliff greets his son with derision, calling the weeping boy a "puling chicken." But Heathcliff tells Nelly to rest assured: "'[M]y son is going to be prospective owner of your place, and I should not wish him to die till I was certain of being his successor.'" This hope of gaining power over the Lintons is, it seems, Heathcliff's only reason for taking the boy in.

Chapter 21
Cathy is distraught at her cousin's absence. Two years will pass, however, before she sees Linton again. On her 16th birthday, Cathy sets out with Nelly to see a colony of moor fowl. Nearing Wuthering Heights, Cathy is stopped by Heathcliff, who accuses her of poaching his game. When Cathy, who does not know Heathcliff, asks if Hareton, whom she recognizes, is his son, Heathcliff replies that he is not. She is intrigued by his suggestion that she accompany him home to meet his real son.

When Nelly protests that Cathy cannot go because Heathcliff has a bad design, he replies straightforwardly: "'My design is as honest as possible. . . . That the two cousins may fall in love, and get married.'" He goes on to clarify matters: Linton's property, including Thrushcross Grange, will go to his father upon his death, "'but, to prevent disputes, I desire their union, and I am resolved to bring it about.'"

Despite Nelly's protestations, Heathcliff leads Cathy to Wuthering Heights, where she meets Linton on the doorstep. At first she does not recognize him, but then she kisses him fervently. Heathcliff acknowledges that he is Cathy's uncle, then exhibits great impatience both with Cathy and Linton. But he confesses to Nelly, "'I covet Hareton, with all his degradation. . . . I'd have loved the lad had he been some one else.'" On some level, Heathcliff clearly cares for Hareton,

who reminds him of his own youthful self. What the older man most enjoys about the younger, however, is his ability to degrade Hareton, to visit on Hindley's son all the abuse the young Heathcliff experienced at Hindley's hand.

Cathy expresses amazement that Hareton is her relation, even going so far as to mock him and his illiteracy. When Linton joins in, Hareton suddenly becomes self-conscious about his seeming inferiority.

After returning home from what she regards as a thoroughly satisfactory outing, Cathy tells her father about the adventure. She chides Edgar for not having told her about Linton's nearness, accepting Heathcliff's explanation that he and Edgar quarrelled long ago because Edgar thought him too poor to marry Isabella. Edgar responds that he has kept his daughter from seeing Linton because to do so would involve her seeing Heathcliff, who would detest Cathy because he detests her father. An attempt to explain briefly how Heathcliff gained possession of Wuthering Heights fails to penetrate Cathy's innocence.

A few hours later, Nelly finds Cathy in tears because she will be unable to keep her promise to visit Linton the next day. When she begs to be able to send a note, Nelly refuses, but Cathy manages nonetheless to send a missive to her cousin through a local delivery boy. Her surreptitious correspondence with Linton becomes a nearly daily occurrence, as Nelly discovers one day by searching through a locked drawer. Finding that Nelly has learned her secret, Cathy begs that her father not be told. Nelly agrees, so long as Cathy promises never to communicate with Linton again. The delivery boy is given one last missive for Linton, telling him Cathy will no longer receive any correspondence from him. The romance that Heathcliff hoped to promote seems at a standstill.

Chapters 22–24
With Edgar suffering from a cold that he cannot shake off, and Cathy suffering from the aftereffects of her aborted romance, Nelly spends as much time as she can with the young girl. One rainy autumn day Nelly and Cathy set out for a walk and encounter Heathcliff. Heathcliff tells Cathy that his son is pining for love of her and encourages her to visit that week during his own absence in order to lift Linton's spirits. Encountering

resistance, Heathcliff goes on to insist that his son is dying.

This news plunges Cathy, already depressed about her father's health, into despair. She insists that she must go to Linton, and the next day she and Nelly visit Wuthering Heights. Upon entering the kitchen, they hear Linton calling peevishly to Joseph to tend the fire. Linton obviously is ill, but not so ill as his whining indicates. Linton complains about everyone in the household—Hareton, Joseph, Zillah—everyone but his father, of whom he is both proud and afraid. Instead of expressing gratitude for Cathy's visit, Linton picks a fight with her about whose father, Edgar or Heathcliff, her mother loved best. The argument ends when Cathy gives his chair a push, causing Linton to fall against one arm and triggering a seizure of coughing. When it passes, he first blames her for his illness, then begs her to nurse him back to health.

Nelly, disgusted with Linton's behavior, tells Cathy that her cousin is not long for this world, adding that Cathy is therefore lucky that there is no chance she will have him as her husband. But Cathy, at nearly 17 feeling in control of her own destiny, tells Nelly defiantly that she is not her jailer. On the way back to the Grange Nelly catches a severe cold that lays her low for three weeks, during which Cathy takes advantage of her lack of supervision.

Nelly eventually spies Cathy stealthily riding home on Minny after dark. When Nelly confronts her, Cathy bursts into tears and confesses that she has been paying evening visits to the Heights. She relates how well, in general, she and Linton have got on, conversing about their individual conceptions of heaven and playing games. She also tells Nelly about Hareton's attempt to decipher the legend over the door to Wuthering Heights. Clearly he has learned the letters—which spell out his own name—to impress her, but Cathy mocks him when he cannot make out the date beneath.

Later, Hareton takes his revenge by throwing Linton and Cathy out of the parlor. Linton's impotent rage at being ousted from what he regards as his rightful home results in a fit of coughing and a hemorrhage. As Joseph and Zillah minister to the boy and Cathy weeps, Hareton makes some attempt to apologize. The girl spurns him then, as she does when he approaches her as she is about to leave for home. Sitting atop Minny, Cathy cuts Hareton with her whip.

After three days, curiosity gets the better of Cathy, and she returns to Wuthering Heights. After Linton ignores her, only addressing her to blame her for Hareton's outburst, Cathy returns home. Two days later, she goes back to see Linton. He begs her forgiveness, telling her that her kindness has made him love her more than ever.

Nelly promptly reports Cathy's confession to Edgar, who forbids his daughter to go back to Wuthering Heights. Linton may come to the Grange, but she is never to go back to the Heights.

Chapters 25–27
Nelly breaks off her story to say that the events she has been relating only go back to the previous winter, when she never would have dreamed she would be relating them to a stranger. Then, coyly, she goes on to suggest that Lockwood may not, in fact, remain a stranger, for who could look on the beautiful Catherine Linton and not fall in love with her?

Then Nelly resumes her tale. Edgar, fearing his own death is near, is eager to provide for his daughter. He wonders if young Linton Heathcliff might not, after all, make her a suitable husband. Edgar has written to Linton, urging him to visit the Grange, but has received no answer. That spring, he writes again, but Linton answers only that his father does not want him to call at the Grange. Linton asks that Edgar occasionally ride with Cathy toward Wuthering Heights, so that the young lovers can exchange a word or two on neutral ground. Because Edgar is too ill to accompany Cathy, he declines this request. He does, however, acquiesce to their correspondence, and by summer he gives his consent for Cathy and Linton to meet once a week in the open air under Nelly's watchful eye.

The first meeting does not go according to plan: When Nelly and Cathy arrive at the crossroads at the appointed hour, they are met by a messenger who tells them that Linton is still near the Heights, where he hopes the women will join him. When they reach Linton, he is no more than a quarter mile from his home, and he is on foot. Nelly and Cathy abandon their mounts and approach Linton, who proves to be more feeble and wan than ever before. He insists, however, that he is better. When Cathy tries to talk with him, she finds him listless and preoccupied.

Linton is finally roused, however, when Cathy suggests that she and Nelly go home. Glancing fearfully over his shoulder at the Heights, he begs her to stay a bit longer. They must, he feverishly insists, tell both her father and his that he is well, and she must promise to come again next Thursday.

When Cathy and Nelly meet Linton the next week, he greets them with an animation induced by fear. Cathy, believing that Linton does not really want her, is angry that his demands have forced her from her dying father's side. When she tries to leave, Linton hangs on to her dress, prompting Cathy to call him "'an abject reptile.'"

Linton then sobs that his life is in her hands, because if she leaves him, he will be killed. While insisting that he dare not tell her why, he says that his father has threatened him.

At that moment Heathcliff appears. Ignoring the two young people, he greets Nelly almost cheerfully, asking whether it is true that Edgar is dying. When she says he is, Heathcliff presses her about how much longer Edgar might last. He is afraid that Linton will die before Edgar does, a sequence of events that could end his plans to inherit the Grange.

Then Heathcliff turns viciously on his ailing son, bullying him into standing. When Heathcliff asks Cathy to walk Linton home, she at first

Although Emily Brontë's Wuthering Heights *was not as successful as her sister Charlotte's* Jane Eyre *upon publication, it has nonetheless inspired five film adaptations. The 1970 version, directed by Robert Fuest, starred Timothy Dalton as Heathcliff and Anne Calder-Marshall as Catherine Earnshaw.* (Movie Star News)

demurs: Her father has forbidden her to go to Wuthering Heights. But when Linton whispers that he has been forbidden to reenter the house without her, she complies. When the foursome reaches Wuthering Heights, Heathcliff locks them inside, saying that he is in need of some interesting company. When Cathy attempts to retrieve the key from him, he slaps her, and when Nelly attempts to come to her rescue, Heathcliff stops her with a tap on the chest. Then Heathcliff proceeds to make them all tea.

Afterward, when Heathcliff leaves, ostensibly to retrieve Cathy's and Nelly's horses, Linton reveals that his father wants Cathy to stay the night and marry him the next morning. When Cathy voices her outrage at this plan, Linton collapses in tears, begging her to save him.

Heathcliff returns, declaring that the horses have disappeared. Sending Linton off to bed, he confronts the women. Cathy begs to be allowed to return to her worried father, promising to come back and marry Linton, which is what her father wants anyway. Heathcliff refuses, declaring that the thought of making Edgar miserable brings him joy. Heathcliff says he will make sure that Cathy either accepts his son or stays imprisoned at Wuthering Heights. When Cathy kneels and begs for her freedom at any cost, Heathcliff reacts with disgust: "'How the devil can you dream of fawning on me? I *detest* you!'"

When some servants arrive from the Grange to ask after Cathy and Nelly, Heathcliff sends them away, then sends the two women upstairs for the night. The next morning, at seven, Heathcliff pulls Cathy out, while locking Nelly in. Nelly remains a prisoner there for five nights and four days.

Chapter 28

On the fifth morning of her imprisonment, Nelly is set free by Zillah, who says that Nelly and Cathy were reported lost in BLACKHORSE MARSH, then found and lodged at Wuthering Heights. Nelly will be allowed to return to the Grange with the news that Cathy will be released in time to attend her father's funeral.

Once downstairs, Nelly finds only Linton, who complains self-indulgently that Cathy, now his wife, keeps him awake at night with her crying. He refuses Nelly's request for the key to Cathy's room, so Nelly leaves to get help at the Grange.

Nelly relates the news of her and Cathy's confinement to Edgar, who is now near death. Edgar knows that part of Heathcliff's plan is to gain control over not only Edgar's estate, but also over his personal property. In an effort to change his will so that Cathy's fortune is put in trust during her lifetime, Edgar sends a servant for Mr. GREEN (2), only to learn that the lawyer will not be able to come to the Grange for some hours. Another party, sent from the Grange to retrieve Cathy from Wuthering Heights, also returns empty handed.

At 3 A.M., however, Cathy comes home. Linton has taken pity on her and let her go. She arrives just in time to see her father die. The lawyer, having been paid off by Heathcliff, arrives too late. He begins to reorder the Grange household to suit its new master.

Chapter 29

The evening after Edgar's funeral, Heathcliff barges in on Cathy and Nelly unannounced. When Cathy makes a move to escape, he stops her, saying he has come to fetch her and take her back to her rightful home. Linton, he says, is entirely her concern now. Furthermore, she must quit the Grange because Heathcliff plans to rent it. Nelly is to remain as housekeeper.

Heathcliff then takes in his surroundings, stopping to focus on a portrait of his late love. He tells Nelly that the day before, while the sexton was digging Edgar's grave, he convinced the grave digger to remove the earth over Catherine's coffin, which lay next to Edgar's grave. Heathcliff opened the coffin in order to look on Catherine's face once more. Then he bribed the sexton someday to bury him alongside her, adding triumphantly, "'[B]y the time Linton gets to us, he'll not know which is which!'"

When Nelly chides Heathcliff for disturbing the dead, he responds viciously: "'Disturbed her? No! she has disturbed me, night and day, through eighteen years. . . .'" He goes on to say that he was wild after Cathy's death, and the only way he was able to gain solace then was by digging the fresh earth off her coffin, trying to get to her. All at once, though, he had felt her presence, which stayed with him while he refilled the grave and went back to Wuthering Heights, fully expecting to see her there. When Hindley and Isabella tried to stop him from entering, he kicked them aside and rushed upstairs to the paneled bed that had been Cathy's, where he could almost, but not quite, gain sight of her. Thus it was night after night, year after year, until last night, when Heathcliff finally saw her again. Worn down with frustrated hope, he is at last appeased, having seen her at rest. Heathcliff leaves on foot with young Cathy for Wuthering Heights, ordering that her mother's portrait be delivered there the following day.

Chapter 30

Nelly tells Lockwood that she has not seen Cathy since the girl left Thrushcross Grange with Heathcliff after Edgar died. She has not been permitted to see her "young lady" and has been forced to rely on Zillah, of whom she is jealous, for information about Cathy. According to Zillah, Cathy has not exhibited entirely admirable behavior, but Nelly dismisses these aspects of her rival's report as the imaginings of a "narrow-minded, selfish woman."

Upon arriving at the Heights, Cathy locks herself in with Linton, emerging the next morning to report that her cousin is ill and needs a doctor. Heathcliff callously responds that his son's life "'is not worth a farthing'" and dismisses her. Zillah, too, declines to help (she has received her instructions from Heathcliff), telling Cathy that it is her job to care for her husband.

When at last Linton dies, Cathy takes to her bed. During the following two weeks, she rebuffs Zillah's attempts to help. Heathcliff shows her Linton's will, which leaves all of his and Cathy's property to his father. With the Linton lands already under Heathcliff's control, Cathy is left virtually penniless.

When Cathy finally comes downstairs, she wears mourning clothes. Heathcliff and Joseph are both out of the house, and she has only Zillah and Hareton for company. Cathy refuses their efforts to make her comfortable. Embittered, she lashes out even at Heathcliff himself, then retreats into stony silence.

Nelly ends her tale by dropping a broad hint, telling Lockwood she fears there is no escape for Cathy unless the girl marries again. Lockwood, taking the hint, decides he is well enough to ride over to Wuthering Heights. He intends to give notice to his landlord of his intention to vacate the Grange.

Chapter 31

One early January morning, Lockwood arrives at the Heights, bearing with him a note from Nelly to Cathy. Not finding Heathcliff in yet, Lockwood resolves to wait for his return. Although Hareton is civil, Cathy barely acknowledges Lockwood's presence. She ignores the missive from Nelly, which Hareton retrieves before she does. Then, taking pity on her, he drops it on the floor beside her.

Cathy cries that she cannot answer Nelly because she has neither pen nor paper, not even a book from which she can tear a page. Hareton has squirreled away all the books she brought for Linton, a great waste, she says, because Hareton cannot learn to read them properly. Humiliated, Hareton leaves the room and returns with an armful of books, which he throws into Cathy's lap. When Cathy opens one and does a mocking imitation of his halting attempts to read, Hareton hurls the other books into the fire.

At this point Heathcliff enters, looking anxious and haggard and muttering about how he sees his lost Cathy in Hareton's features, rather than those of the detested Hindley. When Lockwood gives notice that he will be vacating the Grange, Heathcliff invites him to stay for supper. It is a dreary affair, and as Lockwood leaves, he reflects, "What a realization of something more romantic than a fairy tale it would have been from Mrs. Linton Heathcliff, had she and I struck up an attachment."

Chapter 32

Lockwood resumes his narration in a diary entry dated 1802—several months later when, on a trip to the north of England, he passes near Gimmerton. On a whim, he decides to visit Thrushcross Grange. Upon his arrival, he finds that Nelly Dean has moved to Wuthering Heights, where he then goes.

The exterior of the Heights looks far more welcoming than he remembers it. Before he even enters its doors, he overhears a fond, teasing exchange between Cathy and Hareton. Experiencing a twinge of envy, Lockwood notes both Cathy's beauty and the attention she lavishes on Hareton, who receives both her tutelage and her kisses. As the young couple steps out into the moonlight, Lockwood goes around to the kitchen door, where he finds Nelly and Joseph engaged in teasing banter.

Nelly tells Lockwood that she came to the Heights at Heathcliff's invitation after Lockwood quit the Grange and after Zillah gave her notice at the Heights. Then Nelly reveals the reason for the transformation at Wuthering Heights: Heathcliff has been dead for three months.

Nelly gladly accepted her new assignment, she says, because it allowed her to be near Cathy. At first this companionship seemed enough for the girl, especially since Nelly managed to smuggle books over from the Grange. Then, becoming restless, Cathy began to belittle Hareton, likening him to a cart-horse or a dog. Her reasons for starting up even this type of conversation are mixed, however; when Hareton suffers a hunting injury that forces his confinement indoors, Cathy begins making amends for her past behavior toward him. Hareton is initially wary, even hostile. When Cathy weeps, declaring that it is not she who hates him, but the other way around, Hareton demands to know "'why have I made [Heathcliff] angry, by taking your part then, a hundred times?'" This revelation prompts Cathy first to extend her hand toward her cousin and then, when he refuses to take it, to kiss his cheek. Thereafter they become inseparable companions, as Cathy takes on the job of civilizing the long-oppressed Hareton.

A few days after this incident Cathy gets into trouble, first with Joseph, then with Heathcliff, for clearing away some currant and gooseberry bushes so that she can plant flowers. Hareton attempts to take the blame for her, but Cathy speaks up, challenging Heathcliff by demanding to know how he can begrudge her a few yards of earth when he has taken all her land, as well as Hareton's land and money.

Enraged, Heathcliff grabs Cathy by the hair, only to suddenly release her. After eating his meal in silence, he leaves the house. In his absence, Cathy begins to tell Hareton about Heathcliff's treatment of Hindley, but Hareton silences her, asking how she would like him to speak ill of her father. Cathy then understands for the first time that Heathcliff, despite his mistreatment of Hareton, is the only true father her cousin has ever known.

When Heathcliff returns that evening, he sees Cathy and Hareton bent over a book together. As they look up at him, he responds with agitation, a response Nelly later attributes to the resemblance both bear to Catherine Earnshaw. Dismissing them, Heathcliff turns to Nelly and muses about his inability to "'demolish the two houses'" because he has "'lost the faculty for enjoying their destruction.'" Hareton, who seems to be a personification of Heathcliff's youth, has also become, in his likeness to the dead Cathy, the embodiment of Heathcliff and Cathy's immortal love.

Heathcliff then confesses that in addition to losing the will to destroy, he is losing the will to live. He has to remind himself to breathe, remind his heart to beat. Although he is hale, he yearns for death; indeed, he has yearned for it so long that it has "devoured" his existence. Now, he feels, his "long fight" will soon be over.

Some days later, when Heathcliff returns to Wuthering Heights from a long night away, he is pale and excited. After declaring that he is hungry, he gets up from the dinner table, leaving his meal untouched. When he reenters the house a couple of hours later, he exhibits the same unnatural animation. Nelly, concerned about his health, questions where he was the night before. Heathcliff responds, "'Last night I was on the threshold of hell. Today, I am within sight of my heaven.'" Requesting that everyone stay away from him, he sends her away.

Nelly later brings Heathcliff's supper to him. She finds him sitting in the damp, cold room, leaning against the ledge of an open window. Startled by his unearthly appearance, she lets her candle go out, and he orders her to fetch another. Nelly, frightened by what she has seen, sends Joseph instead. But Joseph quickly returns with his light and Heathcliff's untouched supper tray; the master wants nothing to eat until morning. Then they hear Heathcliff mount the stairs and turn into the room with the paneled bed.

After spending a fitful night half dreaming about Heathcliff's uncertain origins and true nature ("'Is he a ghoul, or a vampire?'"), Nelly wakes and checks the garden to make sure no footprints appear under the master's window. When Heathcliff finally appears at the breakfast table, he is if anything more agitated than the day before. He stares fixedly at something two yards in front of him that Nelly cannot see. Irritated at her attempts to get him to eat, Heathcliff walks out of the house. He does not return until after midnight, when he begins pacing the floor downstairs, muttering words that are for Nelly indistinguishable except for the name Catherine, "'spoken as one would speak to a person present.'"

At 4 A.M. Nelly goes downstairs, where Heathcliff asks her to make a fire for him. He tells her that at dawn he intends to send for Mr. Green so that he can draw up a will. When Nelly chides that instead of seeing Green he should call a minister, Heathcliff tells her how he wishes to be buried. He asks to be carried to the churchyard in the evening, adding that she and Hareton may accompany him if they wish. Above all, she is to see that his instructions to the sexton are carried out; otherwise, he will haunt her.

That afternoon, Heathcliff attempts to get either Nelly or Cathy to sit with him in his den, but both women are afraid to join him. "'Well,'" he declares, "'there is *one* who won't shrink from my company! By God! She is relentless!'" He spends the remainder of the day alone and at dusk retires to his chamber, where he spends the night groaning and murmuring. The next morning, together with Mr. Kenneth, Nelly tries to open Heathcliff's door, only to find it locked. When Heathcliff tells them to go away, they do so.

The next morning, as she walks around the exterior of the house in the driving rain, Nelly sees that Heathcliff's window is open to the elements. Rushing to his room, she opens the panels of the bed to find Heathcliff lying there soaked with rain. His face bears a faint smile, and his hand has a bloodless cut received from the open casement. One touch assures Nelly that he is dead, but she is unable to close his fierce, staring eyes.

Every member of the household is disturbed by Heathcliff's manner of death, and Kenneth is unable to say exactly what caused it. Hareton, however, is the only one to truly mourn Heathcliff's passing. He and Nelly follow the coffin to the grave, where Heathcliff's final wish to be buried beside Cathy is carried out. The neighborhood, Nelly reports, is scandalized, and some report that Heathcliff—sometimes alone, and sometimes in the company of a woman—continues to walk the moor.

Nelly tells Lockwood that she does not believe these reports, but that she will nonetheless rest easier when the household removes to the Grange after Cathy and Hareton marry on New Year's Day. Lockwood makes a hasty exit, heading through the churchyard, where he examines the graves of those whose story has so long intrigued him. Catherine's grave, in the middle, is half buried by heath. Edgar's, on one side, has only begun to be covered with turf. Heathcliff's, on the other side, is still bare. He wonders "how any one could ever imagine unquiet slumbers for the sleepers in that quiet earth."

PUBLICATION HISTORY

On April 6, 1846, Charlotte Brontë wrote to the publishing house AYLOTT & JONES proposing a three-volume set of distinct tales in the process of being written by Currer, Ellis, and Acton BELL, which could be published either together or as separate works. Charlotte's contribution to this effort, THE PROFESSOR, would not be published during her lifetime, but Emily's novel, which itself filled two volumes, together with Anne's AGNES GREY were accepted the next year for publication by T. C. NEWBY. Newby, who was primarily a printer and a sole proprietor, wanted E. and A. Bell to share the risk of publishing their three-volume set by advancing 50 pounds against the costs of producing it.

In the meantime, Charlotte had continued to send out *The Professor* while working on a second novel, JANE EYRE. Smith, Elder & Co., which rejected the first, was quick to accept the second, which was published before either of her sisters' first novels appeared. When Charlotte complained to her publisher about Newby's slowness, the publishing firm Smith, Elder offered to publish *Wuthering Heights* and *Agnes Grey*, but Emily and Anne declined.

When *Jane Eyre* was greeted with a fair number of excellent reviews and brisk sales following its appearance in October 1847, Newby was finally goaded into action—in part, perhaps, to take advantage of the celebrity and mystery surrounding the name "Bell." Early that December, in 1847, he published *Wuthering Heights* and *Agnes Grey* but without incorporating the changes both sisters had made on their proof sheets.

Heathcliff and Cathy on the moors   (Movie Star News)

Of the two novels in the set, *Wuthering Heights* received most of the attention. Some reviewers said *Wuthering Heights,* like *Jane Eyre,* was burdened with a "low tone of behavior." But others clearly saw the originality of Emily's work, commenting on its strangeness and wildness. *Wuthering Heights* sold well enough to make Newby report that Ellis and Acton Bell would probably recoup their initial deposit.

Apparently cheered by this news, Emily and Anne offered Newby the opportunity to publish their second novels, declining Smith, Elder's offer to do so. No manuscript of Emily's second novel survives, but a great deal of circumstantial evidence suggests that she, like her sisters, was indeed working on a second novel in 1847 and 1848. There would be no second novel, however: In autumn 1848, after burying her brother, Emily entered the final stages of TUBERCULOSIS. By the end of the year she too was dead.

The appearance in 1850 of a review praising *Wuthering Heights* while insisting it was the work of Currer Bell prompted William Smith WILLIAMS of Smith, Elder to offer to reprint Emily's novel, together with *Agnes Grey,* in one volume. Charlotte accepted, agreeing to contribute a biographical introduction that would clarify the separate identities of Currer, Ellis, and Acton Bell. Anne, too, had died by this time, and Charlotte decided to edit a selection of her sisters' poems—18 by Emily and seven by Anne—for inclusion in the volume. She also took a hand in revising the texts of the novels, which had been poorly served by Newby. Unfortunately, many of the "corrections" Charlotte made altered what her sisters originally intended, or, in the case of *Wuthering Heights,* mangled Emily's attempts to reproduce Yorkshire dialect.

Most early reprints of *Wuthering Heights* nonetheless followed the text of the second edition, which appeared in December 1850. Starting with an edition put together by Clement SHORTER in 1911, however, modern reprints have had a tendency to reject, or at least modify, Charlotte's emendations. In 1963 W. W. Norton published an authoritative text, edited by William M. Sale, Jr., reconciling the first and second editions.

Wuthering Heights & Agnes Grey, which initially appeared in an edition of only 250 copies, sold far better in the less expensive one-volume second edition put out by Smith, Elder. The popularity of these works, however, only began to assume major proportions with the publication of Elizabeth GASKELL's *THE LIFE OF CHARLOTTE BRONTË* in 1857. In March 1858, for example, 15,000 copies of the volume containing Emily's and Anne's first novels were rushed into print.

Wycoller A ruined house eight miles west of Haworth, just off the HAWORTH-Colne Road, that is said to have provided a model for FERNDEAN in *JANE EYRE.*

Wynne, Samuel Fawthorpe Minor character in *SHIRLEY.* He is a magistrate and a member of the local gentry. He is a kind enough man who courts Shirley KEELDAR. While she likes him, she has no intention of marrying him, and she shocks Mr. SYMPSON, her uncle, when she rejects Wynne's marriage proposal.

Yorke, Jessy Minor character in SHIRLEY. The daughter of Mr. Hiram and Mrs. YORKE and the sister of Rose YORKE, Jessy has a lively and charming personality.

Yorke, Mark Minor character in *SHIRLEY*. He is the younger son of Mr. Hiram and Mrs. YORKE. At 14 he is handsome, down-to-earth, and mature for his years.

Yorke, Martin Minor character in *SHIRLEY*. A son of Mr. Hiram and Mrs. YORKE, he is uncouth and rude but gives promise of knowing how to take what he wants from the world and to be a success.

Yorke, Matthew Minor character in *SHIRLEY*. He is the eldest son of Mr. Hiram and Mrs. YORKE, and as such he arrogantly asserts himself as the heir of the family. He seems to have a perpetual scowl, and his brothers do their best not to antagonize him.

Yorke, Mr. Hiram Major character in *SHIRLEY*. Like Robert MOORE, Mr. Yorke is an opponent of the TORY administration. Yorke and his wife have democratic principles that clash with conservative and monarchical rule. Yorke was once Matthewson HELSTONE's rival for the love of Mary Cave, whom Helstone married. He has never forgiven Helstone, and he despises Helstone's Tory politics.

Yorke, Mrs. Minor character in *SHIRLEY*. The wife of Mr. Hiram YORKE, she is opinionated and a cynic. She finds fault in people and annoys Caroline HELSTONE with her dubious assumptions about Caroline's character. She has two daughters and three sons.

Yorke, Rose Minor character in *SHIRLEY*. Rose takes after her mother, Mrs. YORKE: She is willful and rather contentious.

Young Men's Magazine, The Charlotte Brontë wrote the November 1829 issue of this magazine started by Branwell in January 1829 in imitation of BLACKWOOD'S MAGAZINE (see BRANWELL'S BLACKWOOD'S MAGAZINE). She renamed it and included a fairy story, poetry, and political commentary. For other issues, she wrote a play, *The Poetaster,* attributed to the authorship of Lord Charles Wellesley, one of the main characters in the GLASS TOWN saga. In Charlotte's only full-length play, she satirized her brother's pretensions as a playwright. He had already written *Caractacus: A Dramatic Poem* and *Lausanne: A Dramatic Poem.* After Charlotte's attack, he wrote *The Revenge: A Tragedy in 3 Acts.* Charlotte's protagonist is Henry Ryhmer, who is reminiscent of YOUNG SOULT, Branwell's hero-poet. Ryhmer, as his name implies, can rhyme, but he is no true poet; instead he is a bombastic, foolish figure who eventually becomes the subordinate of Charlotte's fictional hero Wellesley. Charlotte continued her campaign against Branwell in her short novel, THE GREEN DWARF.

In "A Day at Parry's Palace," Charlotte also aimed her criticism at Emily and Anne, who had formed their own writing team and had created their own world, Parrysland, which features a much more sedate, everyday atmosphere than the grand, exotic locations that Charlotte and Branwell favored. To Charlotte, her sisters lacked maturity, and she mocked their tendency to withdraw into neat, tidy places inhabited by dolls rather than soldiers.

Charlotte's own efforts at romantic nature poetry in "Morning by Marquis Douro," one of her favorite characters in the Glass Town saga, hardly suggest that she was a better poet than her siblings. Like their early verse, hers is derivative and conventional: "Lo! The light of the morning is flowing / Through radiant portal of gold / Which Aurora in crimson robes glowing / For the horses of fire doth untold."

Charlotte also tried her hand at art criticism, writing a critique of three engravings published in a magazine, *Friendship's Offering*. Her air of authority and keen eye are evident: "A fine picture engraved in the first style of the art, the tree weeds & grass in the foreground are beautifully etched & throw the rest of the landscape into distance. Campbell Castle is situated upon a rock & with a thick forest that environs it, forms the centre piece, both are in deep shade, thereby setting off the lights around, the distance mountains are not very picturesque, but the Artist has evidently made the best of his materials." The Scottish background of the engravings reflected Charlotte's deep interest in Scottish history and romantic settings, stimulated by the work of Sir Walter SCOTT.

Young Soult   A poet invented by Branwell Brontë and based on a real historical figure, the son of a marshall in Napoléon BONAPARTE's army. The actual Young Soult visited London in 1830 and met with the duke of WELLINGTON, Charlotte's hero and an important figure in the Brontë JUVENILIA. Charlotte later realized that in creating Young Soult, Branwell was virtually predicting his own fate: Young Soult ruins his own life in various escapades that reveal his brutality and deceptiveness. *See also* GLASS TOWN.

Z

Zamorna, duke of *See* ANGRIA.

Zephyrine Minor character in *THE PROFESSOR*. She is one of the French teachers at Mademoiselle Zoraide REUTER's school.

Zillah Minor character in *WUTHERING HEIGHTS*. When Catherine EARNSHAW marries Edgar LINTON, Nelly DEAN, the housekeeper at WUTHERING HEIGHTS, goes with her to her new home at THRUSHCROSS GRANGE. Nelly's place at the Heights is taken over by Zillah, a woman from the nearby village, after the death of Hindley EARNSHAW. Although Nelly has a low opinion of Zillah, she is forced to rely on her for news about Wuthering Heights.

APPENDIXES

MAP OF BRONTË COUNTRY

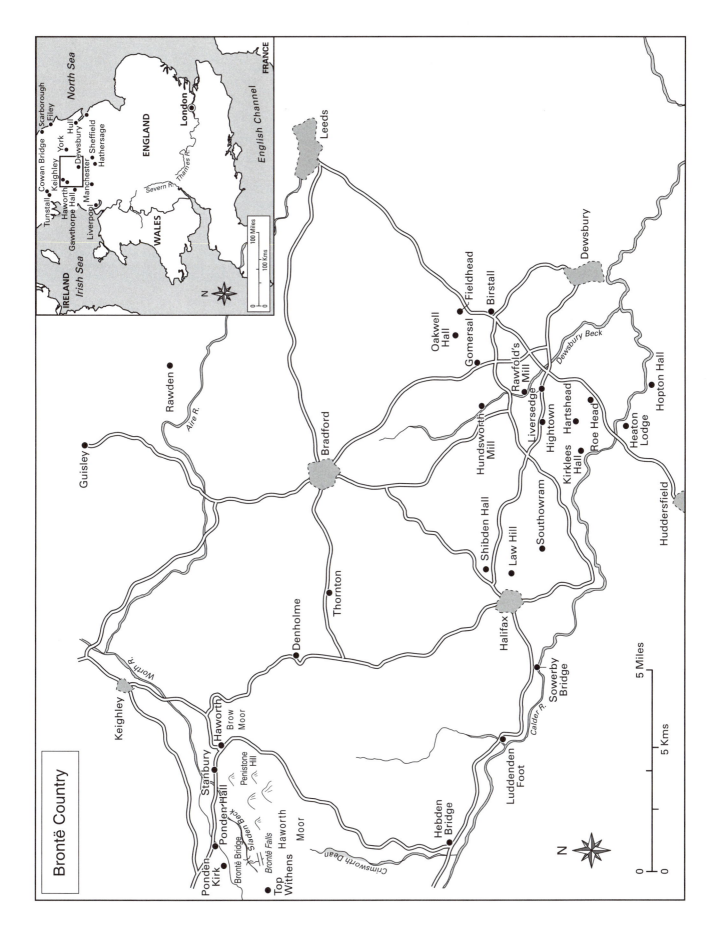

Brontë Country

North Sea

Scarborough
Filey
Cowan Bridge
Tunstall
Keighley
York
Hull
Haworth
Dewsbury
Gawthorpe Hall
Sheffield
Liverpool
Manchester
Hathersage
ENGLAND
IRELAND
Irish Sea
WALES
Severn R.
Thames R.
London
English Channel
FRANCE

N

100 Miles
100 Kms

Leeds

Dewsbury

Fieldhead
Birstall

Oakwell Hall
Gomersal

Rawfold's Mill
Dewsbury Beck

Hopton Hall

Liversedge
Hartshead
Heaton Lodge

Rawden

Hundsworth Mill
Hightown
Kirklees Hall
Roe Head

Aire R.

Bradford

Guisley

Shibden Hall
Southowram

Law Hill

Huddersfield

Thornton

Denholme

Halifax

Worth R.

Keighley

Sowerby Bridge

Calder R.

Haworth
Brow Moor

Stanbury

Luddenden Foot

Penistone Hill

Ponden Hall

Ponden Kirk
Brontë Bridge
Sladen Beck
Brontë Falls
Top Withens
Haworth Moor

Hebden Bridge

Crimsworth Dean

N

5 Miles

5 Kms

0

0

CATEGORICAL APPENDIX

Brontë Authorities

Alexander, Christine and Sellars, Jane
Barker, Juliet
Brontë Society
Fraser, Rebecca
Gaskell, Mrs. Elizabeth
Gérin, Winifred
Miller, Lucasta
Shorter, Clement
Wise, T. J.

Brontë Pets

Black Tom
Flossy
Gasper
Keeper
Little Dick
Tiger

Characters and Fictional Pets

Abbott, Miss
Agnes
Ainley, Miss Mary Ann
Andrews, Miss
Angelique
Archer, Dame
Ashby, Sir Thomas
Barraclough, Moses
Barrett, Mrs.
Bassompierre, M. de (inherited title of Mr. HOME)
Bassompierre, Miss de (inherited title of Paulina HOME)
Bates, Mr.

Batley, Dr.
Beck, Madame
Benson
Bessie
Blanche
"Blatant, Mr."
Bloomfield, Fanny
Bloomfield, Harriet
Bloomfield, Mary Ann
Bloomfield, Mr.
Bloomfield, Mrs.
Bloomfield, Tom
Boarham, Mr.
Boissec, M.
Boultby, Dr. Thomas
Boultby, Mrs.
Branderham, Rev. James
Braun, Anna
Bravey, Sir William
Bretton, John Graham
Bretton, Mrs. Louisa
Briggs, Mr.
Broc, Marie
Brocklehurst, Mr.
Brocklehurst, Mrs.
Brocklehurst, Naomi
Brocklehurst children
Brown, Mr.
Brown, Nancy
Bud, Captain John
Burns, Helen
Caroline (*The Professor*)
Caroline (*The Tenant of Wildfell Hall*)
Carter
Chantry, Henry
Charles
Charlie

Cholmodeley, Mrs.
Crimsworth, Edward
Crimsworth, William
Dean, Ellen
De Lisle, Frederick
Dent, Colonel
Dent, Mrs. Colonel
Desiree
Dindonneau, Duc de
Dolores
Donne, Joseph
Douro, marquis of
Dronsart, Adele
Earnshw, Catherine
Earnshaw, Frances
Earnshaw, Hareton
Earnshaw, Hindley
Earnshaw, Mr.
Emmanuel, Josef
Emmanuel, Paul
Eshton, Amy
Eshton, Louisa
Eshton, Mr.
Eshton, Mrs.
Eulalie
Eyre, Jane
Eyre, John
F ——, Lady
Fairfax, Mrs.
Fanny (*Wuthering Heights*)
Fanny (*Shirley*)
Fanshawe, Ginevra
Farren, William
Fifene
Finic
Fitzgibbon, Matilda
Flower, Captain John
Frank

Reuter, Madame
Reuter, Mademoiselle Zoraide
Richard
Rivers, Diana
Rivers, Mary
Rivers, St. John
Rochemort, M.
Rochester, Mr. Edward Fairfax
Rogue, Alexander
Rover
St. Pierre, Mademoiselle
Sancho
Sara, Lady
Sarah (*Jane Eyre*)
Sarah (*Shirley*)
Sarah (*The Tenant of Wildfell Hall*)
Saveur, Justine Marie (1)
Saveur, Justine Marie (2)
Scatcherd, Miss
Scott, Joe
Seacombe, the Hon. John
Shielders
Silas, Pere
Skulker
Smith, Miss
Sneaky, John
Snowe, Lucy
Sophie
Steighton, Timothy
Sugden
Suzette
Sweeny, Mrs.
Sweeting, David
Sykes, Christopher
Sykes, Dora
Sykes, Hannah
Sykes, Harriet
Sykes, Mary
Sykes, Mrs.
Sylvie (*The Professor*)
Sylvie (*Villette*)
Sympson, Henry
Sympson, Mr.
Sympson, Mrs.
Taylor, Martha
Taylor, Mary
Temple, Miss
Thomas
Throttler

Tree, Captain Andrew
Trista, Juanna
Turner, Miss
Tynedale, Lord
Vandenhuten, Victor
Varens, Adèle
Varens, Céline
Vernet
Virginie
Walravens, Madame
Watsons, the
Wellesley, Lord Charles
Weston, Mr.
Wharton, Mrs.
Whipp, Mrs.
Wilmot
Wilmot, Annabella
Wilmot, Mr.
Wilson, Jane
Wilson, Mary Ann
Wilson, Mr.
Wilson, Mrs.
Wilson, Richard
Wilson, Robert
Wilson, Sir Broadly
Wolf
Wood, Mark
Wood, Mr.
Wynne, Samuel Fawthorpe
Yorke, Jessy
Yorke, Mark
Yorke, Martin
Yorke, Matthew
Yorke, Mr. Hiram
Yorke, Mrs.
Yorke, Rose
Young Soult
Zamorna, duke of
Zephyrine, Mademoiselle
Zillah

People

Austen, Jane
Aykroyd, Tabitha
Bell, Currer, Ellis, and Acton
Blanche, Mademoiselle
Bonaparte, Napoléon
Bossuet, Jacques Bénigne

Bradley, Reverend James
    Chesteron
Branwell, Elizabeth
Brontë, Anne
Brontë, Charlotte
Brontë, Elizabeth
Brontë, Emily Jane
Brontë, Maria
Brontë, Maria Branwell
Brontë, Patrick
Brontë, Patrick Branwell
Brown, Martha
Buckworth, Reverend J.
Burder, Mary
Byron, George Gordon
Carlyle, Thomas
Cartwright, William
Castlereagh, Robert Stewart
Chatterton, Thomas
Coleridge, Hartley
Coriolanus
Cowper, William
Cromwell, Oliver
Crosby, Dr. John
Daniel
Drury, Isobella
Evans, Miss Anne
Fénelon, François de Salignac
    de la Mothe
Garrs, Nancy
Garrs, Sarah
Gaskell, Elizabeth
Goldsmith, Oliver
Greenwood, John
Heald, Reverend William
    Margetson
Ingham family
Jenkins, Reverend Evan
Job
Joseph
Kay Shuttleworth, Sir James and
    Lady Janet
Lewes, George Henry
MacTurk, Dr.
Martineau, Harriet
Milton, John
Morgan, Reverend William
Nicholls, Arthur Bell
Nussey, Ellen

Perceval, Spencer
Pitt, William
Pryce, Reverend David
Raphael
Richardson, Samuel
Robertson, Reverend William
Robinson, Lydia
Robinson family
Rousseau, Jean-Jacques
Samuel
Sand, George
Schiller, (John Christoph)
    Friedrich von
Scott, Sir Walter
Sidgwick, Mrs.
Southey, Robert
Stael, Madame Germaine de
Swift, Jonathan
Taylor, James
Thackeray, William Makepeace
Trollope, Anthony
Weightman, William
Wellington, duke of
Wheelwright family
White family
Williams, William Smith
Wise, Thomas James
Wooler, Miss
Wordsworth, William

Places, Ships, and Institutions— Real and Imaginary

Ambleside
Angria
Antigua
Blackhorse Marsh
Blake Hall
Bradford
Branii Hills
Briarmains
Broughton House
Brussels
Chapel Royal
Chapter Coffee House
Cornhill
Cowan Bridge
Crystal Palace

Edinburgh
Eton College
F ——
Fairy Cave
Ferndean
Fieldhead
Gateshead Hall
Gimmerton
Glass Town
Gondal
Grassdale Manor
Grove, the
Guadeloupe
Halifax
Haworth
Haworth Moor
Haworth Parsonage
Keighley
Knoll, the
L ——
Law Hill
Linden-Car
Lindenhope
Lotherdale
Lowood
M ——
Manchester
Norton Conyers
Nunnely
Parrysland
Paul et Virginie
Penistone Crags
Pensionnat Heger
Philosopher's Island
Quaximina Square
Rawdon
Roe Head
Rue d'Isabelle
Rue Royale
Rydings
Ryecote Farm
Ste. Gudule
St. George's Chapel
St. Paul's Cathedral
Scarborough
Sheffield
Sowerby Bridge
Staningley
Stonegappe

Strand, the
Temple Gardens
Thornfield
Thornton
Thorp Green
Thrushcross Grange
Top Withens
Tower of All Nations
Verdopolis
Villette
Vivid, The
Waterloo Palace
West End, the
Westminster
Whitcross
Wildfell Hall
Woodford
Wuthering Heights
Wycoller

Publishers, Publications, and Organizations

Aylott & Jones
Blackwood's Magazine
Chambers, Robert
Colburn, Henry
Cornhill Magazine
Fraser's Magazine
Halifax Guardian
Keighley Mechanics' Institute
Newby, T. C.
Smith, George

Special Topics

antinomian
art of Anne Brontë
art of Branwell Brontë
art of Charlotte Brontë
art of Emily Brontë
aurora borealis
baptist
bourgeois
Catholicism
Church of England
consumption
dissenter
evangelical

gothic
Highlander
Jacobin
Jesuit
juvenilia
leveller
Luddite
living
materialist
Methodist
orders in council
poems of Anne Brontë
poems of Branwell Brontë
poems of Charlotte Brontë
poems of Emily Brontë
poems of Patrick Brontë
popish
prince regent
Protestant
rector
Reform Bill of 1832
romantic
sermons of Patrick Brontë
Tory
trade
tuberculosis
Whig
Whitsuntide

Titles

"Advantages of Poverty, in
   Religious Concerns"
Agnes Grey

Arabian Nights
"Arthuriana"
Branwell's Blackwood's Magazine
Caroline Vernon
"Cold in the earth—and the
   deep snow piled above thee"
Cottage in the Wood, The
Cottage Poems
"Day at Parry's Palace, A"
"Death is here I feel his power"
"Doubters Hymn, The"
Emma
"Farewell to Angria, The"
"Foundling, The"
Green Dwarf, The
Gulliver's Travels
"High Life in Verdopolis"
"History of the Year, The"
"History of Young Men, The"
Jane Eyre
Life of Charlotte Brontë, The
*Maid of Killarney, or Albion and
   Flora: a modern tale; in which
   are interwoven some cursory
   remarks on religion and politics*
Marmion
"No coward soul is mine"
"Oh, thy bright eyes must
   answer now"
"On Conversion"
Poems
"Philosopher, The"
Pilgrim's Progress, The
Poems

Poetaster, The
"Prisoner, The"
Professor, The
Rasselas
*Rural Minstrel, The: A Miscellany
   of Descriptive Poems*
"Self-Communion"
*Seventy Times Seven, and the First
   of the Seventy-First. A Pious
   Discourse delivered by the
   Reverend Jabes Branderham, in
   the Chapel of Gimmerden Sough*
Shirley
Signs of the Times, The
"Sir Henry Tunstall"
Tales of the Islanders, The
Tenant of Wildfell Hall, The
"Three Guides, The"
"Tract for the Times, A"
Vicar of Wakefield, The
Villette
"We wove a web in childhood"
"Why ask to know the date—
   the clime?"
Winter Evening Thoughts
Wuthering Heights
Young Men's Magazine, The

BIBLIOGRAPHY

Books and Collections of Works by the Brontës

Brontë, Anne. *Agnes Grey.* Ed. Angeline Goreau. London: Penguin Books, 1989.

———. *Poems of Anne Brontë.* Ed. Edward Chitham. London: Macmillan, 1979.

———. *The Tenant of Wildfell Hall.* 2 vols. Oxford, U.K.: Shakespeare Head Press/Basil and Blackwell, 1931.

Brontë, Charlotte. *Five Novelettes.* Ed. Winifred Gérin. London: Folio Press, 1971.

———. *Juvenilia 1829–1835.* London: Penguin Books, 1996.

———. *The Poems of Charlotte Brontë.* Ed. Tom Winnifrith. London: Basil and Blackwell, 1984.

———. *The Professor.* Eds. Margaret Smith and Herbert Rosengarten. Oxford, U.K.: Clarendon Press, 1987.

———. *Shirley.* With introduction by Margaret Lane. New York: Dutton/Everyman's Library, 1975.

———. *Villette.* London: Folio Society, 1967.

Brontë, Emily. *Complete Poems of Emily Brontë.* Ed. C. W. Hatfield. New York: Columbia University Press, 1941.

———. *Wuthering Heights.* Eds. Hilda Marsden and Ian Jack. New York: Pocket Books, 1939.

———. *Wuthering Heights—Text, Sources, Criticism.* Ed. William M. Sale, Jr. New York: Harcourt, Brace, 1962.

Brontë, Patrick. *Brontëana: The Rev. Patrick Brontë, A.B., His Collected Works and Life. The Works; And the Brontës of Ireland.* Ed. J. Horsfall Turner. Bingley, U.K.: T. Harrison and Sons, 1898.

Brontë, Patrick Branwell. *The Poems of Patrick Branwell Brontë.* Ed. Tom Winnifrith. New York: New York University Press, 1983.

Norris, Pamela, ed. *The Brontës.* London: J. M. Dent, 1997.

Ratchford, Fannie E., and William Clyde De Vase, eds. *Legends of Angria.* New Haven, Conn.: Yale University Press, 1933.

Shorter, C. K., and C. W. Hatfield, eds. *The Twelve Adventurers and Other Stories.* London: Hodder and Stoughton, 1925.

Wise, T. J. and J. A. Symington, eds. *The Shakespeare Head Brontë.* 19 vols. Oxford, U.K.: Shakespeare Head Press, 1931–38.

Books about the Brontës and Their Historical Background

Alexander, Christine. *A Bibliography of the Manuscripts of Charlotte Brontë.* Westport, Conn.: Brontë Society/Meckler Publishing, 1982.

———. *The Early Writings of Charlotte Brontë.* New York: Prometheus Books, 1983.

Alexander, Christine, and Jane Sellars. *The Art of the Brontës.* Cambridge, U.K.: Cambridge University Press, 1995.

Allott, Miriam, ed. *The Brontës: The Critical Heritage.* London: Routledge and Kegan Paul, 1974.

Barker, Juliet. *The Brontës.* New York: St. Martin's Press, 1994.

———, ed. *The Brontës: A Life in Letters.* New York: Overlook Press, 1998.

Bell, Arnold Craig. *The Novels of Anne Brontë: A Study and Reappraisal.* Braunton, U.K.: Merlin Books, 1992.

Benson, E. F. *Charlotte Brontë.* London: Longmans, Green, 1932.

Bentley, Phyllis. *The Brontës and Their World.* London: Thames and Hudson, 1969.

Benvenuto, Richard. *Emily Bronte.* Boston: Twayne, 1982.

Berry, Elizabeth Hollis. *Anne Brontë's Radical Vision: Structures of Consciousness*. No. 62, English Literature Studies Monograph Series. Victoria, Canada: University of Victoria, 1994.

Bloom, Harold, ed. *Modern Critical Views: The Brontës*. New York: Chelsea House, 1987.

Bloom, Margaret. *Charlotte Brontë*. Boston: Twayne, 1977.

Birrell, Augustine. *The Life of Charlotte Brontë*. London: Walter Scott, 1887.

Boumelha, Penny. *Charlotte Brontë*. Hemel, U.K.: Harvester, 1990.

Burkhart, Charles. *Charlotte Brontë: A Psychosexual Study of Her Novels*. London: Victor Gollancz, 1973.

Cecil, David. *Early Victorian Novelists*. Chicago: University of Chicago Press, 1964.

Chadwick, Mrs. Ellis H. *In the Footsteps of the Brontës*. London: Sir Isaac Pitman and Sons, 1914.

Chitham, Edward. *The Brontës' Irish Background*. London: Macmillan, 1986.

———. *A Life of Emily Brontë*. Oxford, U.K.: Basil Blackwell, 1987.

Chitham, Edward, and Tom Winnifrith. *Brontë Facts and Brontë Problems*. London: Macmillan, 1983.

Craik, W. A. *The Brontë Novels*. London: Methuen, 1971.

Craven, Joseph. *A Brontë Moorland Village*. Keighley, U.K.: Rydal Press, 1907.

Crump, R. W., ed. *Charlotte and Emily Brontë, 1846–1915: A Reference Guide*. Boston: G. K. Hall, 1982.

Davids, Shirley, and Geoff Moore. *Haworth in Times Past*. Chorley, U.K.: Countryside Publications, 1983.

Davies, Stevie. *Emily Brontë*. New York: Simon and Schuster, 1988.

———. *Emily Brontë: The Artist as a Free Woman*. Manchester: Carcanet Press, 1983.

Dry, F. S. *The Sources of Jane Eyre*. Cambridge, U.K.: Heffer, 1940.

du Maurier, Daphne. *The Infernal World of Branwell Brontë*. New York: Doubleday, 1961.

Duthie, Enid. *The Foreign Vision of Charlotte Brontë*. London: Macmillan, 1975.

Evans, Barbara, and Gareth Lloyd. *The Scribner Companion to the Brontës*. New York: Charles Scribner's Sons, 1982.

Ewbank, Inga-Stina. *Their Proper Sphere. A Study of the Brontë Sisters as Early Victorian Female Novelists*. London: Edward Arnold, 1966.

Frank, Katherine. *Emily Brontë: A Chainless Soul*. New York: Viking Penguin, 1990.

Fraser, Rebecca. *The Brontës: Charlotte Brontë and Her Family*. New York: Crown Publishers, 1988.

Frawley, Maria H. *Anne Brontë*. New York: Twayne, 1996.

Gardiner, Juliet. *The Brontës at Haworth: The World Within*. New York: Clarkson Potter, 1992.

Gaskell, Elizabeth. *The Life of Charlotte Brontë*. London: Penguin, 1975.

Gérin, Winifred. *Anne Brontë*. London: Allen Lane, 1959.

———. *Branwell Brontë*. London: Radius Book/ Hutchinson, 1972.

———. *Emily Brontë: A Biography*. Oxford, U.K.: Clarendon Press, 1971.

———. *The Life of Charlotte Brontë*. Oxford, U.K.: Oxford University Press, 1967.

Glynn, Jennifer. *Prince of Publishers: A Biography of George Smith*. London: Allison and Busby, 1986.

Goodridge, J. F. *Emily Brontë: Wuthering Heights*. London: Edward Arnold, 1964.

Gordon, Lyndall. *Charlotte Brontë: A Passionate Life*. New York: W. W. Norton, 1995.

Haig, Alan. *The Victorian Clergy*. London: Croom Helm, 1984.

Hanson, Lawrence, and E. M. Hanson. *The Four Brontës: The Lives and Works of Charlotte, Branwell, Emily, and Anne Brontë*. London: Oxford University Press, 1949.

Harland, Marian. *Charlotte Brontë at Home*. New York: G. P. Putnam's Sons, 1899.

Hewish, John. *Emily Brontë: A Critical and Biographical Study*. London: Macmillan, 1969.

Hinkley, Laura L. *The Brontës: Charlotte and Emily*. London: Hammond, 1947.

Hopkins, Annette B. *The Father of the Brontës*. Baltimore: Johns Hopkins University Press, 1958.

Hughes, Glyn. *Brontë: A Novel*. New York: St. Martin's Press, 1996.

Jay, Elisabeth. *The Religion of the Heart: Anglican Evangelicalism and the Nineteenth-Century Novel*. Oxford, U.K.: Clarendon Press, 1979.

Keefe, Robert. *Charlotte Brontë's World of Death*. Austin: University of Texas Press, 1979.

Kipling, Lesley, and Nick Hall. *On the Trail of the Luddites.* N.p.: Pennine Heritage Network, n.d.

Knapp, Bettina L. *The Brontës: Branwell, Anne, Emily, Charlotte.* New York: Continuum, 1991.

Knies, Earl A. *The Art of Charlotte Brontë.* Athens: Ohio University Press, 1969.

Lane, Margaret. *The Brontë Story: A Reconsideration of Mrs. Gaskell's "Life of Charlotte Brontë."* London: Heinemann, 1953.

Langland, Elizabeth. *Anne Brontë: The Other One.* London: Macmillan, 1989.

Liddell, Robert. *Twin Spirits: The Novels of Emily and Anne Brontë.* London: Peter Owen, 1990.

Linder, Cynthia A. *Romantic Imagery in the Novels of Charlotte Brontë.* New York: Barnes and Noble, 1978.

Martin, Robert B. *Accents of Persuasion: Charlotte Brontë's Novels.* London: Faber and Faber, 1966.

Maynard, John. *Charlotte Brontë and Sexuality.* Cambridge, U.K.: Cambridge University Press, 1984.

Moers, Ellen. *Literary Women.* London: Women's Press, 1963.

Moglen, Helen. *Charlotte Brontë: The Self Conceived.* New York: W. W. Norton, 1976.

Neufeldt, Victor, ed. *A Bibliography of the Manuscripts of Patrick Branwell Brontë.* New York: Garland, 1993.

Peters, Margot. *Charlotte Brontë: Style in the Novel.* Madison: University of Wisconsin Press, 1973.

———. *Unquiet Soul: A Biography of Charlotte Brontë.* New York: Doubleday, 1975.

Pinion, F. B. *A Brontë Companion: Literary Assessment, Background, and Reference.* London: Macmillan, 1975.

Pollard, Arthur. *Charlotte Brontë.* New York: Humanities Press, 1968.

———. *The Landscape of the Brontës.* Exeter, U.K.: Webb and Bower, 1988.

Ramsden, J. *The Brontë Homeland.* London: Roxburghe Press, 1898.

Ratchford, Fannie E. *The Brontës' Web of Childhood.* New York: Columbia University Press, 1941.

Raymond, E. *In the Steps of the Brontës.* London: Rich and Cowan, 1948.

Rees, Joan. *Profligate Son: Branwell Brontë and His Sisters.* London: Robert Hale, 1986.

Robinson, Mary E. *Emily Brontë.* London: W. H. Allen, 1883.

Sanders, Valerie, ed. *Harriet Martineau: Selected Letters.* Oxford, U.K.: Clarendon Press, 1990.

Sanger, C. P. *The Structure of Wuthering Heights.* London: Hogarth Press, 1926.

Scott, P. J. M. *Anne Brontë: A New Critical Assessment.* London: Barnes and Noble, 1983.

Shorter, Clement K. *The Brontës and Their Circle.* London: J. M. Dent, 1914.

———. *The Brontës: Life and Letters.* London: Hodder and Stoughton, 1908.

Showalter, Elaine. *A Literature of Their Own: British Women Novelists from Brontë to Lessing.* Princeton, N.J.: Princeton University Press, 1977.

Sinclair, May. *The Three Brontës.* London: Hutchinson, 1912.

Smith, Anne, ed. *The Art of Emily Brontë.* New York: Barnes and Noble, 1976.

Spark, Muriel, and Derek Stanford. *Emily Brontë: Her Life and Work.* New York: Coward-McCann, 1966.

Stevenson, W. H. *Emily and Anne Brontë.* New York: Humanities Press, 1968.

Tillotson, Kathleen. *Novels of the Eighteen-Forties.* Oxford, U.K.: Clarendon Press, 1954.

Tully, James. *The Crimes of Charlotte Brontë: A Novel.* New York: Carroll and Graf, 1999.

Uglow, Jenny. *Elizabeth Gaskell: A Habit of Stories.* London: Faber and Faber, 1993.

Visick, Mary. *The Genesis of "Wuthering Heights."* New York: Oxford University Press, 1965.

Wilks, Brian. *The Brontës.* London: Hamlyn, 1975.

Winnifrith, Tom. *The Brontës and Their Background.* London: Macmillan, 1973.

Wright, William. *The Brontës and Ireland.* London: Hodder and Stoughton, 1893.

Yates, W. W. *The Father of the Brontës: His Life and Work at Dewsbury & Hartshead.* Leeds, U.K.: Fred R. Spark and Son, 1897.

Web Sites

The Brontës—http://www.geocities.com/Paris/LeftBank/8723/bronte.html

This site contains an extensive menu of links to materials about Charlotte, Emily, Anne, and Branwell Brontë. Each link is briefly described. The menu also includes links to places to stay near Haworth, concordances to the novels, discussions of juvenilia, and discussion groups.

Brontë Parsonage Museum—http://www.bronte. org.uk/
A good site for those just beginning their study of the family.

Brontë Conference—http://www.spring.net/yapp-bin/public/browse/bronte/all/
An extensive list of discussion topics, including film adaptations, characters, biographies, individual novels, documentaries, and requests for information.

Concordances of Brontë Sisters' Novels—http://www.concordance.com/bronte.htm
Provides links to concordances for all the novels.

Literary Life On-Line—http://www2.sbbs.se/hp/cfalk/brlist.htm
An essay by Susannah Gordon that assesses several web sites.

Angria and Gondal: The Secret World of the Brontë Children—http://hosted.ukoln.ac.uk/msc/org-info/1998/11222/bronwebh.htm
The site is devoted to Angria and Gondal

"Brontë" (The Columbia Electronic Encyclopedia on Infoplease.com)—http://infoplease.com/ce6/people/A0809059.html
This includes sections on lives and works, an appraisal, and bibliography.

"Family-Systems Theory, Addiction, and the Novels of the Brontës" (The Victorian Web)—http://65.107.211.206/victorian/bronte/ebronte/bump5.html
An article by Jerome Bump on the Victorian family with special reference to the sisters and their novels.

The Brontës Live Campfire Chat—http://hatteraslight.com/navy/The Bronteshall/live/chat.cgi
This is a discussion group.

Jean Wainman's Brontë Sisters & Haworth Web Site—http://www.fortunecity.com/victorian/austen/25/index.html
This site includes photographs of Haworth, a family tree, and links to other sites.

Eagle Intermedia's Brontë Country—http://www.eagle.co.uk/Bronte/
Photographs of Haworth and the surrounding territory can be viewed here.

The Brontë Sisters—http://www2.sbbs.se/hp/cfalk/brontele.htm
This site by Cecilia Falk contains entries about all of the novels, selected discussion of the poetry, individual biographies of the sisters, individual chronologies, as well as several links to sites devoted to the family and to "Haworth and the Irish Roots."

The Brontë Sisters Web—http://www.lang.nagoya-u.ac.jp/~matsuoka/Bronte.html
Compiled by Mitsuharu Matsuoka, this site includes electronic texts of all the novels and Mrs. Gaskell's biography of Charlotte, along with links to many articles, concordances, discussion groups, bibliographies, photographs, and reference works on the Brontë sisters. This is one of the most comprehensive Brontë web sites.

Emily Jane Brontë—http://www.geocities.com/CollegePark/1380/emily.htm
Compiled by Jody Allard, this site contains a brief biography of Emily and links to similar sites.

INDEX

Note: **Boldface** numbers indicate primary discussions of a topic. *Italic* numbers indicate illustrations.

DATE DUE